MODESTY
Blaise
CRY WOLF

Modesty Blaise: Cry Wolf

ISBN 1 84023 869 0
ISBN-13: 9781840238693

Published by Titan Books,
a division of Titan Publishing Group Ltd.
144 Southwark St
London SE1 0UP

A CIP catalogue record for this title is available from the British Library.

This edition first published: October 2006
10 9 8 7 6 5 4 3 2

Printed in Italy.

Also available from Titan Books:
Modesty Blaise: The Gabriel Set-Up (ISBN: 1 84023 658 2)
Modesty Blaise: Mister Sun (ISBN: 1 84023 721 X)
Modesty Blaise: Top Traitor (ISBN: 1 84023 684 1)
Modesty Blaise: The Black Pearl (ISBN: 1 84023 842 9)
Modesty Blaise: Bad Suki (ISBN: 1 84023 864 X)
Modesty Blaise: The Hell-Makers (ISBN: 1 84023 865 8)
Modesty Blaise: The Green-Eyed Monster (ISBN: 1 84023 866 6)
Modesty Blaise: The Puppet Master (ISBN 1 84023 867 4)
Modesty Blaise: The Gallows Bird (ISBN 1 84023 868 2)

Grateful thanks to Peter O'Donnell, Rick Norwood, Lawrence Blackmore, Rob van der Nol and Trevor York for their help and support in the production of this book.

Introduction © Russell Mael 2006.
Peter O'Donnell Interview © Comic Media 1974, 2006.

Picture credits:
Modesty Blaise hardback (page 6) published by Souvenir Press.
Modesty Blaise promotional artwork and Monica Vitti photo (pages 7-9) © 20th Century Fox.

What did you think of this book? We love to hear from our readers. Please email us at: readerfeedback@titanemail.com, or write to us at the above address.

www.titanbooks.com

Much of the comic strip material used by Titan in this edition is exceedingly rare. As such, we hope that readers appreciate that the quality of the materials can be variable.

MODESTY Blaise

CRY WOLF

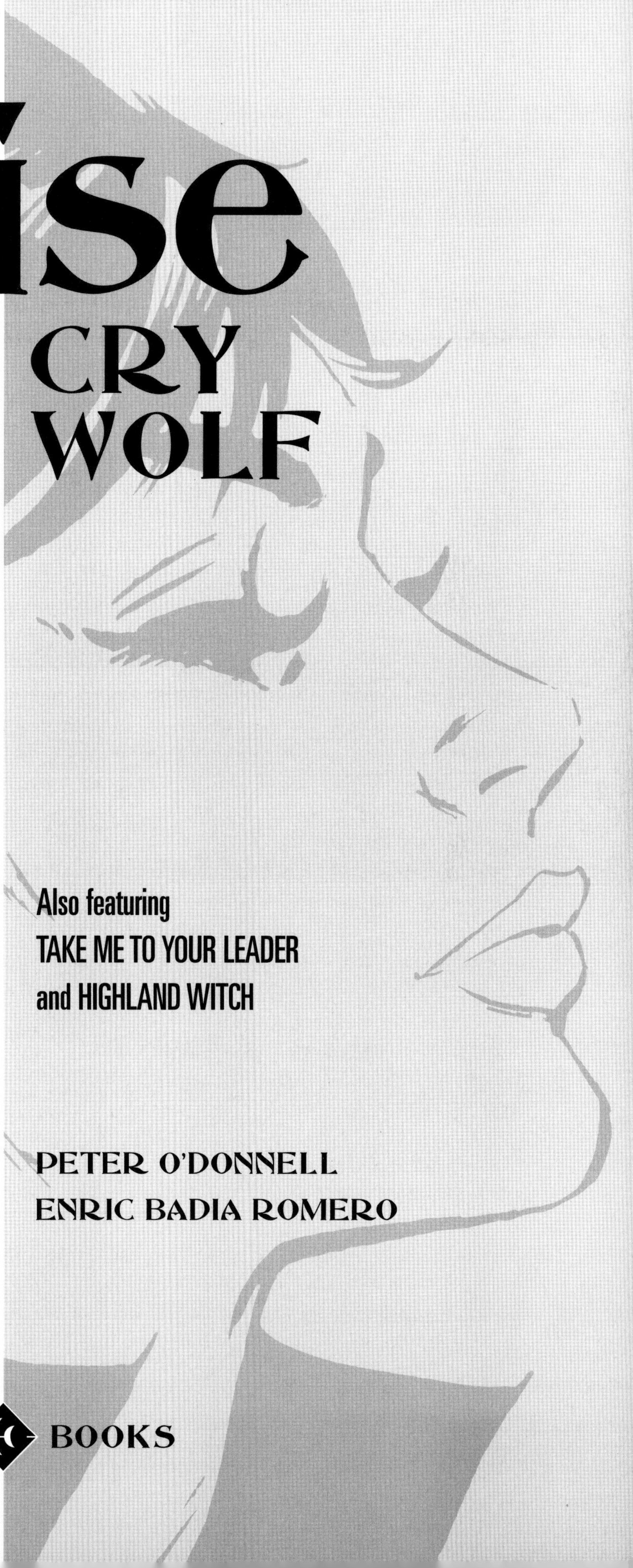

Also featuring
TAKE ME TO YOUR LEADER
and HIGHLAND WITCH

PETER O'DONNELL
ENRIC BADIA ROMERO

TITAN BOOKS

The Truth Behind *Modesty Plays*

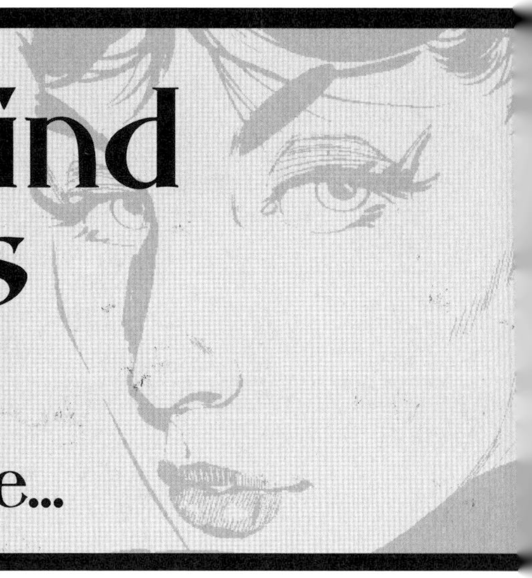

The story behind Sparks' involvement with our heroine...

In 1981, we were approached by Los Angeles screenwriter and producer, Larry Wilson (co-writer and co-producer of Tim Burton's *Beetlejuice*), to compose the theme song for a planned TV series that he was writing, based on the comic book character Modesty Blaise. We happily accepted the assignment and soon thereafter, came up with the melody and lyrics for the song that was to introduce the character to America's masses (and, hopefully, to the rest of the world later on). The song got the thumbs-up from the multitude of execs that need to weigh in and sign off on any Hollywood project. We passed the board-of-review relatively unscathed.

Next came the period that everyone working in Hollywood hopes to avoid, but unfortunately seldom do: development hell. Articles appeared in *The Hollywood Reporter* and *Variety*, the two trade magazines which tout projects that are on the cusp of being made into mega-million-dollar sensations but rarely have a chance of even being made at all, featuring the impending TV smash, *Modesty Blaise*. We believed what we read — silly us. And we read, and we read, and we waited, and we waited.

While waiting to hear that we were the next Bernard Herrmanns of television scores, we distributed the song to friends, loved ones and record companies. What, initially, was to be a TV theme song now turned into something that was standing on its own merits. Record companies were wanting to release it simply because they liked the song.

Shortly thereafter we heard from someone upstairs at Paramount TV that empowered female characters were passé as far as Hollywood was concerned and that the project was going to be shelved. Hey, but we had a theme song that was already being touted as the next Sparks single.

What to do? Afraid of raising any legal issues over the copyrighted name "Modesty Blaise", and not wanting to disappoint the record companies who had already heard the song, we concluded that the refrain I sang over and over throughout the song was really saying, "Modesty Plays," and that no, Your Honour, I absolutely was *not* singing "Modesty Blaise."

So to this day, we have a song called *Modesty Plays*, and any similarity to any female comic-book heroines, living or dead, is strictly coincidental.

Russell Mael/Sparks
Los Angeles, 2006

Russell Mael and his brother Ron comprise the pop group Sparks. Their first UK hit, This Town Ain't Big Enough For The Both Of Us, *reached #2 in 1974, and the band's unique mixture of offbeat lyrics and orchestral influences have thrilled worldwide audiences ever since. The band have recently completed a successful American tour and their twentieth and most recent studio album,* Hello Young Lovers, *was released in February 2006.*

An Interview With PETER O'DONNELL

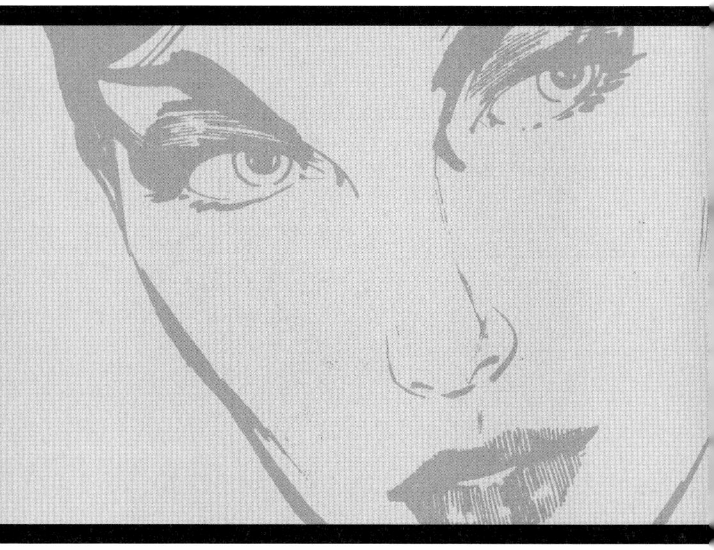

by Nick Landau and Richard Burton

Nick Landau and Richard Burton of *Comic Media* (CM) spoke to the *Modesty Blaise* creator in January 1973. This is the second excerpt from that interview, reprinted with kind permission of *Comic Media*. The first excerpt – covering O'Donnell's meeting and work with Jim Holdaway on *Romeo Brown* and *Modesty Blaise* – is reprinted in *Modesty Blaise: The Hell-Makers*.

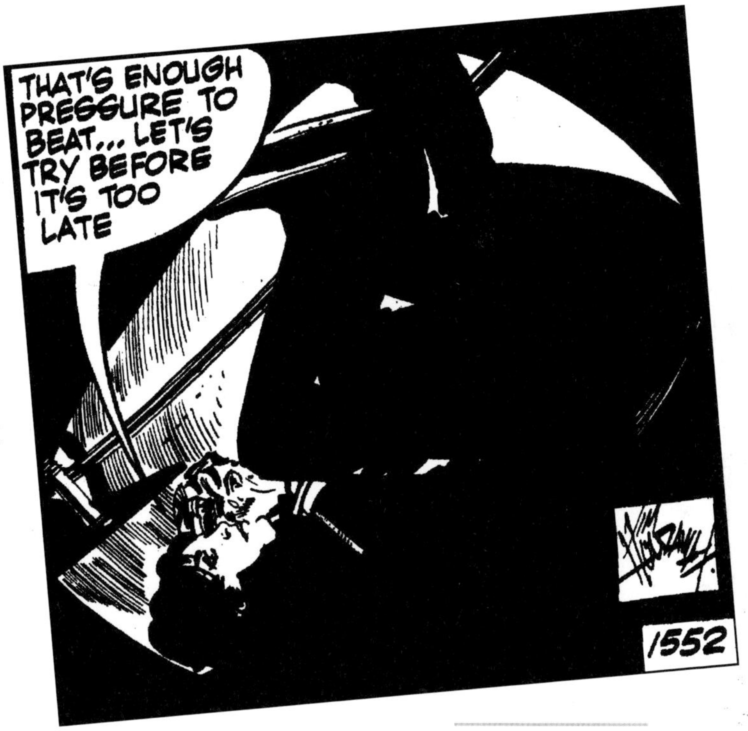
THAT'S ENOUGH PRESSURE TO BEAT... LET'S TRY BEFORE IT'S TOO LATE
1552

Above: Modesty and Willie prepare to defy the laws of physics in *Bad Suki*.

CM: What sort of response do you get to *Modesty*? Do you get many letters?

PO'D: I get more letters regarding the books than the strips. You usually get letters if you've either made a mistake or somebody thinks you've made one. I've only had to eat crow on one occasion in the ten years, and that was when I did something to do with a capsule underwater. Apparently, what I had Modesty and Willie do was completely impossible, because the pressure would have been such that they couldn't have performed the task. I had a very polite and pleasant letter written to me by some scientific boffin pointing this out. Sometimes people jump to the conclusion that you've made a mistake when you haven't. I always answer letters. You don't get a tremendous reader reaction — you get it more when you're in trouble.

CM: Have you ever had any strange letters that you personally remember?

PO'D: Not about *Modesty*. However, a bloke used to write to me every so often when I was doing *Garth*. This was when I had introduced Astra, who was the reincarnation of the goddess Venus, and he wrote long letters to me assuring me that Astra was

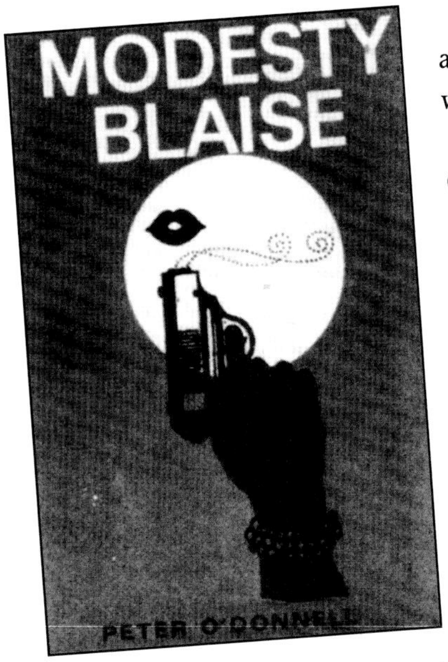
MODESTY
BLAISE

Above: Souvenir Press' first *Modesty Blaise* novel.

alive and well and living in Eastbourne, not far from where he lived, and that he wondered how I'd found out about her. Most amiable letters, but cranky.

CM: She probably had a boarding house there. But back to *Modesty*. What sort of relationship do you envisage between Modesty and Willie?

PO'D: Everybody has to draw their own conclusions. I've had infinite trouble with that question, which has been asked me many, many times. Once, in 1965, to my horror. When I was in France with my publisher — I suddenly found myself in their radio station on — what do they call it —

CM: ORTF.

PO'D: — in a studio, about to be interviewed (I hadn't expected this at all) by a bloke, in French. I can manage alright in French (let's say I can understand it) but it's rather a different thing to be able to speak it fluently. I can get by, but I wouldn't think that what I say is terribly well phrased, to put it mildly, and of course he asked me about this relationship between Modesty and Willie. I think that it had a traumatic effect on me, because I go cold whenever anybody mentions it. It is, of course, more fully dealt with in the books. In a strip you can only touch the ground in spots; you just can't stand still for four or five days with a bighead dialogue going back and forth. It just has to be much more implicit. It is, however, a relationship that women understand much better than men; I can tell this from the letters I get about the books.

CM: How did the books and film originate?

PO'D: The strip started in 1963 and within a year, there was an approach on an option for the film rights. I was then approached to write the script for the film. I did various treatments, and finally one was agreed. By this time there was some publicity about — you know, the *Modesty Blaise* property in general — and I was approached by two or three publishers for books. I went with Ernest Hecht, of Souvenir Press, and I used the story that I had done for the film as the first *Modesty Blaise* book. Of course you wouldn't recognise the film from the book, because the film script went out of my hands and was rewritten — first by an Englishman, then by an Italian lady (in Italian); it was translated back into English by Lord Burkett, then rewritten by a West Indian, and finally polished off by an American.

CM: Polished off is the right phrase!

PO'D: Yes, I had three lines left to read and I couldn't understand the story — and of course I didn't recognise the character; it was one of those disasters.

CM: But why were there so many script changes?

PO'D: It isn't at all unusual for a film script to be written and rewritten and rewritten. You might see on a credit title, "Script by John Jackson and Jack Johnson," and you visualise that these two have been sitting down for months working on it, but they've probably never met. What it means is that one wrote the original screenplay and then, because film people are investing a lot of money and it's rather like throwing dice (you've got to face it), it's high risk money that they're putting into making films; so they're naturally frightened and they think, "Well, this isn't good enough, perhaps if we get old so-and-so to rewrite it, it would improve it." And then maybe that also needs rewriting, they think; I don't suppose it does very often, but that is what used to happen to films in that time. The situation has changed a good bit now.

CM: And the film wasn't very well received?

PO'D: No, it got rather odd reviews. To my mind, the critics didn't like it any more than the public, but they didn't like to say so too strongly because Joseph Losey had directed it and he is a very fine director. I think that the film was completely the wrong kind for him to direct. It was just the wrong subject for him.

CM: It was made in the very camp period of the '60s, though, wasn't it?

PO'D: Yes, well... they were frightened of *Bond*. Having committed themselves to the movie, they didn't want to play it straight — which is the way I felt it should have been done: to base the movie on the characters and to try to find really good actors for the principals. I would have tried to find unknowns, but of course this doesn't suit the box office at all. Terry Stamp had been a big hit in *Billy Budd* and *The Collector*, and by the time this got into their hands, front office at Twentieth Century Fox said that they wanted him for the part. Joseph Losey almost always has Dirk Bogarde in his films, as you know, and Joe Janni, the producer — a very nice man — picked Monica Vitti and cast her for Modesty. I think it was wrong. I'm rather sad; Janni's made a lot of films and they've all been very good and very successful except *Modesty Blaise*, where he slipped out of gear. I never quarrelled with him about it. He's the most amiable man and gave me a lot of his time, but he said, "No, you'll have to do it this way." I think he had a lot of problems, working with a very temperamental actress and, possibly, a difficult director.

CM: Also, I understand that Monica Vitti didn't want to change the colour of her hair to conform to Modesty's.

PO'D: That caused problems because — under the contract to which Beaverbrook were a party — it was stipulated that the essential characteristics of the two principals, Modesty and Willie, must be maintained.

When we first saw the film script, it was quite obvious that the two principals were nothing like the real characters, and there was a meeting up at the *Standard*. The trouble was that the film company's lawyers were prepared to argue interminably about what exactly "essential characteristics" were. If you start going into litigation on a thing like this, you'll go into enormous cost. I know Beaverbrook [Newspapers, owners of the *Evening Standard*] weren't prepared to have a vast battle over it, and reasonably enough. They probably thought, "This is an excellent filmmaking team. It may not come out exactly like Modesty

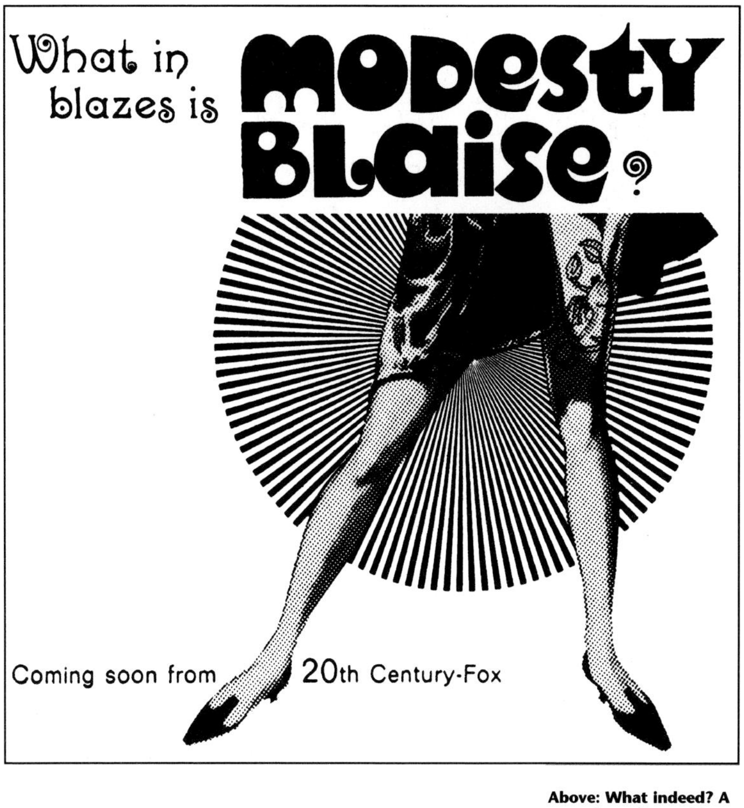
What in blazes is
MODESTY BLAISE?
Coming soon from 20th Century-Fox

Above: What indeed? A pre-release 'teaser' for the 1966 *Modesty Blaise* movie.

Blaise and Willie Garvin, but it should be a success." And I certainly wasn't prepared to fight them on my own. I couldn't stand up to such a weight of money. So we got certain modifications.

You would hardly credit it, but in the titles as scripted they had some dreadful scenes, such as Modesty with long steel talons on her fingers kissing a man and then tearing his throat out! Then dissolve, and she's strangling someone with her hair; then dissolve again, and there's a man, she shoots him and then she goes and kisses the bullet wound in the middle of his forehead! Well, Beaverbrook went mad about this, and got it out — it was sick — but we couldn't really do much more than to just get the worst of it out.

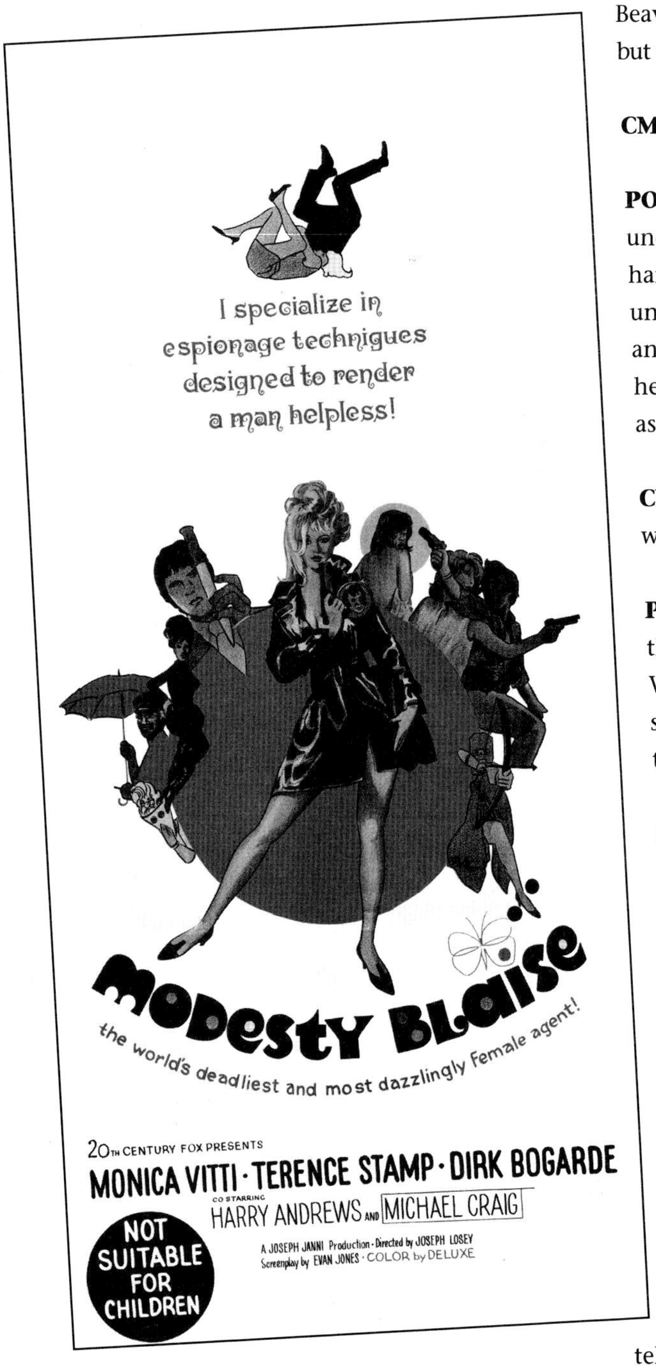
I specialize in espionage techniques designed to render a man helpless!
Modesty Blaise
the world's deadliest and most dazzlingly female agent!
20th CENTURY FOX PRESENTS
MONICA VITTI · TERENCE STAMP · DIRK BOGARDE
CO STARRING
HARRY ANDREWS AND MICHAEL CRAIG
NOT SUITABLE FOR CHILDREN
A JOSEPH JANNI Production · Directed by JOSEPH LOSEY
Screenplay by EVAN JONES · COLOR by DELUXE

Below: The lobby poster from the 1966 *Modesty Blaise* movie. Note that the screenplay is credited to one Evan Jones...

CM: Did you ever go down to the sets much?

PO'D: No. Writers are not very welcome in studios. I suppose it's understandable. Once the thing's in the floor, it's got to be in the hands of one man, the director, and the writer is unwelcome unless he's the useful type who will keep quiet most of the time and only talk quietly to the director about a particular thing that he feels strongly about, in a reasonable sort of way. I suppose it's as well to have a writer off the floor.

CM: Did it come as much of a shock to see the final version, or were you prepared for it?

PO'D: I was prepared for it, having seen the script. I'd hoped that it might have come out a little differently. I'd hoped that Vitti might at least look a little like Modesty, but she didn't — she was kittenish... and when they broke into song I just wanted to get out. I felt like sitting alone for the rest of the film.

CM: But I understand that you've now got the film rights.

PO'D: Oh, yes. I've got a pile of contracts about a foot deep on this, but the rights were eventually vested in a company which was set up to operate the rights by a number of film people, and this was called "Modesty Blaise Ltd.", and they were the production company which operated under finance by Twentieth Century Fox to make the film. After the thing flopped, I let it go for a couple of years, until some of the stink faded — and then I approached them and asked to buy the rights back and they wouldn't listen to that. However, they said that they'd listen to an offer for a shareholding in the company, Modesty Blaise Ltd. After a fair amount of negotiation I bought the whole shareholding of the company, which effectively restores the rights (film, television and merchandising) to me, the idea being that I thought I might have another go, which I'm trying to do now.

CM: You have no idea when?

PO'D: I can't say when. The thing is, since I don't want the same thing to happen all over again and to get out of control, you first have to find a producer whose mind is in tandem with yours. In my view, I've found the right man — the man who can produce the film — and I've had a number of approaches, some vague, some positive, but this man knew precisely what he wanted to do, and it went along with my own thinking. He's also a writer as well as a producer and he wanted to script the thing himself, which he's done from one of the books – *I, Lucifer*. He did the first draft script, and then I worked on it, and when I'd done what I thought necessary, we worked on it together for three or four weeks, fighting over lines here and there, and arguing and hammering it out, but at least we were both aiming for the same thing, and we finally got it out and agreed on the script, so that's ready. The next thing is that we need to raise some money for pre-production to make a package of it, that is to say, to cast principals, to find locations, to estimate all travelling, hotel and film unit costs, screen tests, clips for showing, and then once we've got a package to take it to a major company for financing; at that stage, when you have a package put together, it can't be messed about with very much, so that's the only way we could do it.

It's very difficult because you've got to find all this pre-production money which runs into quite a few thousands and is, undoubtedly, gambling money — and anybody who puts up the dough for this kind of thing has to know before he starts that it could all be lost. That's what films are about.

Above: Monica Vitti in the 1966 *Modesty Blaise* movie.

CM: Do you have anybody in mind?

PO'D: No, I've got a few lines out, but there's nothing specific. I don't think it's a thing for a corporate venture.

I wouldn't go to Beaverbrook or somebody like that; I don't think it's the kind of thing a company should risk shareholders' money on, but there are people with spare money who might like the character, and the script, and would be prepared to gamble.

Before I'd thought of a film on this occasion, I wrote three fifty-minute scripts which I liked quite well, because I have written for a TV series and that sort of thing before. However, there is one rather large problem. To my mind, I think that in any show with Modesty Blaise and Willie Garvin on the screen, you've got to have two to three minutes of effective unarmed combat of some kind or other. This seems to me to be an essential ingredient of the two. Now this would have to be done, for them, better than it's ever been done before. You'd have to use substitutes — gymnasts, wrestlers — have long shots and intercut the close-ups, and it would be a very tricky technical business. Now on film, you might spend ten days shooting your combat scenes, meticulously, shot by shot; you can't afford to spend ten days for a TV series — you can perhaps afford to spend one day and that just isn't enough to do it. The costs would be too great for TV. However, if the film thing didn't work, then I would go back to the TV idea — but I would try to design the thing, write say another three or four episodes, so that all the combat sequences could be shot back to back, as they say; and that then might make it a possibility...

Romero's SKETCHBOOK

As with much of his *Modesty Blaise* work, artist Enric Badia Romero devised close-up head-shots of his main players before beginning to draw the strips (Modesty and Willie aside, of course). Here are some of the designs for *Take Me To Your Leader* and *Highland Witch*.

CARSON

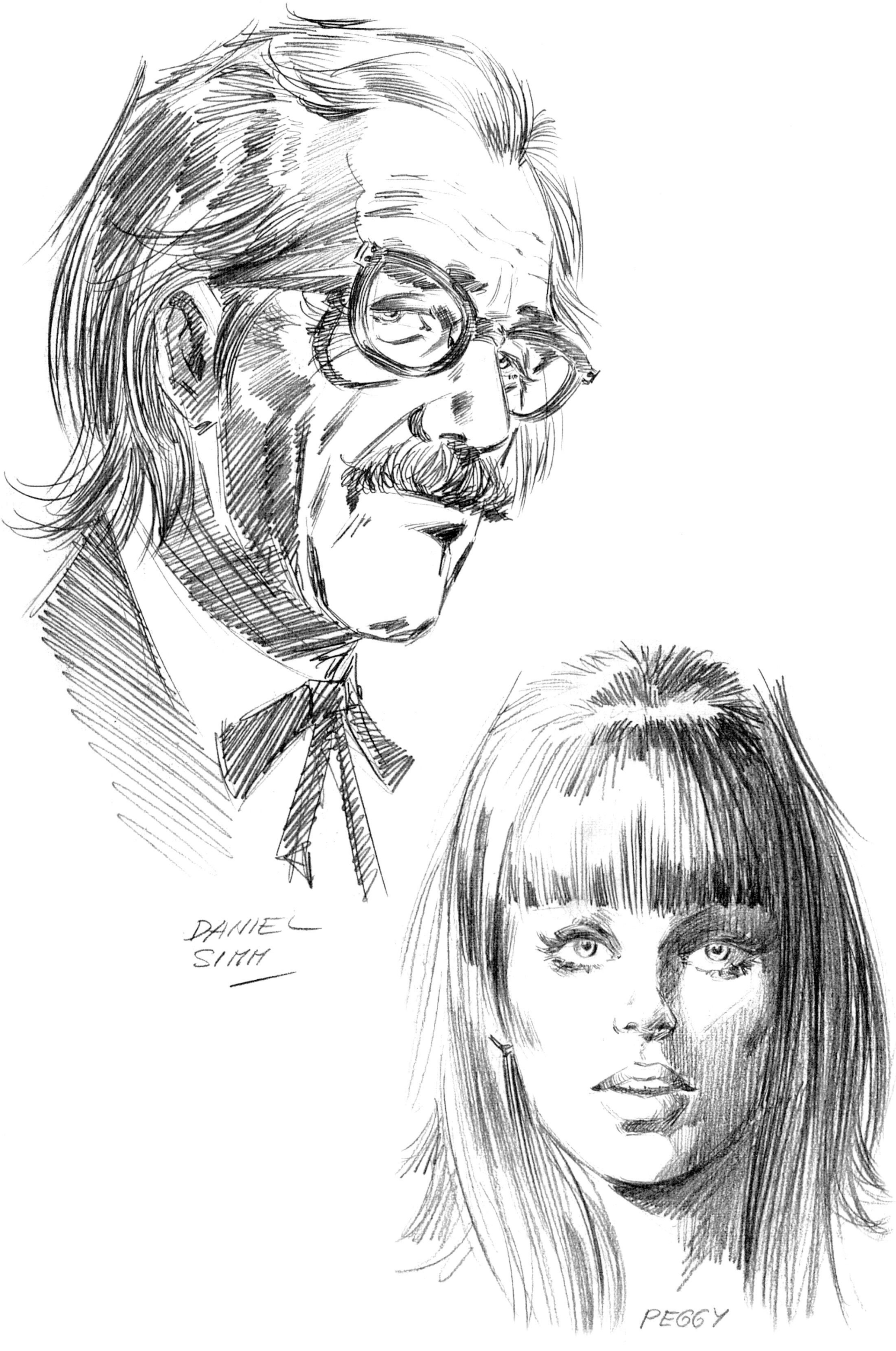
DANIEL SIMM
PEGGY

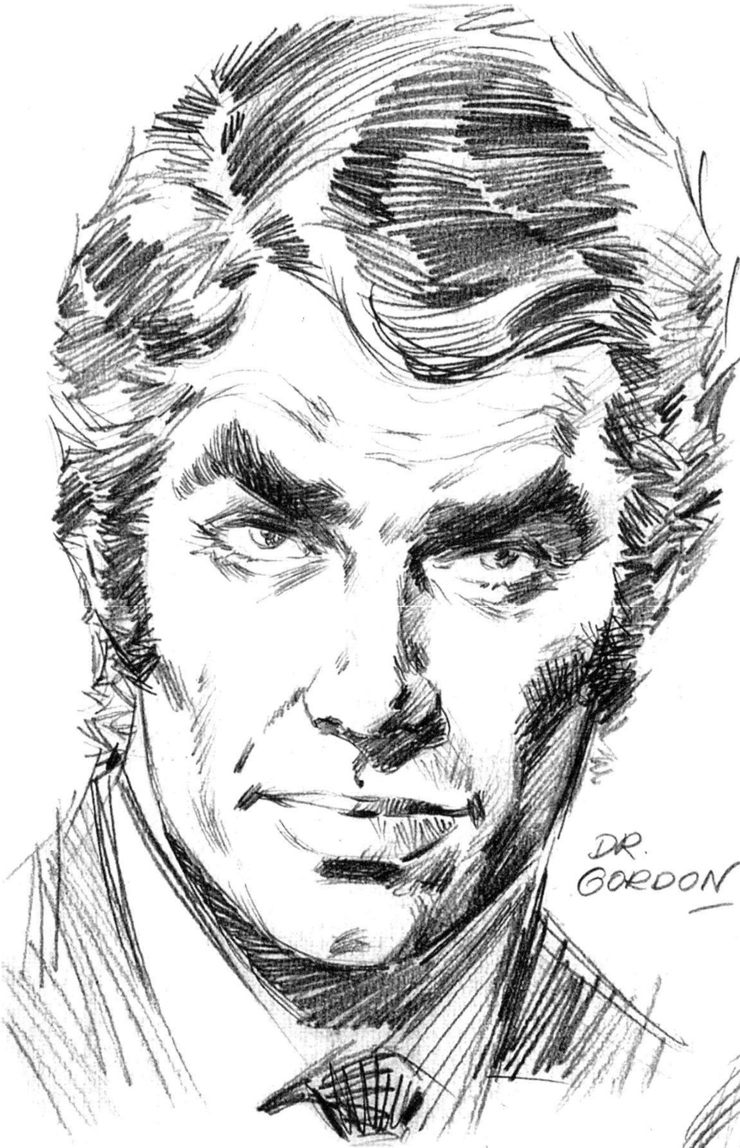
DR. GORDON

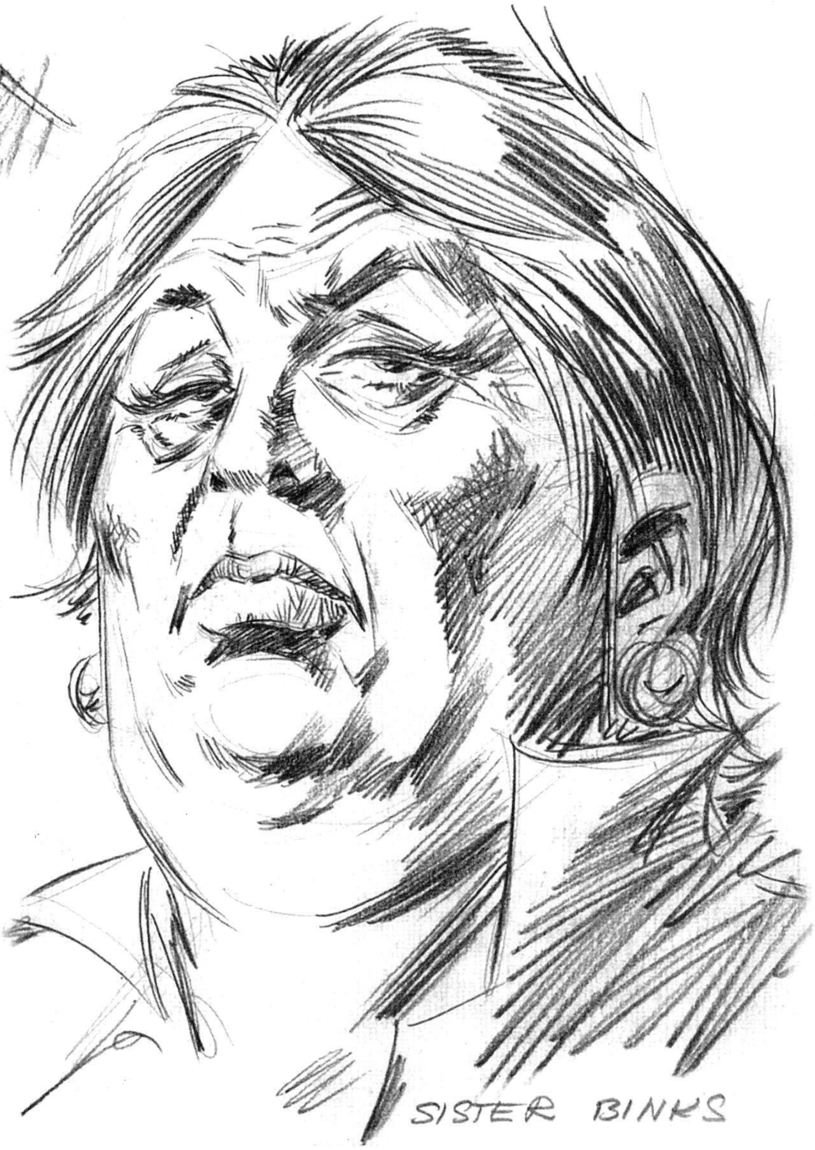
SISTER BINKS

TAKE ME TO YOUR LEADER

Have aliens from another planet landed on Earth in a spaceship? Or is this a gigantic hoax? Or is it neither – whatever that may mean! These are the questions I had to ask myself when I began to write this story. I thought the most likely answer was that it's a hoax, but Modesty and Willie are more open-minded.

They take the view that with a few billion stars in the universe, some must be Earth-type and able to produce life, so with scientific progress there must surely be a probability of contact eventually. In only a few thousand years we might be the first people to reach another populated planet, but if others are smarter than we are, then the reverse could happen. And not just eventually but any time now – like next Tuesday, or even tomorrow.

Or perhaps it already happened somewhere last week, which is why Sir Gerald Tarrant sent Modesty and Willie to confirm or deny an amazing report from an unimpeachable source. If you'd like to join them, read on. It must be quite a caper, whichever.

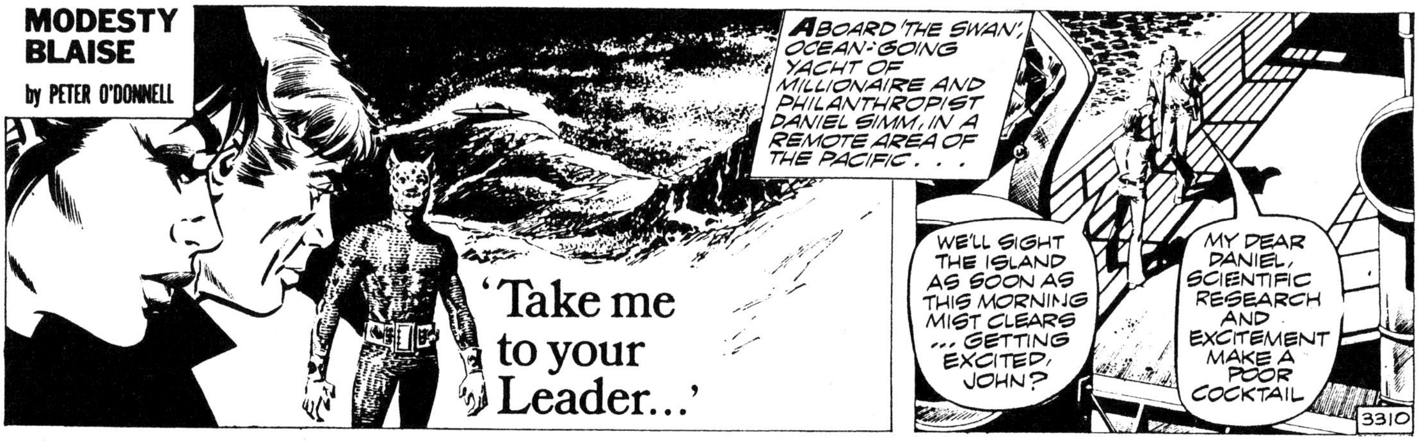
MODESTY BLAISE
by PETER O'DONNELL
'Take me to your Leader…'
ABOARD 'THE SWAN', OCEAN-GOING YACHT OF MILLIONAIRE AND PHILANTHROPIST DANIEL SIMM, IN A REMOTE AREA OF THE PACIFIC . . .
WE'LL SIGHT THE ISLAND AS SOON AS THIS MORNING MIST CLEARS … GETTING EXCITED, JOHN?
MY DEAR DANIEL, SCIENTIFIC RESEARCH AND EXCITEMENT MAKE A POOR COCKTAIL
3310

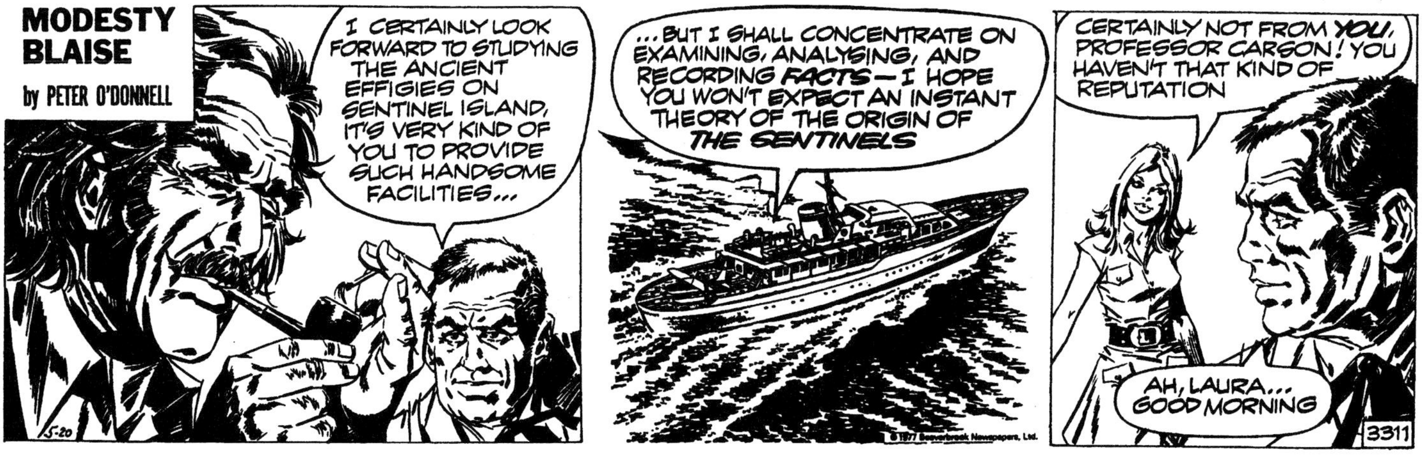
MODESTY BLAISE
by PETER O'DONNELL
I CERTAINLY LOOK FORWARD TO STUDYING THE ANCIENT EFFIGIES ON SENTINEL ISLAND, IT'S VERY KIND OF YOU TO PROVIDE SUCH HANDSOME FACILITIES...
5-20
... BUT I SHALL CONCENTRATE ON EXAMINING, ANALYSING, AND RECORDING FACTS — I HOPE YOU WON'T EXPECT AN INSTANT THEORY OF THE ORIGIN OF THE SENTINELS
© 1977 Beaverbrook Newspapers, Ltd.
CERTAINLY NOT FROM YOU, PROFESSOR CARSON! YOU HAVEN'T THAT KIND OF REPUTATION
AH, LAURA... GOOD MORNING
3311

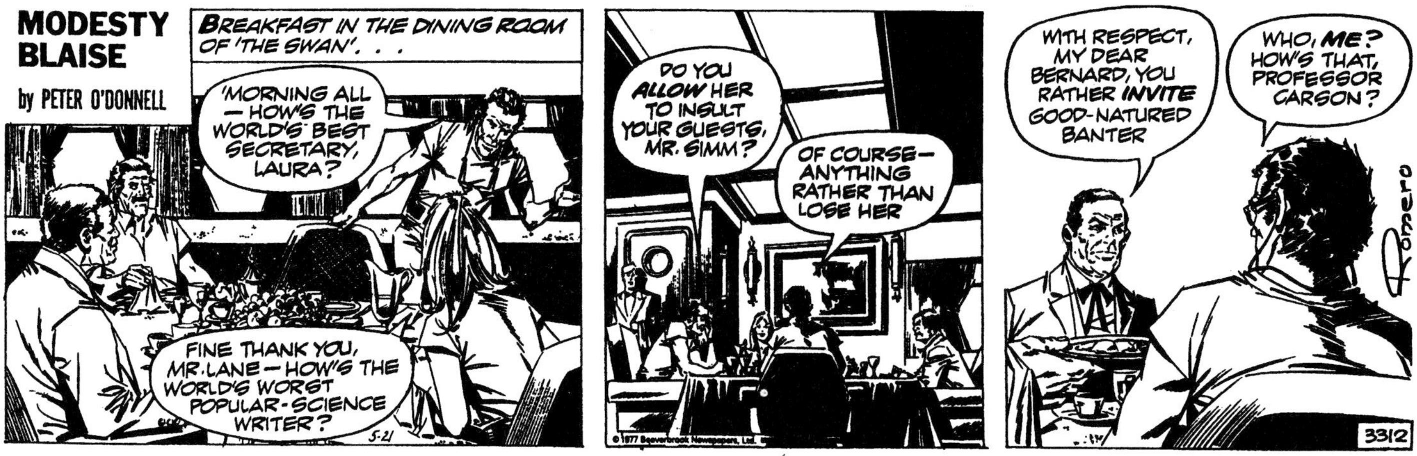
MODESTY BLAISE
by PETER O'DONNELL
BREAKFAST IN THE DINING ROOM OF 'THE SWAN'. . .
'MORNING ALL — HOW'S THE WORLD'S BEST SECRETARY, LAURA?
FINE THANK YOU, MR. LANE — HOW'S THE WORLD'S WORST POPULAR-SCIENCE WRITER?
5-21
DO YOU ALLOW HER TO INSULT YOUR GUESTS, MR. SIMM?
OF COURSE — ANYTHING RATHER THAN LOSE HER
© 1977 Beaverbrook Newspapers, Ltd.
WITH RESPECT, MY DEAR BERNARD, YOU RATHER INVITE GOOD-NATURED BANTER
WHO, ME? HOW'S THAT, PROFESSOR CARSON?
Romero
3312

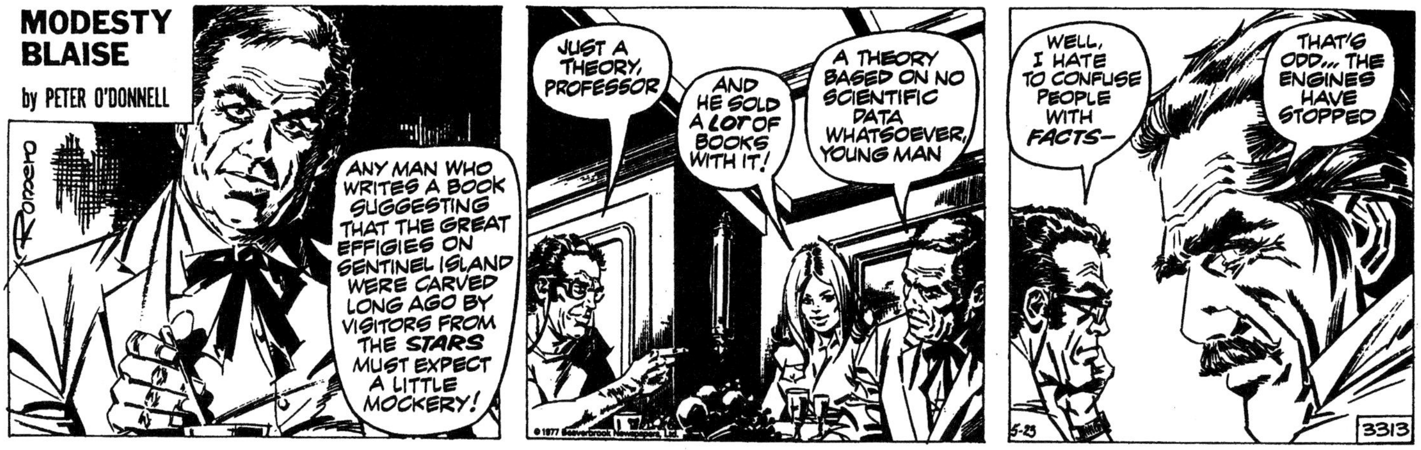
MODESTY BLAISE
by PETER O'DONNELL
Romero
ANY MAN WHO WRITES A BOOK SUGGESTING THAT THE GREAT EFFIGIES ON SENTINEL ISLAND WERE CARVED LONG AGO BY VISITORS FROM THE STARS MUST EXPECT A LITTLE MOCKERY!
JUST A THEORY, PROFESSOR
AND HE SOLD A LOT OF BOOKS WITH IT!
A THEORY BASED ON NO SCIENTIFIC DATA WHATSOEVER, YOUNG MAN
© 1977 Beaverbrook Newspapers, Ltd.
WELL, I HATE TO CONFUSE PEOPLE WITH FACTS—
THAT'S ODD... THE ENGINES HAVE STOPPED
5-23
3313

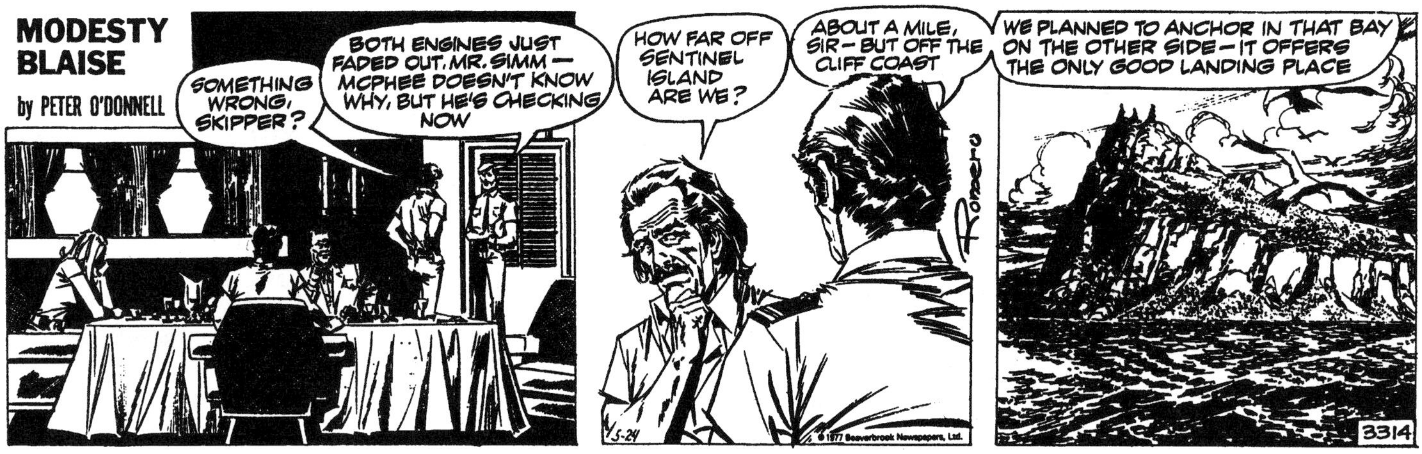
MODESTY BLAISE
by PETER O'DONNELL
SOMETHING WRONG, SKIPPER?
BOTH ENGINES JUST FADED OUT, MR. SIMM — McPHEE DOESN'T KNOW WHY, BUT HE'S CHECKING NOW
HOW FAR OFF SENTINEL ISLAND ARE WE?
ABOUT A MILE, SIR — BUT OFF THE CLIFF COAST
WE PLANNED TO ANCHOR IN THAT BAY ON THE OTHER SIDE — IT OFFERS THE ONLY GOOD LANDING PLACE
Romero
5-24
© 1977 Beaverbrook Newspapers, Ltd.
3314

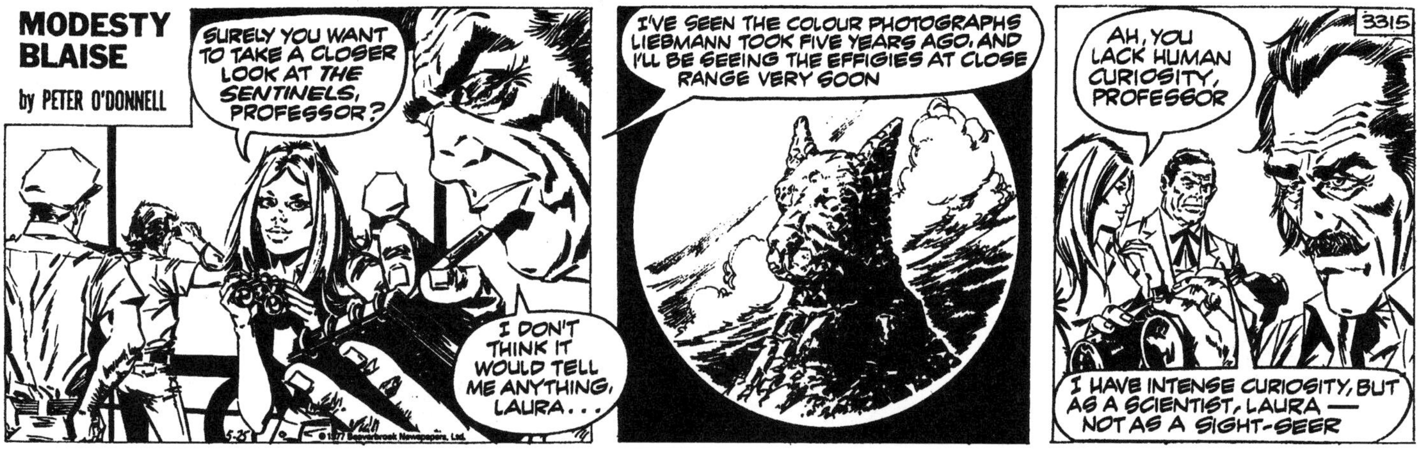
MODESTY BLAISE
by PETER O'DONNELL
SURELY YOU WANT TO TAKE A CLOSER LOOK AT THE SENTINELS, PROFESSOR?
I DON'T THINK IT WOULD TELL ME ANYTHING, LAURA . . .
I'VE SEEN THE COLOUR PHOTOGRAPHS LIEBMANN TOOK FIVE YEARS AGO, AND I'LL BE SEEING THE EFFIGIES AT CLOSE RANGE VERY SOON
AH, YOU LACK HUMAN CURIOSITY, PROFESSOR
I HAVE INTENSE CURIOSITY, BUT AS A SCIENTIST, LAURA — NOT AS A SIGHT-SEER
5-25
© 1977 Beaverbrook Newspapers, Ltd.
3315

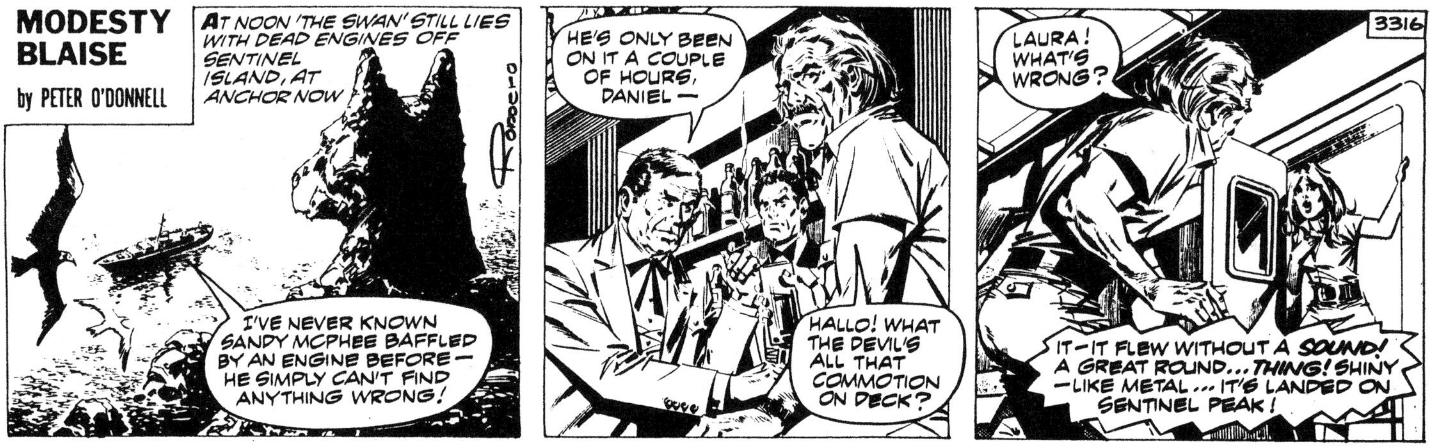
MODESTY BLAISE
by PETER O'DONNELL
AT NOON 'THE SWAN' STILL LIES WITH DEAD ENGINES OFF SENTINEL ISLAND, AT ANCHOR NOW
I'VE NEVER KNOWN SANDY McPHEE BAFFLED BY AN ENGINE BEFORE — HE SIMPLY CAN'T FIND ANYTHING WRONG!
Romero
HE'S ONLY BEEN ON IT A COUPLE OF HOURS, DANIEL —
HALLO! WHAT THE DEVIL'S ALL THAT COMMOTION ON DECK?
LAURA! WHAT'S WRONG?
IT — IT FLEW WITHOUT A SOUND! A GREAT ROUND... THING! SHINY — LIKE METAL ... IT'S LANDED ON SENTINEL PEAK!
3316

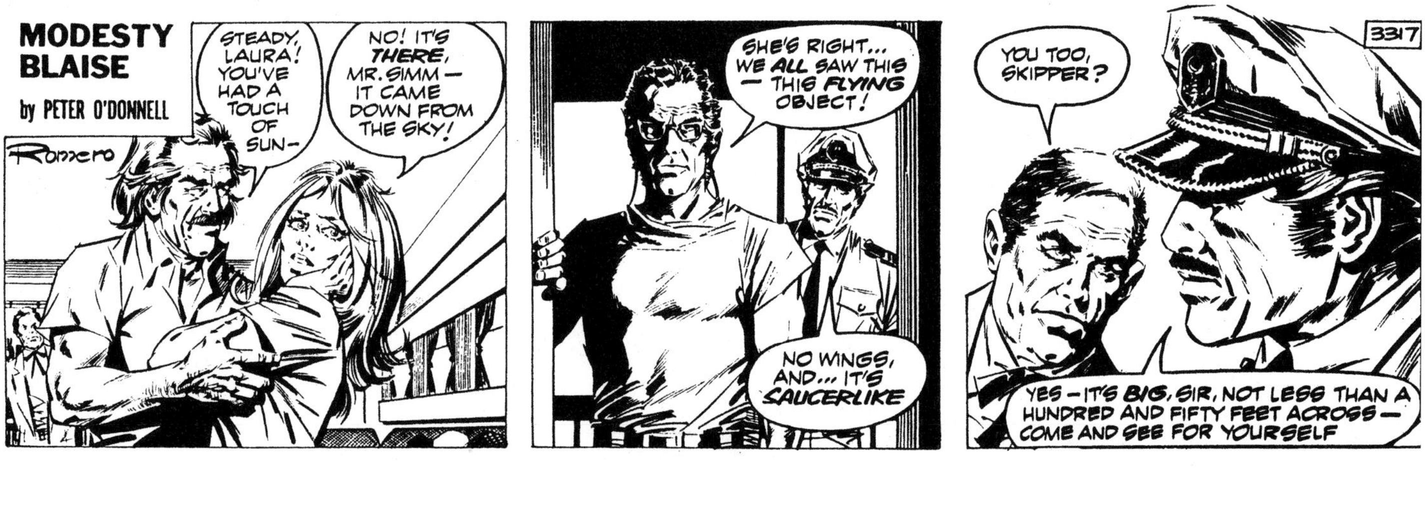
MODESTY BLAISE
by PETER O'DONNELL
Romero
STEADY, LAURA! YOU'VE HAD A TOUCH OF SUN —
NO! IT'S THERE, MR. SIMM — IT CAME DOWN FROM THE SKY!
SHE'S RIGHT... WE ALL SAW THIS — THIS FLYING OBJECT!
NO WINGS, AND... IT'S SAUCERLIKE
YOU TOO, SKIPPER?
YES — IT'S BIG, SIR, NOT LESS THAN A HUNDRED AND FIFTY FEET ACROSS — COME AND SEE FOR YOURSELF
3317

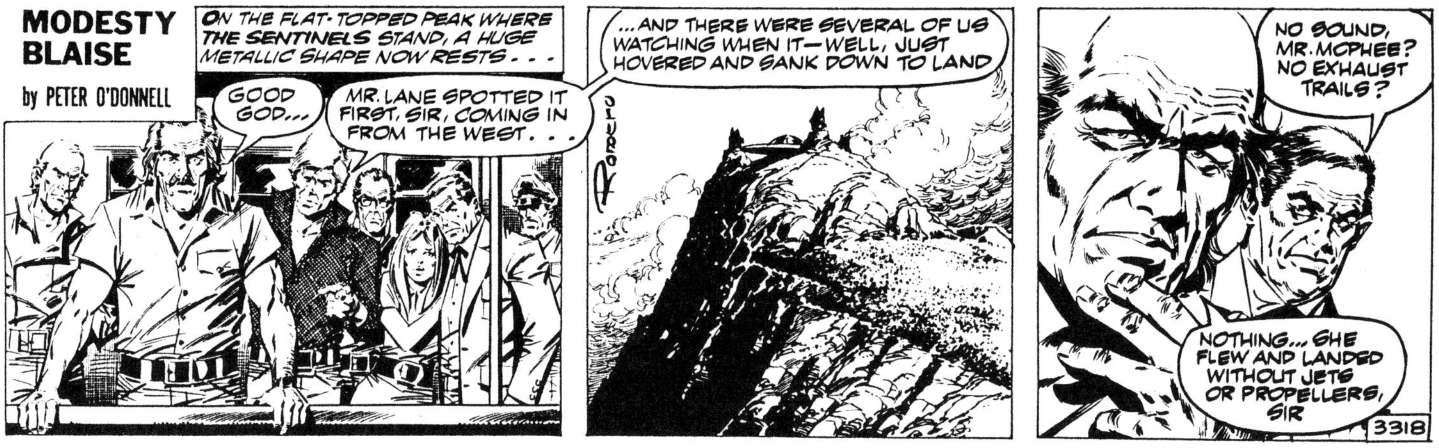
MODESTY BLAISE
by PETER O'DONNELL
ON THE FLAT-TOPPED PEAK WHERE THE SENTINELS STAND, A HUGE METALLIC SHAPE NOW RESTS . . .
GOOD GOD...
MR. LANE SPOTTED IT FIRST, SIR, COMING IN FROM THE WEST . . .
...AND THERE WERE SEVERAL OF US WATCHING WHEN IT—WELL, JUST HOVERED AND SANK DOWN TO LAND
NO SOUND, MR. MCPHEE? NO EXHAUST TRAILS?
NOTHING... SHE FLEW AND LANDED WITHOUT JETS OR PROPELLERS, SIR
3318

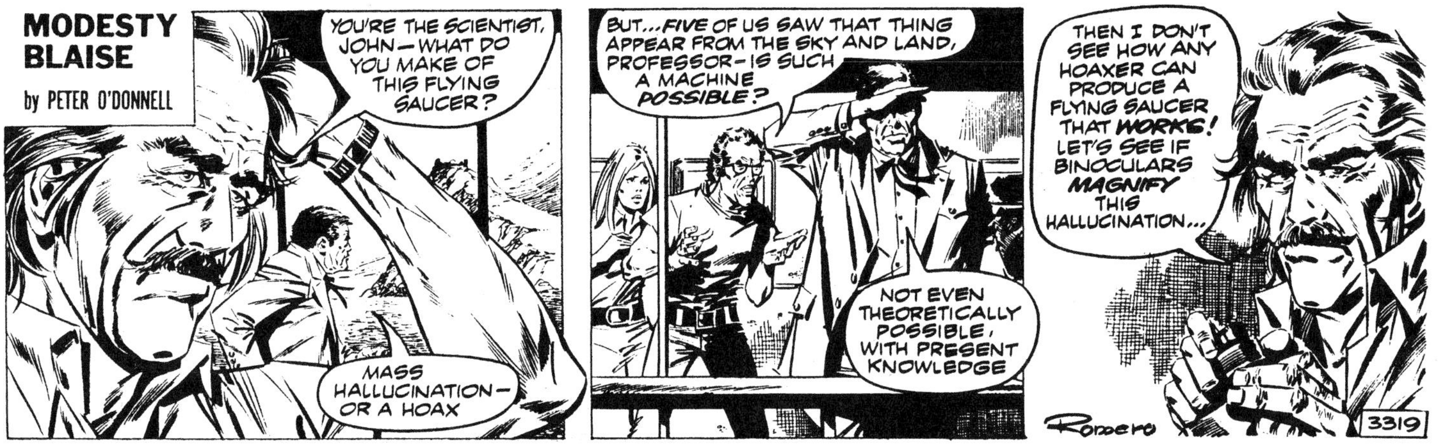
MODESTY BLAISE
by PETER O'DONNELL
YOU'RE THE SCIENTIST, JOHN—WHAT DO YOU MAKE OF THIS FLYING SAUCER?
MASS HALLUCINATION—OR A HOAX
BUT... FIVE OF US SAW THAT THING APPEAR FROM THE SKY AND LAND, PROFESSOR—IS SUCH A MACHINE POSSIBLE?
NOT EVEN THEORETICALLY POSSIBLE, WITH PRESENT KNOWLEDGE
THEN I DON'T SEE HOW ANY HOAXER CAN PRODUCE A FLYING SAUCER THAT WORKS! LET'S SEE IF BINOCULARS MAGNIFY THIS HALLUCINATION...
Romero
3319

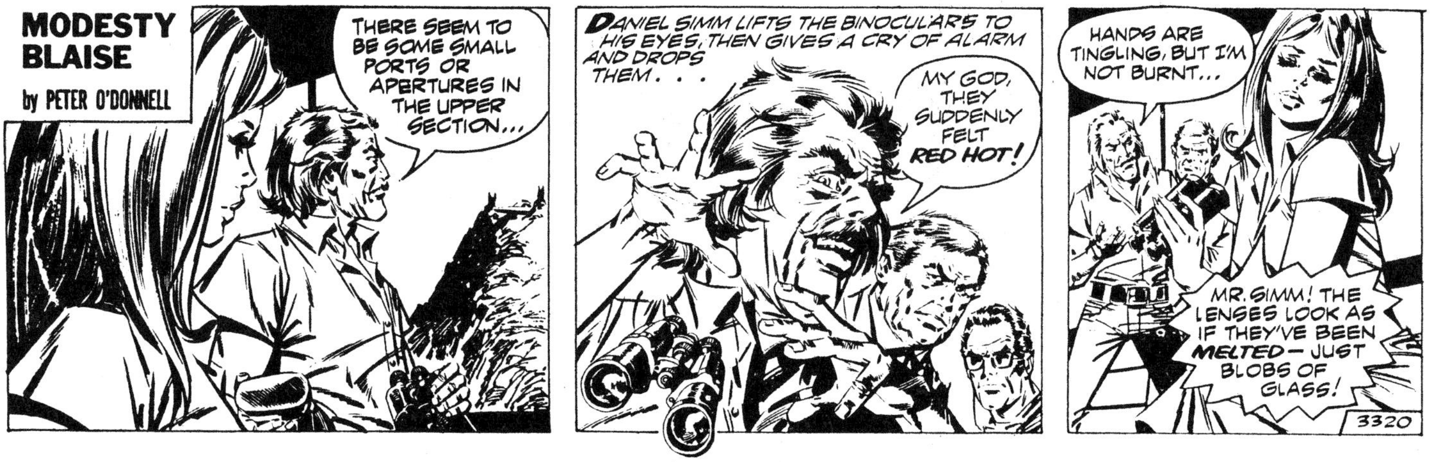
MODESTY BLAISE
by PETER O'DONNELL
THERE SEEM TO BE SOME SMALL PORTS OR APERTURES IN THE UPPER SECTION...
DANIEL SIMM LIFTS THE BINOCULARS TO HIS EYES, THEN GIVES A CRY OF ALARM AND DROPS THEM . . .
MY GOD, THEY SUDDENLY FELT RED HOT!
HANDS ARE TINGLING, BUT I'M NOT BURNT...
MR. SIMM! THE LENSES LOOK AS IF THEY'VE BEEN MELTED—JUST BLOBS OF GLASS!
3320

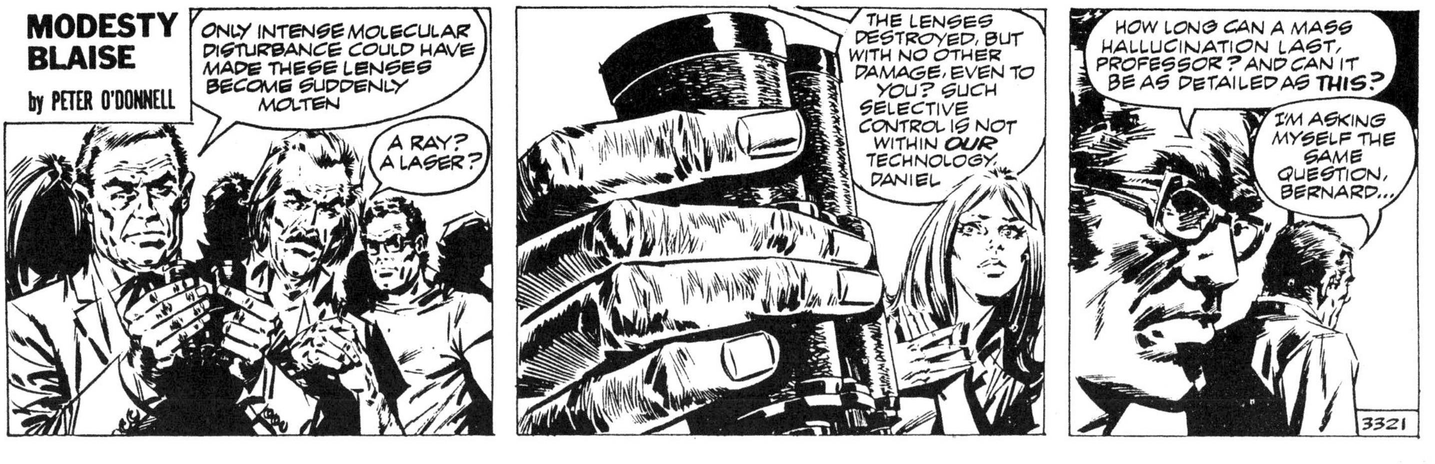
MODESTY BLAISE
by PETER O'DONNELL
ONLY INTENSE MOLECULAR DISTURBANCE COULD HAVE MADE THESE LENSES BECOME SUDDENLY MOLTEN
A RAY? A LASER?
THE LENSES DESTROYED, BUT WITH NO OTHER DAMAGE, EVEN TO YOU? SUCH SELECTIVE CONTROL IS NOT WITHIN OUR TECHNOLOGY, DANIEL
HOW LONG CAN A MASS HALLUCINATION LAST, PROFESSOR? AND CAN IT BE AS DETAILED AS THIS?
I'M ASKING MYSELF THE SAME QUESTION, BERNARD...
3321

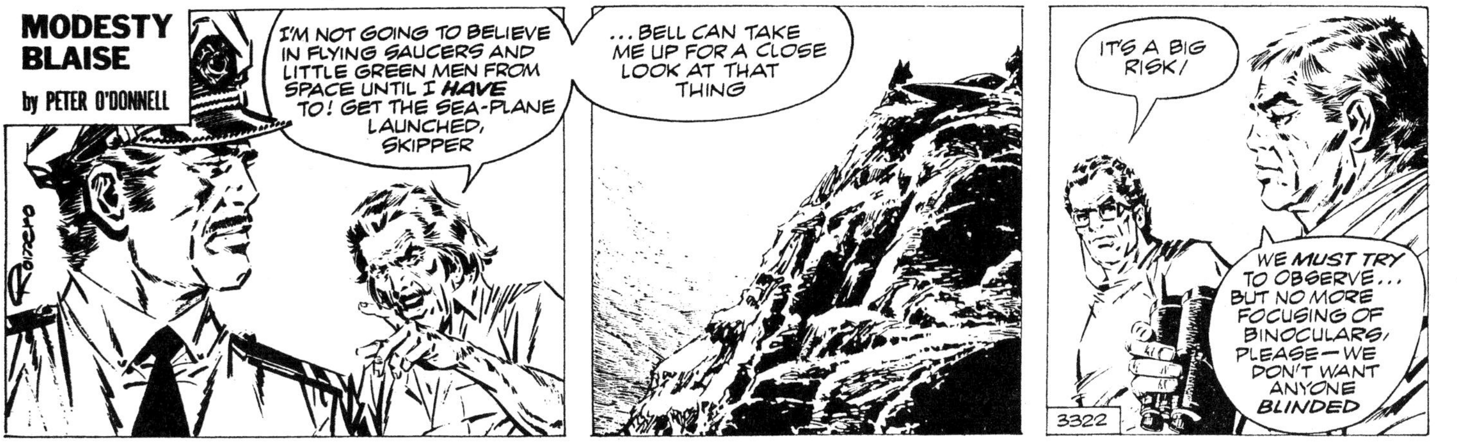
MODESTY BLAISE
by PETER O'DONNELL
I'M NOT GOING TO BELIEVE IN FLYING SAUCERS AND LITTLE GREEN MEN FROM SPACE UNTIL I HAVE TO! GET THE SEA-PLANE LAUNCHED, SKIPPER
...BELL CAN TAKE ME UP FOR A CLOSE LOOK AT THAT THING
IT'S A BIG RISK!
WE MUST TRY TO OBSERVE... BUT NO MORE FOCUSING OF BINOCULARS, PLEASE—WE DON'T WANT ANYONE BLINDED
3322

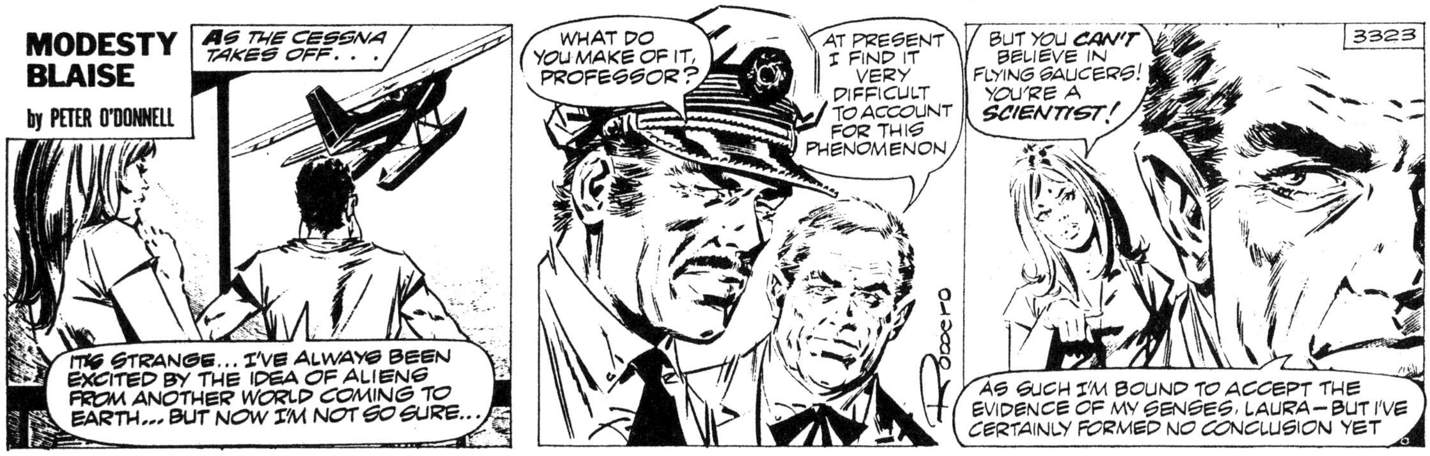
MODESTY BLAISE
by PETER O'DONNELL
AS THE CESSNA TAKES OFF...
IT'S STRANGE... I'VE ALWAYS BEEN EXCITED BY THE IDEA OF ALIENS FROM ANOTHER WORLD COMING TO EARTH... BUT NOW I'M NOT SO SURE...
WHAT DO YOU MAKE OF IT, PROFESSOR?
AT PRESENT I FIND IT VERY DIFFICULT TO ACCOUNT FOR THIS PHENOMENON
3323
BUT YOU CAN'T BELIEVE IN FLYING SAUCERS! YOU'RE A SCIENTIST!
AS SUCH I'M BOUND TO ACCEPT THE EVIDENCE OF MY SENSES, LAURA—BUT I'VE CERTAINLY FORMED NO CONCLUSION YET

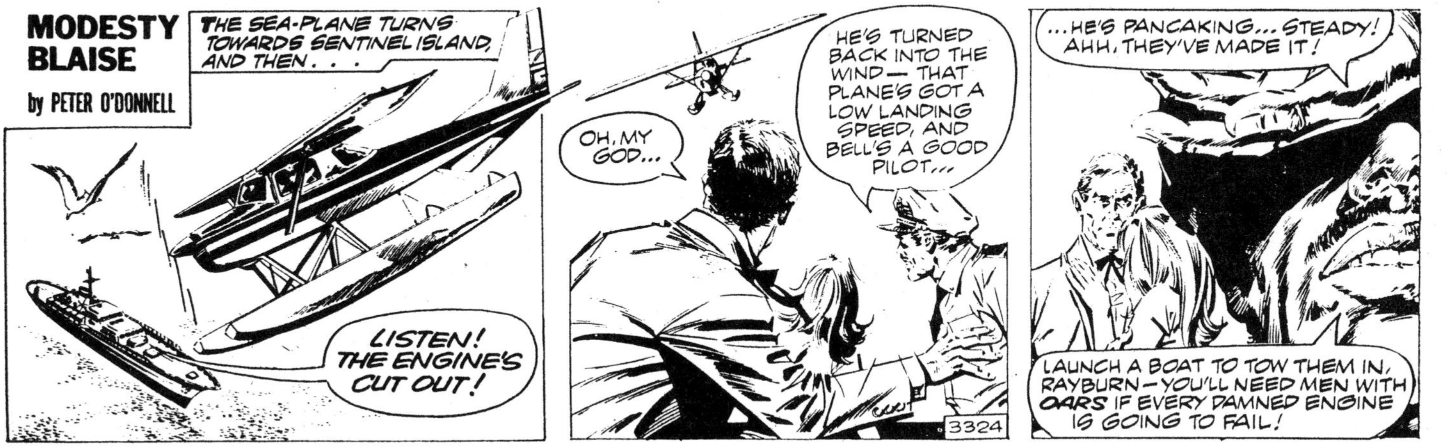
MODESTY BLAISE
by PETER O'DONNELL
THE SEA-PLANE TURNS TOWARDS SENTINEL ISLAND, AND THEN...
LISTEN! THE ENGINE'S CUT OUT!
OH, MY GOD...
HE'S TURNED BACK INTO THE WIND— THAT PLANE'S GOT A LOW LANDING SPEED, AND BELL'S A GOOD PILOT...
3324
...HE'S PANCAKING... STEADY! AHH, THEY'VE MADE IT!
LAUNCH A BOAT TO TOW THEM IN, RAYBURN—YOU'LL NEED MEN WITH OARS IF EVERY DAMNED ENGINE IS GOING TO FAIL!

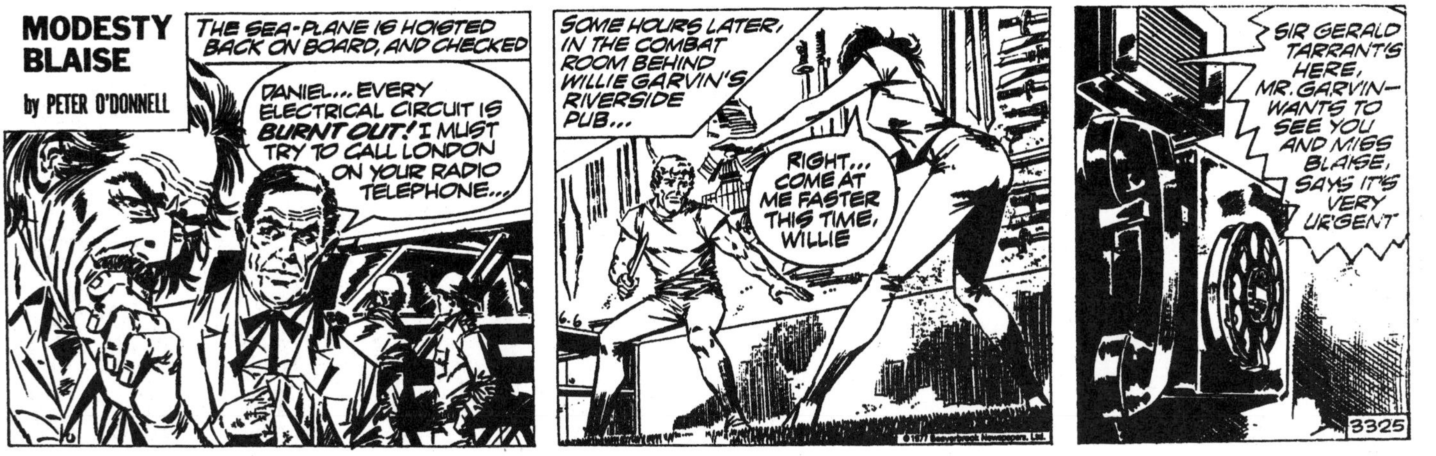
MODESTY BLAISE
by PETER O'DONNELL
THE SEA-PLANE IS HOISTED BACK ON BOARD, AND CHECKED
DANIEL... EVERY ELECTRICAL CIRCUIT IS BURNT OUT! I MUST TRY TO CALL LONDON ON YOUR RADIO TELEPHONE...
SOME HOURS LATER, IN THE COMBAT ROOM BEHIND WILLIE GARVIN'S RIVERSIDE PUB...
RIGHT... COME AT ME FASTER THIS TIME, WILLIE
© 1977 Beaverbrook Newspapers Ltd.
SIR GERALD TARRANT'S HERE, MR. GARVIN— WANTS TO SEE YOU AND MISS BLAISE. SAYS IT'S VERY URGENT
3325

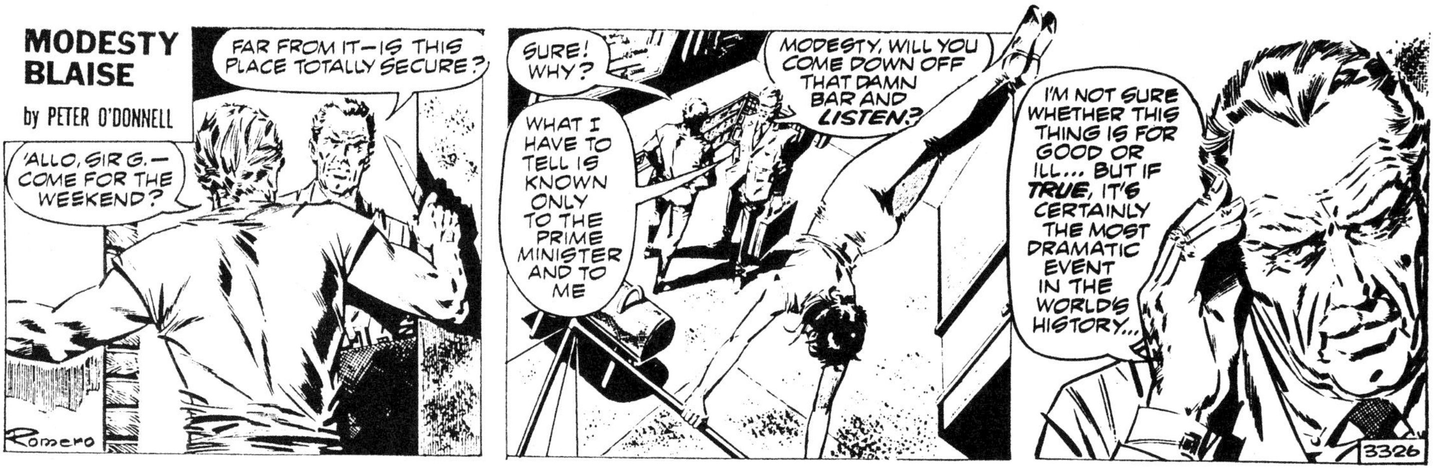
MODESTY BLAISE
by PETER O'DONNELL
FAR FROM IT—IS THIS PLACE TOTALLY SECURE?
'ALLO, SIR G.—COME FOR THE WEEKEND?
Romero
SURE! WHY?
MODESTY, WILL YOU COME DOWN OFF THAT DAMN BAR AND LISTEN?
WHAT I HAVE TO TELL IS KNOWN ONLY TO THE PRIME MINISTER AND TO ME
I'M NOT SURE WHETHER THIS THING IS FOR GOOD OR ILL... BUT IF TRUE, IT'S CERTAINLY THE MOST DRAMATIC EVENT IN THE WORLD'S HISTORY...
3326

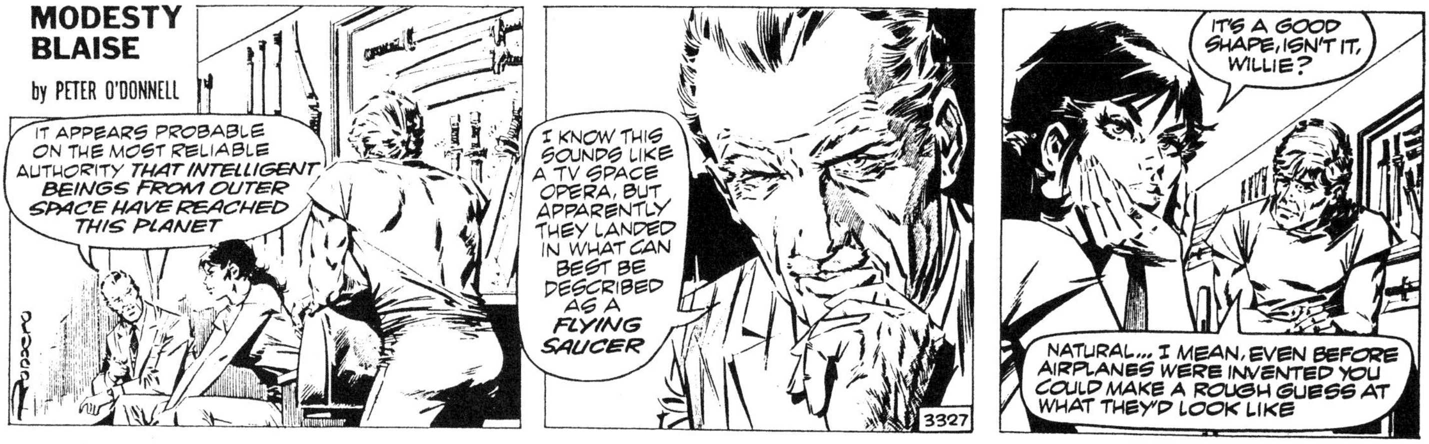
MODESTY BLAISE
by PETER O'DONNELL
IT APPEARS PROBABLE ON THE MOST RELIABLE AUTHORITY THAT INTELLIGENT BEINGS FROM OUTER SPACE HAVE REACHED THIS PLANET
I KNOW THIS SOUNDS LIKE A TV SPACE OPERA, BUT APPARENTLY THEY LANDED IN WHAT CAN BEST BE DESCRIBED AS A FLYING SAUCER
3327
IT'S A GOOD SHAPE, ISN'T IT, WILLIE?
NATURAL... I MEAN, EVEN BEFORE AIRPLANES WERE INVENTED YOU COULD MAKE A ROUGH GUESS AT WHAT THEY'D LOOK LIKE

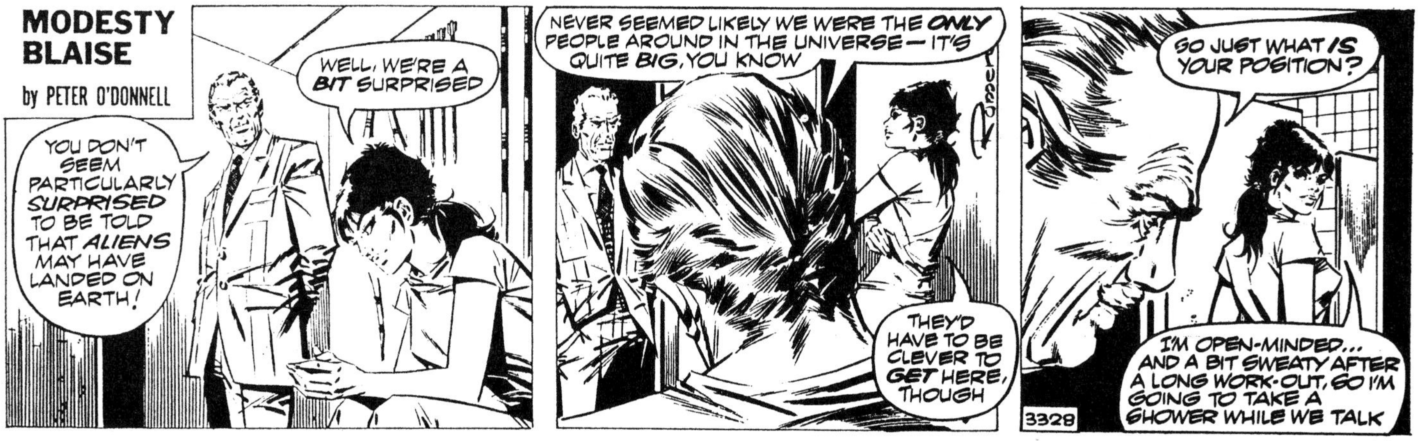
MODESTY BLAISE
by PETER O'DONNELL
YOU DON'T SEEM PARTICULARLY SURPRISED TO BE TOLD THAT ALIENS MAY HAVE LANDED ON EARTH!
WELL, WE'RE A BIT SURPRISED
NEVER SEEMED LIKELY WE WERE THE ONLY PEOPLE AROUND IN THE UNIVERSE—IT'S QUITE BIG, YOU KNOW
THEY'D HAVE TO BE CLEVER TO GET HERE, THOUGH
3328
SO JUST WHAT IS YOUR POSITION?
I'M OPEN-MINDED... AND A BIT SWEATY AFTER A LONG WORK-OUT, SO I'M GOING TO TAKE A SHOWER WHILE WE TALK

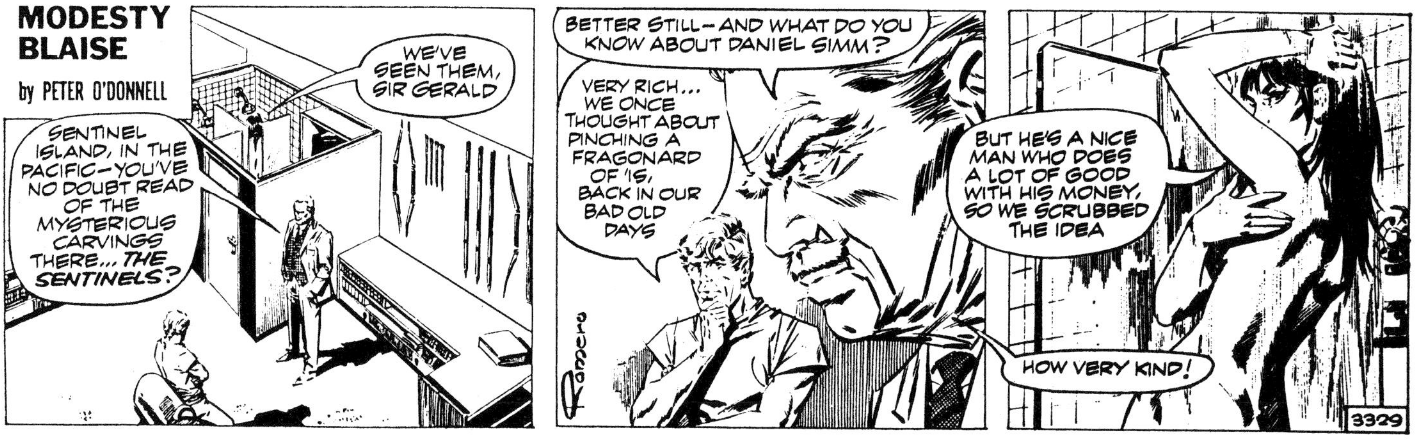
MODESTY BLAISE
by PETER O'DONNELL
SENTINEL ISLAND, IN THE PACIFIC—YOU'VE NO DOUBT READ OF THE MYSTERIOUS CARVINGS THERE... THE SENTINELS?
WE'VE SEEN THEM, SIR GERALD
BETTER STILL—AND WHAT DO YOU KNOW ABOUT DANIEL SIMM?
VERY RICH... WE ONCE THOUGHT ABOUT PINCHING A FRAGONARD OF 'IS, BACK IN OUR BAD OLD DAYS
Romero
BUT HE'S A NICE MAN WHO DOES A LOT OF GOOD WITH HIS MONEY, SO WE SCRUBBED THE IDEA
HOW VERY KIND!
3329

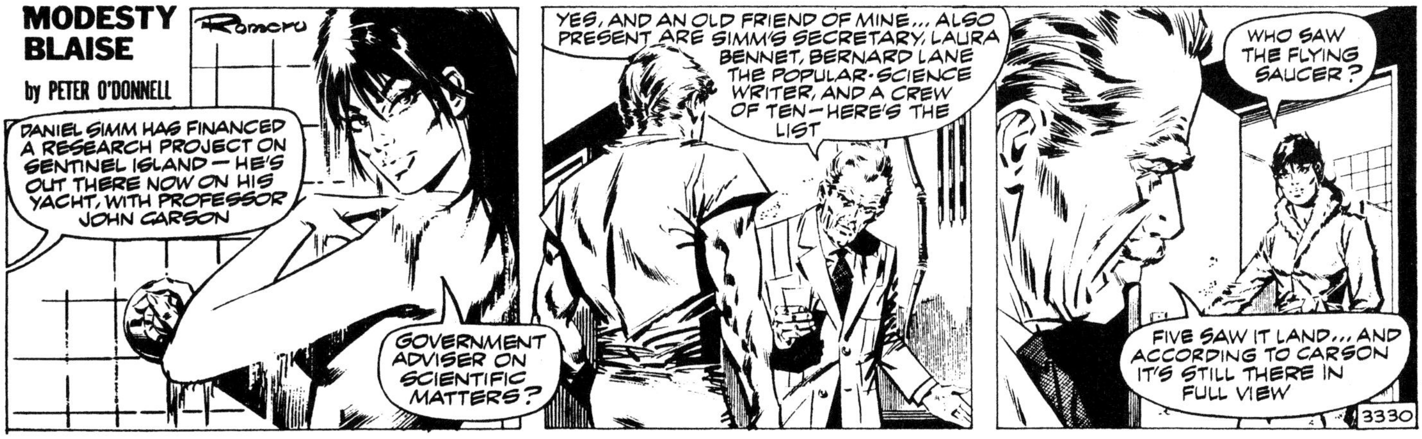
MODESTY BLAISE
by PETER O'DONNELL
DANIEL SIMM HAS FINANCED A RESEARCH PROJECT ON SENTINEL ISLAND — HE'S OUT THERE NOW ON HIS YACHT, WITH PROFESSOR JOHN CARSON
GOVERNMENT ADVISER ON SCIENTIFIC MATTERS?
YES, AND AN OLD FRIEND OF MINE... ALSO PRESENT ARE SIMM'S SECRETARY, LAURA BENNET, BERNARD LANE THE POPULAR-SCIENCE WRITER, AND A CREW OF TEN — HERE'S THE LIST
WHO SAW THE FLYING SAUCER?
FIVE SAW IT LAND... AND ACCORDING TO CARSON IT'S STILL THERE IN FULL VIEW
3330

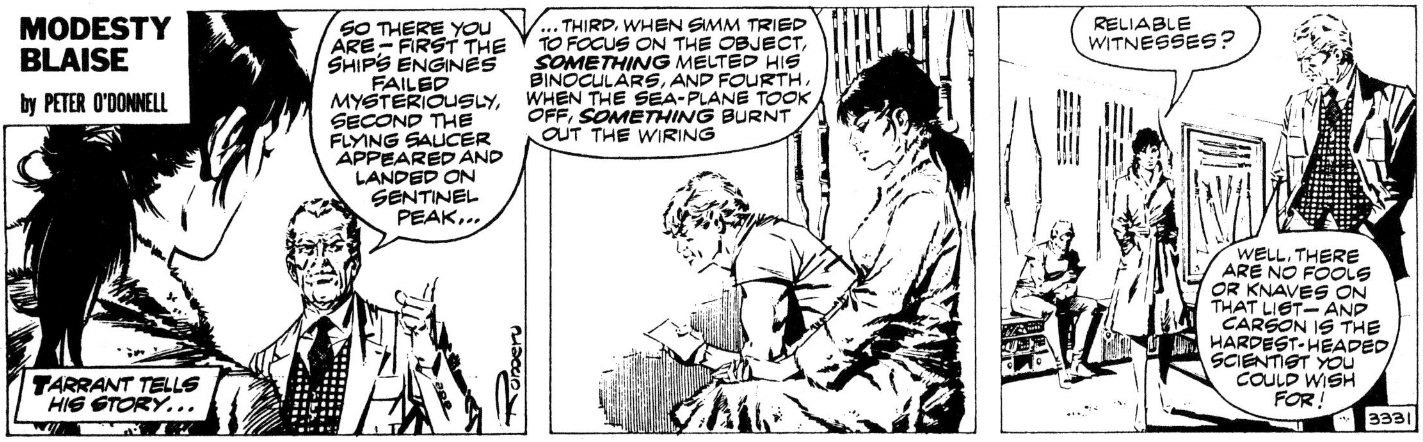
MODESTY BLAISE
by PETER O'DONNELL
TARRANT TELLS HIS STORY...
SO THERE YOU ARE — FIRST THE SHIP'S ENGINES FAILED MYSTERIOUSLY, SECOND THE FLYING SAUCER APPEARED AND LANDED ON SENTINEL PEAK...
...THIRD, WHEN SIMM TRIED TO FOCUS ON THE OBJECT, SOMETHING MELTED HIS BINOCULARS, AND FOURTH, WHEN THE SEA-PLANE TOOK OFF, SOMETHING BURNT OUT THE WIRING
RELIABLE WITNESSES?
WELL, THERE ARE NO FOOLS OR KNAVES ON THAT LIST — AND CARSON IS THE HARDEST-HEADED SCIENTIST YOU COULD WISH FOR!
3331

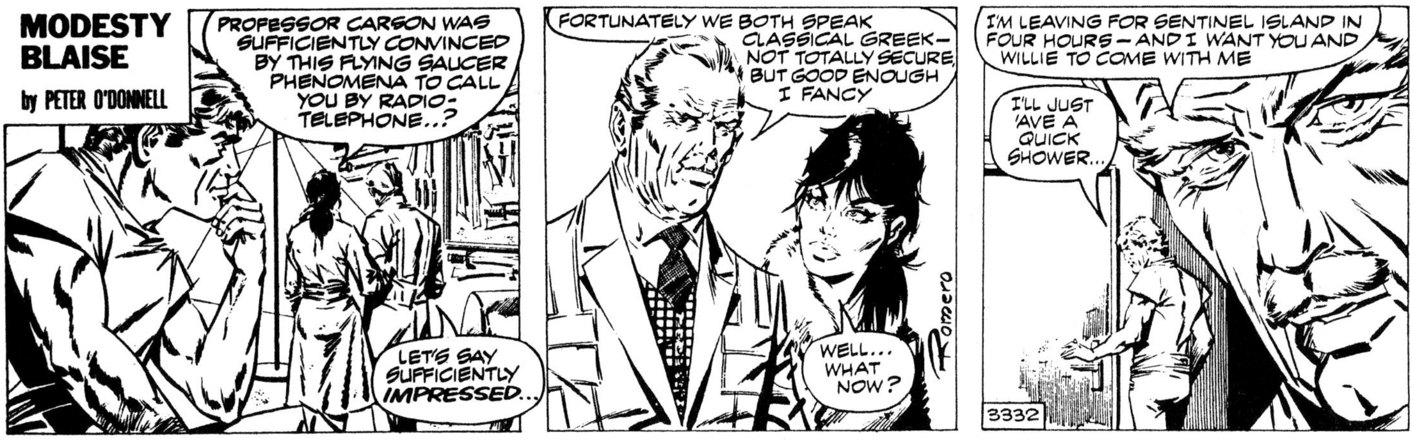
MODESTY BLAISE
by PETER O'DONNELL
PROFESSOR CARSON WAS SUFFICIENTLY CONVINCED BY THIS FLYING SAUCER PHENOMENA TO CALL YOU BY RADIO-TELEPHONE..?
LET'S SAY SUFFICIENTLY IMPRESSED...
FORTUNATELY WE BOTH SPEAK CLASSICAL GREEK — NOT TOTALLY SECURE, BUT GOOD ENOUGH I FANCY
WELL... WHAT NOW?
I'M LEAVING FOR SENTINEL ISLAND IN FOUR HOURS — AND I WANT YOU AND WILLIE TO COME WITH ME
I'LL JUST 'AVE A QUICK SHOWER...
3332

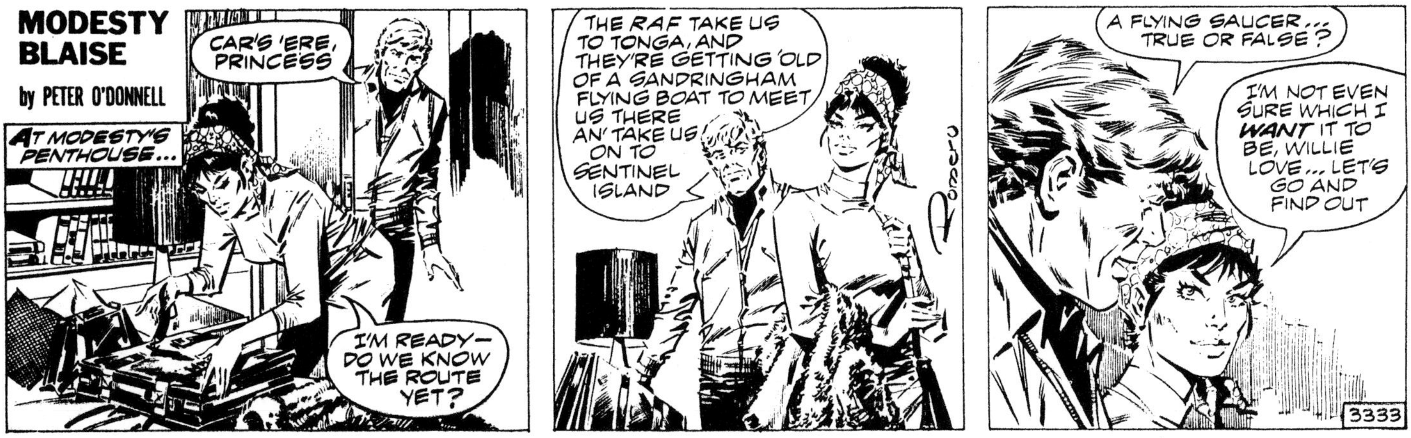
MODESTY BLAISE
by PETER O'DONNELL
AT MODESTY'S PENTHOUSE...
CAR'S 'ERE, PRINCESS
I'M READY — DO WE KNOW THE ROUTE YET?
THE RAF TAKE US TO TONGA, AND THEY'RE GETTING 'OLD OF A SANDRINGHAM FLYING BOAT TO MEET US THERE AN' TAKE US ON TO SENTINEL ISLAND
A FLYING SAUCER... TRUE OR FALSE?
I'M NOT EVEN SURE WHICH I WANT IT TO BE, WILLIE LOVE... LET'S GO AND FIND OUT
3333

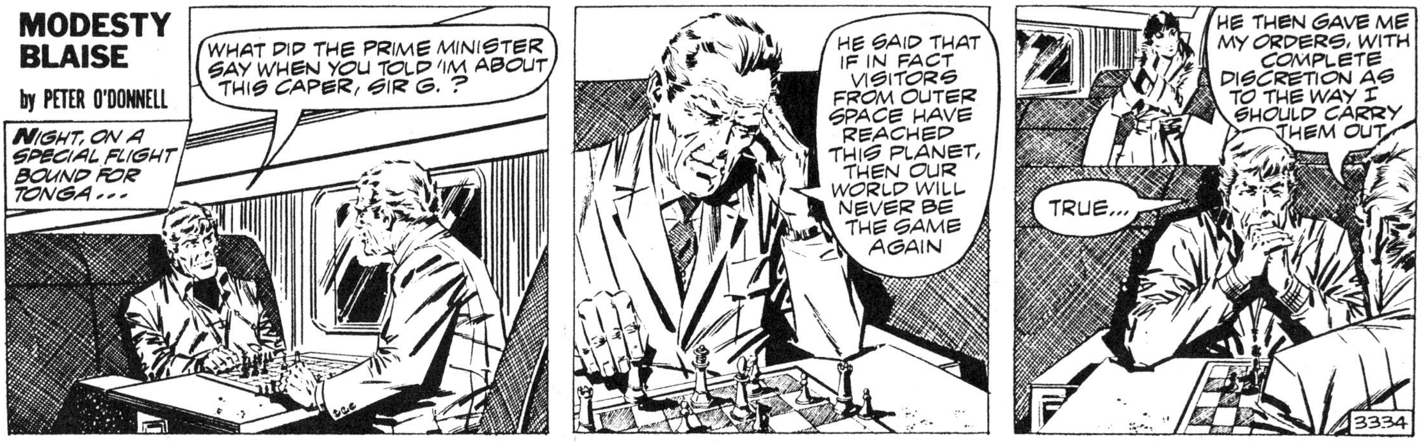
MODESTY BLAISE
by PETER O'DONNELL
NIGHT, ON A SPECIAL FLIGHT BOUND FOR TONGA . . .
WHAT DID THE PRIME MINISTER SAY WHEN YOU TOLD 'IM ABOUT THIS CAPER, SIR G. ?
HE SAID THAT IF IN FACT VISITORS FROM OUTER SPACE HAVE REACHED THIS PLANET, THEN OUR WORLD WILL NEVER BE THE SAME AGAIN
HE THEN GAVE ME MY ORDERS, WITH COMPLETE DISCRETION AS TO THE WAY I SHOULD CARRY THEM OUT
TRUE...
3334

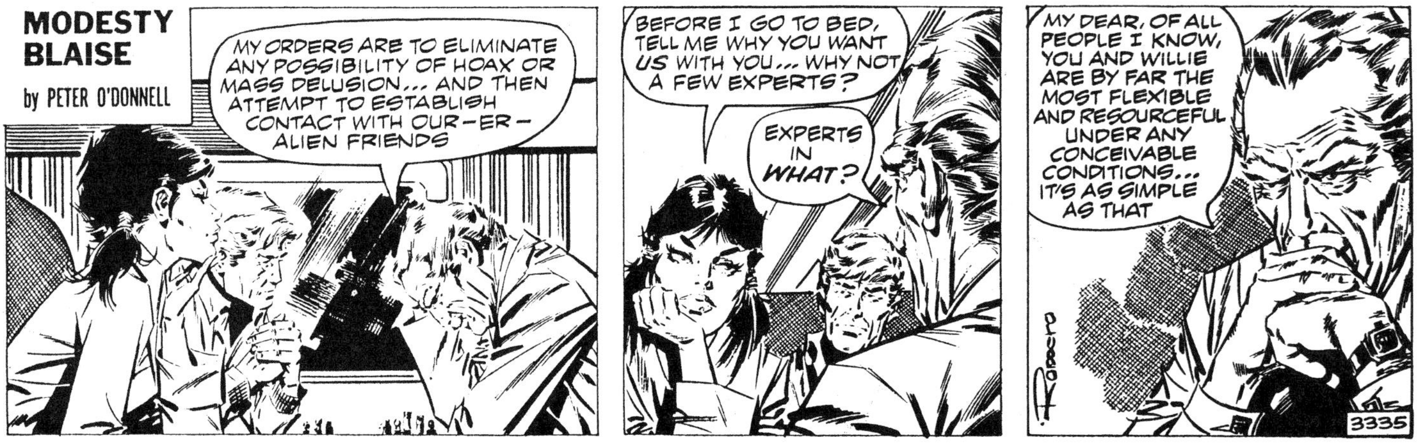
MODESTY BLAISE
by PETER O'DONNELL
MY ORDERS ARE TO ELIMINATE ANY POSSIBILITY OF HOAX OR MASS DELUSION... AND THEN ATTEMPT TO ESTABLISH CONTACT WITH OUR—ER— ALIEN FRIENDS
BEFORE I GO TO BED, TELL ME WHY YOU WANT US WITH YOU... WHY NOT A FEW EXPERTS?
EXPERTS IN WHAT?
MY DEAR, OF ALL PEOPLE I KNOW, YOU AND WILLIE ARE BY FAR THE MOST FLEXIBLE AND RESOURCEFUL UNDER ANY CONCEIVABLE CONDITIONS... IT'S AS SIMPLE AS THAT
3335

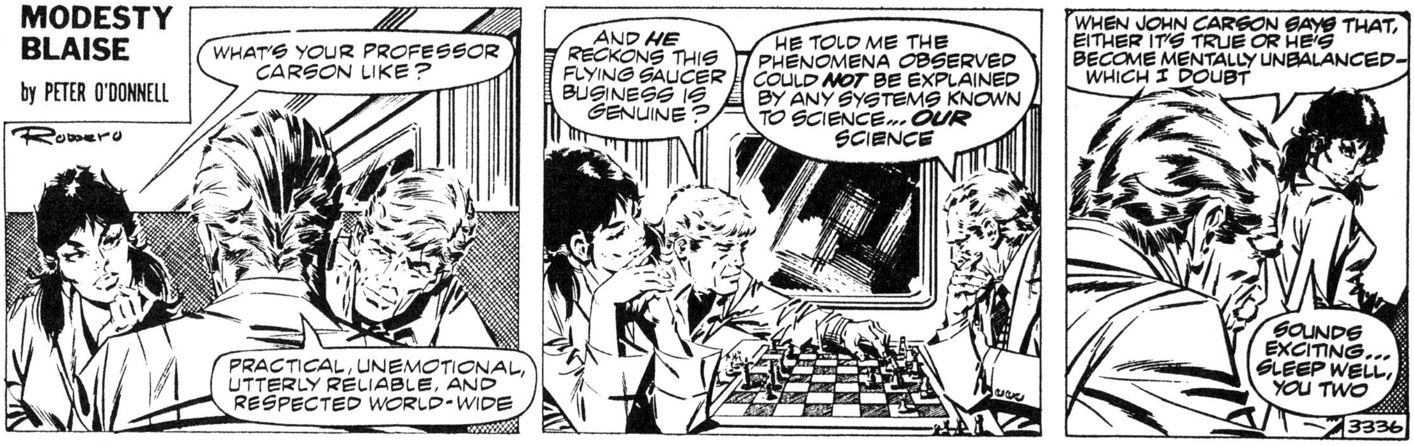
MODESTY BLAISE
by PETER O'DONNELL
WHAT'S YOUR PROFESSOR CARSON LIKE?
PRACTICAL, UNEMOTIONAL, UTTERLY RELIABLE, AND RESPECTED WORLD-WIDE
AND HE RECKONS THIS FLYING SAUCER BUSINESS IS GENUINE?
HE TOLD ME THE PHENOMENA OBSERVED COULD NOT BE EXPLAINED BY ANY SYSTEMS KNOWN TO SCIENCE... OUR SCIENCE
WHEN JOHN CARSON SAYS THAT, EITHER IT'S TRUE OR HE'S BECOME MENTALLY UNBALANCED— WHICH I DOUBT
SOUNDS EXCITING... SLEEP WELL, YOU TWO
3336

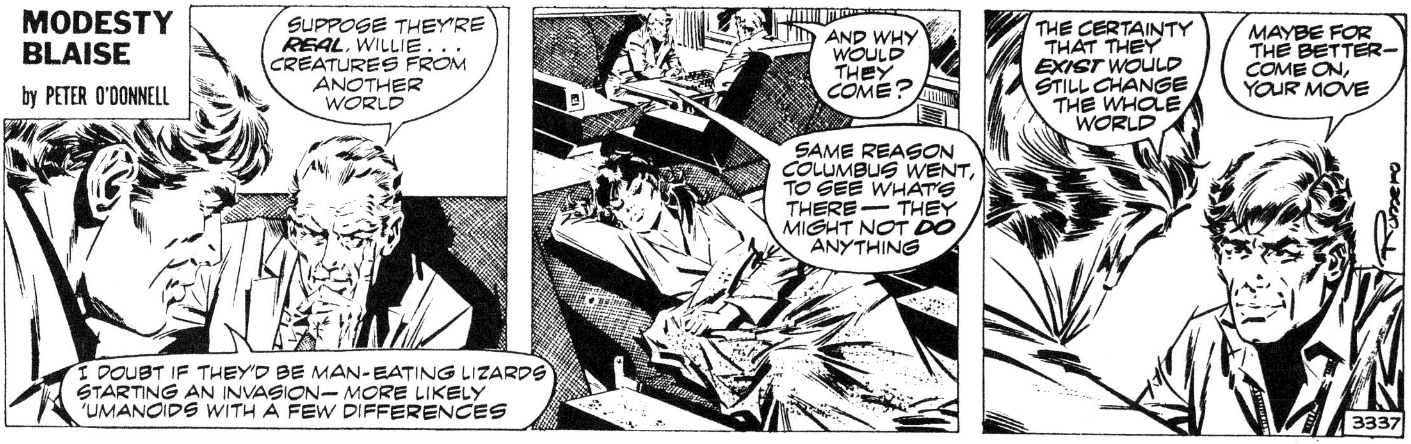
MODESTY BLAISE
by PETER O'DONNELL
SUPPOSE THEY'RE REAL, WILLIE . . . CREATURES FROM ANOTHER WORLD
I DOUBT IF THEY'D BE MAN-EATING LIZARDS STARTING AN INVASION— MORE LIKELY 'UMANOIDS WITH A FEW DIFFERENCES
AND WHY WOULD THEY COME?
SAME REASON COLUMBUS WENT, TO SEE WHAT'S THERE— THEY MIGHT NOT DO ANYTHING
THE CERTAINTY THAT THEY EXIST WOULD STILL CHANGE THE WHOLE WORLD
MAYBE FOR THE BETTER— COME ON, YOUR MOVE
3337

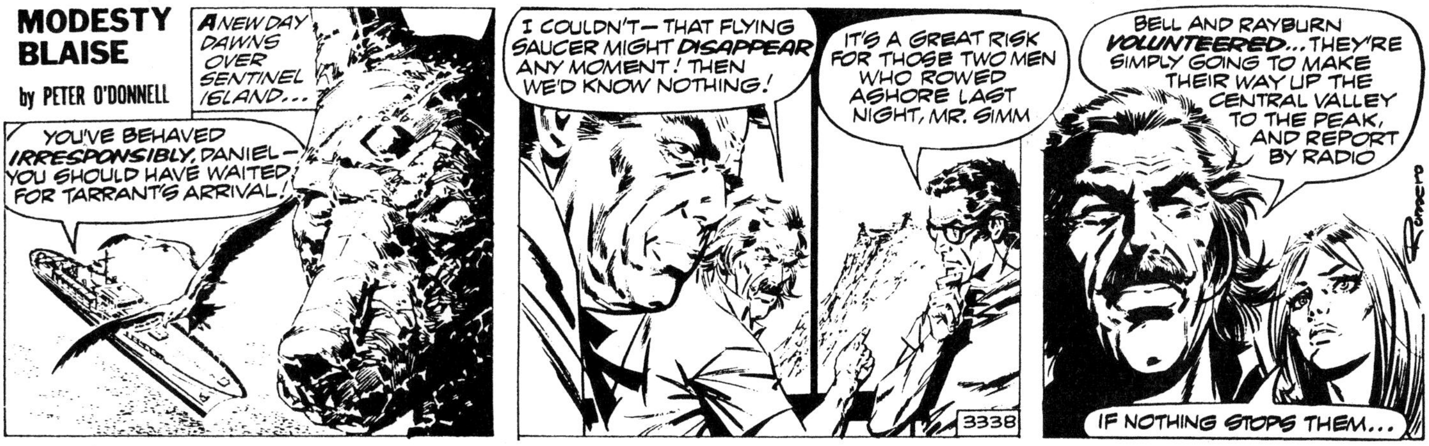
MODESTY BLAISE
by PETER O'DONNELL
A NEW DAY DAWNS OVER SENTINEL ISLAND...
YOU'VE BEHAVED IRRESPONSIBLY, DANIEL— YOU SHOULD HAVE WAITED FOR TARRANT'S ARRIVAL!
I COULDN'T— THAT FLYING SAUCER MIGHT DISAPPEAR ANY MOMENT! THEN WE'D KNOW NOTHING!
IT'S A GREAT RISK FOR THOSE TWO MEN WHO ROWED ASHORE LAST NIGHT, MR. SIMM
BELL AND RAYBURN VOLUNTEERED... THEY'RE SIMPLY GOING TO MAKE THEIR WAY UP THE CENTRAL VALLEY TO THE PEAK, AND REPORT BY RADIO
IF NOTHING STOPS THEM...
3338

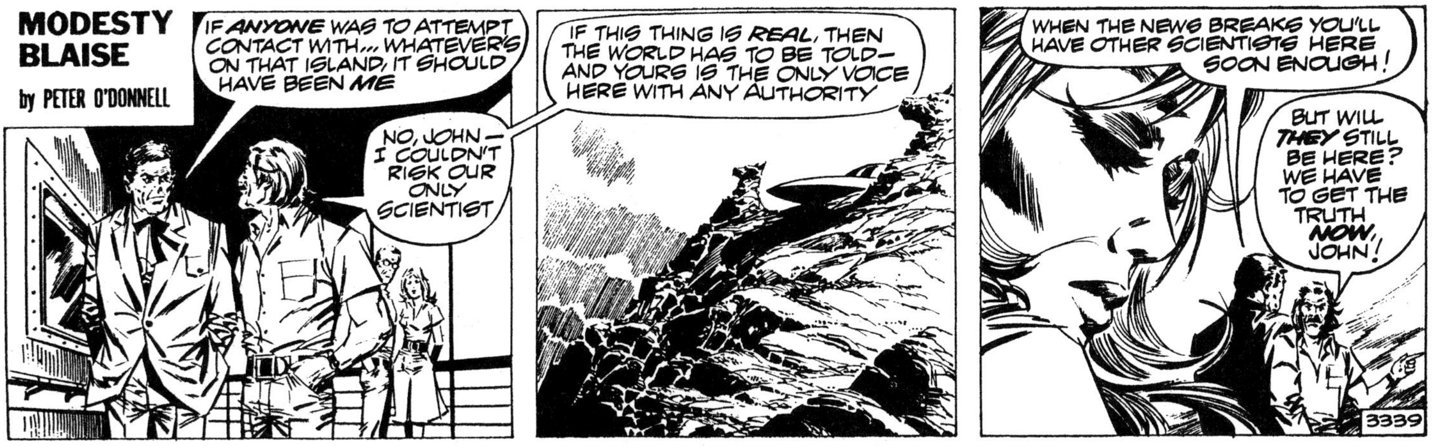
MODESTY BLAISE
by PETER O'DONNELL
IF ANYONE WAS TO ATTEMPT CONTACT WITH... WHATEVER'S ON THAT ISLAND, IT SHOULD HAVE BEEN ME
NO, JOHN— I COULDN'T RISK OUR ONLY SCIENTIST
IF THIS THING IS REAL, THEN THE WORLD HAS TO BE TOLD— AND YOURS IS THE ONLY VOICE HERE WITH ANY AUTHORITY
WHEN THE NEWS BREAKS YOU'LL HAVE OTHER SCIENTISTS HERE SOON ENOUGH!
BUT WILL THEY STILL BE HERE? WE HAVE TO GET THE TRUTH NOW, JOHN!
3339

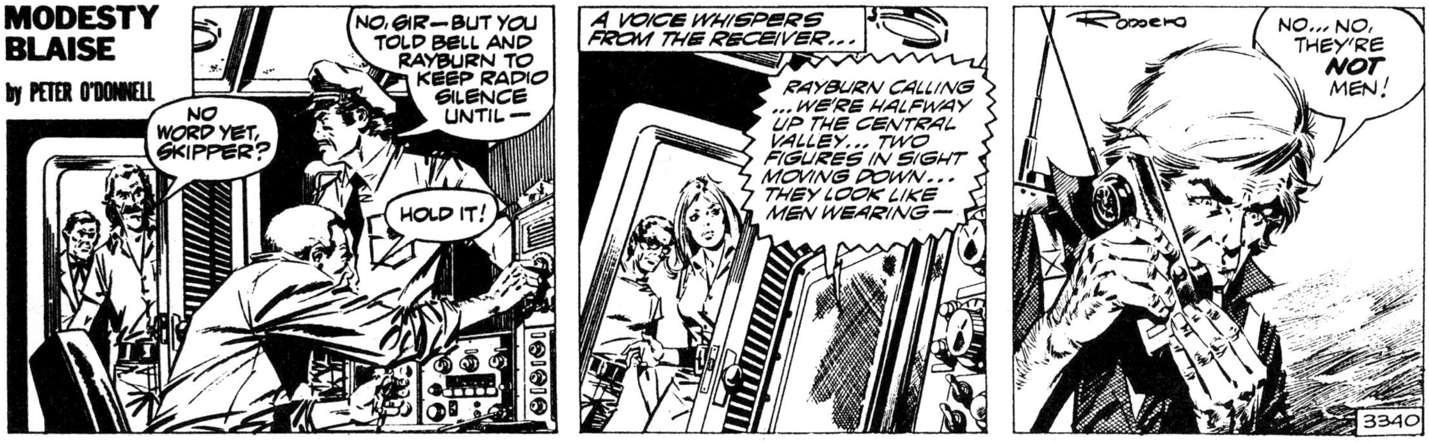
MODESTY BLAISE
by PETER O'DONNELL
NO WORD YET, SKIPPER?
NO, SIR— BUT YOU TOLD BELL AND RAYBURN TO KEEP RADIO SILENCE UNTIL—
HOLD IT!
A VOICE WHISPERS FROM THE RECEIVER...
RAYBURN CALLING ...WE'RE HALFWAY UP THE CENTRAL VALLEY... TWO FIGURES IN SIGHT MOVING DOWN... THEY LOOK LIKE MEN WEARING—
NO... NO, THEY'RE NOT MEN!
3340

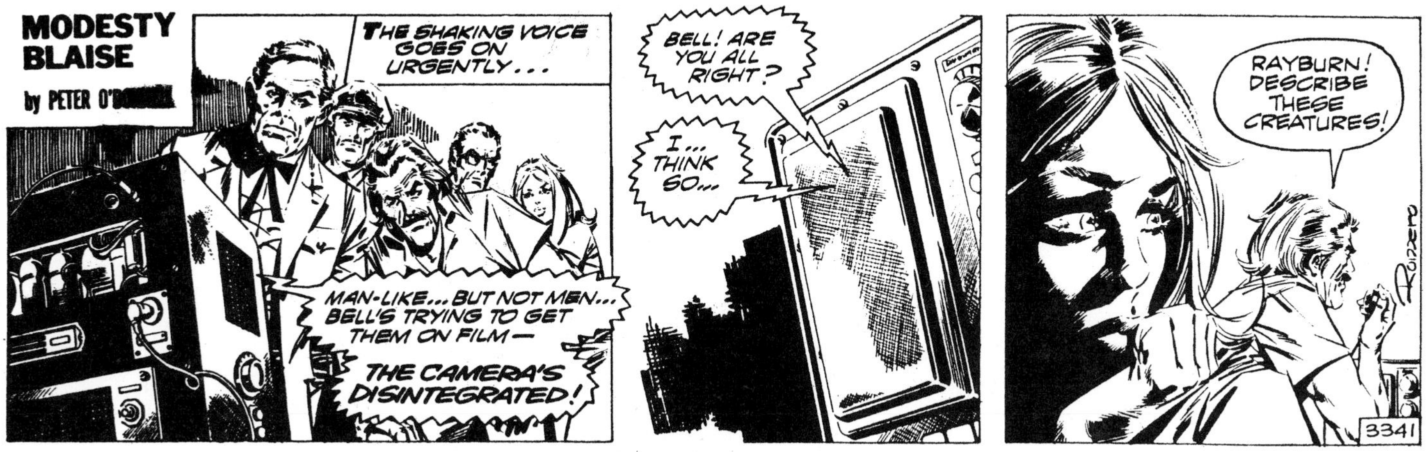
MODESTY BLAISE
by PETER O'
THE SHAKING VOICE GOES ON URGENTLY...
MAN-LIKE... BUT NOT MEN... BELL'S TRYING TO GET THEM ON FILM—
THE CAMERA'S DISINTEGRATED!
BELL! ARE YOU ALL RIGHT?
I... THINK SO...
RAYBURN! DESCRIBE THESE CREATURES!
3341

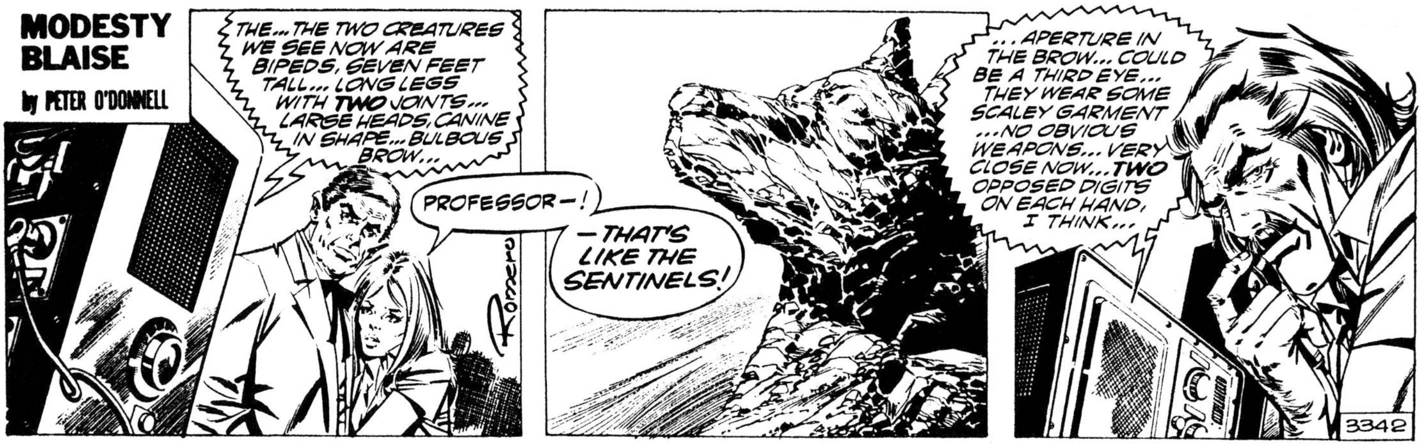
MODESTY BLAISE
by PETER O'DONNELL
THE... THE TWO CREATURES WE SEE NOW ARE BIPEDS, SEVEN FEET TALL... LONG LEGS WITH TWO JOINTS... LARGE HEADS, CANINE IN SHAPE... BULBOUS BROW...
PROFESSOR—!
—THAT'S LIKE THE SENTINELS!
... APERTURE IN THE BROW... COULD BE A THIRD EYE... THEY WEAR SOME SCALEY GARMENT ...NO OBVIOUS WEAPONS... VERY CLOSE NOW... TWO OPPOSED DIGITS ON EACH HAND, I THINK...
3342

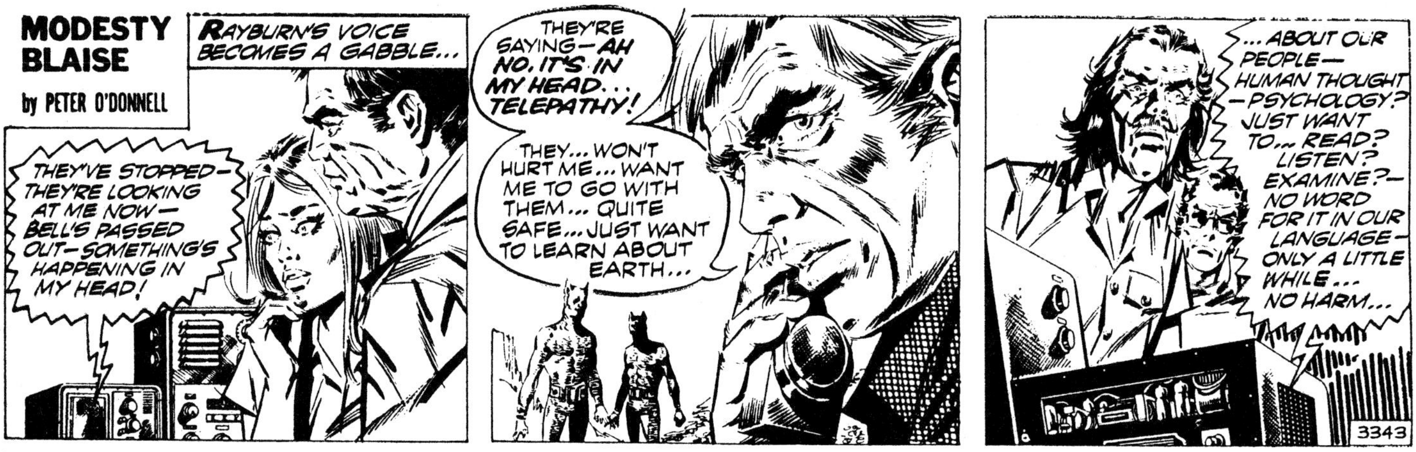
MODESTY BLAISE
by PETER O'DONNELL
RAYBURN'S VOICE BECOMES A GABBLE...
THEY'VE STOPPED— THEY'RE LOOKING AT ME NOW— BELL'S PASSED OUT— SOMETHING'S HAPPENING IN MY HEAD!
THEY'RE SAYING— AH NO, IT'S IN MY HEAD... TELEPATHY!
THEY... WON'T HURT ME... WANT ME TO GO WITH THEM... QUITE SAFE... JUST WANT TO LEARN ABOUT EARTH...
... ABOUT OUR PEOPLE— HUMAN THOUGHT —PSYCHOLOGY? JUST WANT TO... READ? LISTEN? EXAMINE?— NO WORD FOR IT IN OUR LANGUAGE— ONLY A LITTLE WHILE... NO HARM...
3343

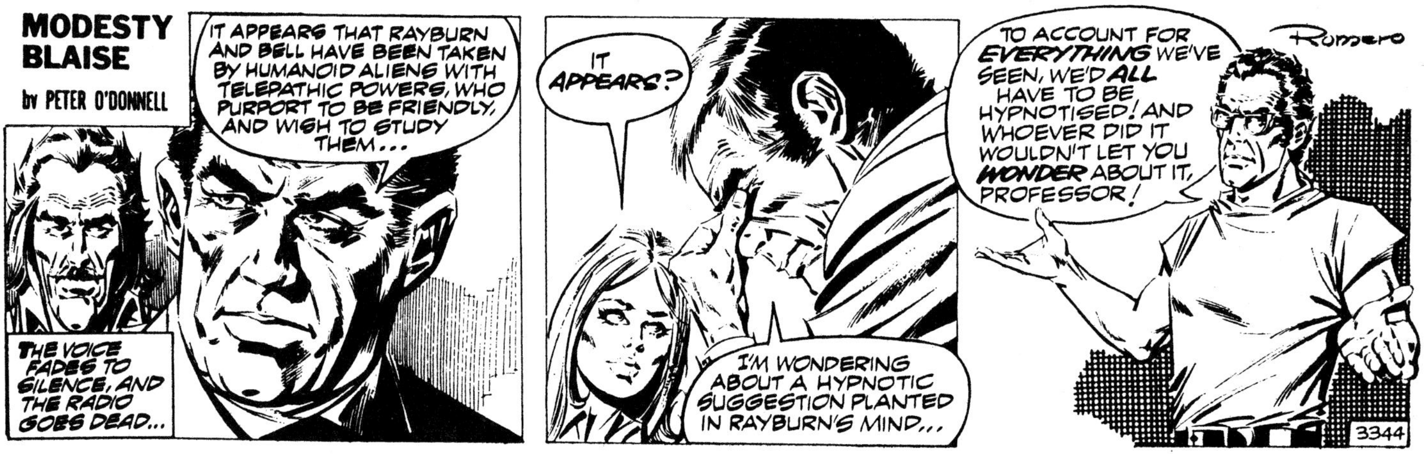
MODESTY BLAISE
by PETER O'DONNELL
IT APPEARS THAT RAYBURN AND BELL HAVE BEEN TAKEN BY HUMANOID ALIENS WITH TELEPATHIC POWERS, WHO PURPORT TO BE FRIENDLY, AND WISH TO STUDY THEM...
THE VOICE FADES TO SILENCE, AND THE RADIO GOES DEAD...
IT APPEARS?
I'M WONDERING ABOUT A HYPNOTIC SUGGESTION PLANTED IN RAYBURN'S MIND...
TO ACCOUNT FOR EVERYTHING WE'VE SEEN, WE'D ALL HAVE TO BE HYPNOTISED! AND WHOEVER DID IT WOULDN'T LET YOU WONDER ABOUT IT, PROFESSOR!
3344

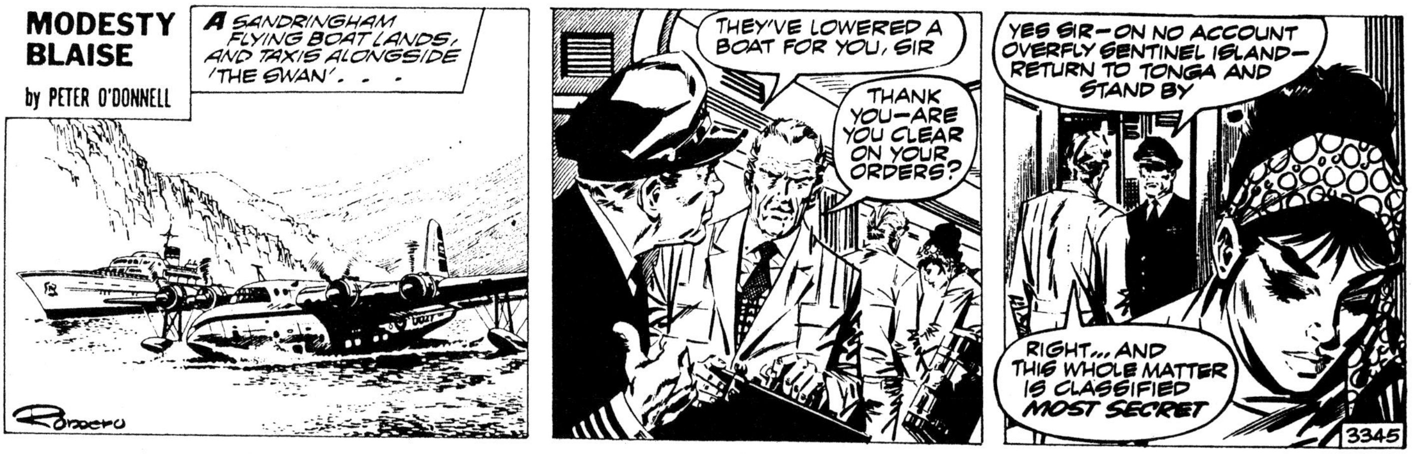
MODESTY BLAISE
by PETER O'DONNELL
A SANDRINGHAM FLYING BOAT LANDS, AND TAXIS ALONGSIDE 'THE SWAN'...
THEY'VE LOWERED A BOAT FOR YOU, SIR
THANK YOU—ARE YOU CLEAR ON YOUR ORDERS?
YES SIR—ON NO ACCOUNT OVERFLY SENTINEL ISLAND— RETURN TO TONGA AND STAND BY
RIGHT... AND THIS WHOLE MATTER IS CLASSIFIED MOST SECRET
3345

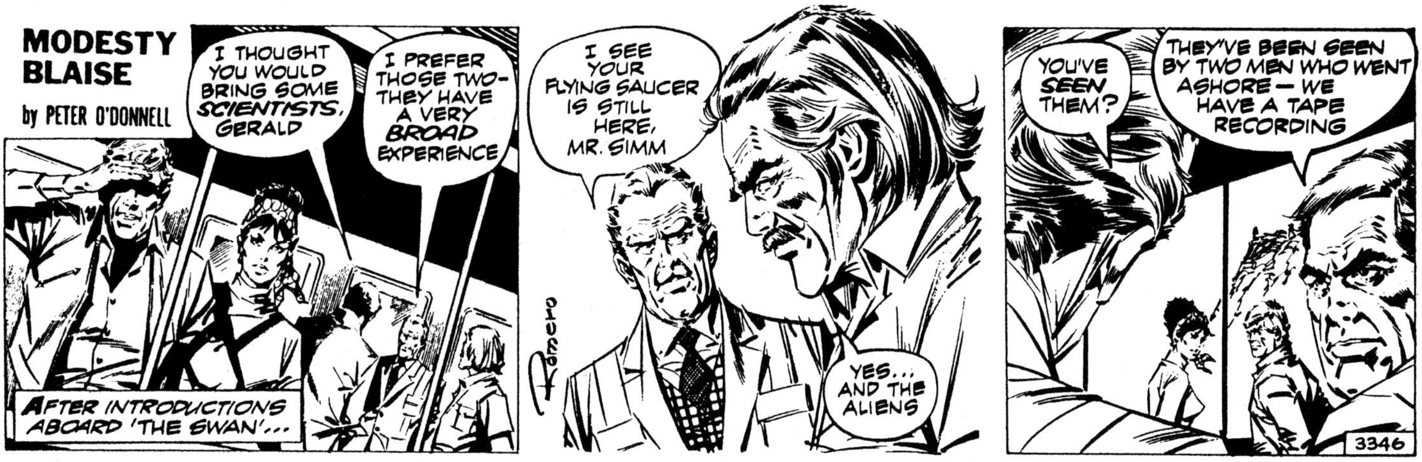
MODESTY BLAISE
by PETER O'DONNELL
AFTER INTRODUCTIONS ABOARD 'THE SWAN'...
I THOUGHT YOU WOULD BRING SOME SCIENTISTS, GERALD
I PREFER THOSE TWO— THEY HAVE A VERY BROAD EXPERIENCE
I SEE YOUR FLYING SAUCER IS STILL HERE, MR. SIMM
YES... AND THE ALIENS
YOU'VE SEEN THEM?
THEY'VE BEEN SEEN BY TWO MEN WHO WENT ASHORE — WE HAVE A TAPE RECORDING
3346

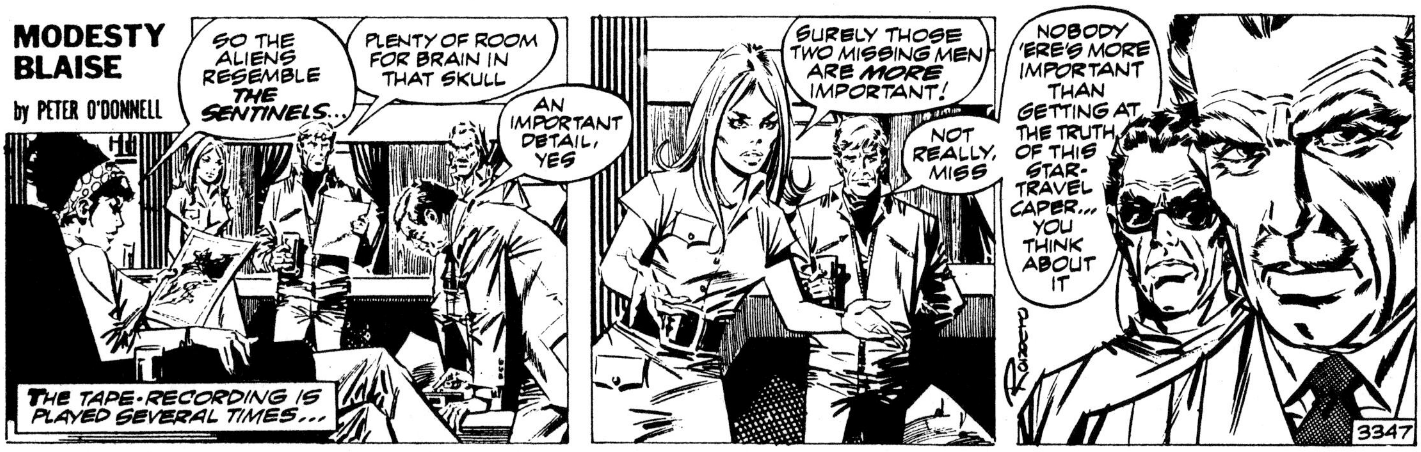
MODESTY BLAISE
by PETER O'DONNELL
THE TAPE-RECORDING IS PLAYED SEVERAL TIMES...
SO THE ALIENS RESEMBLE THE SENTINELS...
PLENTY OF ROOM FOR BRAIN IN THAT SKULL
AN IMPORTANT DETAIL, YES
SURELY THOSE TWO MISSING MEN ARE MORE IMPORTANT!
NOT REALLY, MISS
NOBODY 'ERE'S MORE IMPORTANT THAN GETTING AT THE TRUTH OF THIS STAR-TRAVEL CAPER... YOU THINK ABOUT IT
3347

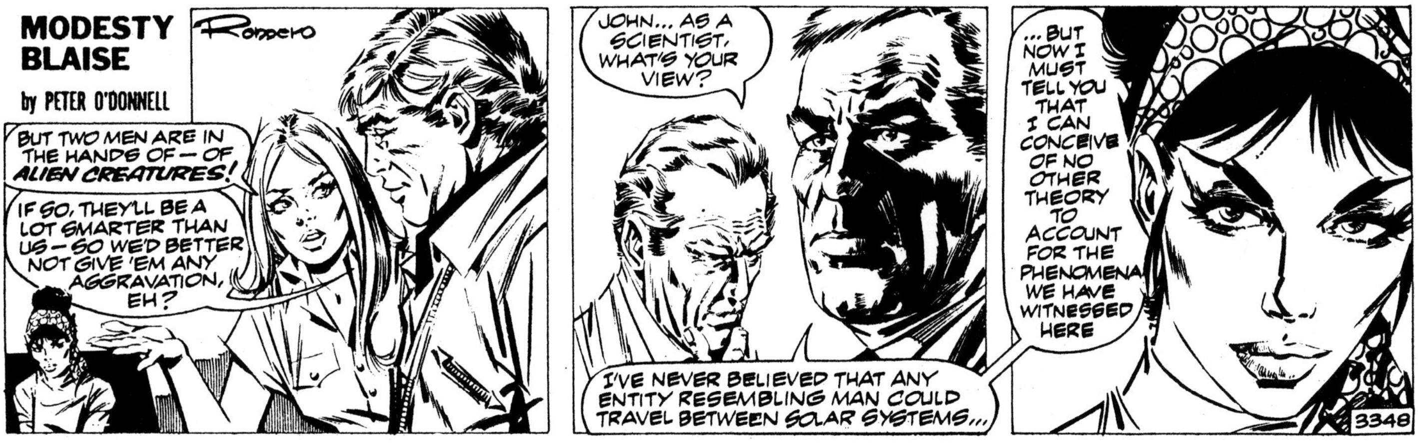
MODESTY BLAISE
by PETER O'DONNELL
BUT TWO MEN ARE IN THE HANDS OF — OF ALIEN CREATURES!
IF SO, THEY'LL BE A LOT SMARTER THAN US — SO WE'D BETTER NOT GIVE 'EM ANY AGGRAVATION, EH?
JOHN... AS A SCIENTIST, WHAT'S YOUR VIEW?
I'VE NEVER BELIEVED THAT ANY ENTITY RESEMBLING MAN COULD TRAVEL BETWEEN SOLAR SYSTEMS...
...BUT NOW I MUST TELL YOU THAT I CAN CONCEIVE OF NO OTHER THEORY TO ACCOUNT FOR THE PHENOMENA WE HAVE WITNESSED HERE
3348

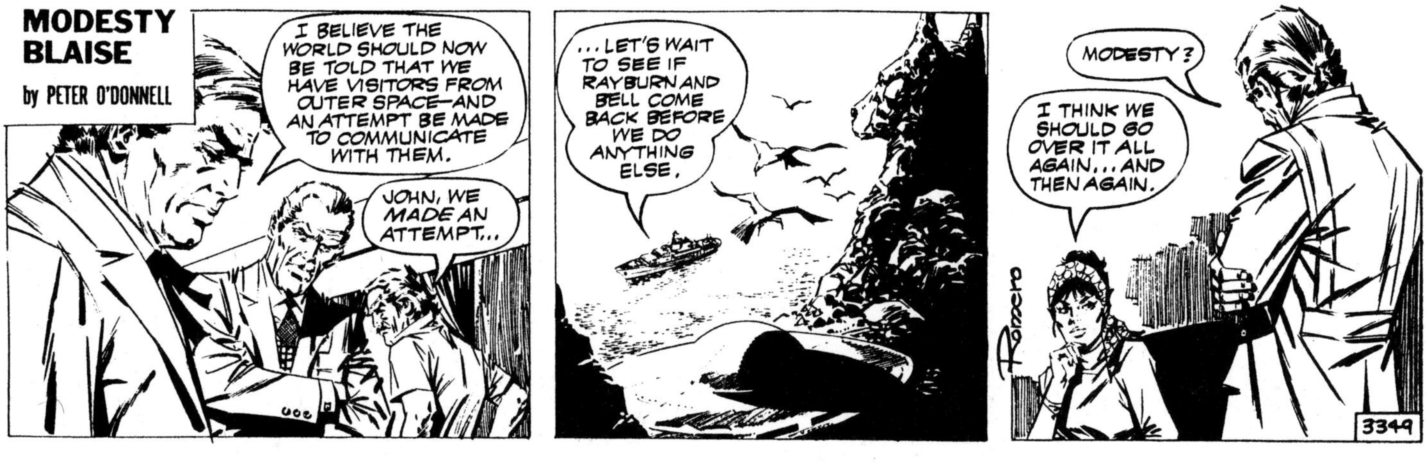
MODESTY BLAISE
by PETER O'DONNELL
I BELIEVE THE WORLD SHOULD NOW BE TOLD THAT WE HAVE VISITORS FROM OUTER SPACE—AND AN ATTEMPT BE MADE TO COMMUNICATE WITH THEM.
JOHN, WE MADE AN ATTEMPT...
...LET'S WAIT TO SEE IF RAYBURN AND BELL COME BACK BEFORE WE DO ANYTHING ELSE.
MODESTY?
I THINK WE SHOULD GO OVER IT ALL AGAIN... AND THEN AGAIN.
3349

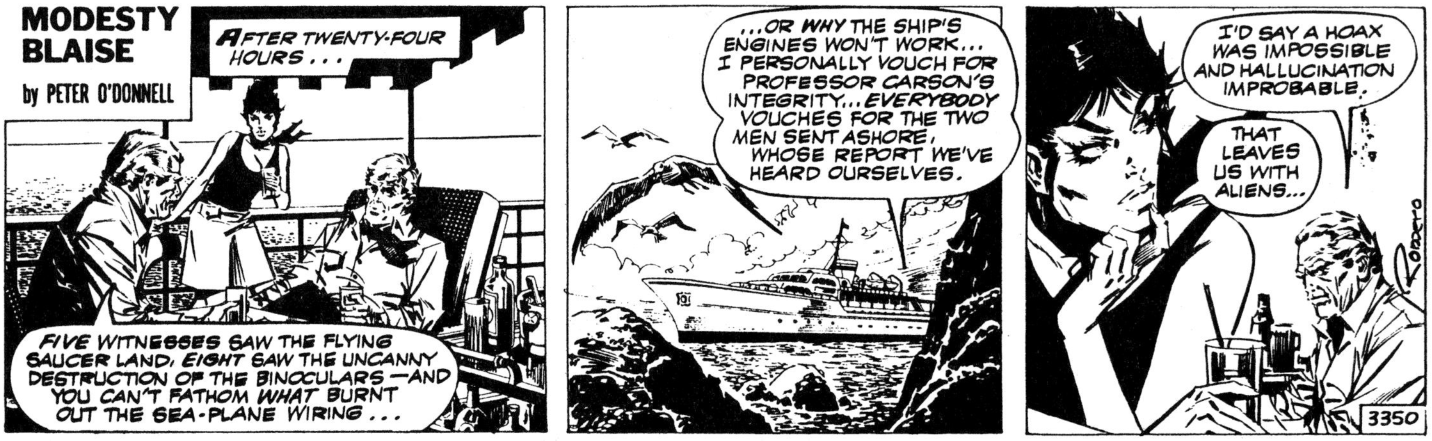
MODESTY BLAISE
by PETER O'DONNELL
AFTER TWENTY-FOUR HOURS . . .
FIVE WITNESSES SAW THE FLYING SAUCER LAND, EIGHT SAW THE UNCANNY DESTRUCTION OF THE BINOCULARS — AND YOU CAN'T FATHOM WHAT BURNT OUT THE SEA-PLANE WIRING . . .
...OR WHY THE SHIP'S ENGINES WON'T WORK... I PERSONALLY VOUCH FOR PROFESSOR CARSON'S INTEGRITY... EVERYBODY VOUCHES FOR THE TWO MEN SENT ASHORE, WHOSE REPORT WE'VE HEARD OURSELVES.
I'D SAY A HOAX WAS IMPOSSIBLE AND HALLUCINATION IMPROBABLE.
THAT LEAVES US WITH ALIENS...
3350

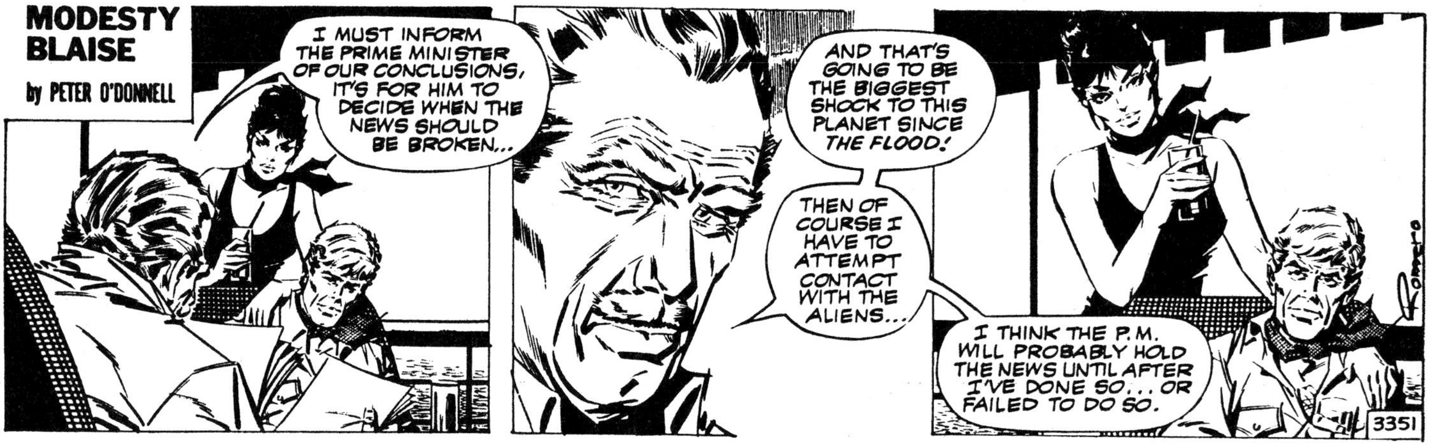
MODESTY BLAISE
by PETER O'DONNELL
I MUST INFORM THE PRIME MINISTER OF OUR CONCLUSIONS, IT'S FOR HIM TO DECIDE WHEN THE NEWS SHOULD BE BROKEN...
AND THAT'S GOING TO BE THE BIGGEST SHOCK TO THIS PLANET SINCE THE FLOOD!
THEN OF COURSE I HAVE TO ATTEMPT CONTACT WITH THE ALIENS...
I THINK THE P.M. WILL PROBABLY HOLD THE NEWS UNTIL AFTER I'VE DONE SO... OR FAILED TO DO SO.
3351

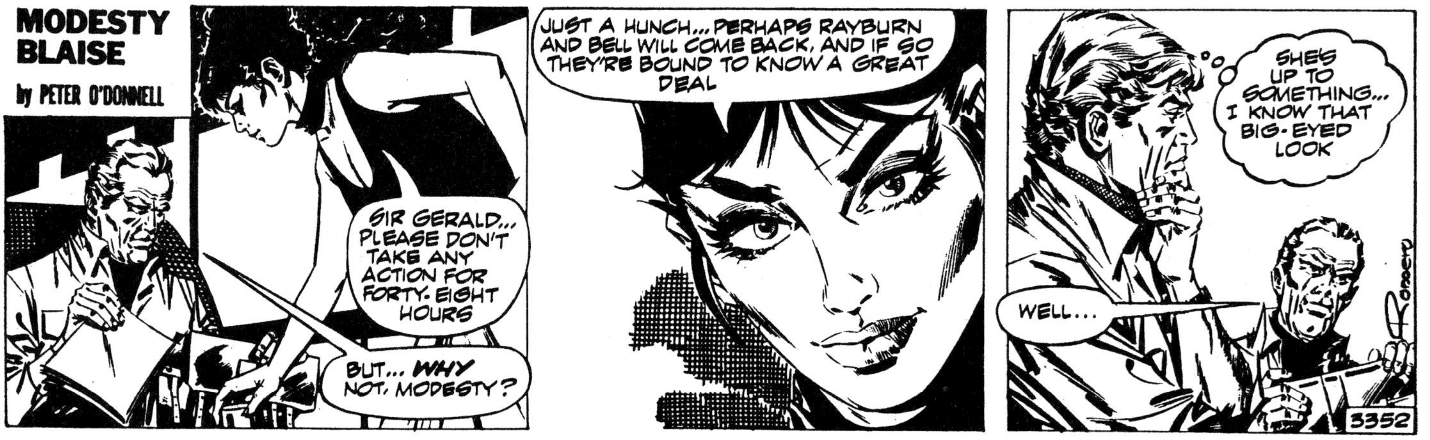
MODESTY BLAISE
by PETER O'DONNELL
SIR GERALD... PLEASE DON'T TAKE ANY ACTION FOR FORTY-EIGHT HOURS
BUT... WHY NOT, MODESTY?
JUST A HUNCH... PERHAPS RAYBURN AND BELL WILL COME BACK, AND IF SO THEY'RE BOUND TO KNOW A GREAT DEAL
SHE'S UP TO SOMETHING... I KNOW THAT BIG-EYED LOOK
WELL...
3352

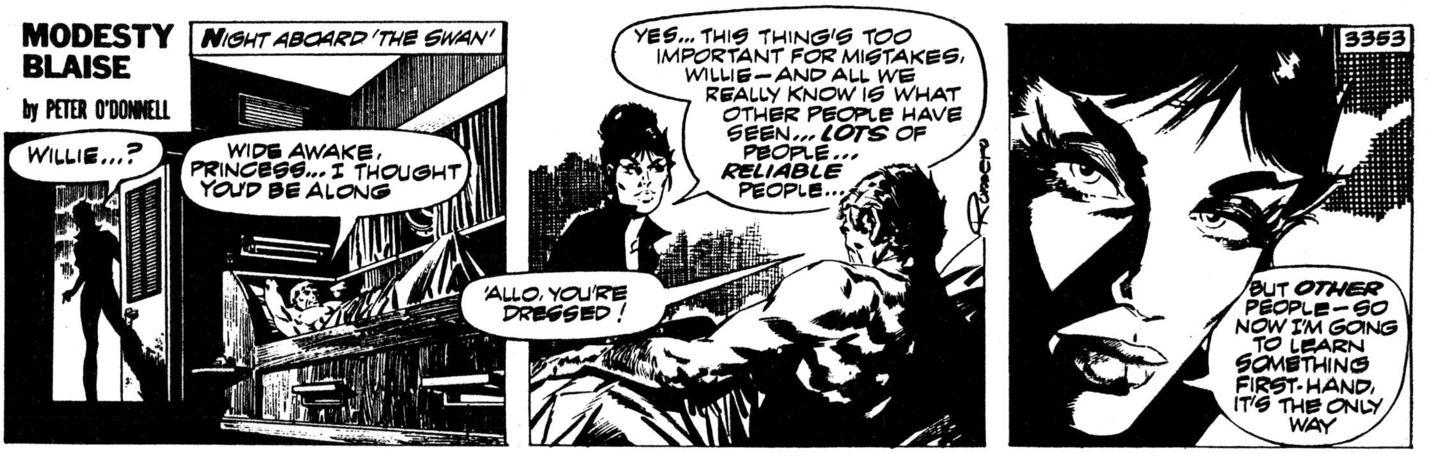
MODESTY BLAISE
by PETER O'DONNELL
NIGHT ABOARD 'THE SWAN'
WILLIE...?
WIDE AWAKE, PRINCESS... I THOUGHT YOU'D BE ALONG
'ALLO, YOU'RE DRESSED!
YES... THIS THING'S TOO IMPORTANT FOR MISTAKES, WILLIE — AND ALL WE REALLY KNOW IS WHAT OTHER PEOPLE HAVE SEEN... LOTS OF PEOPLE... RELIABLE PEOPLE...
3353
BUT OTHER PEOPLE — SO NOW I'M GOING TO LEARN SOMETHING FIRST-HAND, IT'S THE ONLY WAY

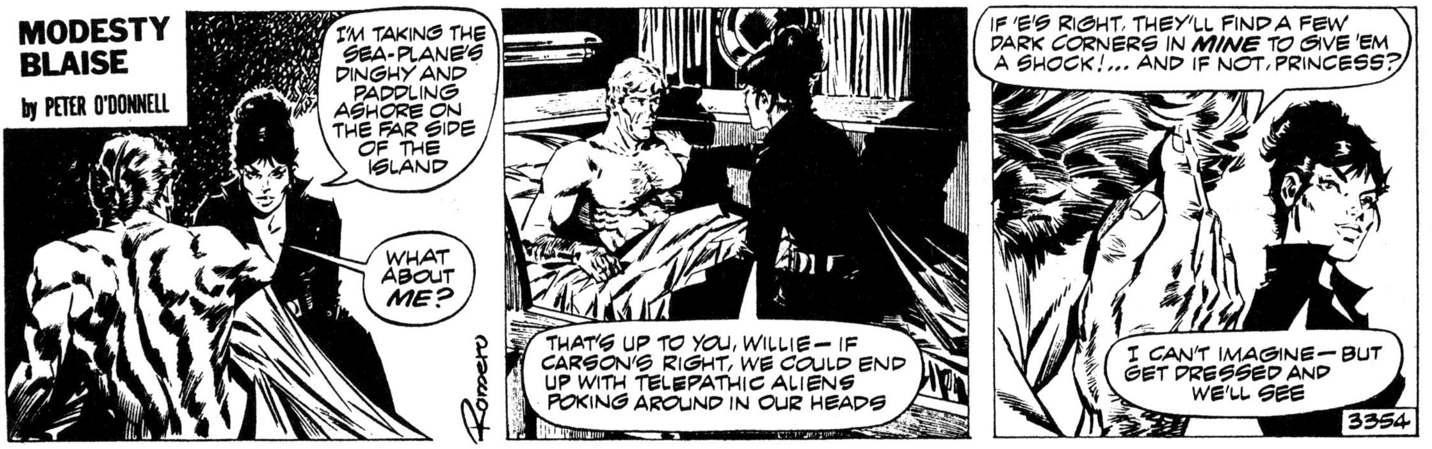
MODESTY BLAISE
by PETER O'DONNELL
I'M TAKING THE SEA-PLANE'S DINGHY AND PADDLING ASHORE ON THE FAR SIDE OF THE ISLAND
WHAT ABOUT ME?
THAT'S UP TO YOU, WILLIE — IF CARSON'S RIGHT, WE COULD END UP WITH TELEPATHIC ALIENS POKING AROUND IN OUR HEADS
IF 'E'S RIGHT, THEY'LL FIND A FEW DARK CORNERS IN MINE TO GIVE 'EM A SHOCK! ... AND IF NOT, PRINCESS?
I CAN'T IMAGINE — BUT GET DRESSED AND WE'LL SEE
3354

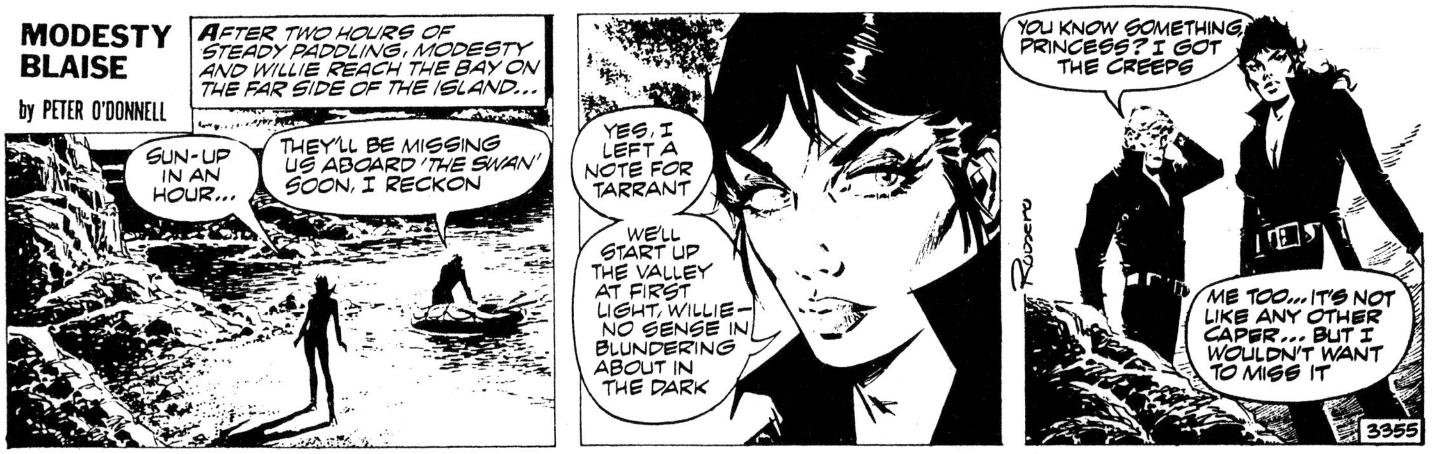
MODESTY BLAISE
by PETER O'DONNELL
AFTER TWO HOURS OF STEADY PADDLING, MODESTY AND WILLIE REACH THE BAY ON THE FAR SIDE OF THE ISLAND...
SUN-UP IN AN HOUR...
THEY'LL BE MISSING US ABOARD 'THE SWAN' SOON, I RECKON
YES, I LEFT A NOTE FOR TARRANT
WE'LL START UP THE VALLEY AT FIRST LIGHT, WILLIE — NO SENSE IN BLUNDERING ABOUT IN THE DARK
YOU KNOW SOMETHING, PRINCESS? I GOT THE CREEPS
ME TOO... IT'S NOT LIKE ANY OTHER CAPER... BUT I WOULDN'T WANT TO MISS IT
3355

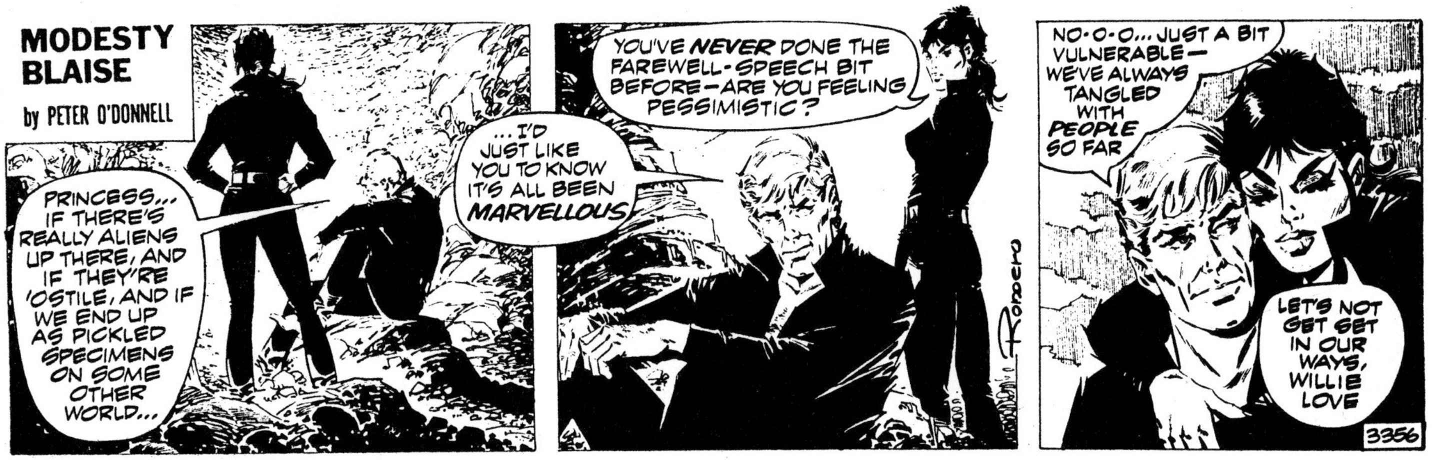
MODESTY BLAISE
by PETER O'DONNELL
PRINCESS... IF THERE'S REALLY ALIENS UP THERE, AND IF THEY'RE 'OSTILE, AND IF WE END UP AS PICKLED SPECIMENS ON SOME OTHER WORLD...
...I'D JUST LIKE YOU TO KNOW IT'S ALL BEEN MARVELLOUS
YOU'VE NEVER DONE THE FAREWELL-SPEECH BIT BEFORE — ARE YOU FEELING PESSIMISTIC?
NO-O-O... JUST A BIT VULNERABLE — WE'VE ALWAYS TANGLED WITH PEOPLE SO FAR
LET'S NOT GET SET IN OUR WAYS, WILLIE LOVE
3356

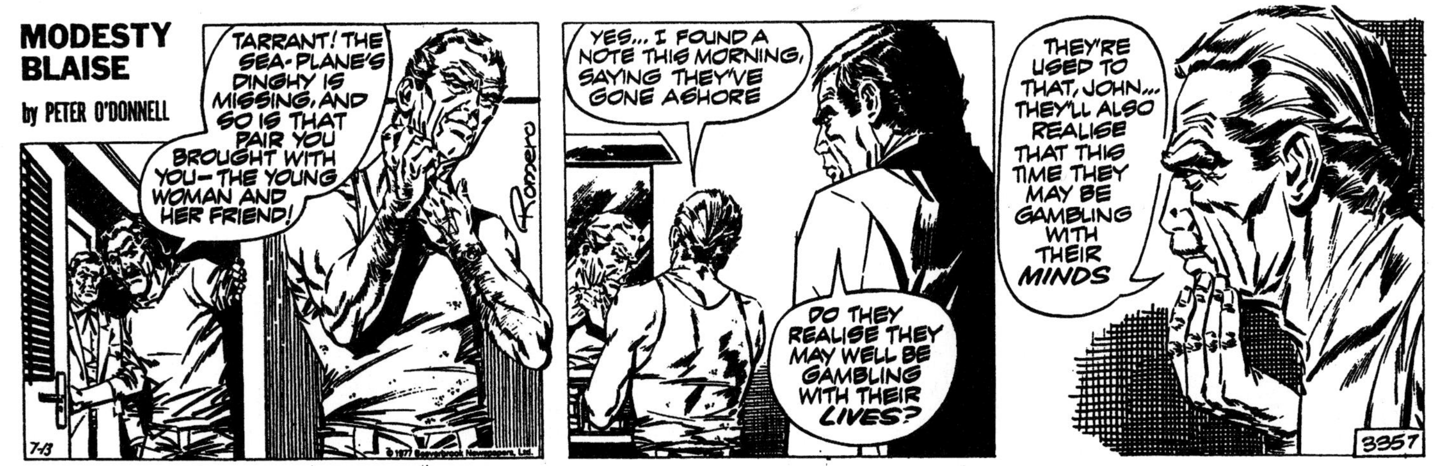
MODESTY BLAISE
by PETER O'DONNELL
TARRANT! THE SEA-PLANE'S DINGHY IS MISSING, AND SO IS THAT PAIR YOU BROUGHT WITH YOU — THE YOUNG WOMAN AND HER FRIEND!
7-13
© 1977 Beaverbrook Newspapers, Ltd.
YES... I FOUND A NOTE THIS MORNING, SAYING THEY'VE GONE ASHORE
DO THEY REALISE THEY MAY WELL BE GAMBLING WITH THEIR LIVES?
THEY'RE USED TO THAT, JOHN... THEY'LL ALSO REALISE THAT THIS TIME THEY MAY BE GAMBLING WITH THEIR MINDS
3357

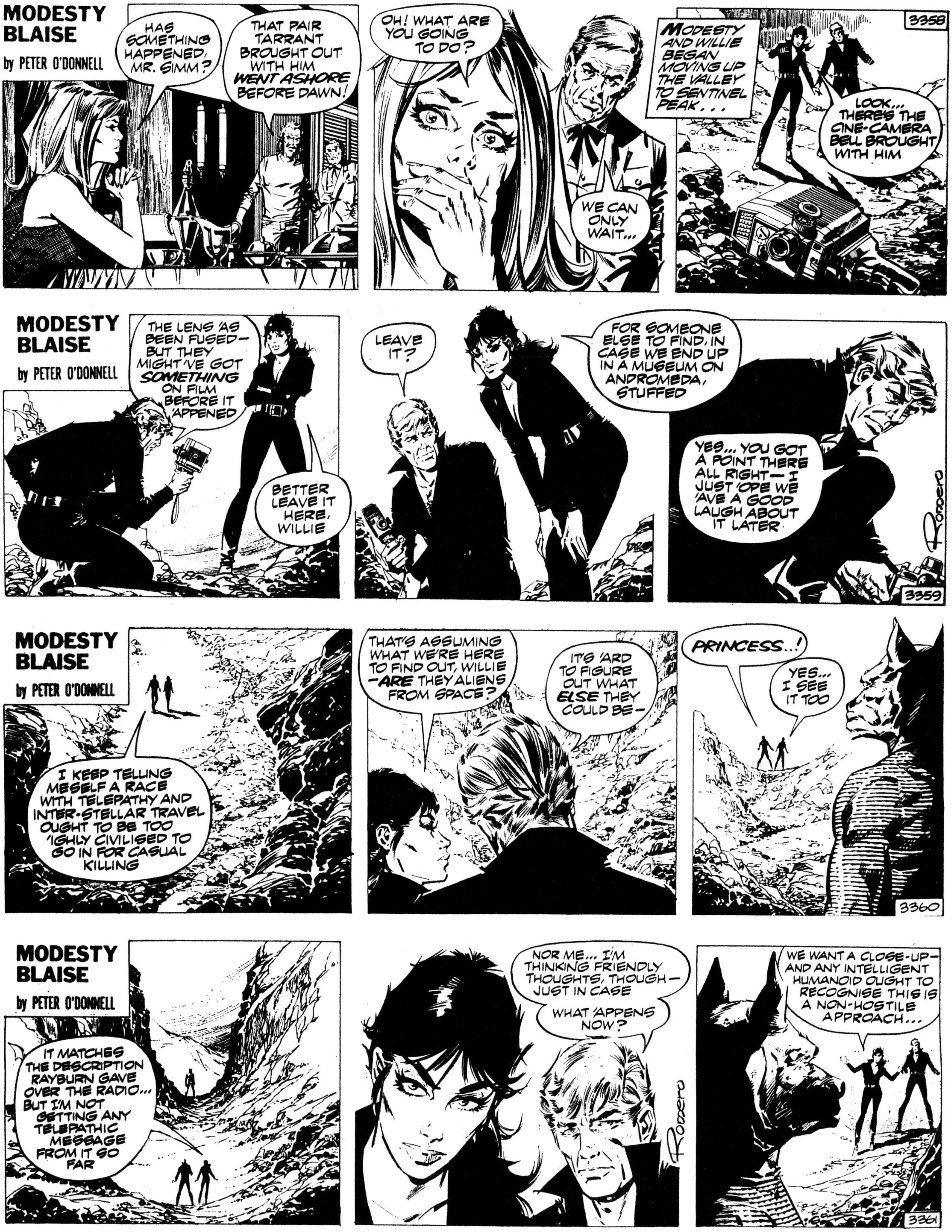
MODESTY BLAISE
by PETER O'DONNELL
HAS SOMETHING HAPPENED, MR. SIMM?
THAT PAIR TARRANT BROUGHT OUT WITH HIM WENT ASHORE BEFORE DAWN!
OH! WHAT ARE YOU GOING TO DO?
WE CAN ONLY WAIT...
3358
MODESTY AND WILLIE BEGAN MOVING UP THE VALLEY TO SENTINEL PEAK . . .
LOOK... THERE'S THE CINE-CAMERA BELL BROUGHT WITH HIM
MODESTY BLAISE
by PETER O'DONNELL
THE LENS 'AS BEEN FUSED— BUT THEY MIGHT 'VE GOT SOMETHING ON FILM BEFORE IT 'APPENED
BETTER LEAVE IT HERE, WILLIE
LEAVE IT?
FOR SOMEONE ELSE TO FIND, IN CASE WE END UP IN A MUSEUM ON ANDROMEDA, STUFFED
YES... YOU GOT A POINT THERE ALL RIGHT— I JUST 'OPE WE 'AVE A GOOD LAUGH ABOUT IT LATER
Romero
3359
MODESTY BLAISE
by PETER O'DONNELL
I KEEP TELLING MESELF A RACE WITH TELEPATHY AND INTER-STELLAR TRAVEL OUGHT TO BE TOO 'IGHLY CIVILISED TO GO IN FOR CASUAL KILLING
THAT'S ASSUMING WHAT WE'RE HERE TO FIND OUT, WILLIE —ARE THEY ALIENS FROM SPACE?
IT'S 'ARD TO FIGURE OUT WHAT ELSE THEY COULD BE—
PRINCESS...!
YES... I SEE IT TOO
3360
MODESTY BLAISE
by PETER O'DONNELL
IT MATCHES THE DESCRIPTION RAYBURN GAVE OVER THE RADIO... BUT I'M NOT GETTING ANY TELEPATHIC MESSAGE FROM IT SO FAR
NOR ME... I'M THINKING FRIENDLY THOUGHTS, THOUGH— JUST IN CASE
WHAT 'APPENS NOW?
Romero
WE WANT A CLOSE-UP— AND ANY INTELLIGENT HUMANOID OUGHT TO RECOGNISE THIS IS A NON-HOSTILE APPROACH...
3361

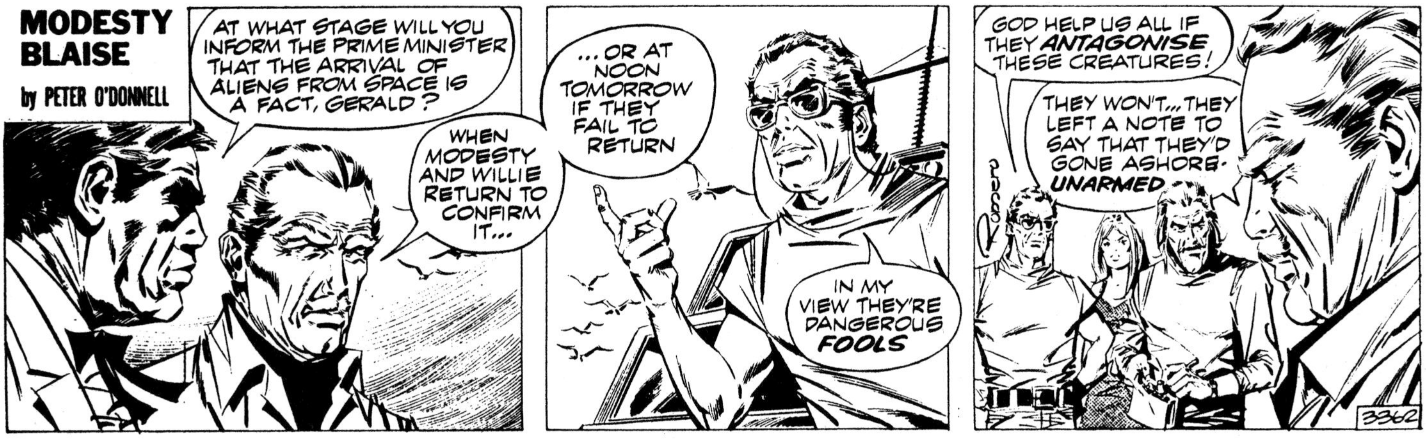
MODESTY BLAISE
by PETER O'DONNELL
AT WHAT STAGE WILL YOU INFORM THE PRIME MINISTER THAT THE ARRIVAL OF ALIENS FROM SPACE IS A FACT, GERALD?
WHEN MODESTY AND WILLIE RETURN TO CONFIRM IT...
...OR AT NOON TOMORROW IF THEY FAIL TO RETURN
IN MY VIEW THEY'RE DANGEROUS FOOLS
GOD HELP US ALL IF THEY ANTAGONISE THESE CREATURES!
THEY WON'T... THEY LEFT A NOTE TO SAY THAT THEY'D GONE ASHORE-UNARMED
3362

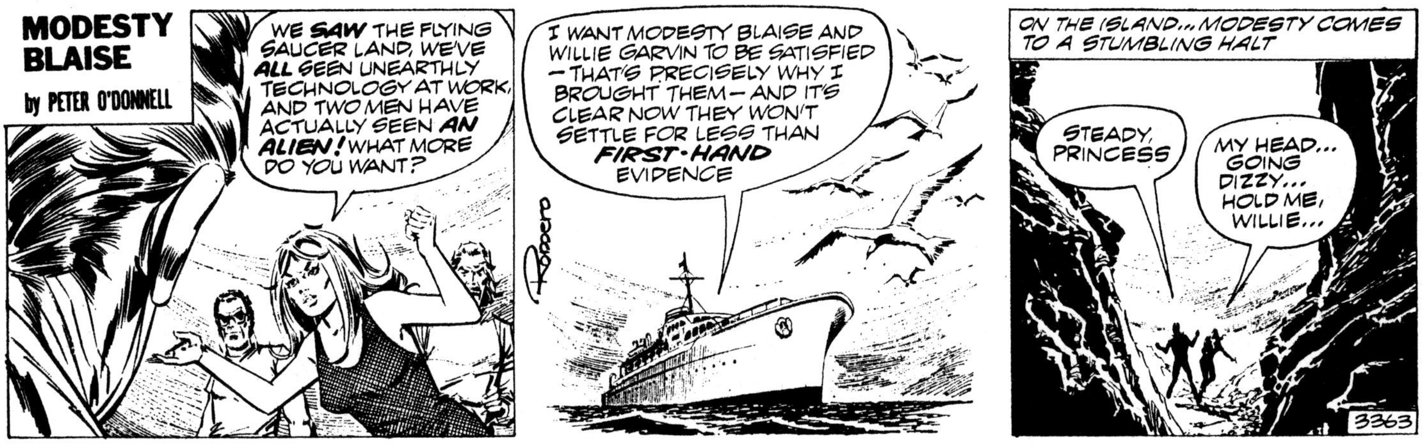
MODESTY BLAISE
by PETER O'DONNELL
WE SAW THE FLYING SAUCER LAND, WE'VE ALL SEEN UNEARTHLY TECHNOLOGY AT WORK, AND TWO MEN HAVE ACTUALLY SEEN AN ALIEN! WHAT MORE DO YOU WANT?
I WANT MODESTY BLAISE AND WILLIE GARVIN TO BE SATISFIED — THAT'S PRECISELY WHY I BROUGHT THEM — AND IT'S CLEAR NOW THEY WON'T SETTLE FOR LESS THAN FIRST-HAND EVIDENCE
ON THE ISLAND... MODESTY COMES TO A STUMBLING HALT
STEADY, PRINCESS
MY HEAD... GOING DIZZY... HOLD ME, WILLIE...
3363

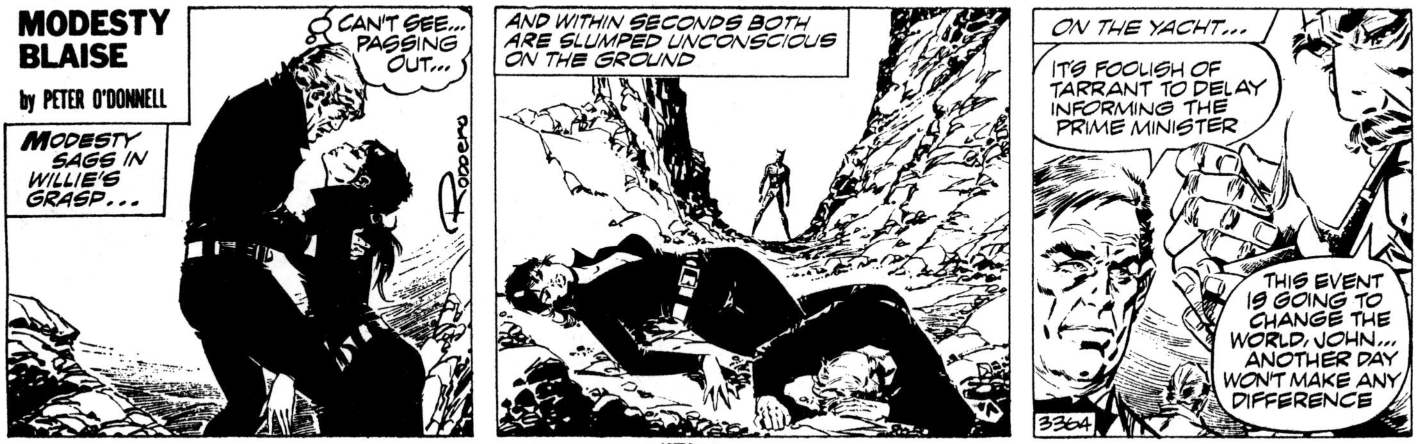
MODESTY BLAISE
by PETER O'DONNELL
MODESTY SAGS IN WILLIE'S GRASP...
CAN'T SEE... PASSING OUT...
AND WITHIN SECONDS BOTH ARE SLUMPED UNCONSCIOUS ON THE GROUND
ON THE YACHT...
IT'S FOOLISH OF TARRANT TO DELAY INFORMING THE PRIME MINISTER
THIS EVENT IS GOING TO CHANGE THE WORLD, JOHN... ANOTHER DAY WON'T MAKE ANY DIFFERENCE
3364

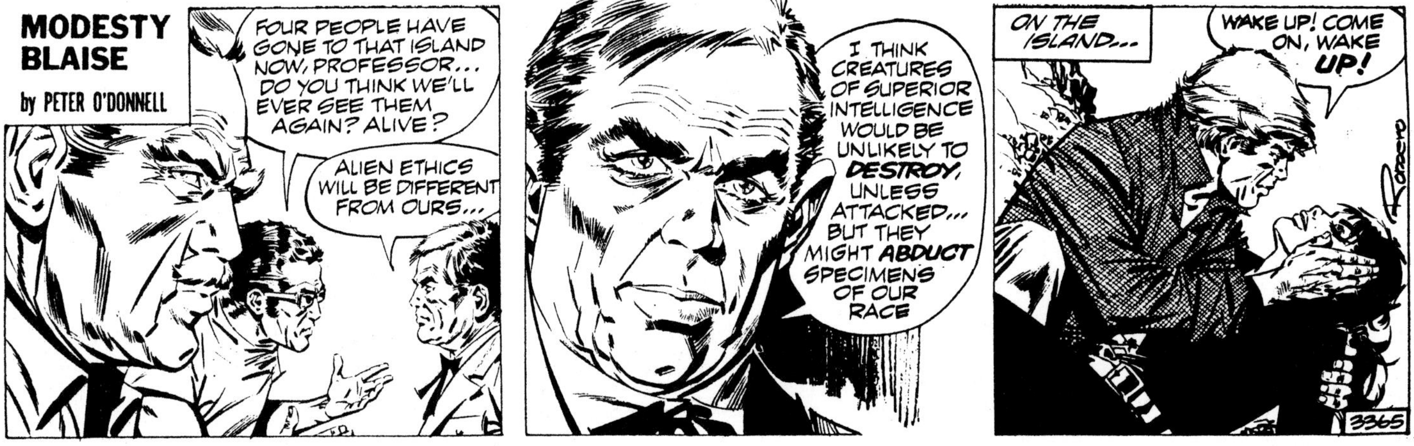
MODESTY BLAISE
by PETER O'DONNELL
FOUR PEOPLE HAVE GONE TO THAT ISLAND NOW, PROFESSOR... DO YOU THINK WE'LL EVER SEE THEM AGAIN? ALIVE?
ALIEN ETHICS WILL BE DIFFERENT FROM OURS...
I THINK CREATURES OF SUPERIOR INTELLIGENCE WOULD BE UNLIKELY TO DESTROY, UNLESS ATTACKED... BUT THEY MIGHT ABDUCT SPECIMENS OF OUR RACE
ON THE ISLAND...
WAKE UP! COME ON, WAKE UP!
3365

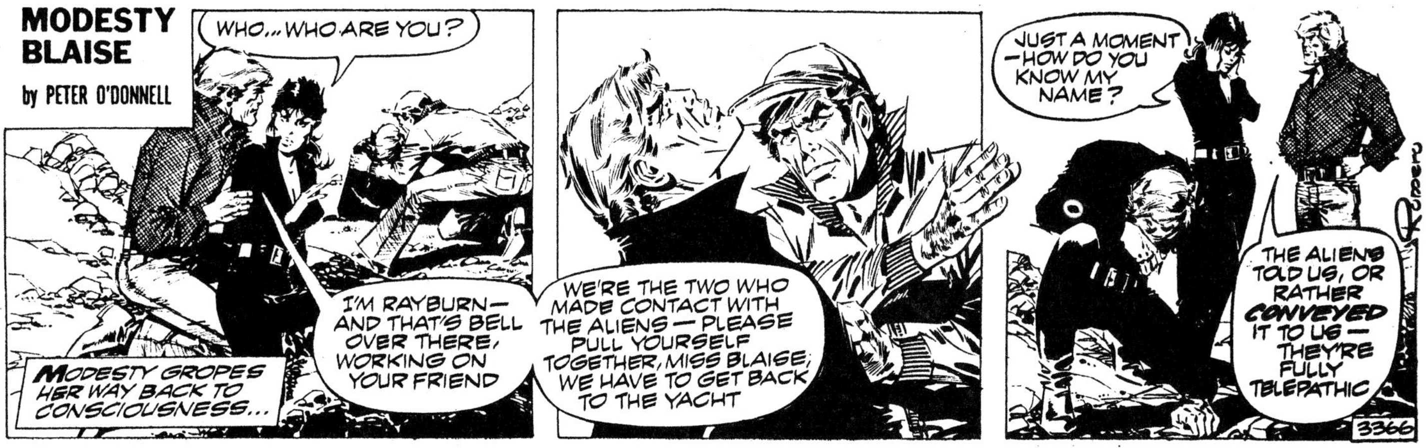
MODESTY BLAISE
by PETER O'DONNELL
WHO... WHO ARE YOU?
MODESTY GROPES HER WAY BACK TO CONSCIOUSNESS...
I'M RAYBURN— AND THAT'S BELL OVER THERE, WORKING ON YOUR FRIEND
WE'RE THE TWO WHO MADE CONTACT WITH THE ALIENS — PLEASE PULL YOURSELF TOGETHER, MISS BLAISE, WE HAVE TO GET BACK TO THE YACHT
JUST A MOMENT —HOW DO YOU KNOW MY NAME?
THE ALIENS TOLD US, OR RATHER CONVEYED IT TO US — THEY'RE FULLY TELEPATHIC
3366

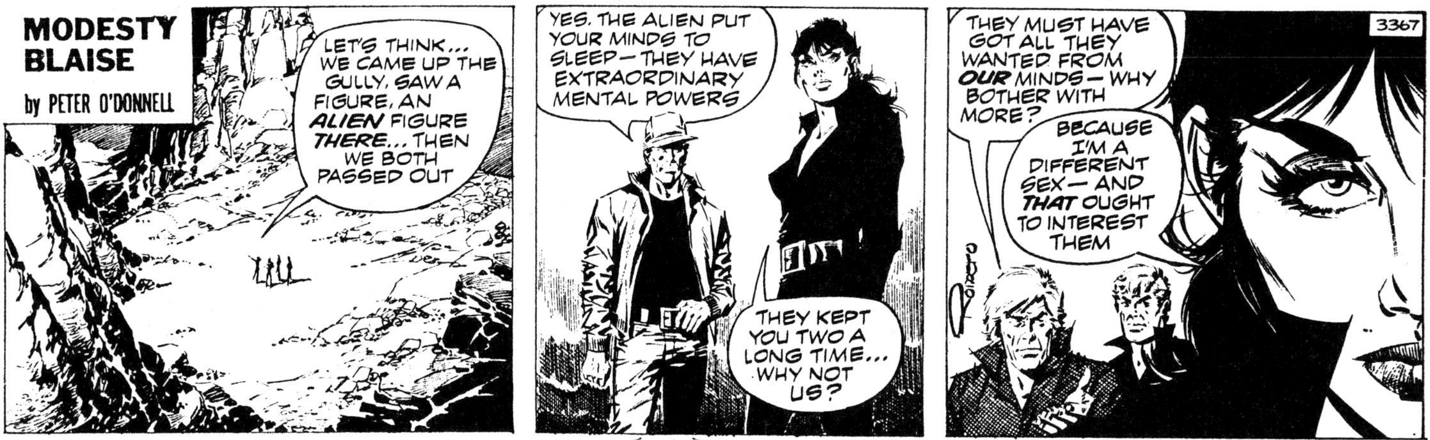
MODESTY BLAISE
by PETER O'DONNELL
LET'S THINK... WE CAME UP THE GULLY, SAW A FIGURE, AN ALIEN FIGURE THERE... THEN WE BOTH PASSED OUT
YES. THE ALIEN PUT YOUR MINDS TO SLEEP— THEY HAVE EXTRAORDINARY MENTAL POWERS
THEY KEPT YOU TWO A LONG TIME... WHY NOT US?
3367
THEY MUST HAVE GOT ALL THEY WANTED FROM OUR MINDS— WHY BOTHER WITH MORE?
BECAUSE I'M A DIFFERENT SEX— AND THAT OUGHT TO INTEREST THEM

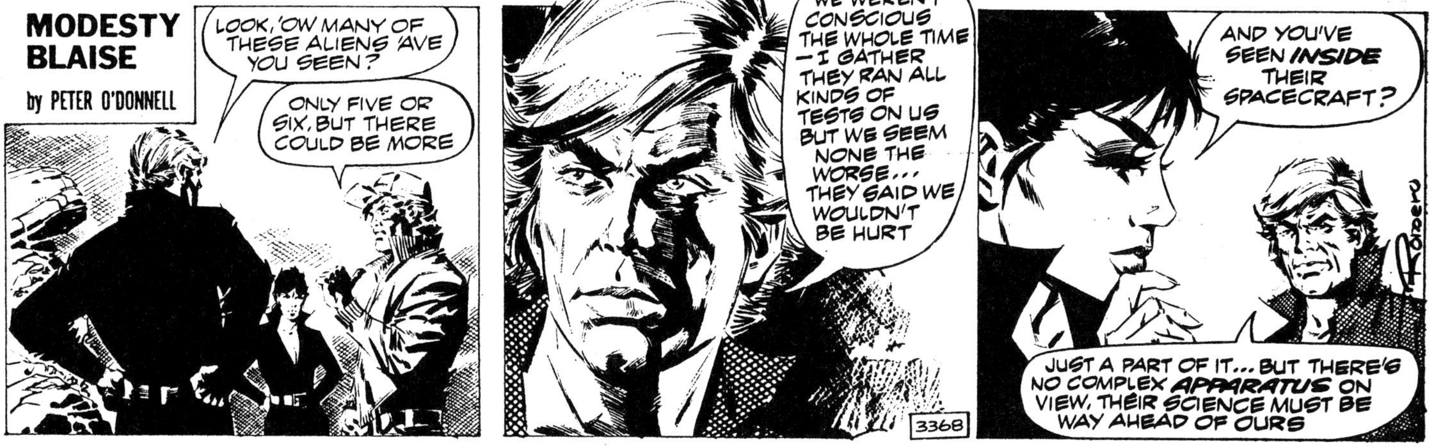
MODESTY BLAISE
by PETER O'DONNELL
LOOK, 'OW MANY OF THESE ALIENS 'AVE YOU SEEN?
ONLY FIVE OR SIX, BUT THERE COULD BE MORE
WE WEREN'T CONSCIOUS THE WHOLE TIME —I GATHER THEY RAN ALL KINDS OF TESTS ON US BUT WE SEEM NONE THE WORSE... THEY SAID WE WOULDN'T BE HURT
3368
AND YOU'VE SEEN INSIDE THEIR SPACECRAFT?
JUST A PART OF IT... BUT THERE'S NO COMPLEX APPARATUS ON VIEW. THEIR SCIENCE MUST BE WAY AHEAD OF OURS

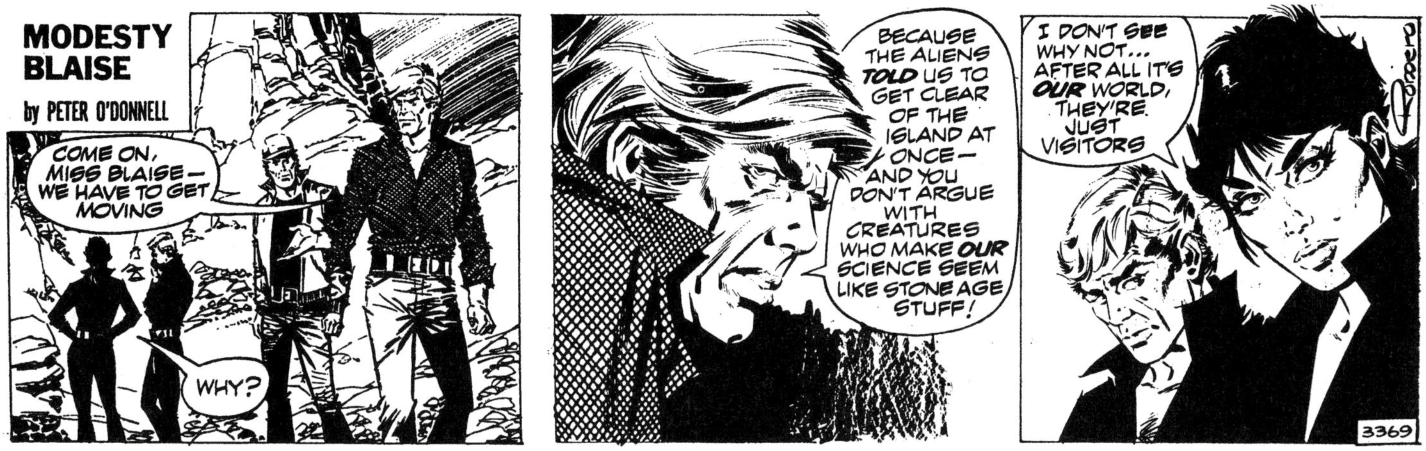
MODESTY BLAISE
by PETER O'DONNELL
COME ON, MISS BLAISE— WE HAVE TO GET MOVING
WHY?
BECAUSE THE ALIENS TOLD US TO GET CLEAR OF THE ISLAND AT ONCE— AND YOU DON'T ARGUE WITH CREATURES WHO MAKE OUR SCIENCE SEEM LIKE STONE AGE STUFF!
I DON'T SEE WHY NOT... AFTER ALL IT'S OUR WORLD, THEY'RE JUST VISITORS
3369

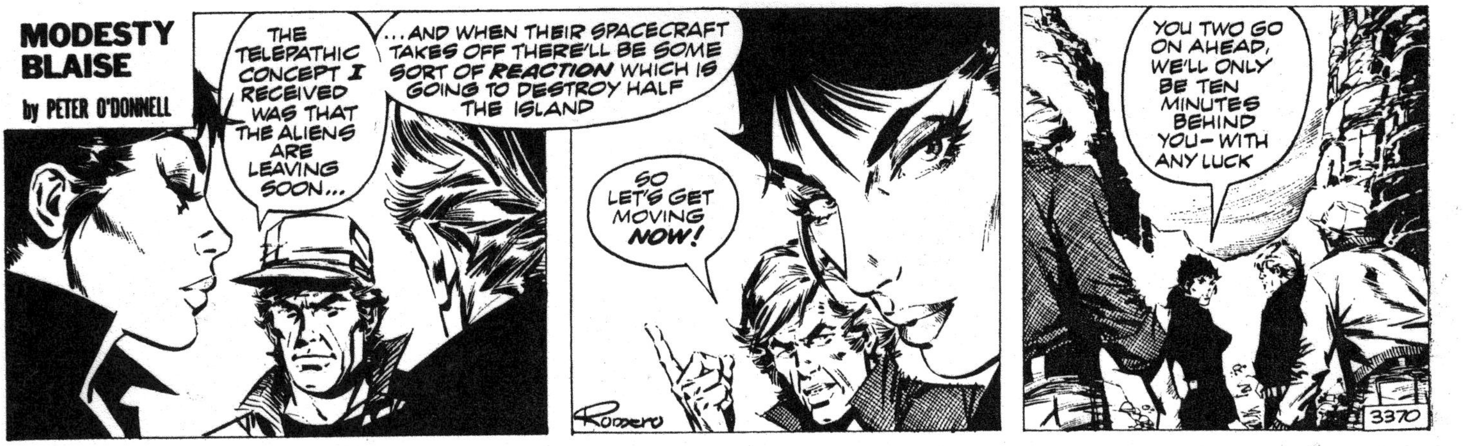
MODESTY BLAISE
by PETER O'DONNELL
THE TELEPATHIC CONCEPT I RECEIVED WAS THAT THE ALIENS ARE LEAVING SOON...
...AND WHEN THEIR SPACECRAFT TAKES OFF THERE'LL BE SOME SORT OF REACTION WHICH IS GOING TO DESTROY HALF THE ISLAND
SO LET'S GET MOVING NOW!
YOU TWO GO ON AHEAD, WE'LL ONLY BE TEN MINUTES BEHIND YOU—WITH ANY LUCK
3370

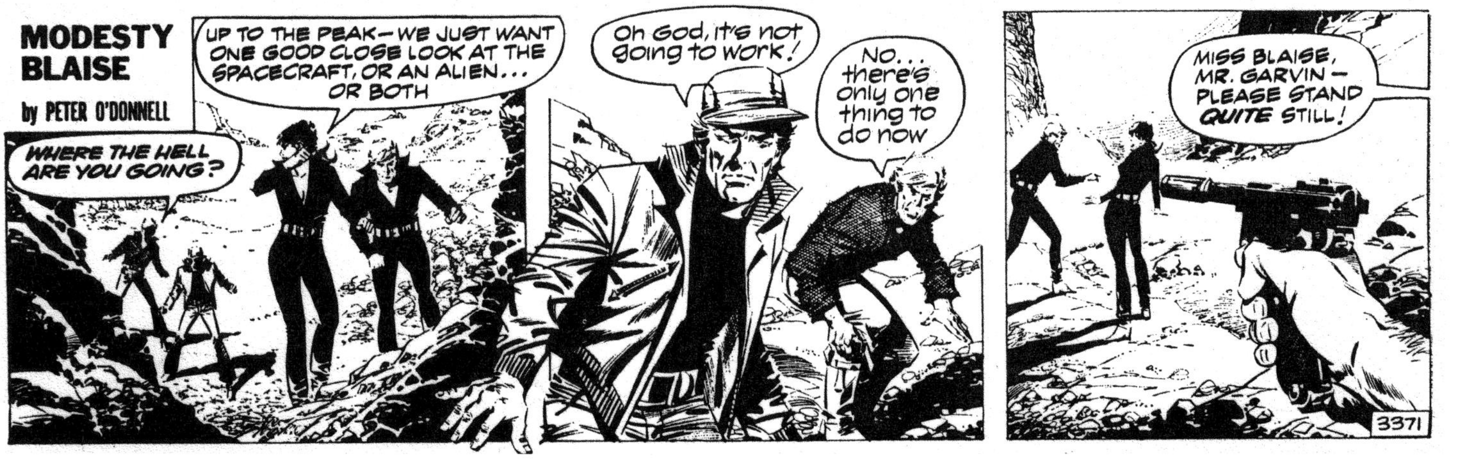
MODESTY BLAISE
by PETER O'DONNELL
UP TO THE PEAK—WE JUST WANT ONE GOOD CLOSE LOOK AT THE SPACECRAFT, OR AN ALIEN... OR BOTH
WHERE THE HELL ARE YOU GOING?
Oh God, it's not going to work!
No... there's only one thing to do now
MISS BLAISE, MR. GARVIN—PLEASE STAND QUITE STILL!
3371

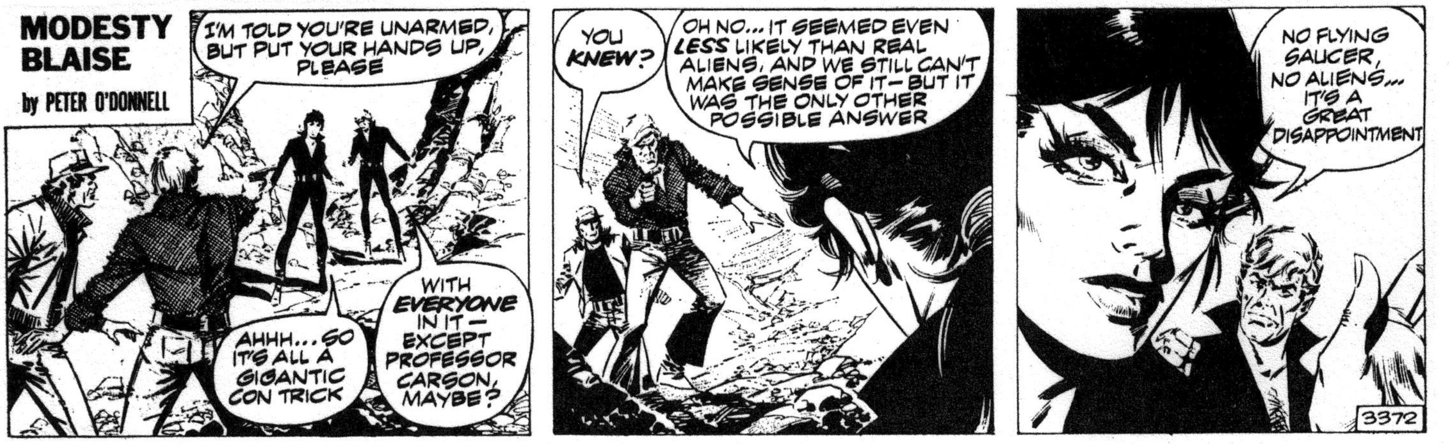
MODESTY BLAISE
by PETER O'DONNELL
I'M TOLD YOU'RE UNARMED, BUT PUT YOUR HANDS UP, PLEASE
AHHH... SO IT'S ALL A GIGANTIC CON TRICK
WITH EVERYONE IN IT—EXCEPT PROFESSOR CARSON, MAYBE?
YOU KNEW?
OH NO... IT SEEMED EVEN LESS LIKELY THAN REAL ALIENS, AND WE STILL CAN'T MAKE SENSE OF IT—BUT IT WAS THE ONLY OTHER POSSIBLE ANSWER
NO FLYING SAUCER, NO ALIENS... IT'S A GREAT DISAPPOINTMENT
3372

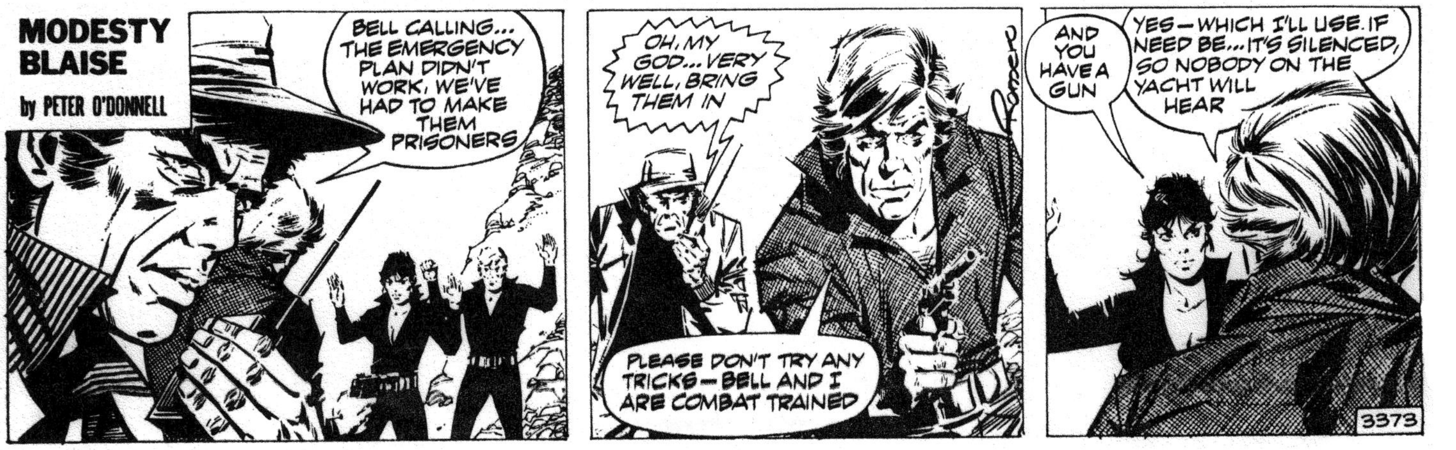
MODESTY BLAISE
by PETER O'DONNELL
BELL CALLING... THE EMERGENCY PLAN DIDN'T WORK, WE'VE HAD TO MAKE THEM PRISONERS
OH, MY GOD... VERY WELL, BRING THEM IN
PLEASE DON'T TRY ANY TRICKS—BELL AND I ARE COMBAT TRAINED
AND YOU HAVE A GUN
YES—WHICH I'LL USE, IF NEED BE... IT'S SILENCED, SO NOBODY ON THE YACHT WILL HEAR
3373

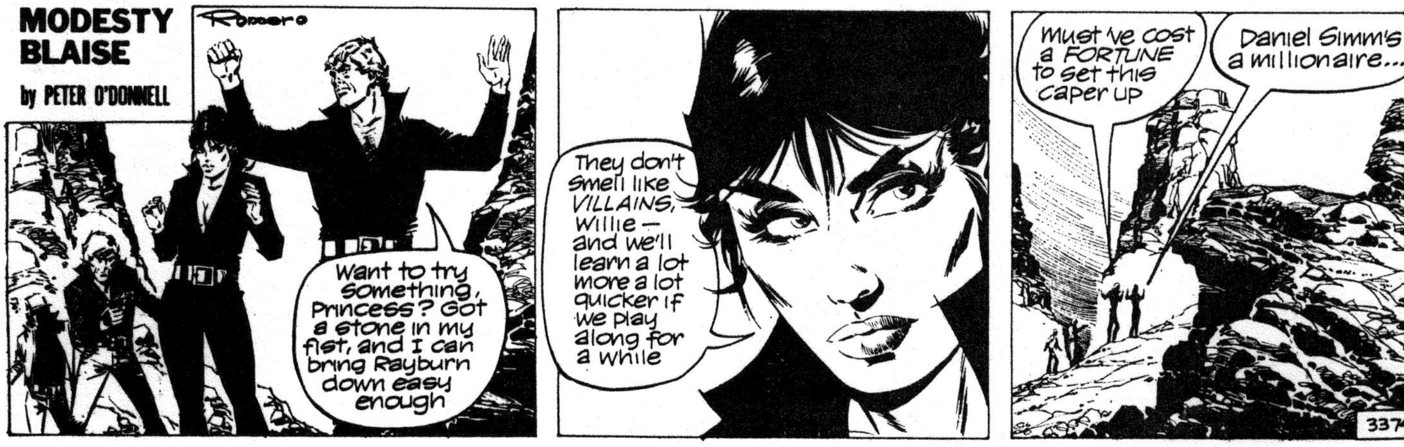
MODESTY BLAISE
by PETER O'DONNELL
Romero
Want to try something, Princess? Got a stone in my fist, and I can bring Rayburn down easy enough
They don't smell like VILLAINS, Willie — and we'll learn a lot more a lot quicker if we play along for a while
Must 've cost a FORTUNE to set this caper up
Daniel Simm's a millionaire...
3374

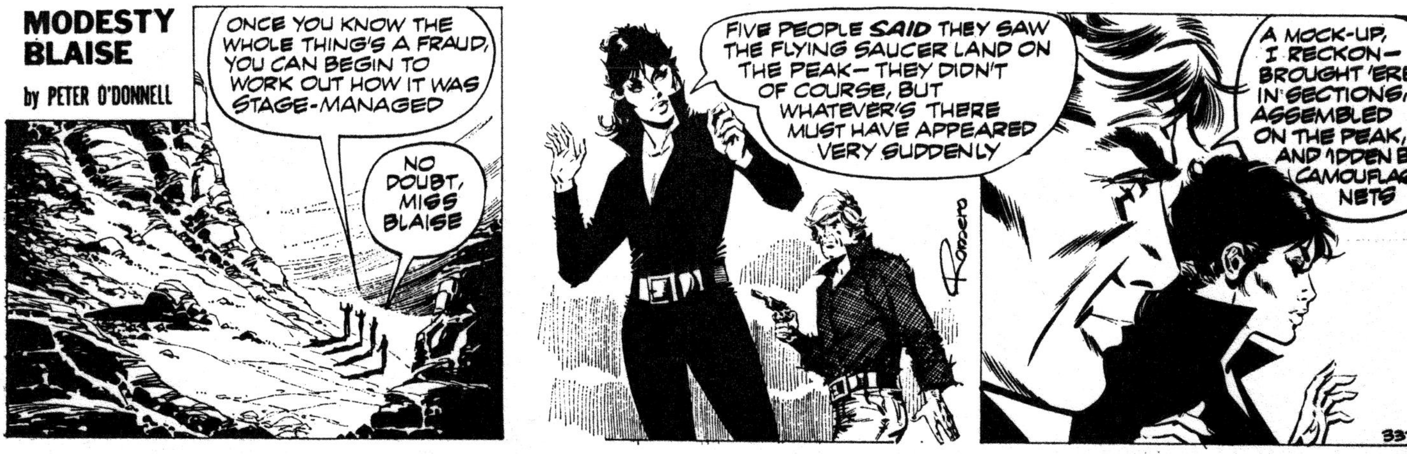
MODESTY BLAISE
by PETER O'DONNELL
ONCE YOU KNOW THE WHOLE THING'S A FRAUD, YOU CAN BEGIN TO WORK OUT HOW IT WAS STAGE-MANAGED
NO DOUBT, MISS BLAISE
FIVE PEOPLE SAID THEY SAW THE FLYING SAUCER LAND ON THE PEAK— THEY DIDN'T OF COURSE, BUT WHATEVER'S THERE MUST HAVE APPEARED VERY SUDDENLY
Romero
A MOCK-UP, I RECKON— BROUGHT 'ERE IN SECTIONS, ASSEMBLED ON THE PEAK, AND 'IDDEN BY CAMOUFLAGE NETS
3375

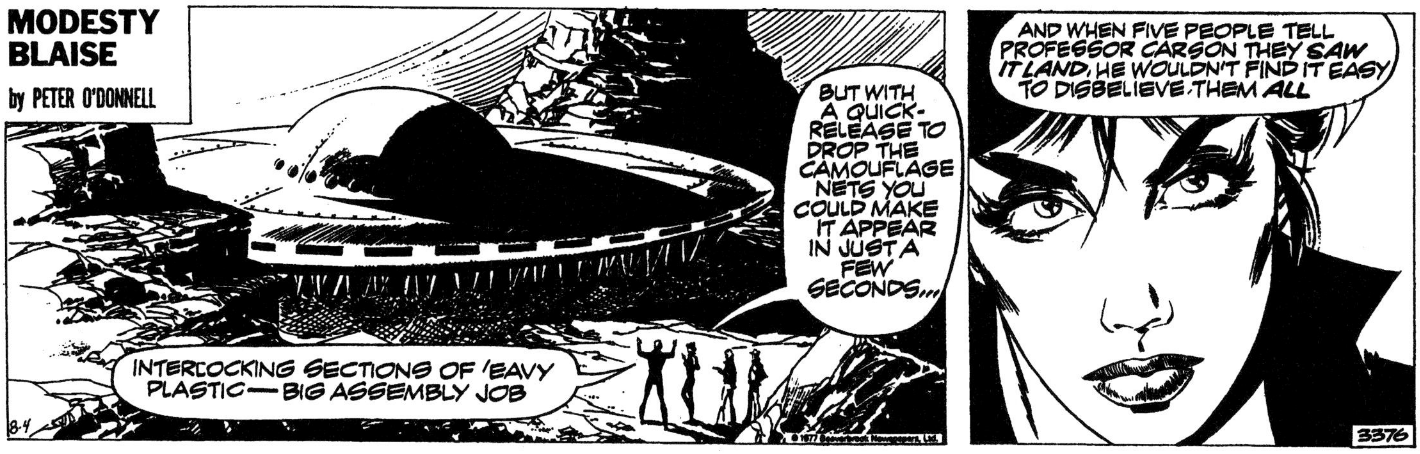
MODESTY BLAISE
by PETER O'DONNELL
INTERLOCKING SECTIONS OF 'EAVY PLASTIC— BIG ASSEMBLY JOB
BUT WITH A QUICK-RELEASE TO DROP THE CAMOUFLAGE NETS YOU COULD MAKE IT APPEAR IN JUST A FEW SECONDS...
8-4
© 1977 Beaverbrook Newspapers, Ltd.
AND WHEN FIVE PEOPLE TELL PROFESSOR CARSON THEY SAW IT LAND, HE WOULDN'T FIND IT EASY TO DISBELIEVE THEM ALL
3376

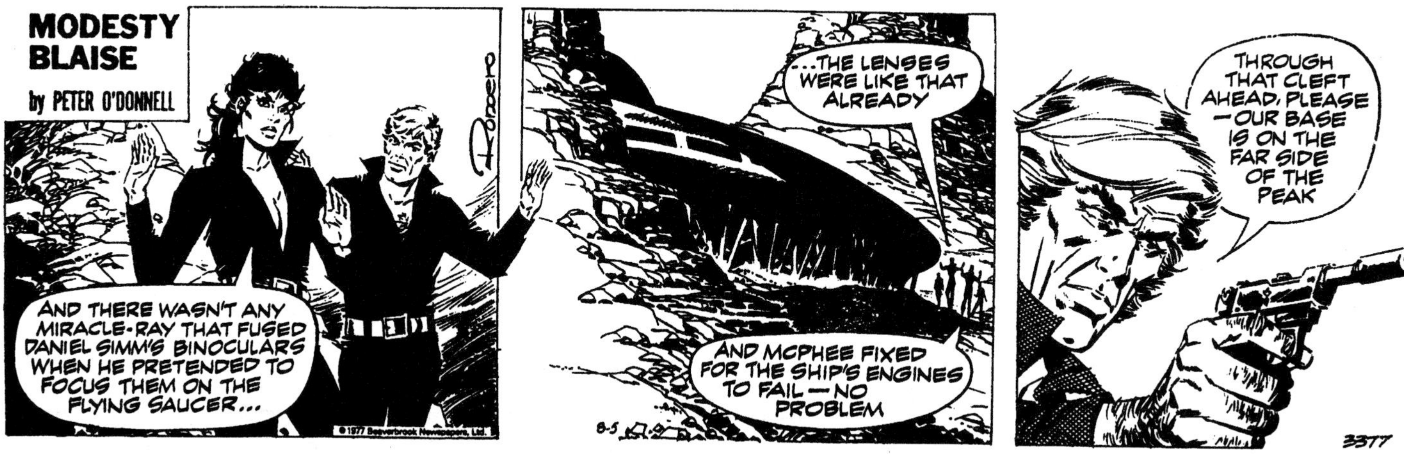
MODESTY BLAISE
by PETER O'DONNELL
Romero
AND THERE WASN'T ANY MIRACLE-RAY THAT FUSED DANIEL SIMM'S BINOCULARS WHEN HE PRETENDED TO FOCUS THEM ON THE FLYING SAUCER...
© 1977 Beaverbrook Newspapers, Ltd.
...THE LENSES WERE LIKE THAT ALREADY
AND McPHEE FIXED FOR THE SHIP'S ENGINES TO FAIL — NO PROBLEM
8-5
THROUGH THAT CLEFT AHEAD, PLEASE — OUR BASE IS ON THE FAR SIDE OF THE PEAK
3377

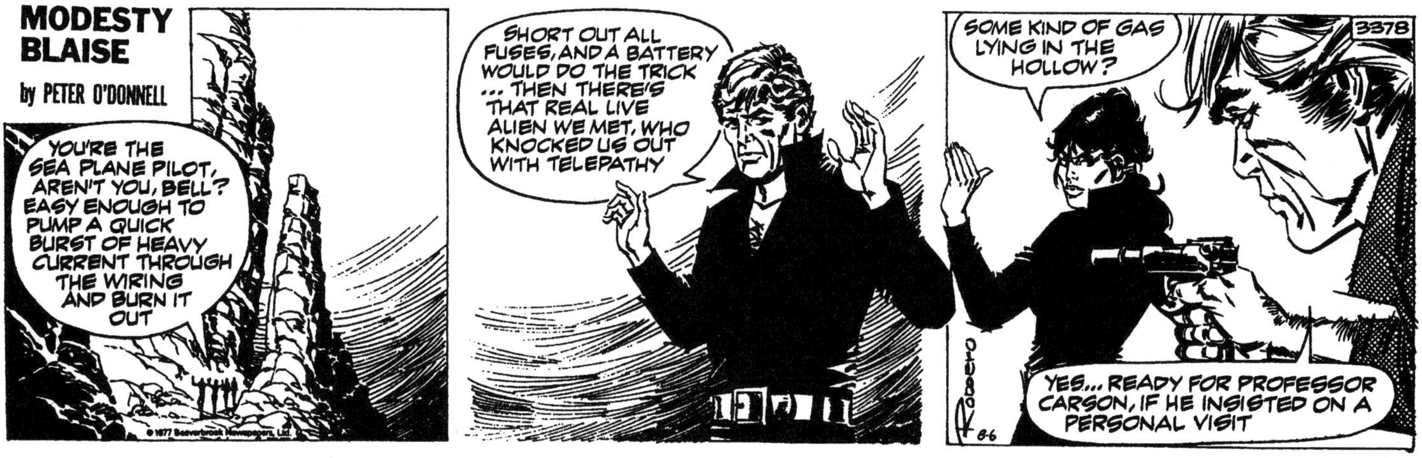
MODESTY BLAISE
by PETER O'DONNELL
YOU'RE THE SEA PLANE PILOT, AREN'T YOU, BELL? EASY ENOUGH TO PUMP A QUICK BURST OF HEAVY CURRENT THROUGH THE WIRING AND BURN IT OUT
© 1977 Beaverbrook Newspapers, Ltd.
SHORT OUT ALL FUSES, AND A BATTERY WOULD DO THE TRICK ... THEN THERE'S THAT REAL LIVE ALIEN WE MET, WHO KNOCKED US OUT WITH TELEPATHY
3378
SOME KIND OF GAS LYING IN THE HOLLOW?
YES... READY FOR PROFESSOR CARSON, IF HE INSISTED ON A PERSONAL VISIT
8-6

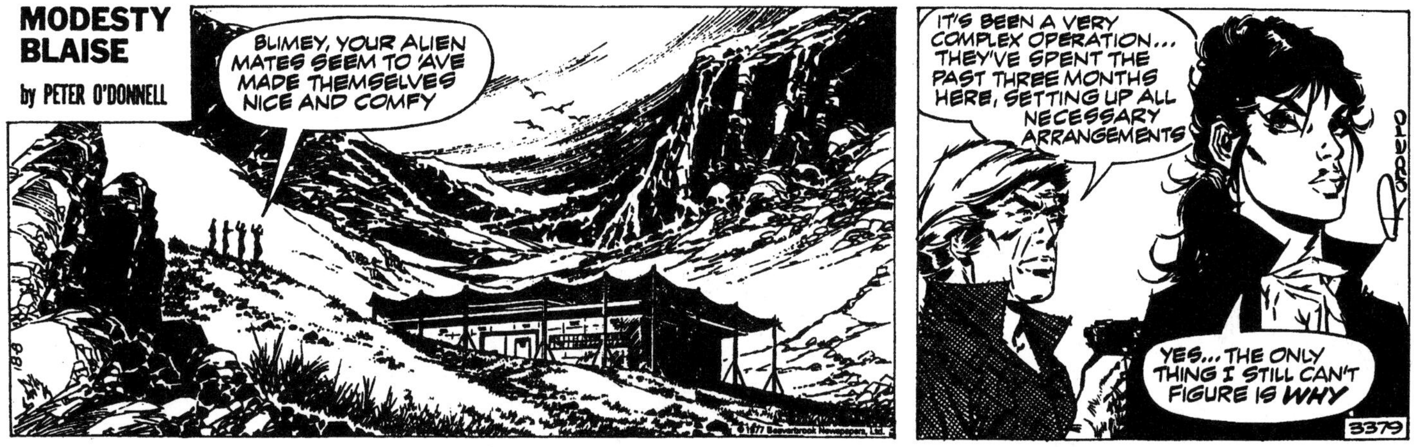
MODESTY BLAISE
by PETER O'DONNELL
BLIMEY, YOUR ALIEN MATES SEEM TO 'AVE MADE THEMSELVES NICE AND COMFY
© 1977 Beaverbrook Newspapers, Ltd.
IT'S BEEN A VERY COMPLEX OPERATION... THEY'VE SPENT THE PAST THREE MONTHS HERE, SETTING UP ALL NECESSARY ARRANGEMENTS
YES... THE ONLY THING I STILL CAN'T FIGURE IS WHY
3379

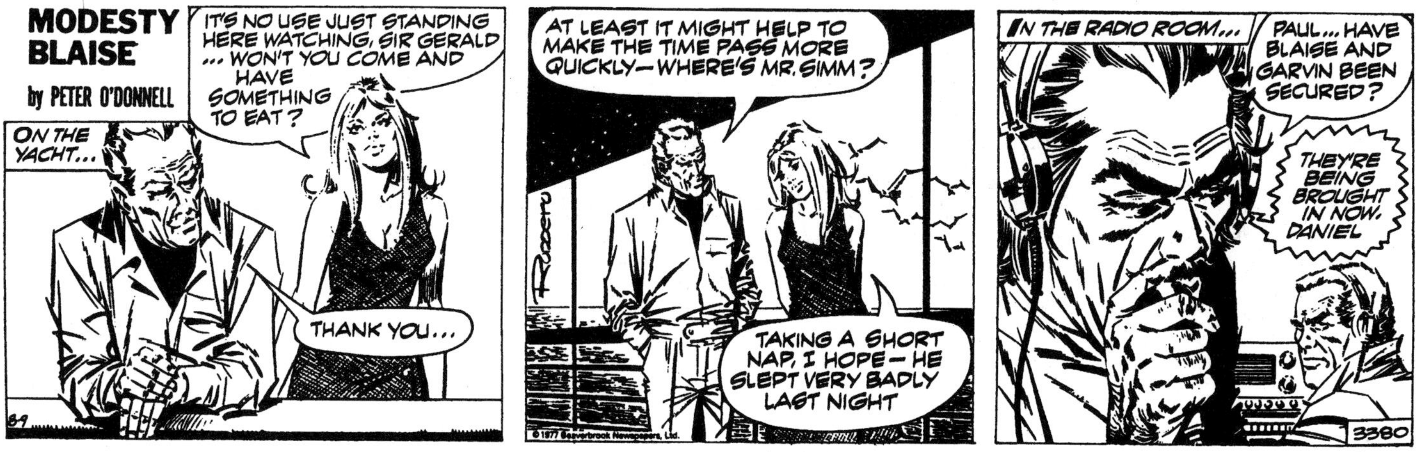
MODESTY BLAISE
by PETER O'DONNELL
ON THE YACHT...
IT'S NO USE JUST STANDING HERE WATCHING, SIR GERALD ... WON'T YOU COME AND HAVE SOMETHING TO EAT?
THANK YOU...
8-9
AT LEAST IT MIGHT HELP TO MAKE THE TIME PASS MORE QUICKLY—WHERE'S MR. SIMM?
TAKING A SHORT NAP, I HOPE—HE SLEPT VERY BADLY LAST NIGHT
© 1977 Beaverbrook Newspapers, Ltd.
IN THE RADIO ROOM...
PAUL... HAVE BLAISE AND GARVIN BEEN SECURED?
THEY'RE BEING BROUGHT IN NOW, DANIEL
3380

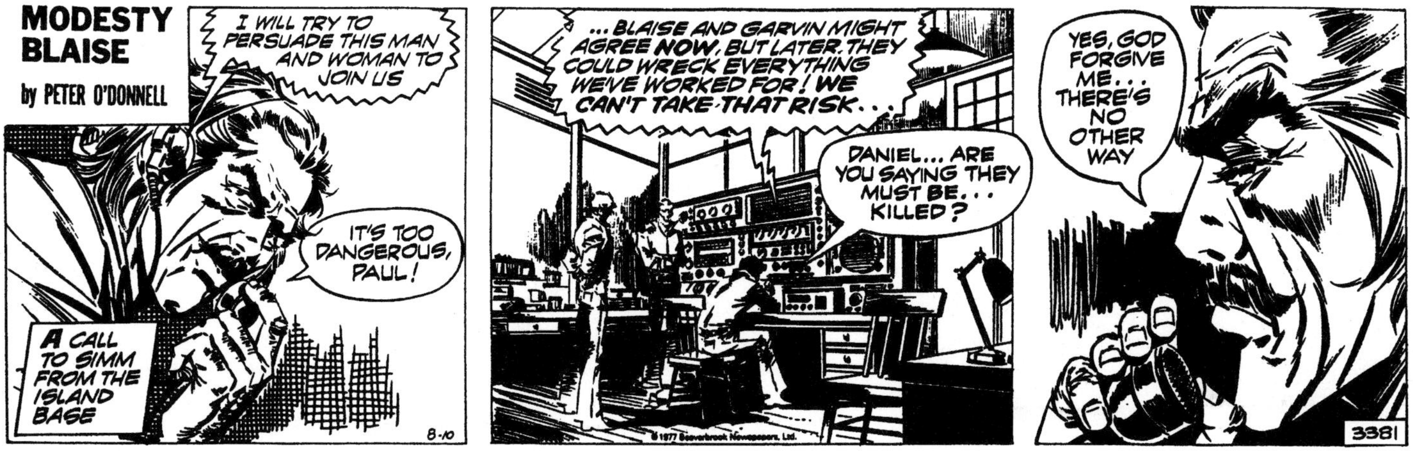
MODESTY BLAISE
by PETER O'DONNELL
I WILL TRY TO PERSUADE THIS MAN AND WOMAN TO JOIN US
IT'S TOO DANGEROUS, PAUL!
A CALL TO SIMM FROM THE ISLAND BASE
8-10
... BLAISE AND GARVIN MIGHT AGREE NOW, BUT LATER, THEY COULD WRECK EVERYTHING WE'VE WORKED FOR! WE CAN'T TAKE THAT RISK...
DANIEL... ARE YOU SAYING THEY MUST BE... KILLED?
© 1977 Beaverbrook Newspapers, Ltd.
YES, GOD FORGIVE ME... THERE'S NO OTHER WAY
3381

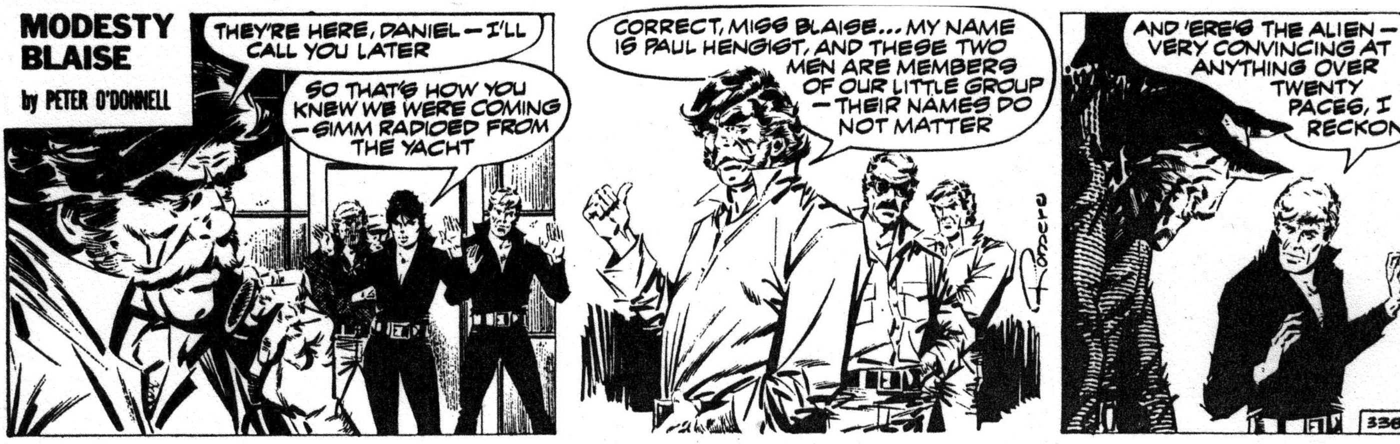
MODESTY BLAISE
by PETER O'DONNELL
THEY'RE HERE, DANIEL — I'LL CALL YOU LATER
SO THAT'S HOW YOU KNEW WE WERE COMING — SIMM RADIOED FROM THE YACHT
CORRECT, MISS BLAISE... MY NAME IS PAUL HENGIST, AND THESE TWO MEN ARE MEMBERS OF OUR LITTLE GROUP — THEIR NAMES DO NOT MATTER
AND 'ERE'S THE ALIEN — VERY CONVINCING AT ANYTHING OVER TWENTY PACES, I RECKON
3382

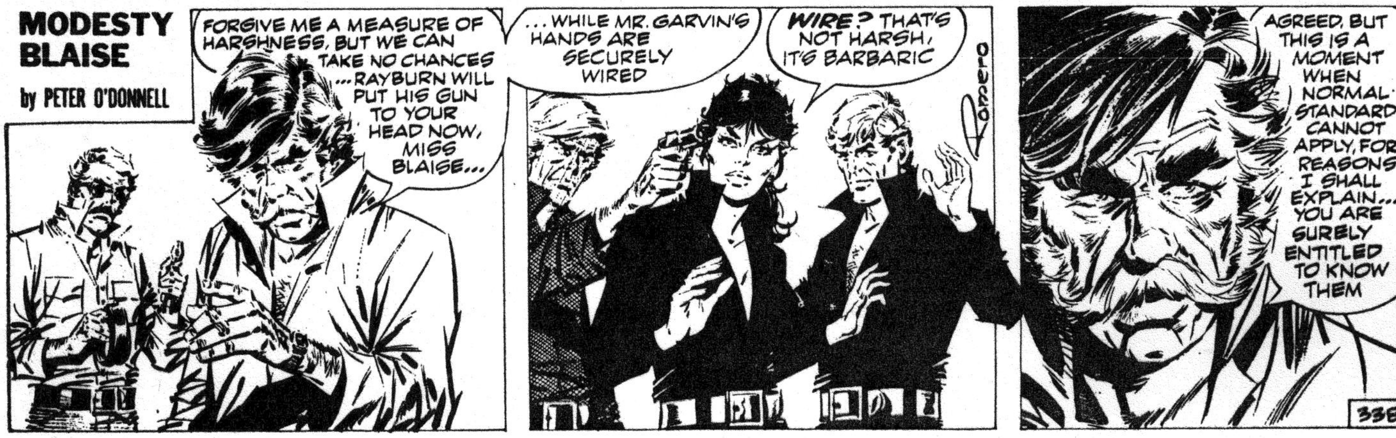
MODESTY BLAISE
by PETER O'DONNELL
FORGIVE ME A MEASURE OF HARSHNESS, BUT WE CAN TAKE NO CHANCES ...RAYBURN WILL PUT HIS GUN TO YOUR HEAD NOW, MISS BLAISE...
...WHILE MR. GARVIN'S HANDS ARE SECURELY WIRED
WIRE? THAT'S NOT HARSH, IT'S BARBARIC
AGREED, BUT THIS IS A MOMENT WHEN NORMAL STANDARDS CANNOT APPLY, FOR REASONS I SHALL EXPLAIN... YOU ARE SURELY ENTITLED TO KNOW THEM
3383

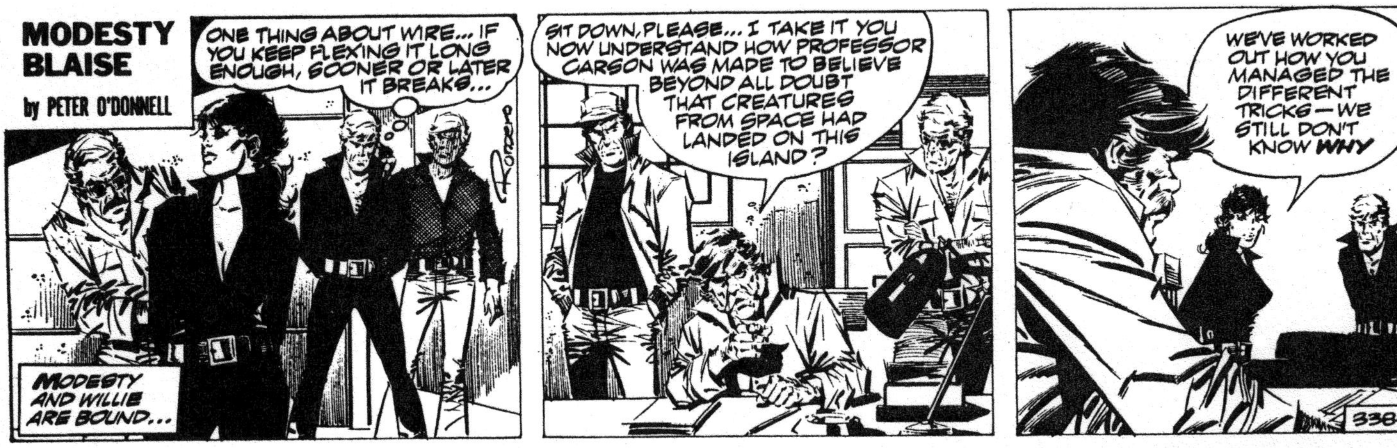
MODESTY BLAISE
by PETER O'DONNELL
ONE THING ABOUT WIRE... IF YOU KEEP FLEXING IT LONG ENOUGH, SOONER OR LATER IT BREAKS...
MODESTY AND WILLIE ARE BOUND...
SIT DOWN, PLEASE... I TAKE IT YOU NOW UNDERSTAND HOW PROFESSOR CARSON WAS MADE TO BELIEVE BEYOND ALL DOUBT THAT CREATURES FROM SPACE HAD LANDED ON THIS ISLAND?
WE'VE WORKED OUT HOW YOU MANAGED THE DIFFERENT TRICKS — WE STILL DON'T KNOW WHY
3384

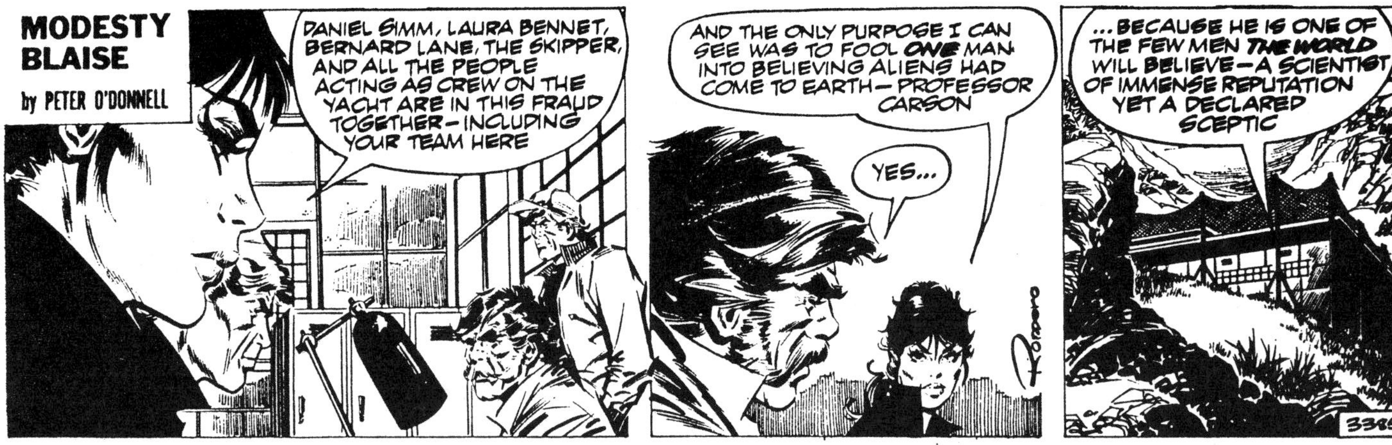
MODESTY BLAISE
by PETER O'DONNELL
DANIEL SIMM, LAURA BENNET, BERNARD LANE, THE SKIPPER, AND ALL THE PEOPLE ACTING AS CREW ON THE YACHT ARE IN THIS FRAUD TOGETHER — INCLUDING YOUR TEAM HERE
AND THE ONLY PURPOSE I CAN SEE WAS TO FOOL ONE MAN INTO BELIEVING ALIENS HAD COME TO EARTH — PROFESSOR CARSON
YES...
...BECAUSE HE IS ONE OF THE FEW MEN THE WORLD WILL BELIEVE — A SCIENTIST OF IMMENSE REPUTATION YET A DECLARED SCEPTIC
3385

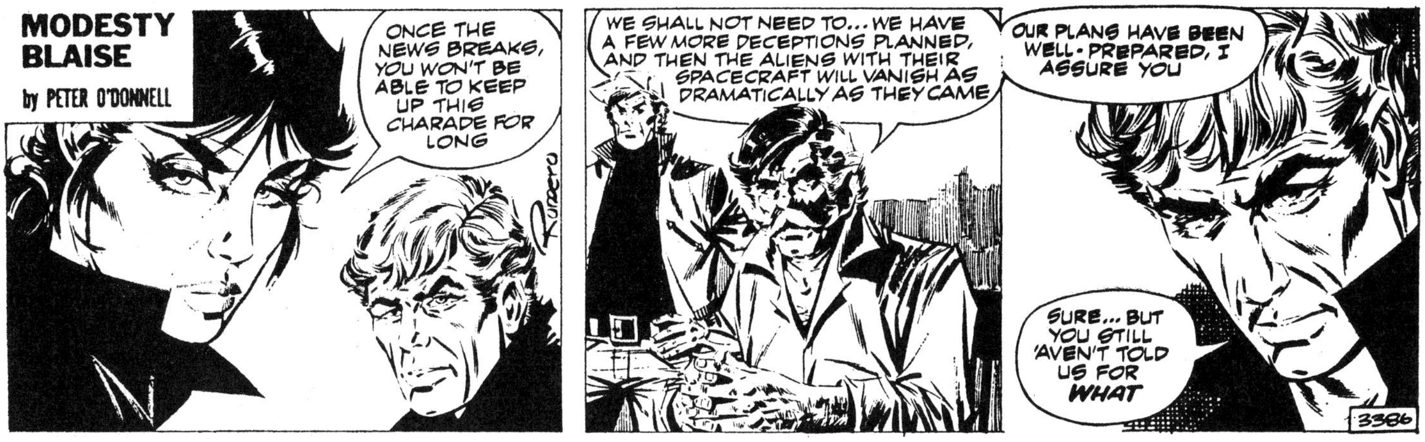
MODESTY BLAISE
by PETER O'DONNELL
ONCE THE NEWS BREAKS, YOU WON'T BE ABLE TO KEEP UP THIS CHARADE FOR LONG
WE SHALL NOT NEED TO... WE HAVE A FEW MORE DECEPTIONS PLANNED, AND THEN THE ALIENS WITH THEIR SPACECRAFT WILL VANISH AS DRAMATICALLY AS THEY CAME
OUR PLANS HAVE BEEN WELL-PREPARED, I ASSURE YOU
SURE... BUT YOU STILL 'AVEN'T TOLD US FOR WHAT
3386

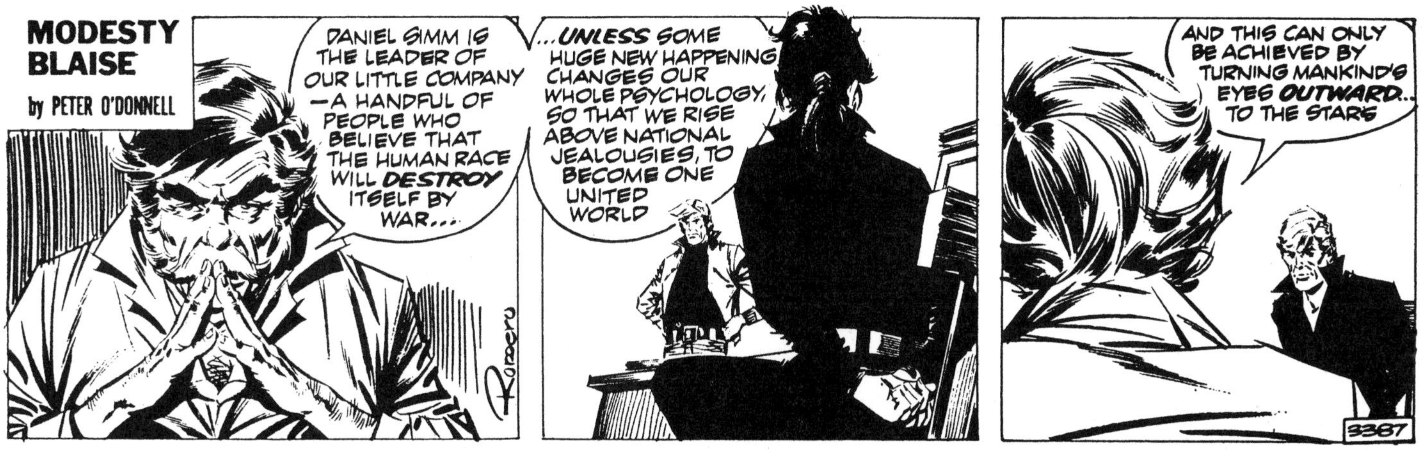
MODESTY BLAISE
by PETER O'DONNELL
DANIEL SIMM IS THE LEADER OF OUR LITTLE COMPANY —A HANDFUL OF PEOPLE WHO BELIEVE THAT THE HUMAN RACE WILL DESTROY ITSELF BY WAR...
...UNLESS SOME HUGE NEW HAPPENING CHANGES OUR WHOLE PSYCHOLOGY, SO THAT WE RISE ABOVE NATIONAL JEALOUSIES, TO BECOME ONE UNITED WORLD
AND THIS CAN ONLY BE ACHIEVED BY TURNING MANKIND'S EYES OUTWARD... TO THE STARS
3387

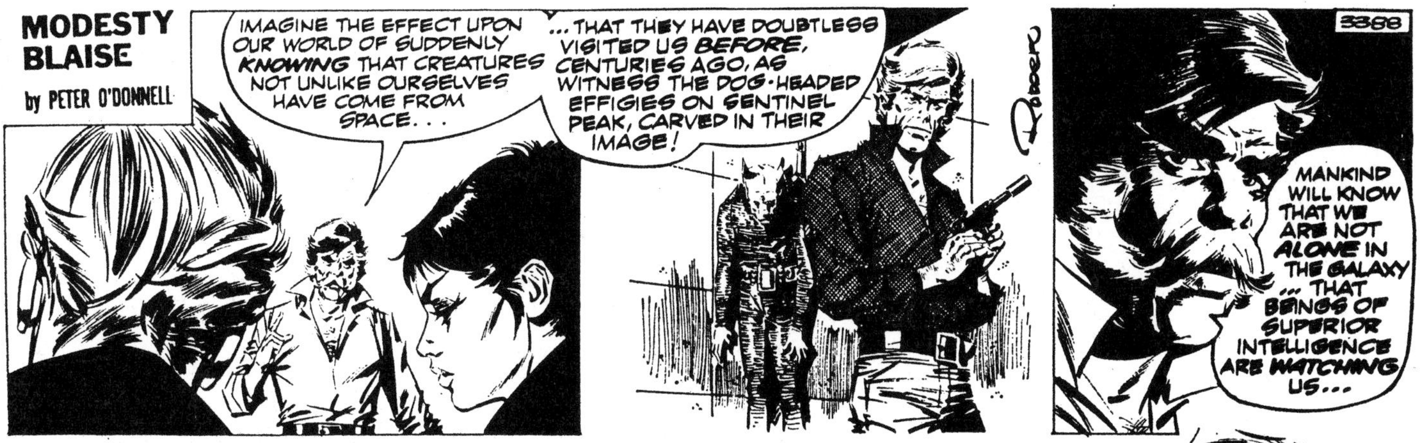
MODESTY BLAISE
by PETER O'DONNELL
IMAGINE THE EFFECT UPON OUR WORLD OF SUDDENLY KNOWING THAT CREATURES NOT UNLIKE OURSELVES HAVE COME FROM SPACE...
...THAT THEY HAVE DOUBTLESS VISITED US BEFORE, CENTURIES AGO, AS WITNESS THE DOG-HEADED EFFIGIES ON SENTINEL PEAK, CARVED IN THEIR IMAGE!
3388
MANKIND WILL KNOW THAT WE ARE NOT ALONE IN THE GALAXY ... THAT BEINGS OF SUPERIOR INTELLIGENCE ARE WATCHING US...

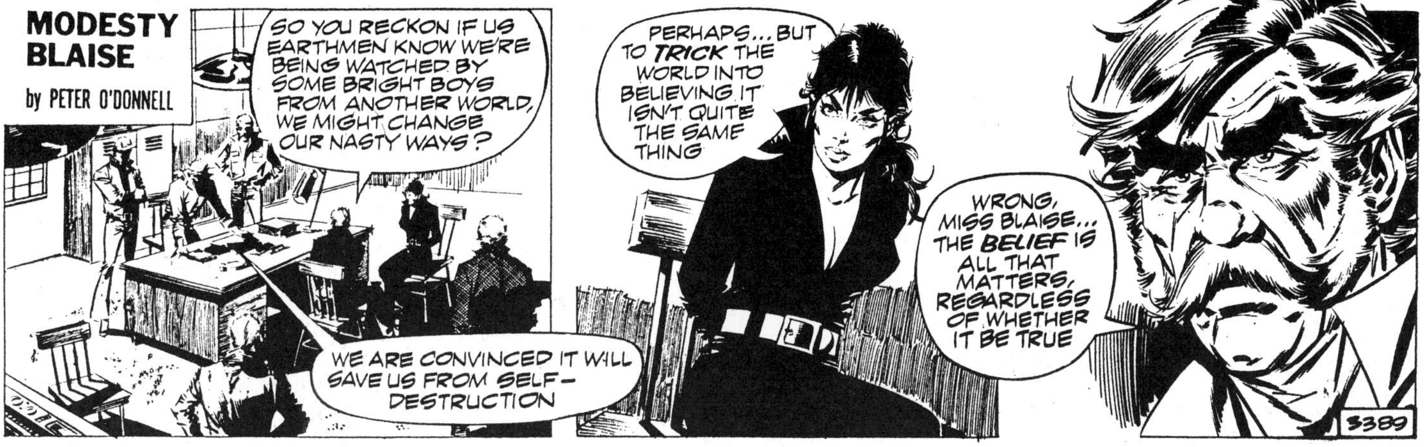
MODESTY BLAISE
by PETER O'DONNELL
SO YOU RECKON IF US EARTHMEN KNOW WE'RE BEING WATCHED BY SOME BRIGHT BOYS FROM ANOTHER WORLD, WE MIGHT CHANGE OUR NASTY WAYS?
WE ARE CONVINCED IT WILL SAVE US FROM SELF-DESTRUCTION
PERHAPS... BUT TO TRICK THE WORLD INTO BELIEVING IT ISN'T QUITE THE SAME THING
WRONG, MISS BLAISE... THE BELIEF IS ALL THAT MATTERS, REGARDLESS OF WHETHER IT BE TRUE
3389

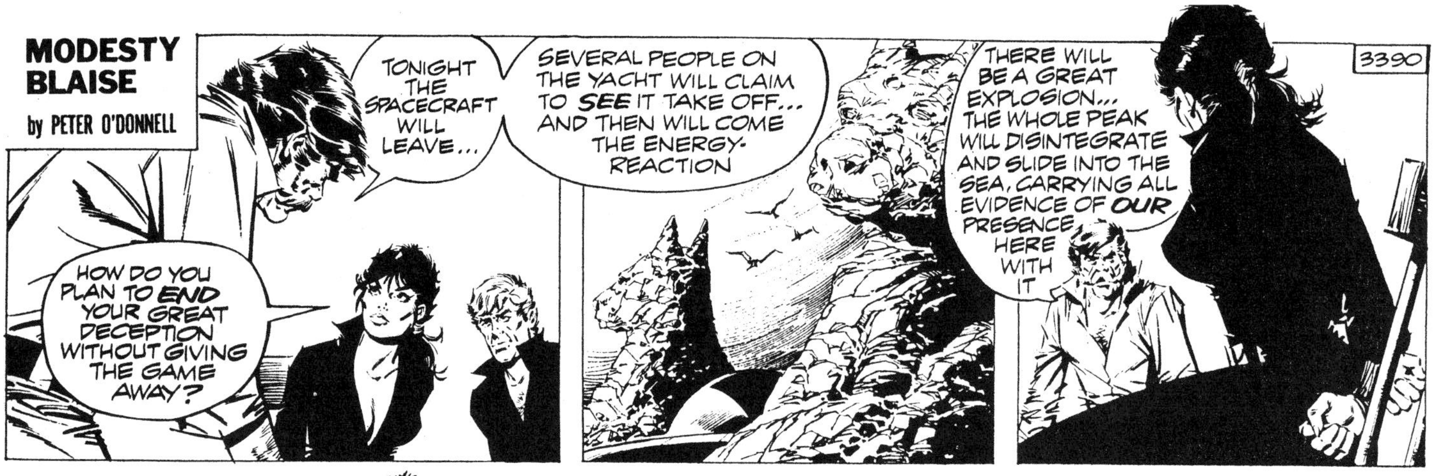
MODESTY BLAISE
by PETER O'DONNELL
HOW DO YOU PLAN TO END YOUR GREAT DECEPTION WITHOUT GIVING THE GAME AWAY?
TONIGHT THE SPACECRAFT WILL LEAVE...
SEVERAL PEOPLE ON THE YACHT WILL CLAIM TO SEE IT TAKE OFF... AND THEN WILL COME THE ENERGY-REACTION
3390
THERE WILL BE A GREAT EXPLOSION... THE WHOLE PEAK WILL DISINTEGRATE AND SLIDE INTO THE SEA, CARRYING ALL EVIDENCE OF OUR PRESENCE HERE WITH IT

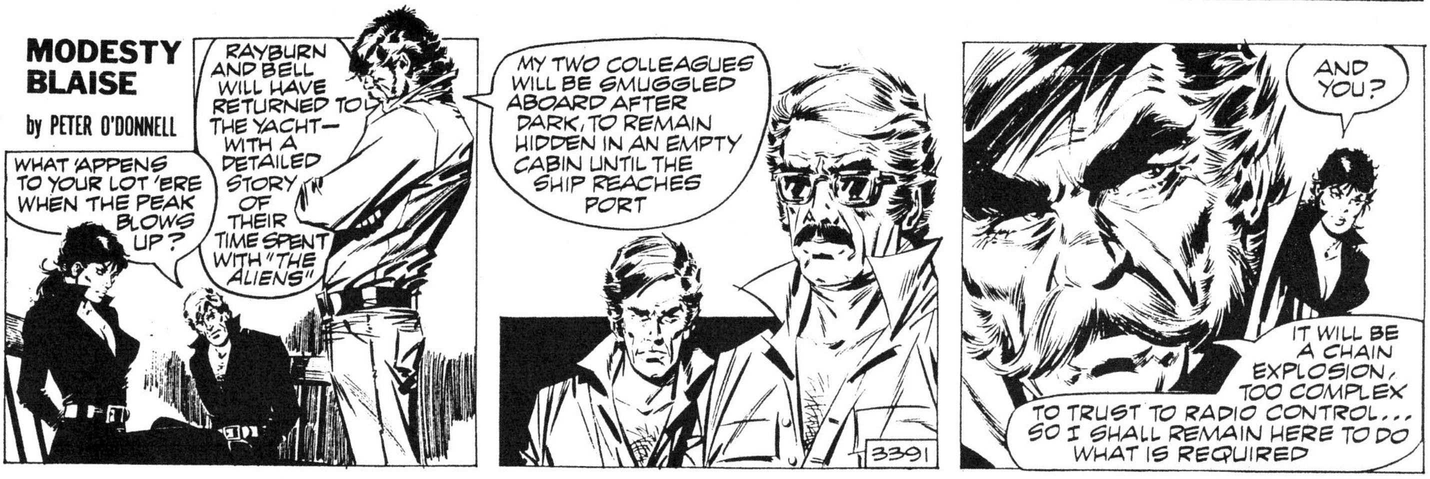
MODESTY BLAISE
by PETER O'DONNELL
WHAT 'APPENS TO YOUR LOT 'ERE WHEN THE PEAK BLOWS UP?
RAYBURN AND BELL WILL HAVE RETURNED TO THE YACHT— WITH A DETAILED STORY OF THEIR TIME SPENT WITH "THE ALIENS"
MY TWO COLLEAGUES WILL BE SMUGGLED ABOARD AFTER DARK, TO REMAIN HIDDEN IN AN EMPTY CABIN UNTIL THE SHIP REACHES PORT
3391
AND YOU?
IT WILL BE A CHAIN EXPLOSION, TOO COMPLEX TO TRUST TO RADIO CONTROL... SO I SHALL REMAIN HERE TO DO WHAT IS REQUIRED

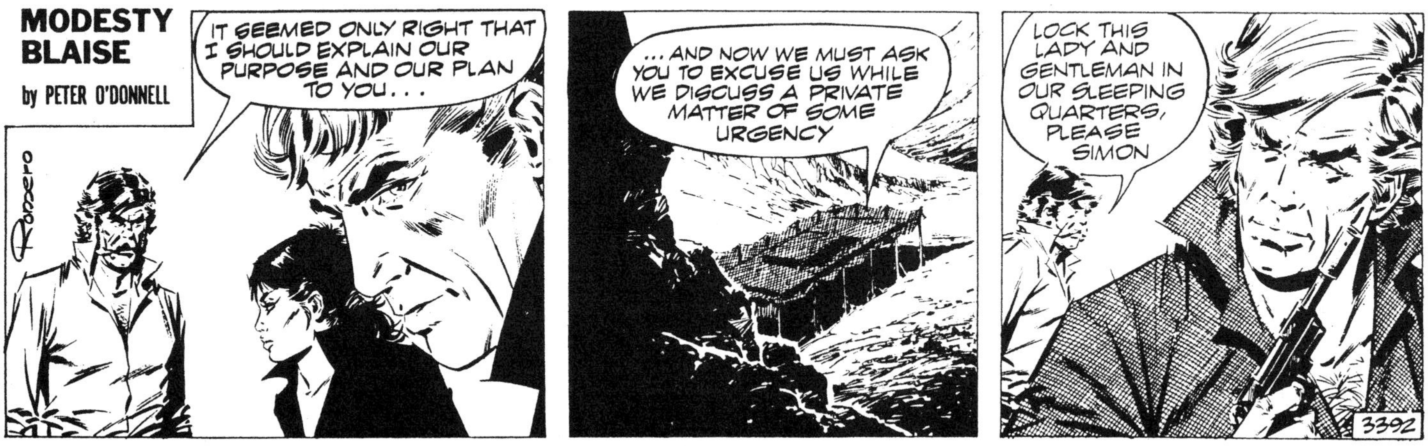
MODESTY BLAISE
by PETER O'DONNELL
Romero
IT SEEMED ONLY RIGHT THAT I SHOULD EXPLAIN OUR PURPOSE AND OUR PLAN TO YOU...
... AND NOW WE MUST ASK YOU TO EXCUSE US WHILE WE DISCUSS A PRIVATE MATTER OF SOME URGENCY
LOCK THIS LADY AND GENTLEMAN IN OUR SLEEPING QUARTERS, PLEASE SIMON
3392

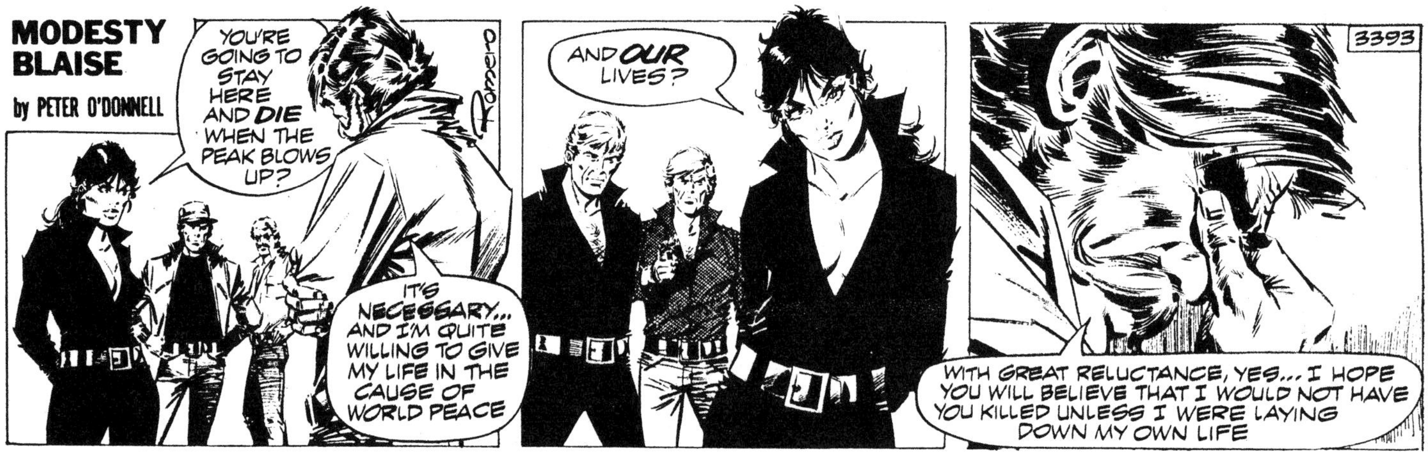
MODESTY BLAISE
by PETER O'DONNELL
Romero
YOU'RE GOING TO STAY HERE AND DIE WHEN THE PEAK BLOWS UP?
IT'S NECESSARY... AND I'M QUITE WILLING TO GIVE MY LIFE IN THE CAUSE OF WORLD PEACE
AND OUR LIVES?
3393
WITH GREAT RELUCTANCE, YES... I HOPE YOU WILL BELIEVE THAT I WOULD NOT HAVE YOU KILLED UNLESS I WERE LAYING DOWN MY OWN LIFE

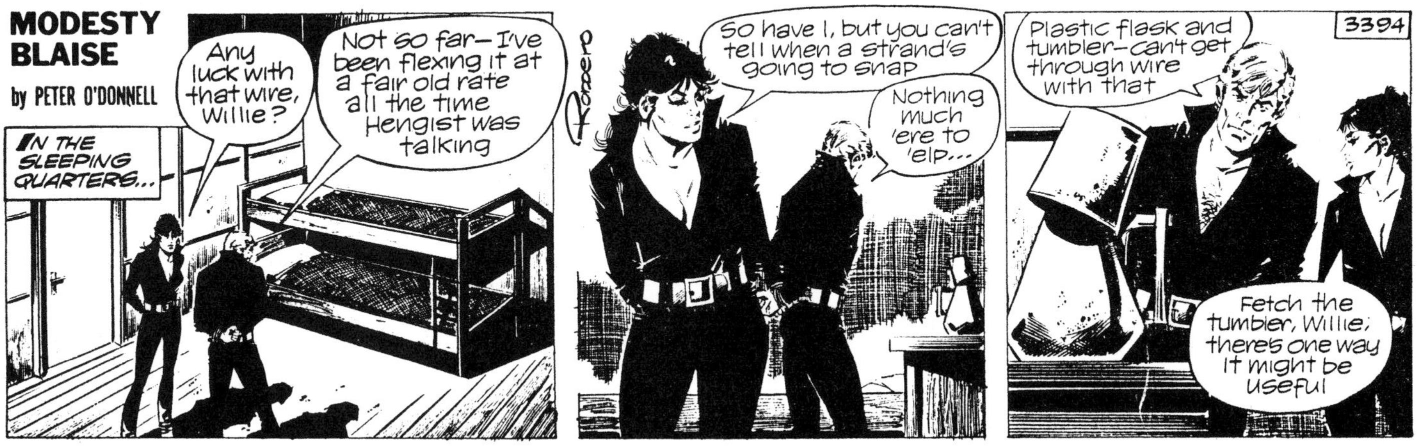
MODESTY BLAISE
by PETER O'DONNELL
IN THE SLEEPING QUARTERS...
Any luck with that wire, Willie?
Not so far—I've been flexing it at a fair old rate all the time Hengist was talking
Romero
So have I, but you can't tell when a strand's going to snap
Nothing much 'ere to 'elp...
3394
Plastic flask and tumbler—can't get through wire with that
Fetch the tumbler, Willie; there's one way it might be useful

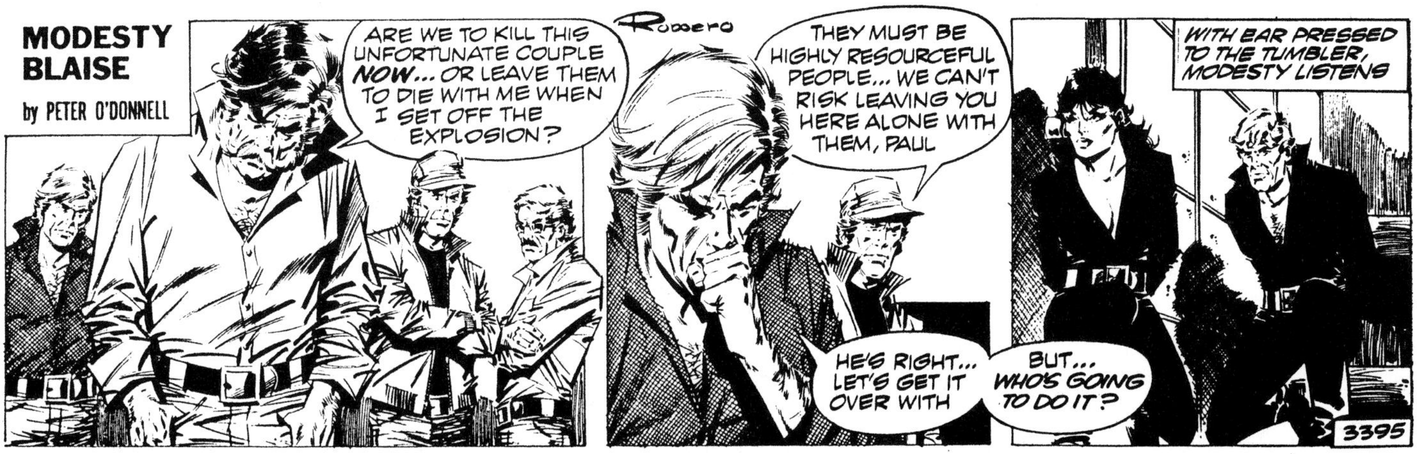
MODESTY BLAISE
by PETER O'DONNELL
ARE WE TO KILL THIS UNFORTUNATE COUPLE NOW... OR LEAVE THEM TO DIE WITH ME WHEN I SET OFF THE EXPLOSION?
Romero
THEY MUST BE HIGHLY RESOURCEFUL PEOPLE... WE CAN'T RISK LEAVING YOU HERE ALONE WITH THEM, PAUL
HE'S RIGHT... LET'S GET IT OVER WITH
BUT... WHO'S GOING TO DO IT?
WITH EAR PRESSED TO THE TUMBLER, MODESTY LISTENS
3395

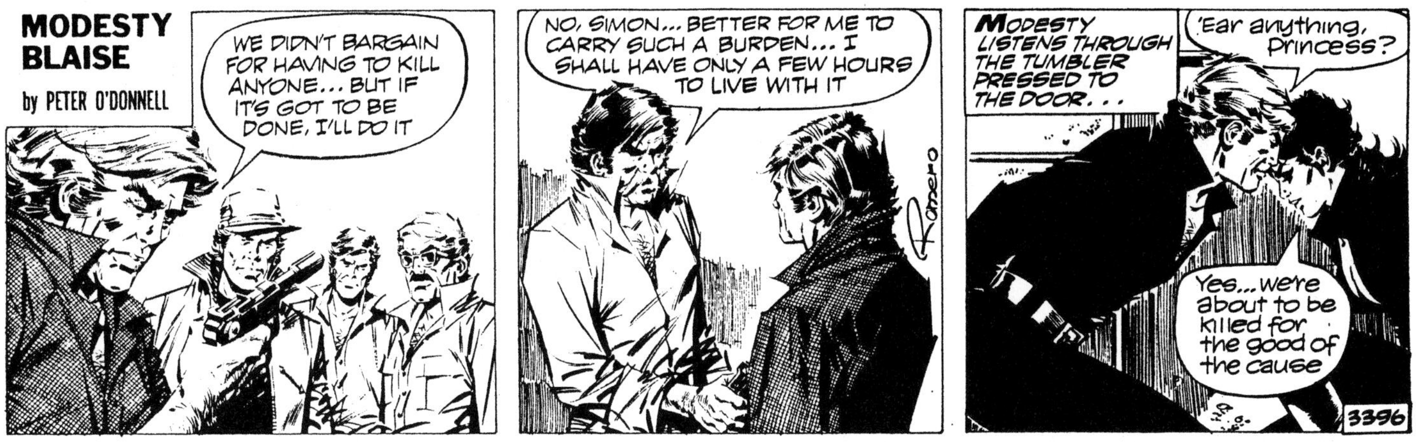
MODESTY BLAISE
by PETER O'DONNELL
WE DIDN'T BARGAIN FOR HAVING TO KILL ANYONE... BUT IF IT'S GOT TO BE DONE, I'LL DO IT
NO, SIMON... BETTER FOR ME TO CARRY SUCH A BURDEN... I SHALL HAVE ONLY A FEW HOURS TO LIVE WITH IT
Romero
MODESTY LISTENS THROUGH THE TUMBLER PRESSED TO THE DOOR...
'Ear anything, Princess?
Yes... we're about to be killed for the good of the cause
3396

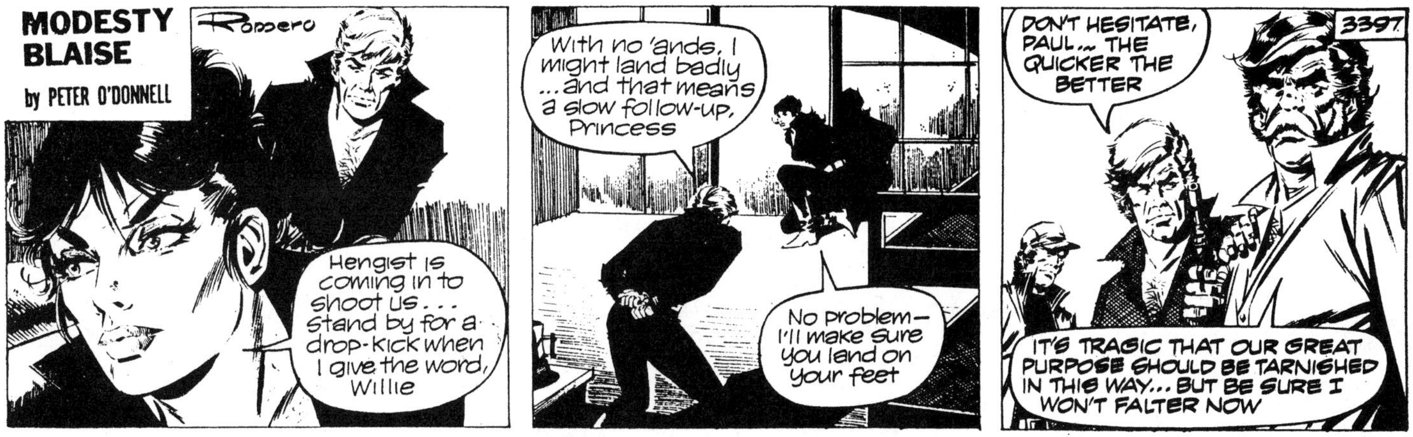
MODESTY BLAISE
by PETER O'DONNELL
Romero
Hengist is coming in to shoot us... stand by for a drop-kick when I give the word, Willie
With no 'ands, I might land badly ...and that means a slow follow-up, Princess
No problem—I'll make sure you land on your feet
3397
DON'T HESITATE, PAUL... THE QUICKER THE BETTER
IT'S TRAGIC THAT OUR GREAT PURPOSE SHOULD BE TARNISHED IN THIS WAY... BUT BE SURE I WON'T FALTER NOW

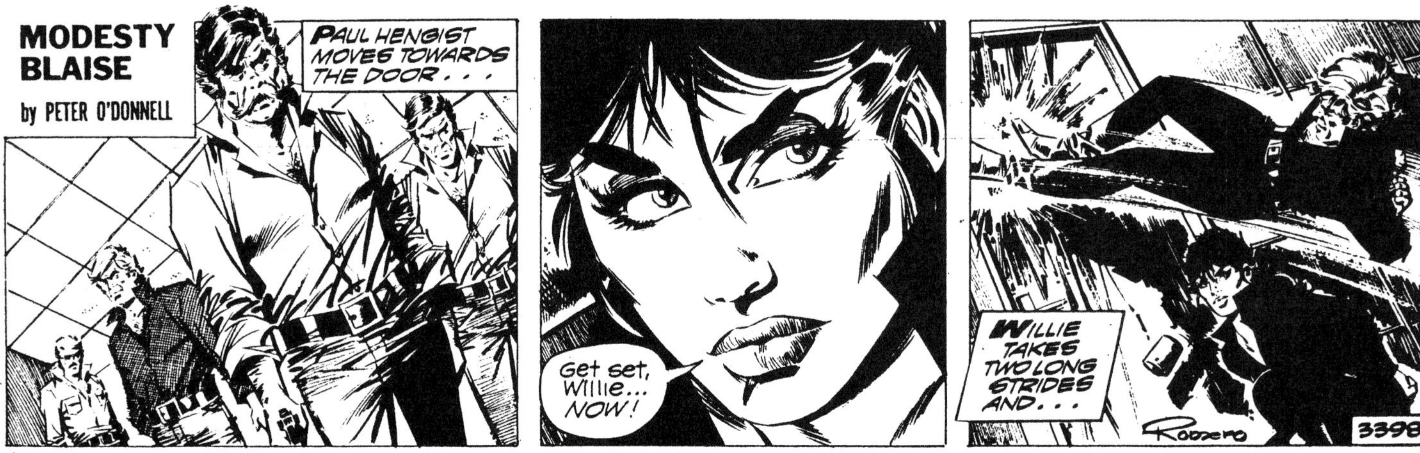
MODESTY BLAISE
by PETER O'DONNELL
PAUL HENGIST MOVES TOWARDS THE DOOR . . .
Get set, Willie... NOW!
WILLIE TAKES TWO LONG STRIDES AND . . .
Romero
3398

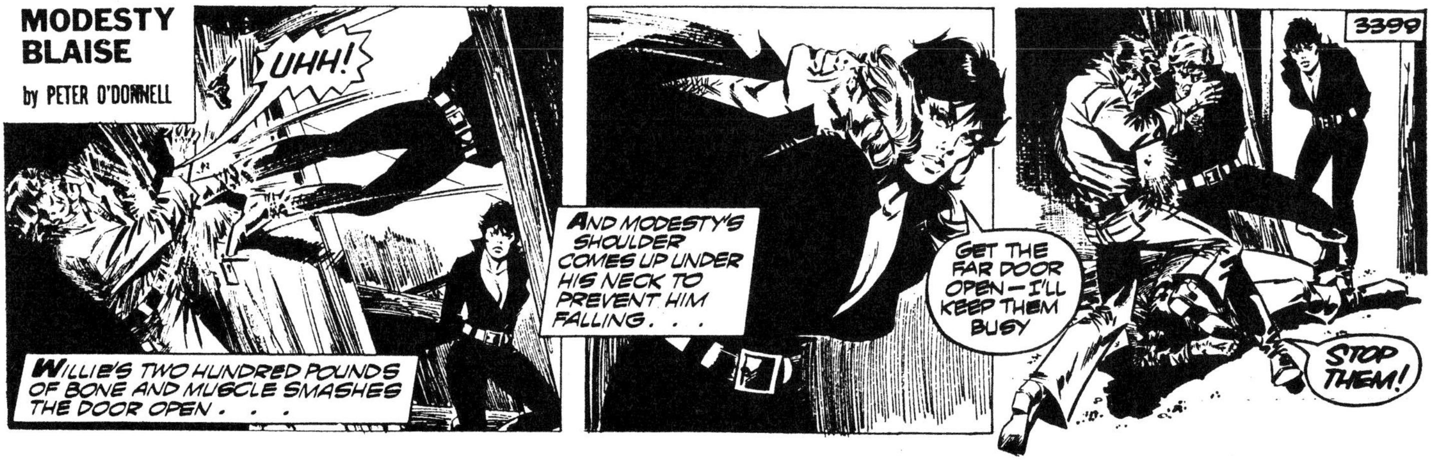
MODESTY BLAISE
by PETER O'DONNELL
UHH!
WILLIE'S TWO HUNDRED POUNDS OF BONE AND MUSCLE SMASHES THE DOOR OPEN . . .
AND MODESTY'S SHOULDER COMES UP UNDER HIS NECK TO PREVENT HIM FALLING . . .
GET THE FAR DOOR OPEN — I'LL KEEP THEM BUSY
3399
STOP THEM!

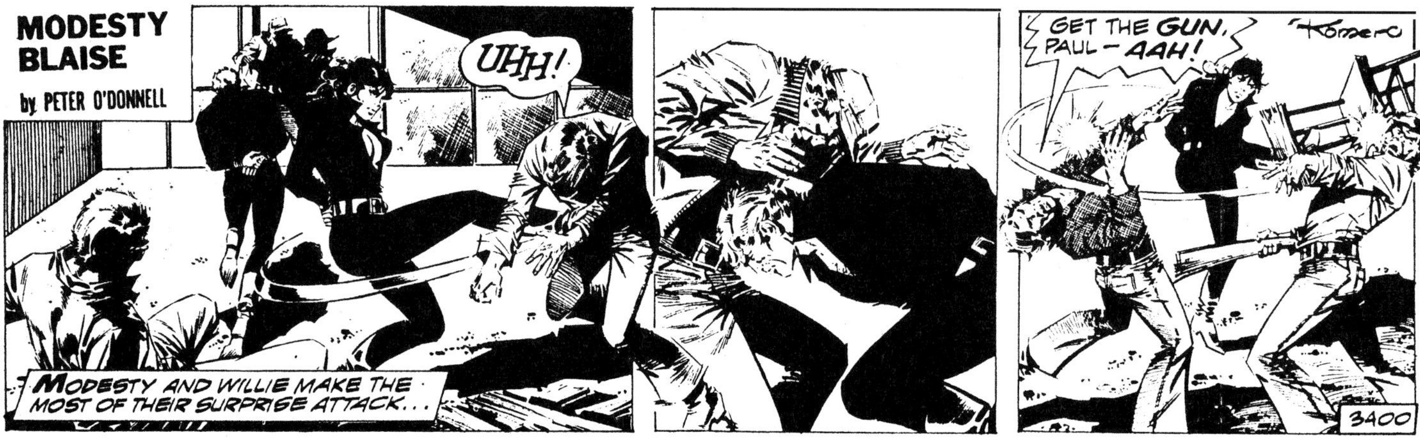
MODESTY BLAISE
by PETER O'DONNELL
UHH!
MODESTY AND WILLIE MAKE THE MOST OF THEIR SURPRISE ATTACK...
GET THE GUN, PAUL — AAH!
Romero
3400

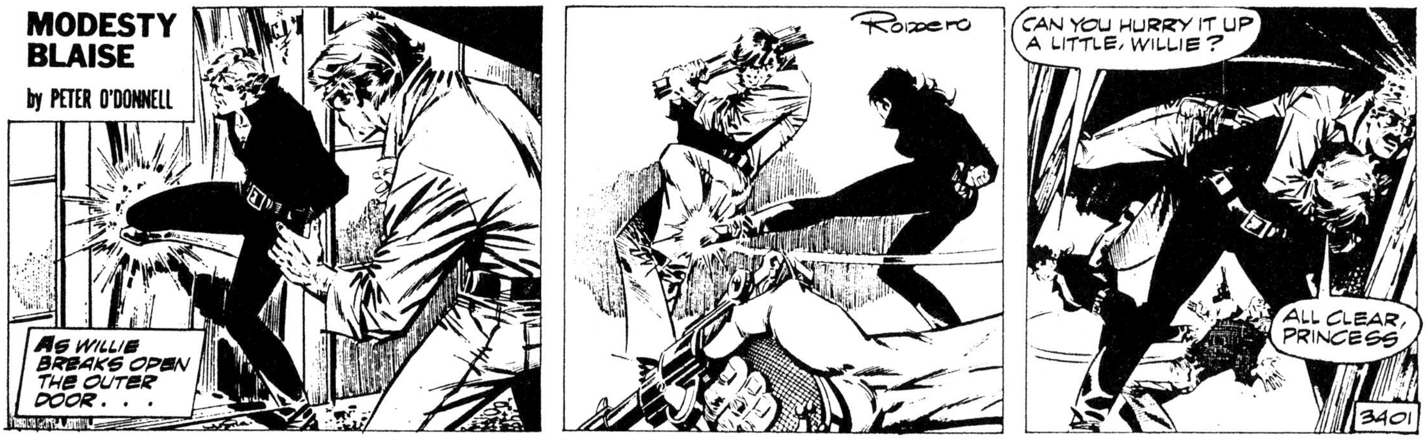
MODESTY BLAISE
by PETER O'DONNELL
AS WILLIE BREAKS OPEN THE OUTER DOOR . . .
Romero
CAN YOU HURRY IT UP A LITTLE, WILLIE?
ALL CLEAR, PRINCESS
3401

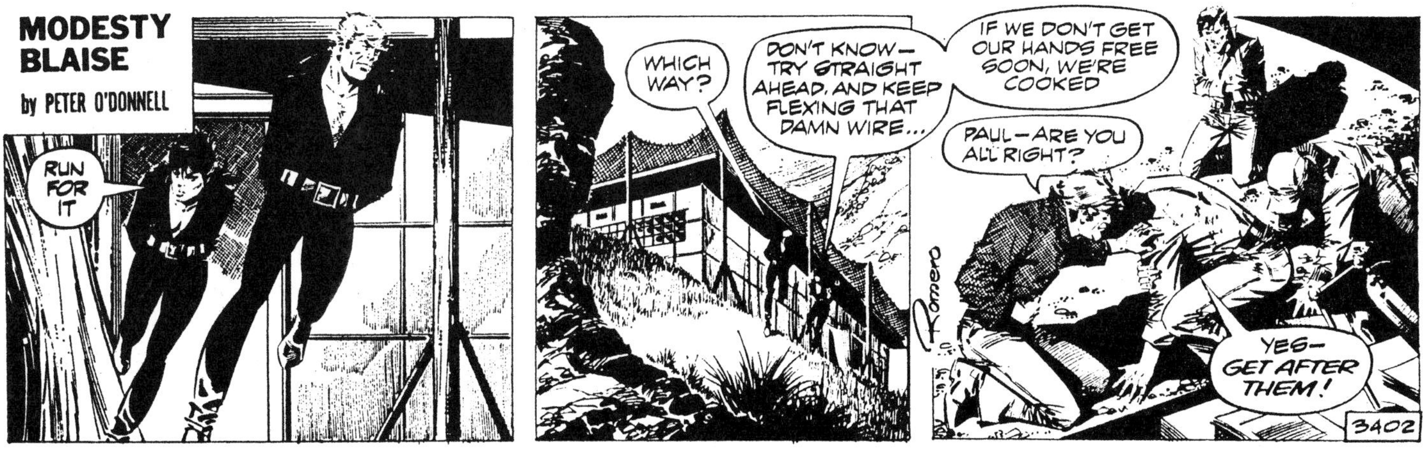
MODESTY BLAISE
by PETER O'DONNELL
RUN FOR IT
WHICH WAY?
DON'T KNOW— TRY STRAIGHT AHEAD, AND KEEP FLEXING THAT DAMN WIRE...
IF WE DON'T GET OUR HANDS FREE SOON, WE'RE COOKED
PAUL—ARE YOU ALL RIGHT?
YES— GET AFTER THEM!
Romero
3402

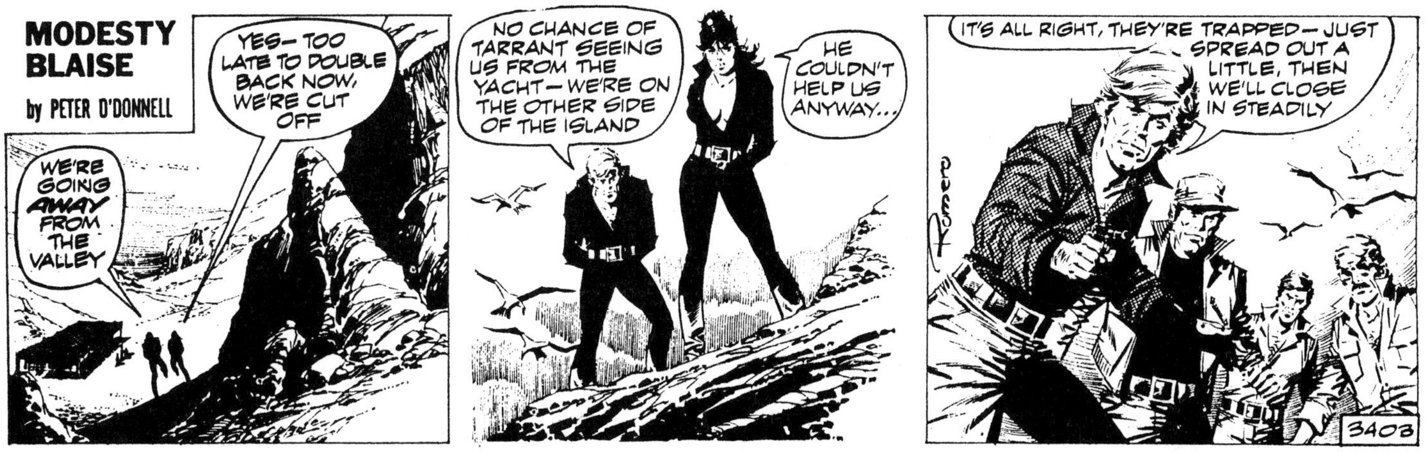
MODESTY BLAISE
by PETER O'DONNELL
YES— TOO LATE TO DOUBLE BACK NOW, WE'RE CUT OFF
WE'RE GOING AWAY FROM THE VALLEY
NO CHANCE OF TARRANT SEEING US FROM THE YACHT—WE'RE ON THE OTHER SIDE OF THE ISLAND
HE COULDN'T HELP US ANYWAY...
IT'S ALL RIGHT, THEY'RE TRAPPED—JUST SPREAD OUT A LITTLE, THEN WE'LL CLOSE IN STEADILY
Romero
3403

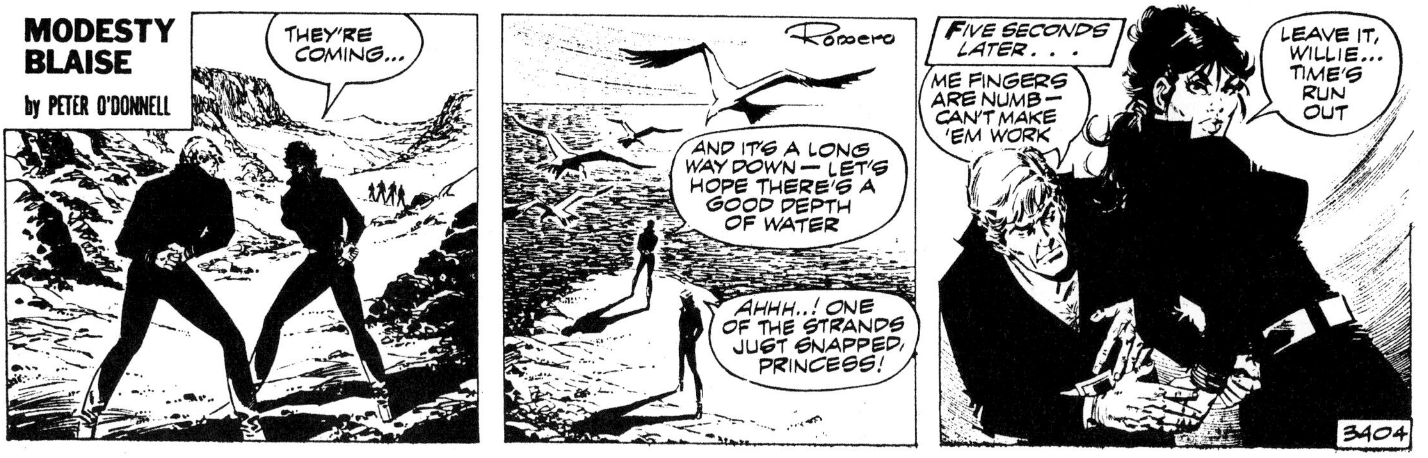
MODESTY BLAISE
by PETER O'DONNELL
THEY'RE COMING...
Romero
AND IT'S A LONG WAY DOWN—LET'S HOPE THERE'S A GOOD DEPTH OF WATER
AHHH..! ONE OF THE STRANDS JUST SNAPPED, PRINCESS!
FIVE SECONDS LATER . . .
ME FINGERS ARE NUMB— CAN'T MAKE 'EM WORK
LEAVE IT, WILLIE... TIME'S RUN OUT
3404

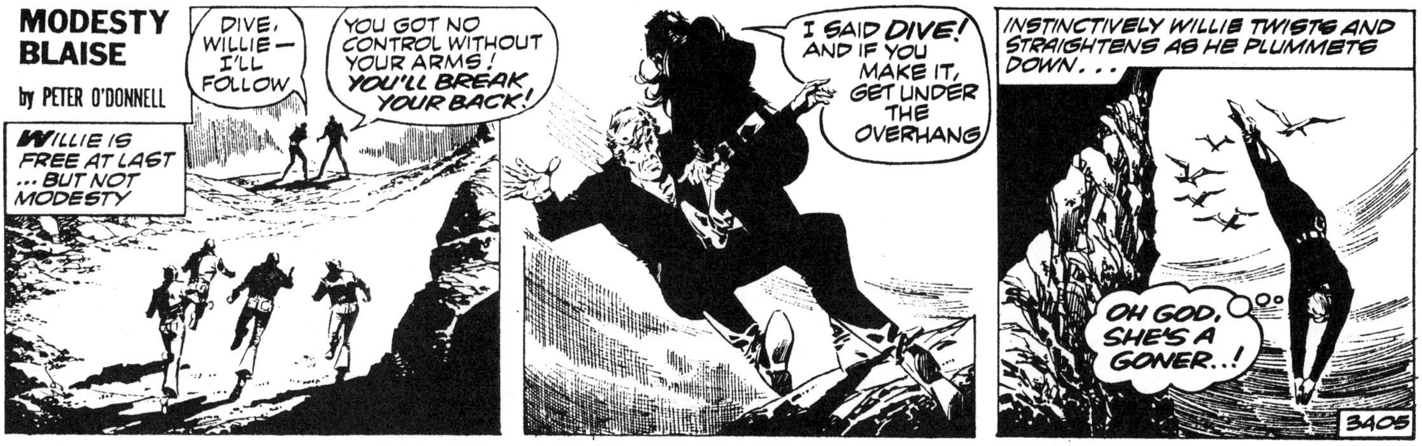
MODESTY BLAISE
by PETER O'DONNELL
DIVE, WILLIE— I'LL FOLLOW
YOU GOT NO CONTROL WITHOUT YOUR ARMS! YOU'LL BREAK YOUR BACK!
WILLIE IS FREE AT LAST ...BUT NOT MODESTY
I SAID DIVE! AND IF YOU MAKE IT, GET UNDER THE OVERHANG
INSTINCTIVELY WILLIE TWISTS AND STRAIGHTENS AS HE PLUMMETS DOWN . . .
OH GOD, SHE'S A GONER..!
3405

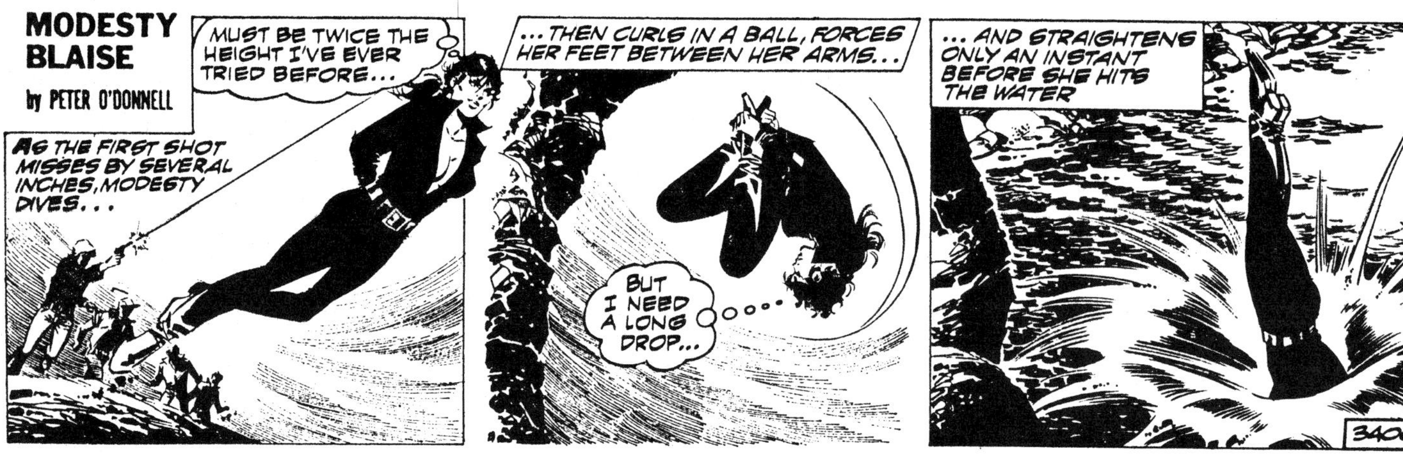

MODESTY BLAISE
by PETER O'DONNELL
MUST BE TWICE THE HEIGHT I'VE EVER TRIED BEFORE...
AS THE FIRST SHOT MISSES BY SEVERAL INCHES, MODESTY DIVES...
...THEN CURLS IN A BALL, FORCES HER FEET BETWEEN HER ARMS...
BUT I NEED A LONG DROP...
...AND STRAIGHTENS ONLY AN INSTANT BEFORE SHE HITS THE WATER
3406

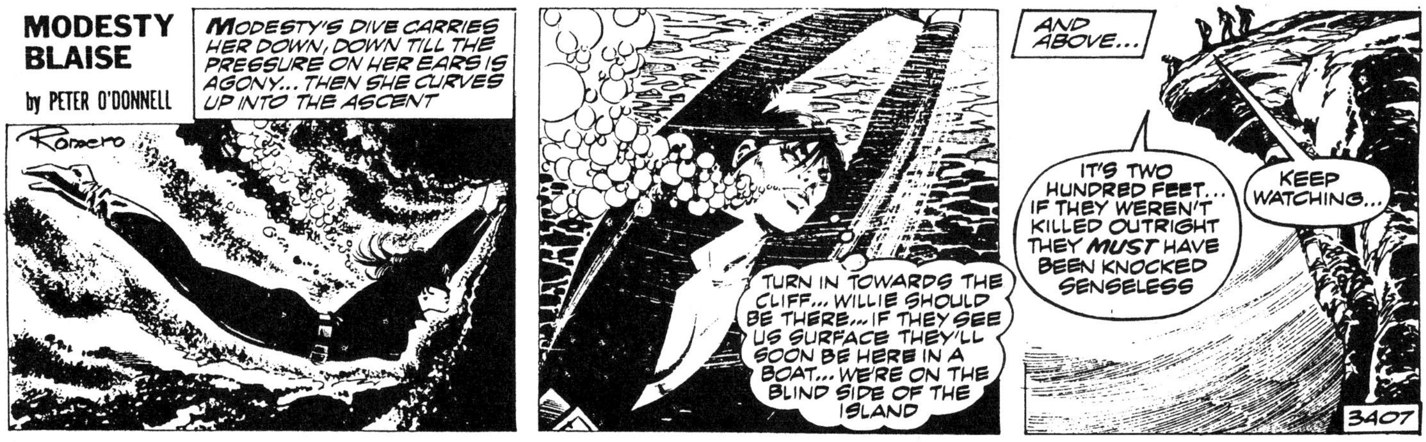

MODESTY BLAISE
by PETER O'DONNELL
MODESTY'S DIVE CARRIES HER DOWN, DOWN TILL THE PRESSURE ON HER EARS IS AGONY... THEN SHE CURVES UP INTO THE ASCENT
Romero
TURN IN TOWARDS THE CLIFF... WILLIE SHOULD BE THERE... IF THEY SEE US SURFACE THEY'LL SOON BE HERE IN A BOAT... WE'RE ON THE BLIND SIDE OF THE ISLAND
AND ABOVE...
IT'S TWO HUNDRED FEET... IF THEY WEREN'T KILLED OUTRIGHT THEY MUST HAVE BEEN KNOCKED SENSELESS
KEEP WATCHING...
3407

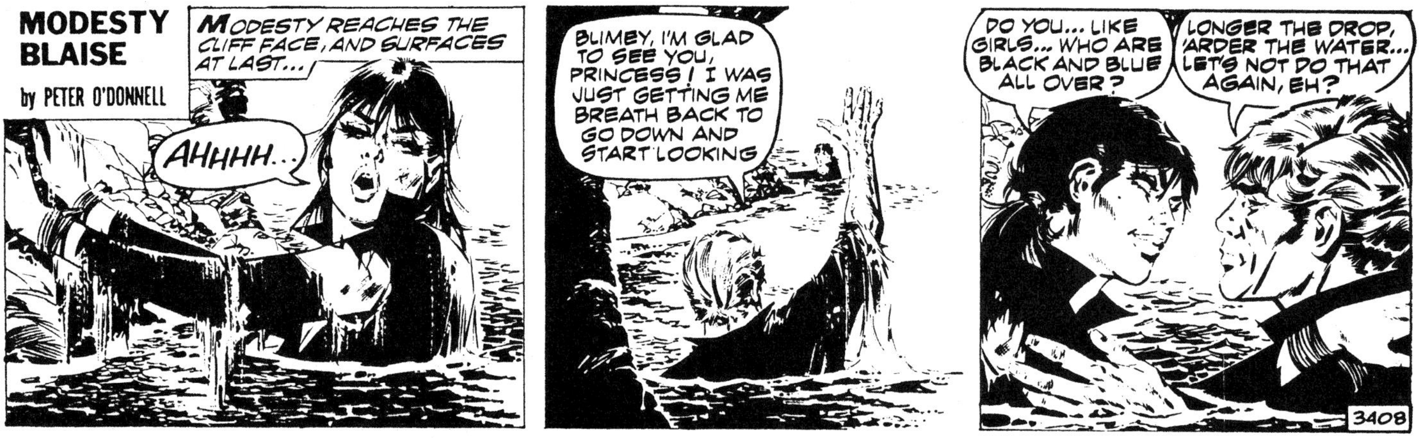

MODESTY BLAISE
by PETER O'DONNELL
MODESTY REACHES THE CLIFF FACE, AND SURFACES AT LAST...
AHHHH...
BLIMEY, I'M GLAD TO SEE YOU, PRINCESS! I WAS JUST GETTING ME BREATH BACK TO GO DOWN AND START LOOKING
DO YOU... LIKE GIRLS... WHO ARE BLACK AND BLUE ALL OVER?
LONGER THE DROP, 'ARDER THE WATER... LET'S NOT DO THAT AGAIN, EH?
3408

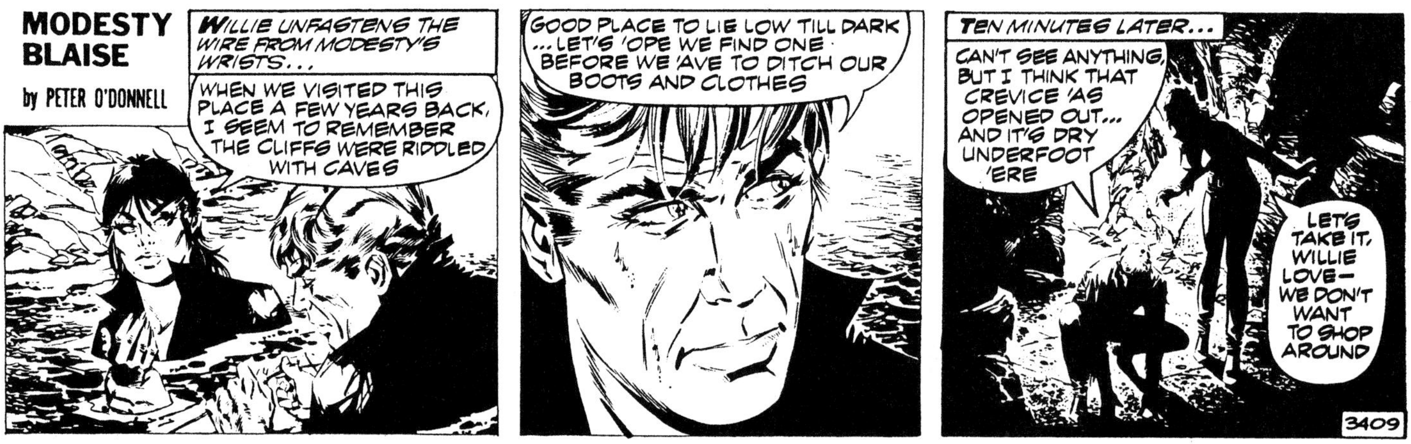

MODESTY BLAISE
by PETER O'DONNELL
WILLIE UNFASTENS THE WIRE FROM MODESTY'S WRISTS...
WHEN WE VISITED THIS PLACE A FEW YEARS BACK, I SEEM TO REMEMBER THE CLIFFS WERE RIDDLED WITH CAVES
GOOD PLACE TO LIE LOW TILL DARK ...LET'S 'OPE WE FIND ONE BEFORE WE 'AVE TO DITCH OUR BOOTS AND CLOTHES
TEN MINUTES LATER...
CAN'T SEE ANYTHING, BUT I THINK THAT CREVICE 'AS OPENED OUT... AND IT'S DRY UNDERFOOT 'ERE
LET'S TAKE IT, WILLIE LOVE— WE DON'T WANT TO SHOP AROUND
3409

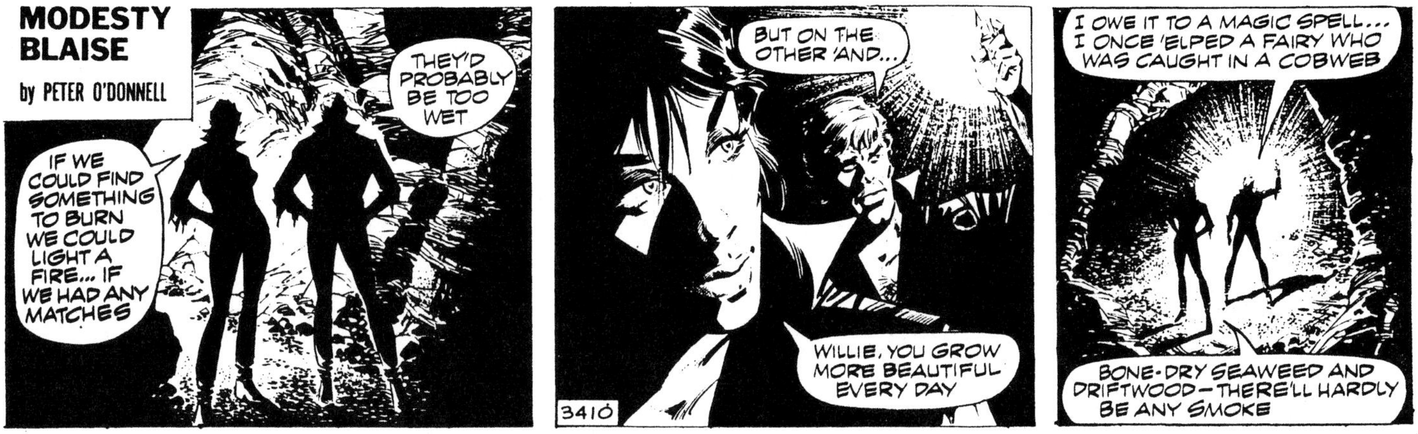
MODESTY BLAISE
by PETER O'DONNELL
IF WE COULD FIND SOMETHING TO BURN WE COULD LIGHT A FIRE... IF WE HAD ANY MATCHES
THEY'D PROBABLY BE TOO WET
BUT ON THE OTHER 'AND...
WILLIE, YOU GROW MORE BEAUTIFUL EVERY DAY
3410
I OWE IT TO A MAGIC SPELL... I ONCE 'ELPED A FAIRY WHO WAS CAUGHT IN A COBWEB
BONE-DRY SEAWEED AND DRIFTWOOD—THERE'LL HARDLY BE ANY SMOKE

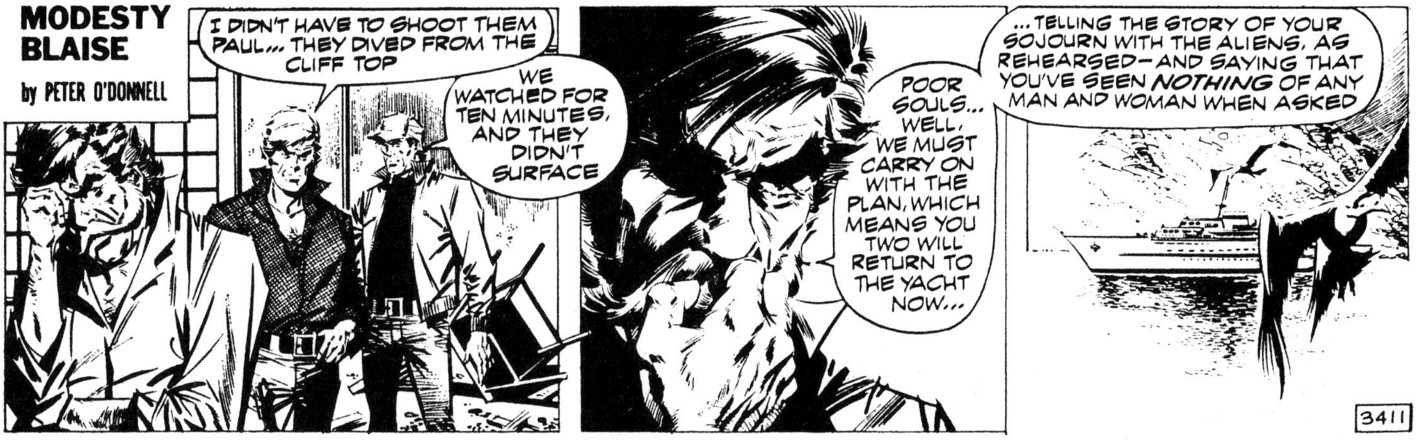
MODESTY BLAISE
by PETER O'DONNELL
I DIDN'T HAVE TO SHOOT THEM PAUL... THEY DIVED FROM THE CLIFF TOP
WE WATCHED FOR TEN MINUTES, AND THEY DIDN'T SURFACE
POOR SOULS... WELL, WE MUST CARRY ON WITH THE PLAN, WHICH MEANS YOU TWO WILL RETURN TO THE YACHT NOW...
...TELLING THE STORY OF YOUR SOJOURN WITH THE ALIENS, AS REHEARSED—AND SAYING THAT YOU'VE SEEN NOTHING OF ANY MAN AND WOMAN WHEN ASKED
3411

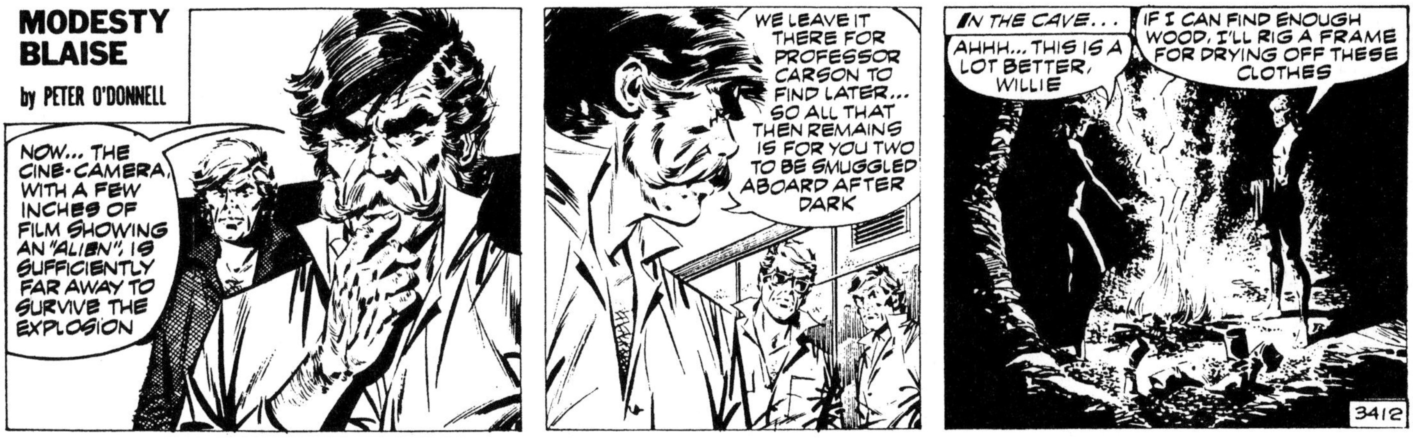
MODESTY BLAISE
by PETER O'DONNELL
NOW... THE CINE-CAMERA, WITH A FEW INCHES OF FILM SHOWING AN "ALIEN", IS SUFFICIENTLY FAR AWAY TO SURVIVE THE EXPLOSION
WE LEAVE IT THERE FOR PROFESSOR CARSON TO FIND LATER... SO ALL THAT THEN REMAINS IS FOR YOU TWO TO BE SMUGGLED ABOARD AFTER DARK
IN THE CAVE...
AHHH... THIS IS A LOT BETTER, WILLIE
IF I CAN FIND ENOUGH WOOD, I'LL RIG A FRAME FOR DRYING OFF THESE CLOTHES
3412

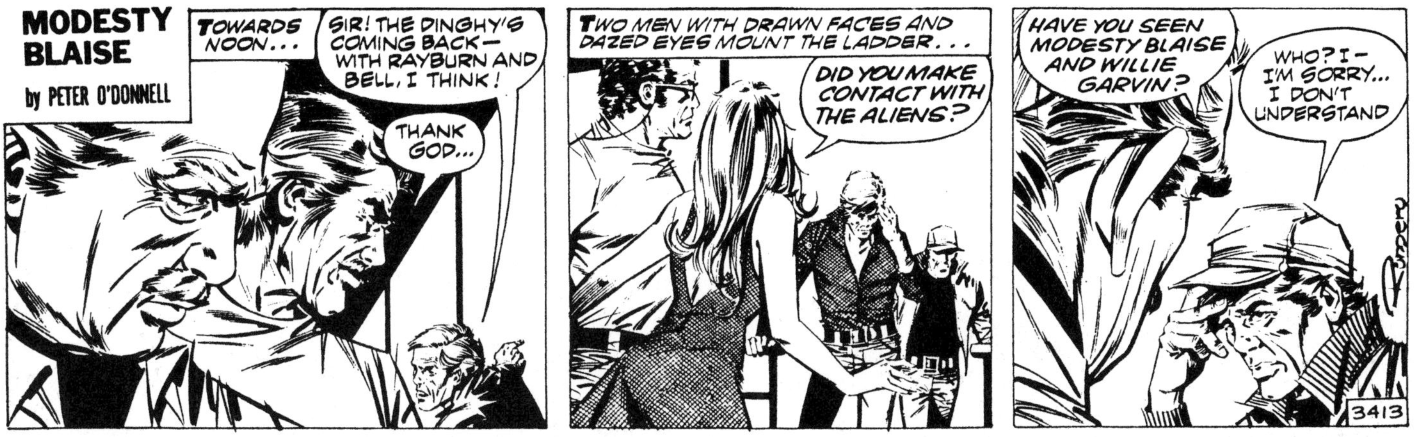
MODESTY BLAISE
by PETER O'DONNELL
TOWARDS NOON...
SIR! THE DINGHY'S COMING BACK—WITH RAYBURN AND BELL, I THINK!
THANK GOD...
TWO MEN WITH DRAWN FACES AND DAZED EYES MOUNT THE LADDER...
DID YOU MAKE CONTACT WITH THE ALIENS?
HAVE YOU SEEN MODESTY BLAISE AND WILLIE GARVIN?
WHO? I—I'M SORRY... I DON'T UNDERSTAND
3413

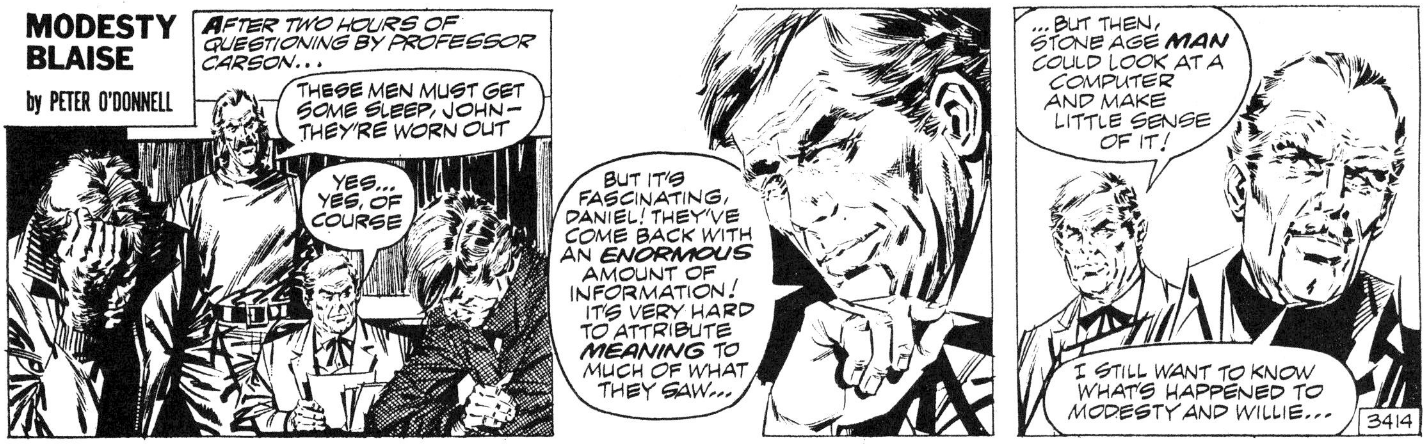
MODESTY BLAISE
by PETER O'DONNELL
AFTER TWO HOURS OF QUESTIONING BY PROFESSOR CARSON...
THESE MEN MUST GET SOME SLEEP, JOHN— THEY'RE WORN OUT
YES... YES, OF COURSE
BUT IT'S FASCINATING, DANIEL! THEY'VE COME BACK WITH AN ENORMOUS AMOUNT OF INFORMATION! IT'S VERY HARD TO ATTRIBUTE MEANING TO MUCH OF WHAT THEY SAW...
...BUT THEN, STONE AGE MAN COULD LOOK AT A COMPUTER AND MAKE LITTLE SENSE OF IT!
I STILL WANT TO KNOW WHAT'S HAPPENED TO MODESTY AND WILLIE...
3414

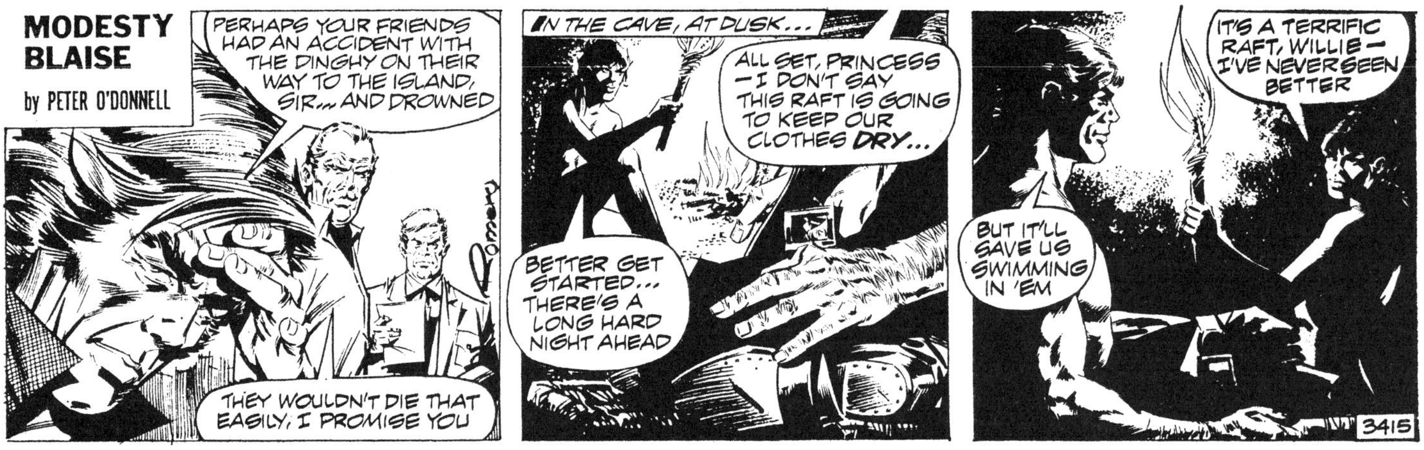
MODESTY BLAISE
by PETER O'DONNELL
PERHAPS YOUR FRIENDS HAD AN ACCIDENT WITH THE DINGHY ON THEIR WAY TO THE ISLAND, SIR... AND DROWNED
THEY WOULDN'T DIE THAT EASILY, I PROMISE YOU
IN THE CAVE, AT DUSK...
ALL SET, PRINCESS —I DON'T SAY THIS RAFT IS GOING TO KEEP OUR CLOTHES DRY...
BETTER GET STARTED... THERE'S A LONG HARD NIGHT AHEAD
IT'S A TERRIFIC RAFT, WILLIE— I'VE NEVER SEEN BETTER
BUT IT'LL SAVE US SWIMMING IN 'EM
3415

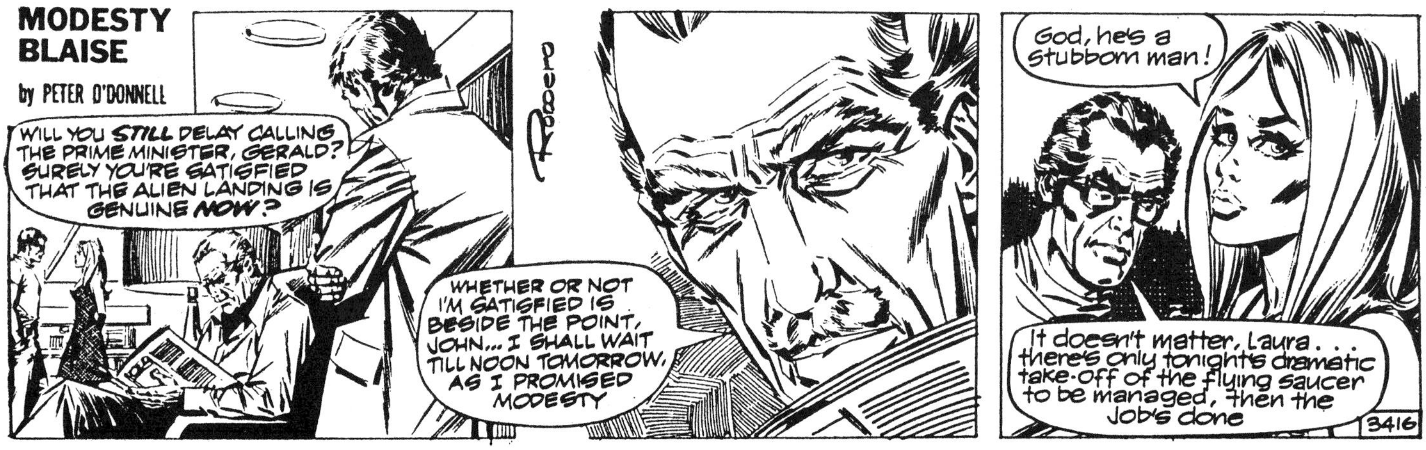
MODESTY BLAISE
by PETER O'DONNELL
WILL YOU STILL DELAY CALLING THE PRIME MINISTER, GERALD? SURELY YOU'RE SATISFIED THAT THE ALIEN LANDING IS GENUINE NOW?
WHETHER OR NOT I'M SATISFIED IS BESIDE THE POINT, JOHN... I SHALL WAIT TILL NOON TOMORROW, AS I PROMISED MODESTY
God, he's a stubborn man!
It doesn't matter, Laura... there's only tonight's dramatic take-off of the flying saucer to be managed, then the job's done
3416

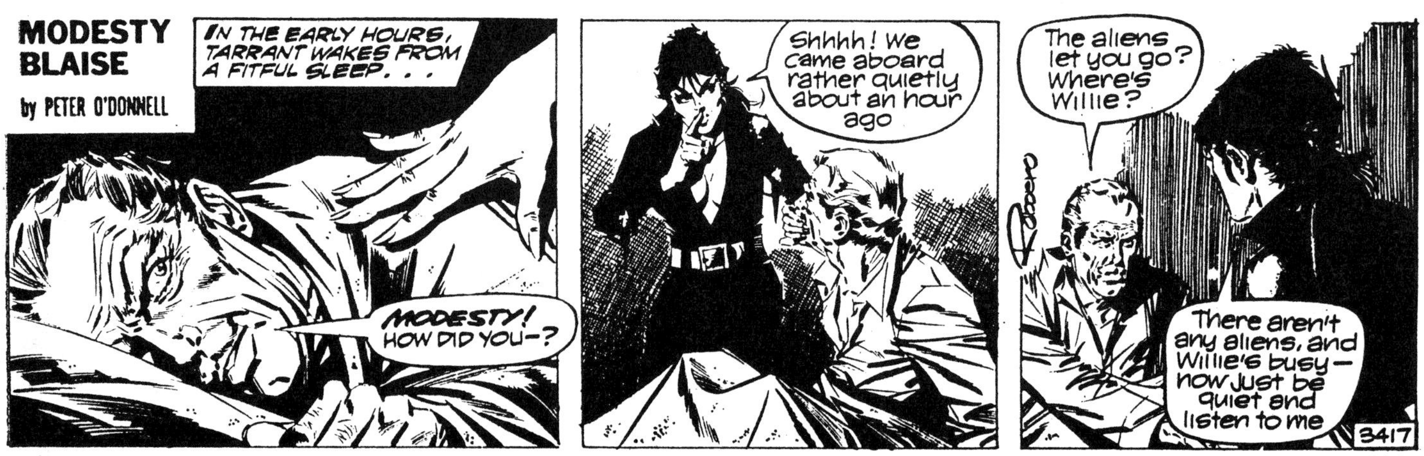
MODESTY BLAISE
by PETER O'DONNELL
IN THE EARLY HOURS, TARRANT WAKES FROM A FITFUL SLEEP...
MODESTY! HOW DID YOU—?
Shhhh! We came aboard rather quietly about an hour ago
The aliens let you go? Where's Willie?
There aren't any aliens, and Willie's busy— now just be quiet and listen to me
3417

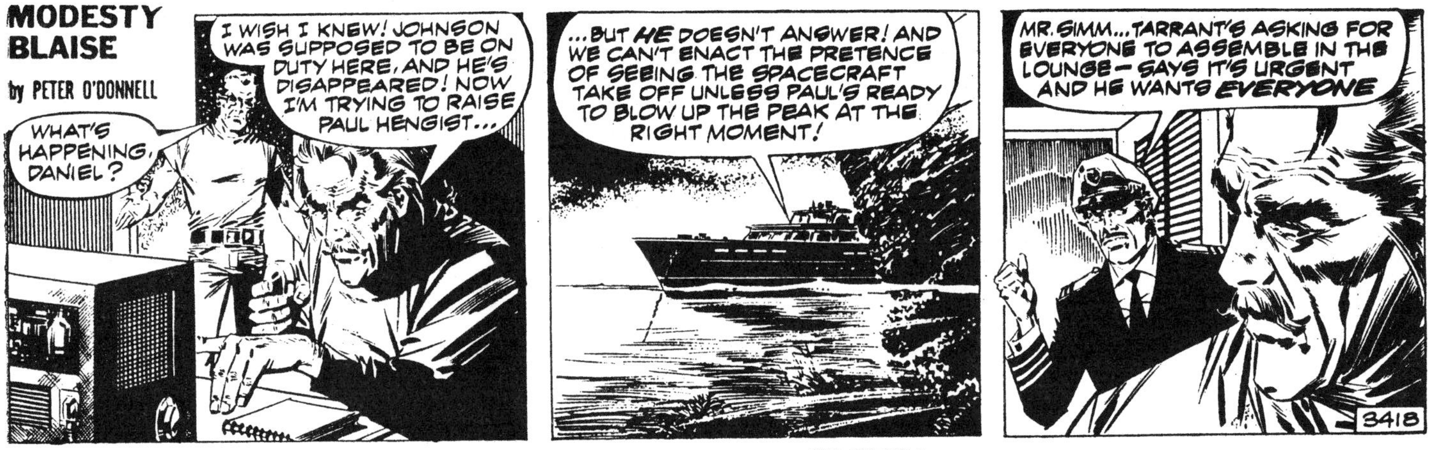
MODESTY BLAISE
by PETER O'DONNELL
WHAT'S HAPPENING, DANIEL?
I WISH I KNEW! JOHNSON WAS SUPPOSED TO BE ON DUTY HERE, AND HE'S DISAPPEARED! NOW I'M TRYING TO RAISE PAUL HENGIST...
...BUT HE DOESN'T ANSWER! AND WE CAN'T ENACT THE PRETENCE OF SEEING THE SPACECRAFT TAKE OFF UNLESS PAUL'S READY TO BLOW UP THE PEAK AT THE RIGHT MOMENT!
MR. SIMM...TARRANT'S ASKING FOR EVERYONE TO ASSEMBLE IN THE LOUNGE — SAYS IT'S URGENT AND HE WANTS EVERYONE
3418

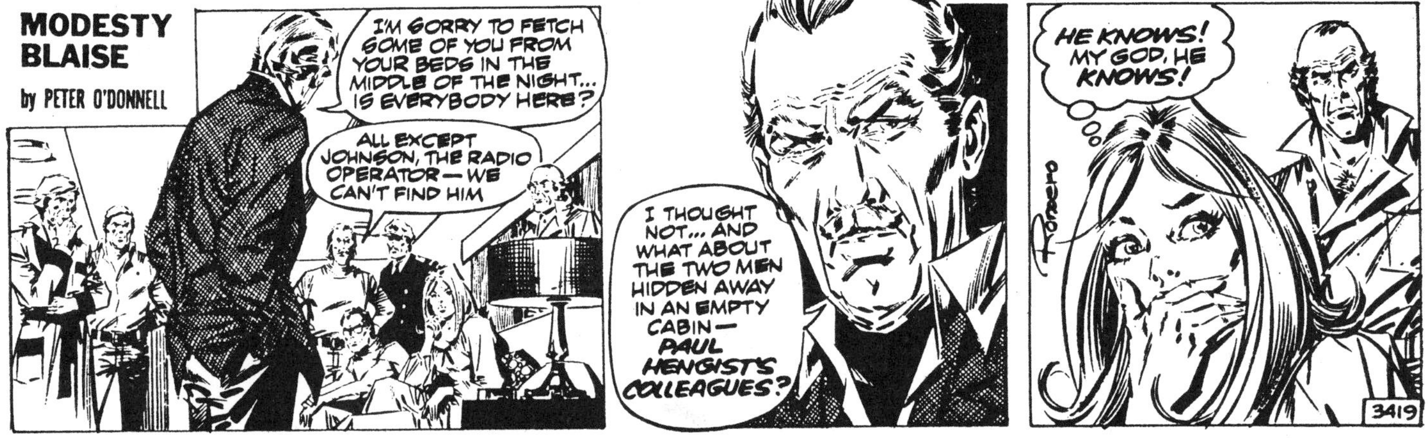
MODESTY BLAISE
by PETER O'DONNELL
I'M SORRY TO FETCH SOME OF YOU FROM YOUR BEDS IN THE MIDDLE OF THE NIGHT... IS EVERYBODY HERE?
ALL EXCEPT JOHNSON, THE RADIO OPERATOR — WE CAN'T FIND HIM
I THOUGHT NOT... AND WHAT ABOUT THE TWO MEN HIDDEN AWAY IN AN EMPTY CABIN — PAUL HENGIST'S COLLEAGUES?
HE KNOWS! MY GOD, HE KNOWS!
3419

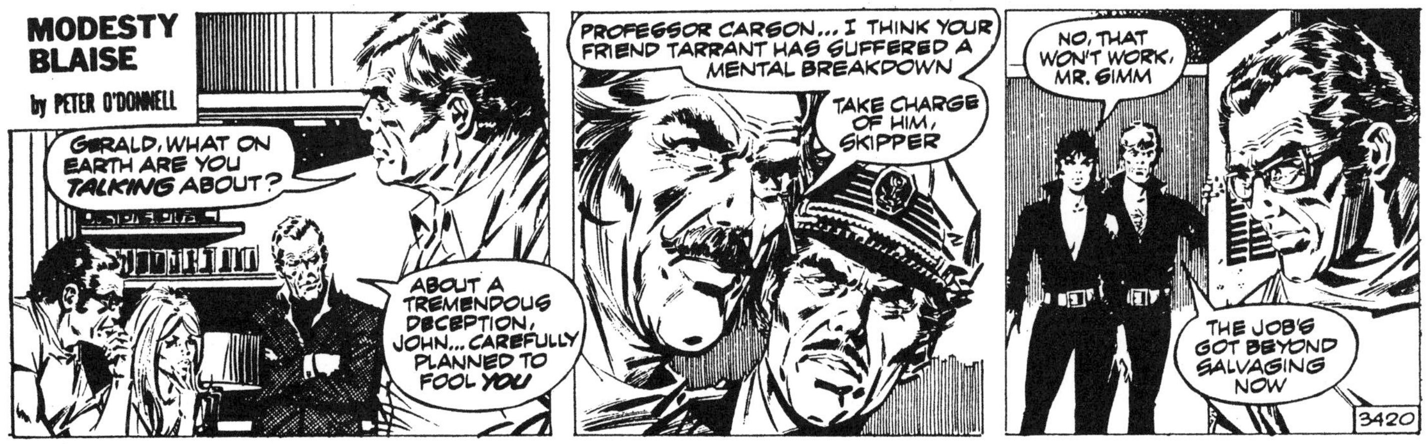
MODESTY BLAISE
by PETER O'DONNELL
GERALD, WHAT ON EARTH ARE YOU TALKING ABOUT?
ABOUT A TREMENDOUS DECEPTION, JOHN... CAREFULLY PLANNED TO FOOL YOU
PROFESSOR CARSON... I THINK YOUR FRIEND TARRANT HAS SUFFERED A MENTAL BREAKDOWN
TAKE CHARGE OF HIM, SKIPPER
NO, THAT WON'T WORK, MR. SIMM
THE JOB'S GOT BEYOND SALVAGING NOW
3420

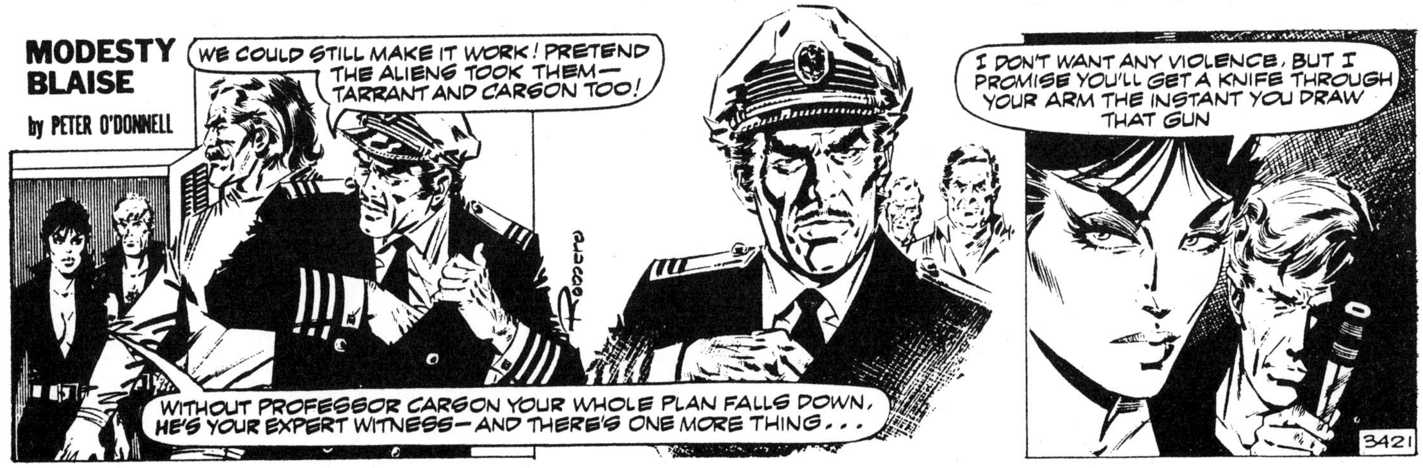
MODESTY BLAISE
by PETER O'DONNELL
WE COULD STILL MAKE IT WORK! PRETEND THE ALIENS TOOK THEM — TARRANT AND CARSON TOO!
WITHOUT PROFESSOR CARSON YOUR WHOLE PLAN FALLS DOWN. HE'S YOUR EXPERT WITNESS — AND THERE'S ONE MORE THING...
I DON'T WANT ANY VIOLENCE, BUT I PROMISE YOU'LL GET A KNIFE THROUGH YOUR ARM THE INSTANT YOU DRAW THAT GUN
3421

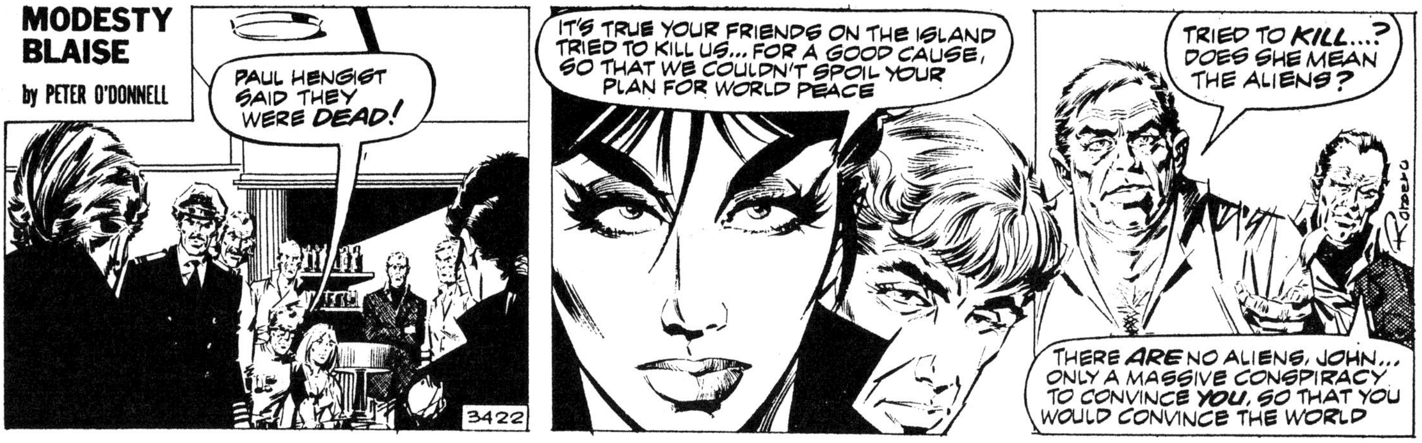
MODESTY BLAISE
by PETER O'DONNELL
PAUL HENGIST SAID THEY WERE DEAD!
IT'S TRUE YOUR FRIENDS ON THE ISLAND TRIED TO KILL US... FOR A GOOD CAUSE, SO THAT WE COULDN'T SPOIL YOUR PLAN FOR WORLD PEACE
TRIED TO KILL...? DOES SHE MEAN THE ALIENS?
THERE ARE NO ALIENS, JOHN... ONLY A MASSIVE CONSPIRACY TO CONVINCE YOU, SO THAT YOU WOULD CONVINCE THE WORLD
3422

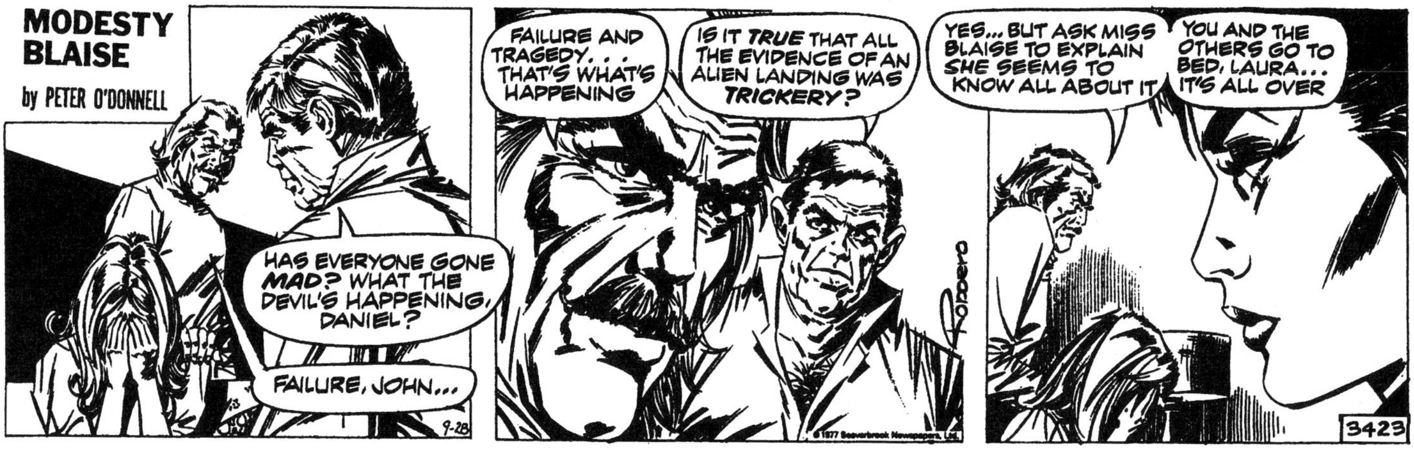
MODESTY BLAISE
by PETER O'DONNELL
HAS EVERYONE GONE MAD? WHAT THE DEVIL'S HAPPENING, DANIEL?
FAILURE, JOHN...
9-28
FAILURE AND TRAGEDY. . . THAT'S WHAT'S HAPPENING
IS IT TRUE THAT ALL THE EVIDENCE OF AN ALIEN LANDING WAS TRICKERY?
YES... BUT ASK MISS BLAISE TO EXPLAIN SHE SEEMS TO KNOW ALL ABOUT IT
YOU AND THE OTHERS GO TO BED, LAURA... IT'S ALL OVER
3423

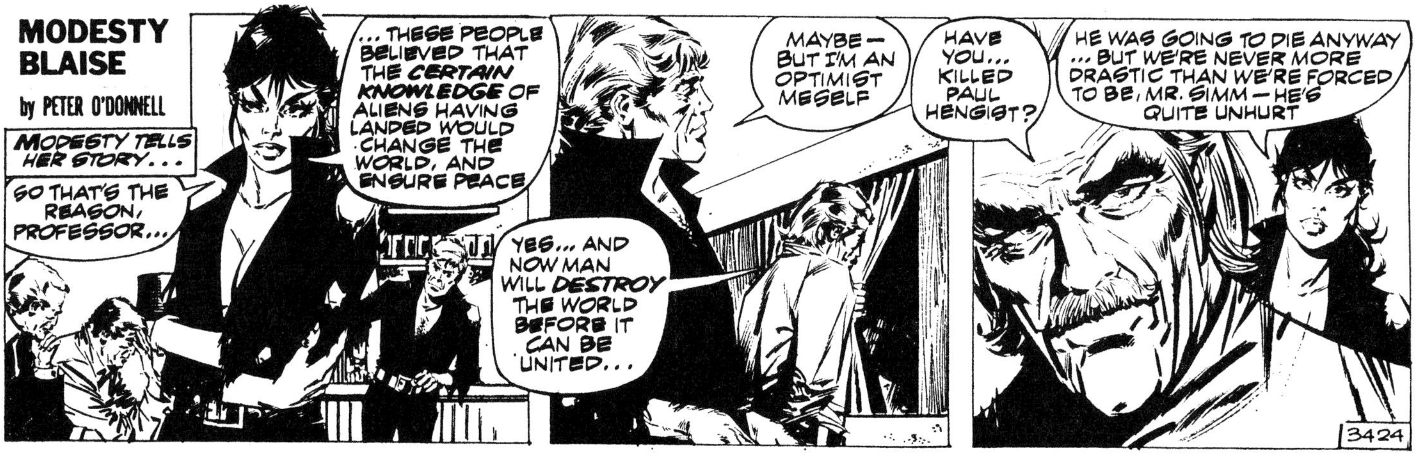
MODESTY BLAISE
by PETER O'DONNELL
MODESTY TELLS HER STORY...
SO THAT'S THE REASON, PROFESSOR...
... THESE PEOPLE BELIEVED THAT THE CERTAIN KNOWLEDGE OF ALIENS HAVING LANDED WOULD CHANGE THE WORLD, AND ENSURE PEACE
YES... AND NOW MAN WILL DESTROY THE WORLD BEFORE IT CAN BE UNITED...
MAYBE — BUT I'M AN OPTIMIST MESELF
HAVE YOU... KILLED PAUL HENGIST?
HE WAS GOING TO DIE ANYWAY ... BUT WE'RE NEVER MORE DRASTIC THAN WE'RE FORCED TO BE, MR. SIMM — HE'S QUITE UNHURT
3424

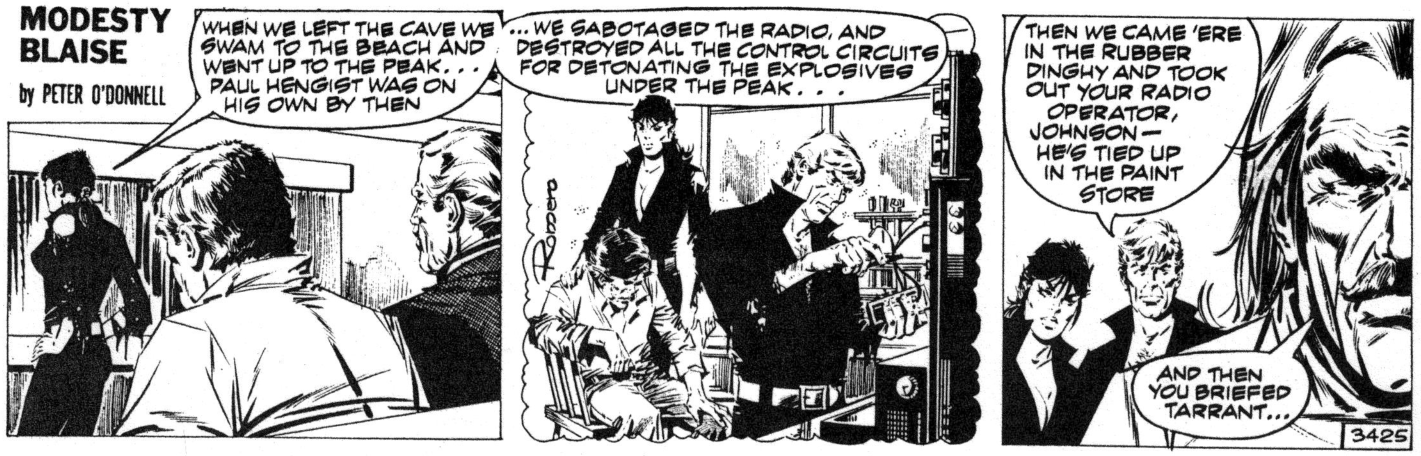
MODESTY BLAISE
by PETER O'DONNELL
WHEN WE LEFT THE CAVE WE SWAM TO THE BEACH AND WENT UP TO THE PEAK. . . PAUL HENGIST WAS ON HIS OWN BY THEN
... WE SABOTAGED THE RADIO, AND DESTROYED ALL THE CONTROL CIRCUITS FOR DETONATING THE EXPLOSIVES UNDER THE PEAK. . .
THEN WE CAME 'ERE IN THE RUBBER DINGHY AND TOOK OUT YOUR RADIO OPERATOR, JOHNSON — HE'S TIED UP IN THE PAINT STORE
AND THEN YOU BRIEFED TARRANT...
3425

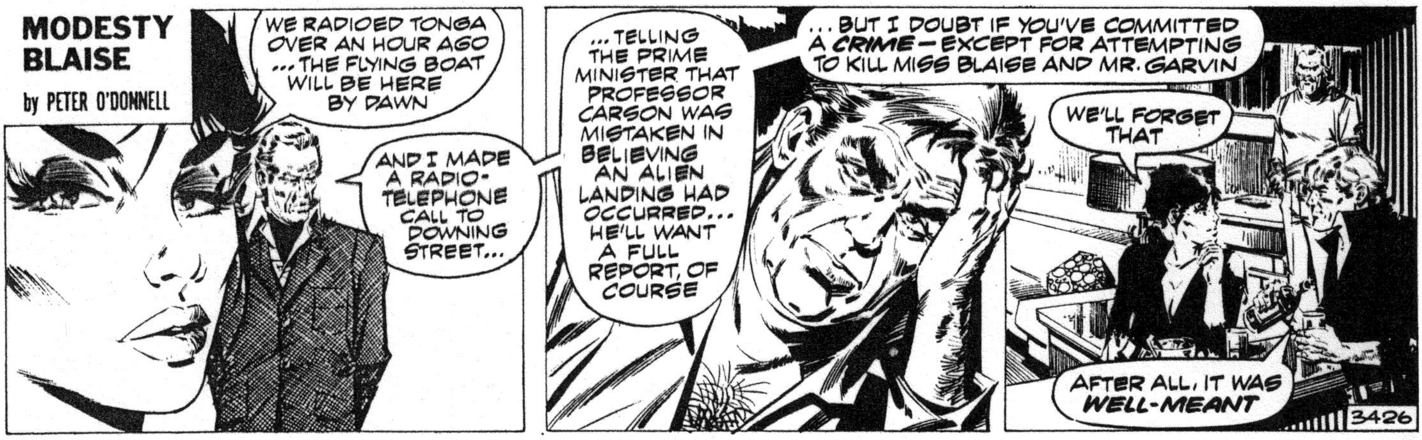
MODESTY BLAISE
by PETER O'DONNELL
WE RADIOED TONGA OVER AN HOUR AGO ...THE FLYING BOAT WILL BE HERE BY DAWN
AND I MADE A RADIO-TELEPHONE CALL TO DOWNING STREET...
...TELLING THE PRIME MINISTER THAT PROFESSOR CARSON WAS MISTAKEN IN BELIEVING AN ALIEN LANDING HAD OCCURRED... HE'LL WANT A FULL REPORT, OF COURSE
... BUT I DOUBT IF YOU'VE COMMITTED A CRIME — EXCEPT FOR ATTEMPTING TO KILL MISS BLAISE AND MR. GARVIN
WE'LL FORGET THAT
AFTER ALL, IT WAS WELL-MEANT
3426

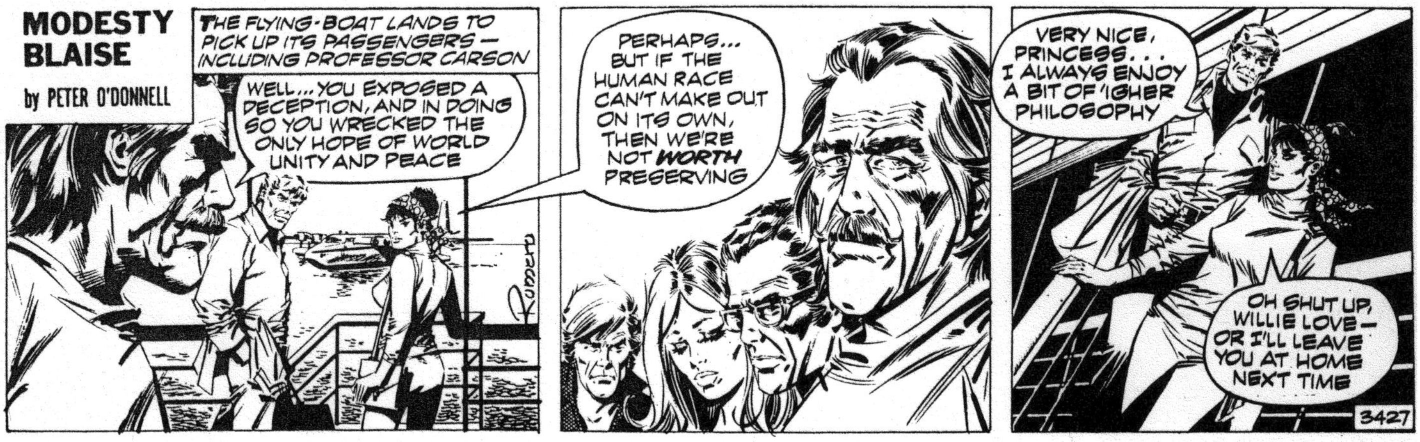
MODESTY BLAISE
by PETER O'DONNELL
THE FLYING-BOAT LANDS TO PICK UP ITS PASSENGERS — INCLUDING PROFESSOR CARSON
WELL...YOU EXPOSED A DECEPTION, AND IN DOING SO YOU WRECKED THE ONLY HOPE OF WORLD UNITY AND PEACE
PERHAPS... BUT IF THE HUMAN RACE CAN'T MAKE OUT ON ITS OWN, THEN WE'RE NOT WORTH PRESERVING
VERY NICE, PRINCESS... I ALWAYS ENJOY A BIT OF 'IGHER PHILOSOPHY
OH SHUT UP, WILLIE LOVE — OR I'LL LEAVE YOU AT HOME NEXT TIME
3427

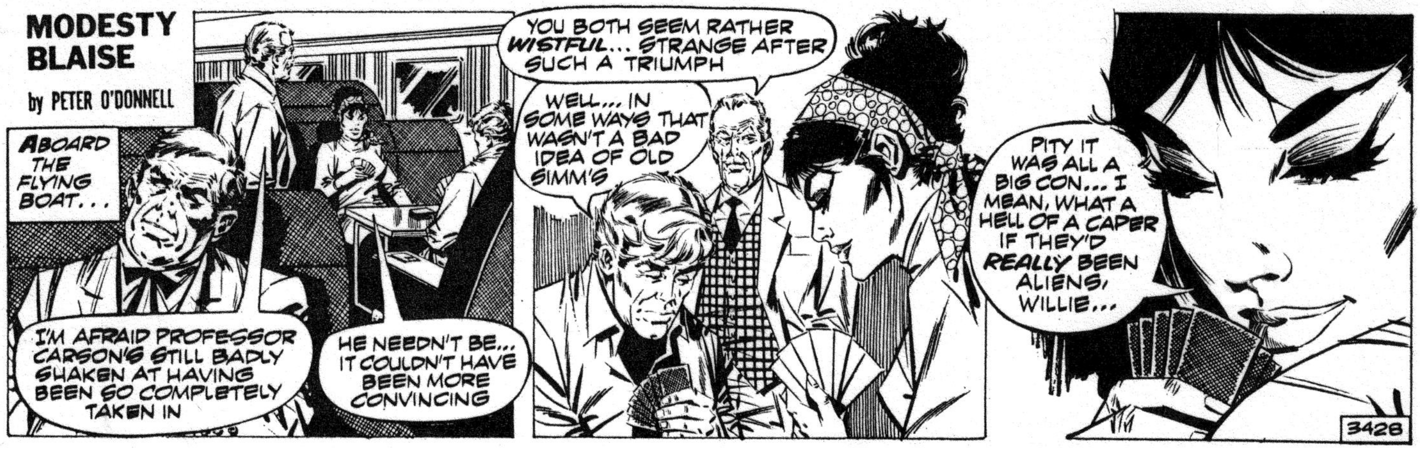
MODESTY BLAISE
by PETER O'DONNELL
ABOARD THE FLYING BOAT...
I'M AFRAID PROFESSOR CARSON'S STILL BADLY SHAKEN AT HAVING BEEN SO COMPLETELY TAKEN IN
HE NEEDN'T BE... IT COULDN'T HAVE BEEN MORE CONVINCING
YOU BOTH SEEM RATHER WISTFUL... STRANGE AFTER SUCH A TRIUMPH
WELL... IN SOME WAYS THAT WASN'T A BAD IDEA OF OLD SIMM'S
PITY IT WAS ALL A BIG CON... I MEAN, WHAT A HELL OF A CAPER IF THEY'D REALLY BEEN ALIENS, WILLIE...
3428

HIGHLAND WITCH

I f you've read 'The Stone Age Caper' in an earlier Titan book of this series you'll recall that Modesty and Willie sometimes go walkabout with an Aborigine tribe led by Jacko, who has managed to absorb education without losing any of the instinctive abilities he was born with. Here he is with them in Scotland, and they need his help to track a car over several miles by scent alone, which is impossible of course. It's interesting to watch him do it.

I'd forgotten all about this story until I re-read it in order to write the foreword, so I was somewhat startled to find that Modesty has a new boyfriend. It wasn't surprising that she has one. After all she has several long-term male escorts and none of them is exclusive. No, it was the *kind* of boyfriend that startled me because he, Gordon Ritchie, has an obsession, and Modesty isn't that obsession, as I discovered in the first few strips. In fact she comes a bad second to it. I wondered how she would react to this, and was again surprised to find that she was in no way put out but treats him as an entertaining curiosity, a new experience, a joke.

This did give me the opportunity for a little light humour, and in fact the Gordon Ritchie joke theme continued through all the murderous mayhem that follows, and I was greatly amused to find that in the finale its none other than Gordon himself who is called on by Modesty to save the day — with a vital skill that derives from his obsession.

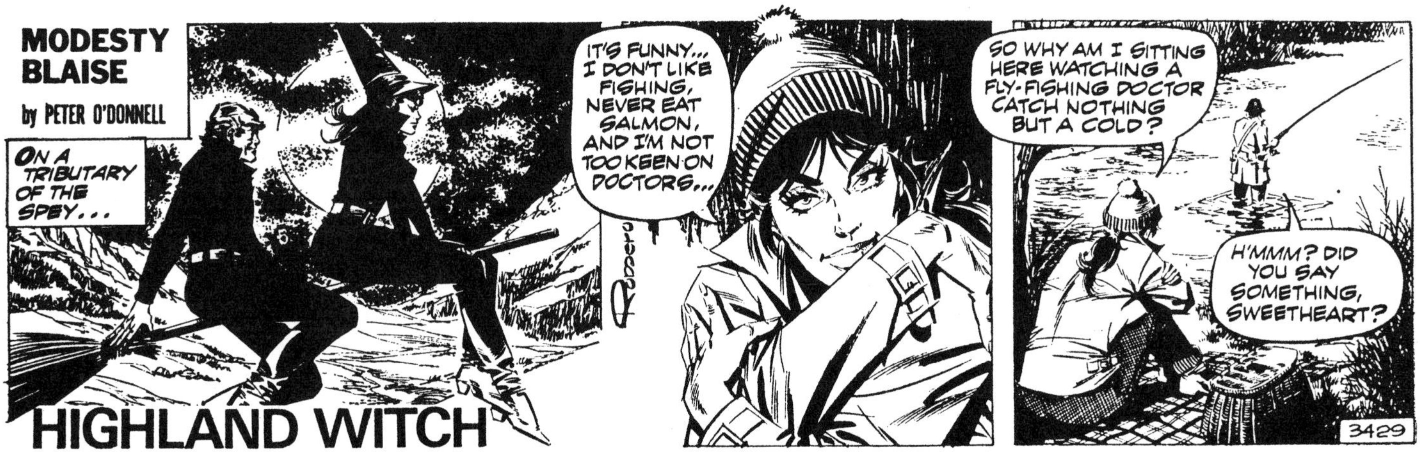
MODESTY BLAISE
by PETER O'DONNELL
ON A TRIBUTARY OF THE SPEY...
HIGHLAND WITCH
IT'S FUNNY... I DON'T LIKE FISHING, NEVER EAT SALMON, AND I'M NOT TOO KEEN ON DOCTORS...
SO WHY AM I SITTING HERE WATCHING A FLY-FISHING DOCTOR CATCH NOTHING BUT A COLD?
H'MMM? DID YOU SAY SOMETHING, SWEETHEART?
3429

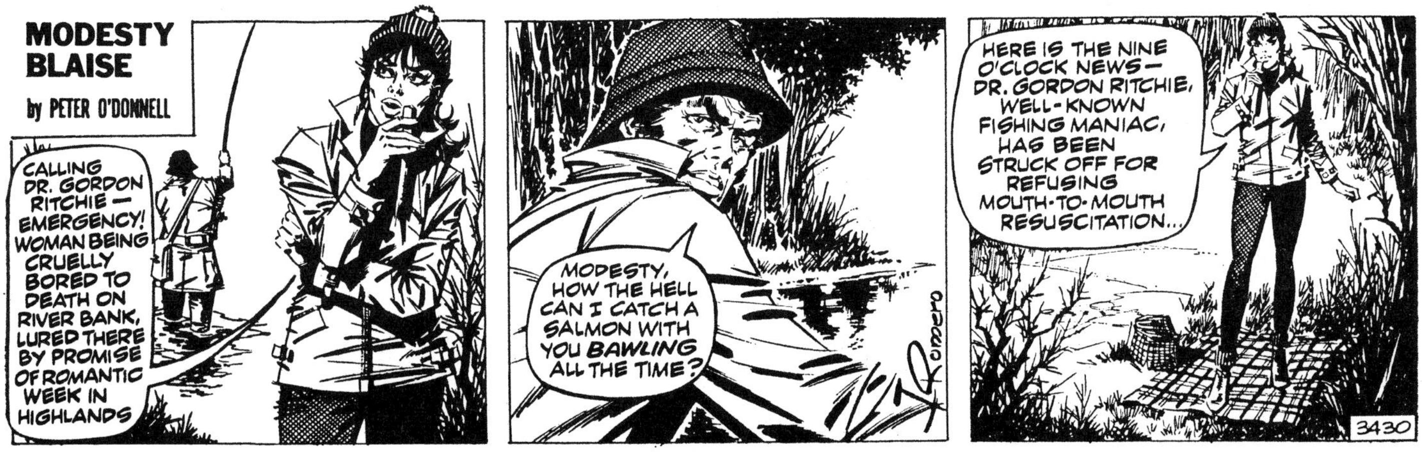
MODESTY BLAISE
by PETER O'DONNELL
CALLING DR. GORDON RITCHIE — EMERGENCY! WOMAN BEING CRUELLY BORED TO DEATH ON RIVER BANK, LURED THERE BY PROMISE OF ROMANTIC WEEK IN HIGHLANDS
MODESTY, HOW THE HELL CAN I CATCH A SALMON WITH YOU BAWLING ALL THE TIME?
HERE IS THE NINE O'CLOCK NEWS — DR. GORDON RITCHIE, WELL-KNOWN FISHING MANIAC, HAS BEEN STRUCK OFF FOR REFUSING MOUTH-TO-MOUTH RESUSCITATION...
3430

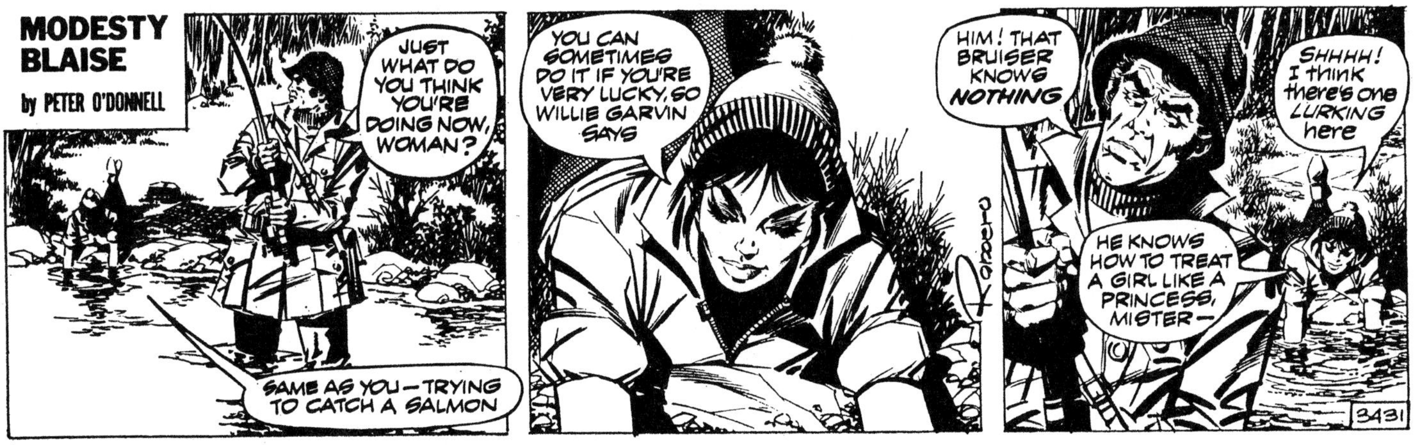
MODESTY BLAISE
by PETER O'DONNELL
JUST WHAT DO YOU THINK YOU'RE DOING NOW, WOMAN?
SAME AS YOU — TRYING TO CATCH A SALMON
YOU CAN SOMETIMES DO IT IF YOU'RE VERY LUCKY, SO WILLIE GARVIN SAYS
HIM! THAT BRUISER KNOWS NOTHING
SHHHH! I think there's one LURKING here
HE KNOWS HOW TO TREAT A GIRL LIKE A PRINCESS, MISTER —
3431

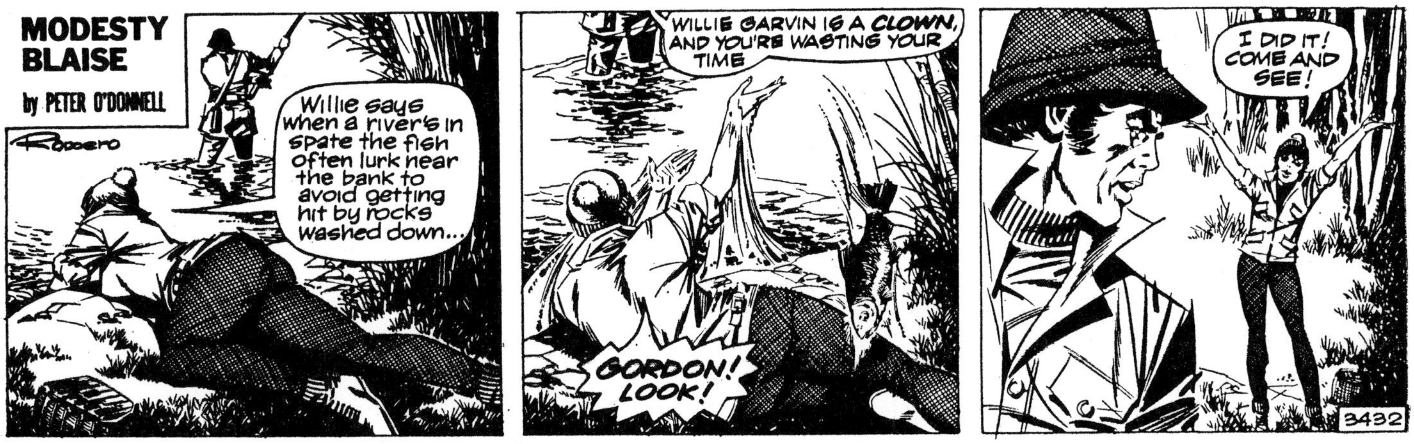
MODESTY BLAISE
by PETER O'DONNELL
Willie says when a river's in spate the fish often lurk near the bank to avoid getting hit by rocks washed down...
WILLIE GARVIN IS A CLOWN, AND YOU'RE WASTING YOUR TIME
GORDON! LOOK!
I DID IT! COME AND SEE!
3432

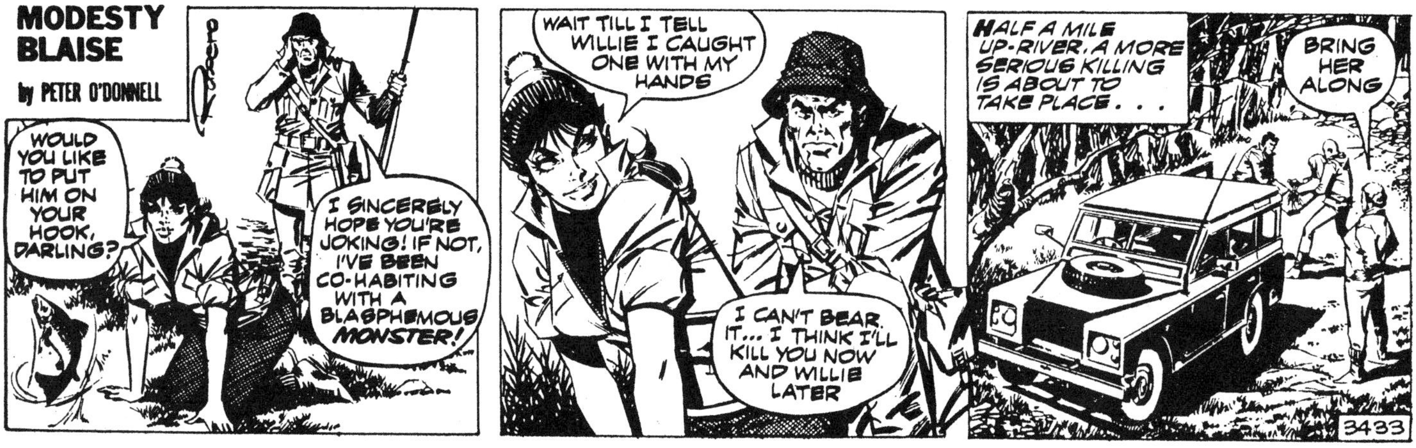
MODESTY BLAISE
by PETER O'DONNELL
Romero
WOULD YOU LIKE TO PUT HIM ON YOUR HOOK, DARLING?
I SINCERELY HOPE YOU'RE JOKING! IF NOT, I'VE BEEN CO-HABITING WITH A BLASPHEMOUS MONSTER!
WAIT TILL I TELL WILLIE I CAUGHT ONE WITH MY HANDS
I CAN'T BEAR IT... I THINK I'LL KILL YOU NOW AND WILLIE LATER
HALF A MILE UP-RIVER, A MORE SERIOUS KILLING IS ABOUT TO TAKE PLACE . . .
BRING HER ALONG
3433

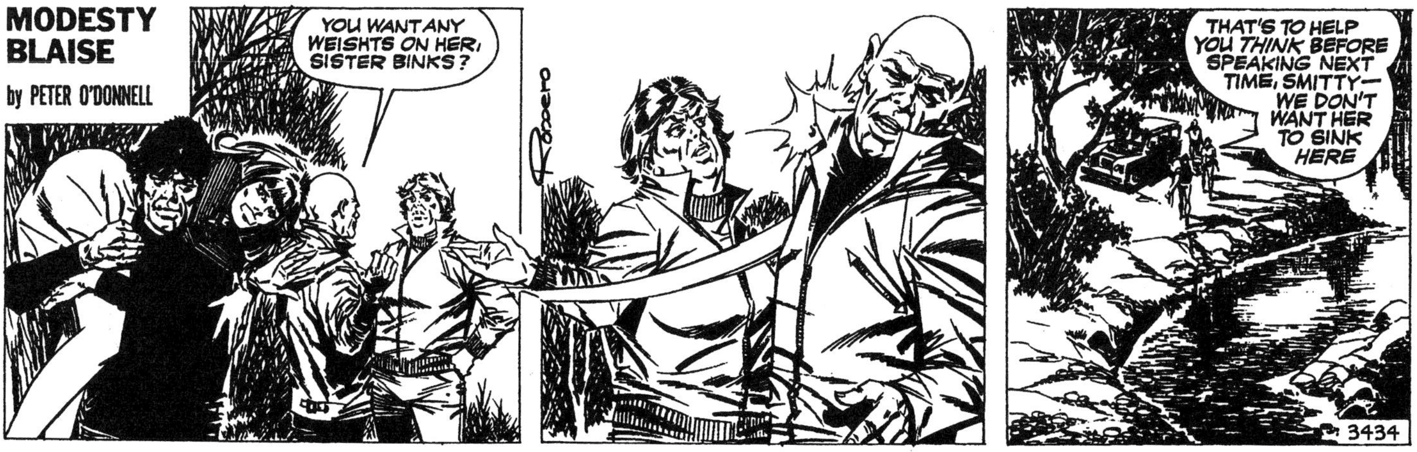
MODESTY BLAISE
by PETER O'DONNELL
YOU WANT ANY WEIGHTS ON HER, SISTER BINKS?
Romero
THAT'S TO HELP YOU THINK BEFORE SPEAKING NEXT TIME, SMITTY— WE DON'T WANT HER TO SINK HERE
3434

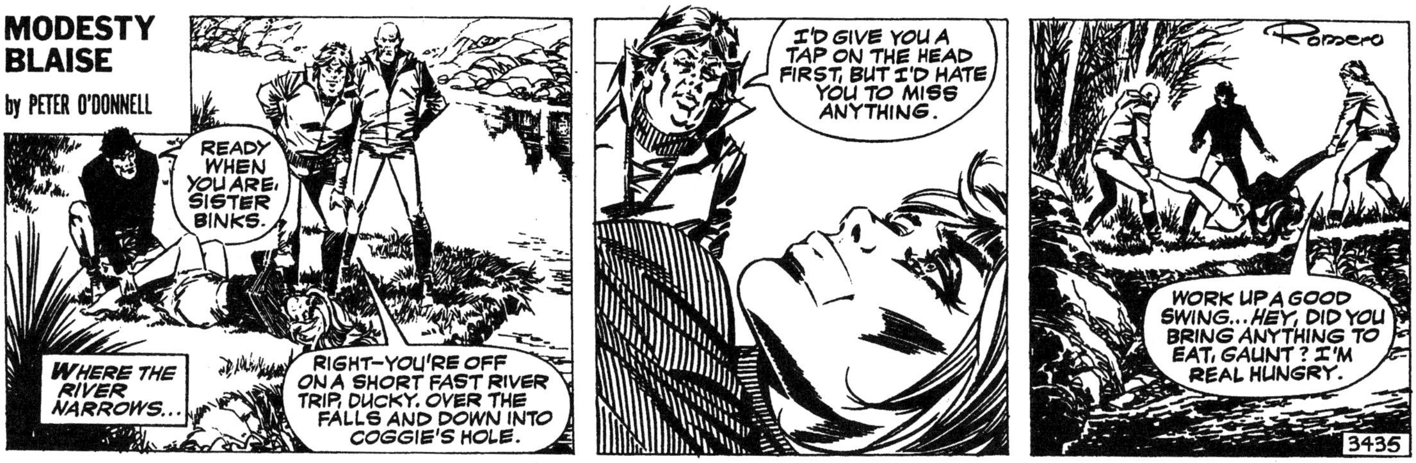
MODESTY BLAISE
by PETER O'DONNELL
READY WHEN YOU ARE, SISTER BINKS.
WHERE THE RIVER NARROWS...
RIGHT—YOU'RE OFF ON A SHORT FAST RIVER TRIP, DUCKY. OVER THE FALLS AND DOWN INTO COGGIE'S HOLE.
I'D GIVE YOU A TAP ON THE HEAD FIRST, BUT I'D HATE YOU TO MISS ANYTHING.
Romero
WORK UP A GOOD SWING... HEY, DID YOU BRING ANYTHING TO EAT, GAUNT? I'M REAL HUNGRY.
3435

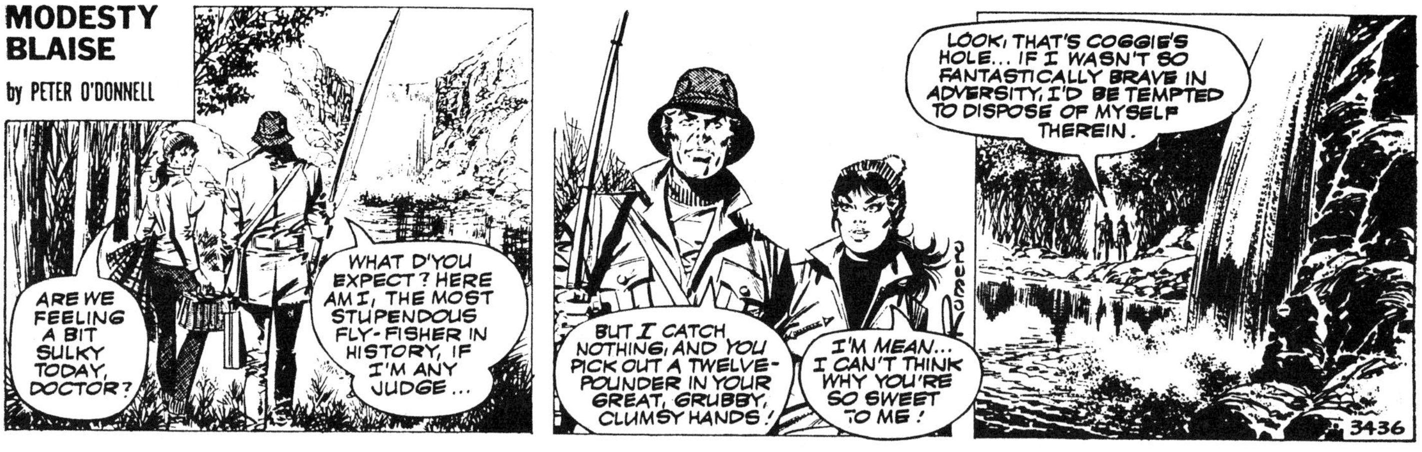
MODESTY BLAISE
by PETER O'DONNELL
ARE WE FEELING A BIT SULKY TODAY, DOCTOR?
WHAT D'YOU EXPECT? HERE AM I, THE MOST STUPENDOUS FLY-FISHER IN HISTORY, IF I'M ANY JUDGE ...
BUT I CATCH NOTHING, AND YOU PICK OUT A TWELVE-POUNDER IN YOUR GREAT, GRUBBY, CLUMSY HANDS!
I'M MEAN... I CAN'T THINK WHY YOU'RE SO SWEET TO ME!
Romero
LOOK, THAT'S COGGIE'S HOLE... IF I WASN'T SO FANTASTICALLY BRAVE IN ADVERSITY, I'D BE TEMPTED TO DISPOSE OF MYSELF THEREIN.
3436

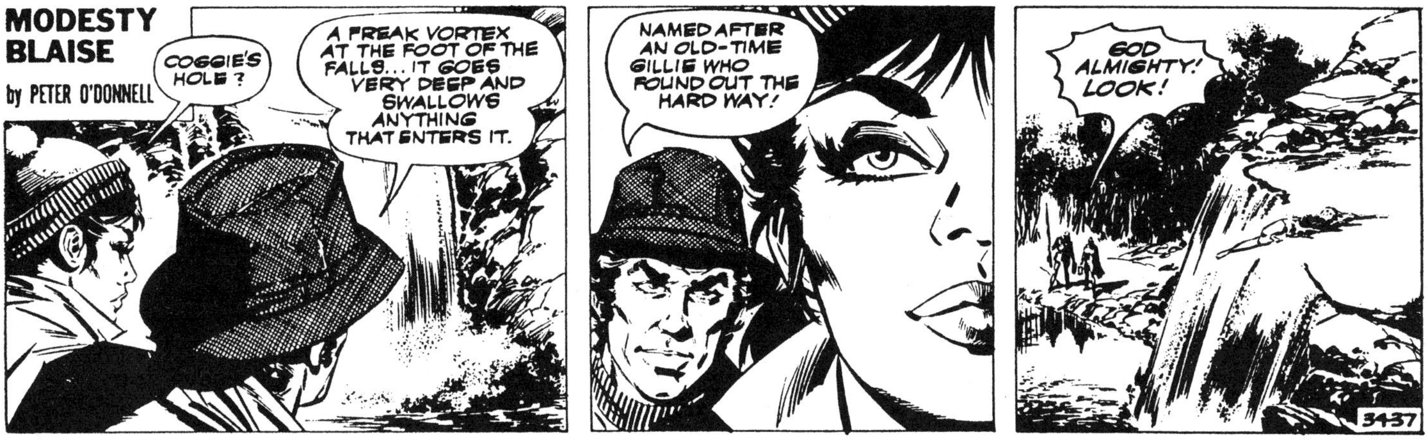
MODESTY BLAISE
by PETER O'DONNELL
COGGIE'S HOLE ?
A FREAK VORTEX AT THE FOOT OF THE FALLS... IT GOES VERY DEEP AND SWALLOWS ANYTHING THAT ENTERS IT.
NAMED AFTER AN OLD-TIME GILLIE WHO FOUND OUT THE HARD WAY!
GOD ALMIGHTY! LOOK!
3437

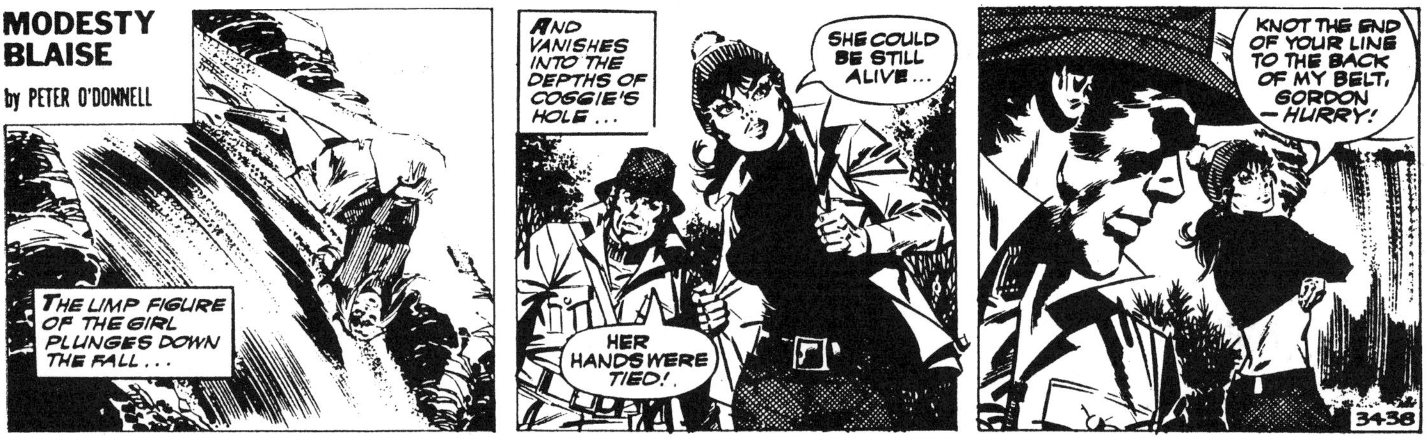
MODESTY BLAISE
by PETER O'DONNELL
THE LIMP FIGURE OF THE GIRL PLUNGES DOWN THE FALL...
AND VANISHES INTO THE DEPTHS OF COGGIE'S HOLE...
SHE COULD BE STILL ALIVE...
HER HANDS WERE TIED!
KNOT THE END OF YOUR LINE TO THE BACK OF MY BELT, GORDON —HURRY!
3438

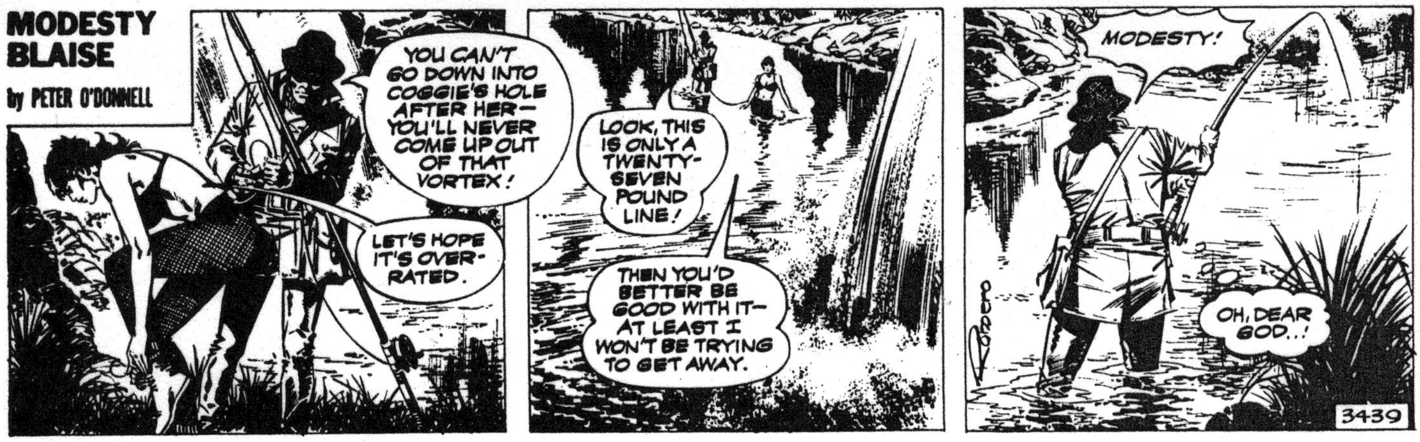
MODESTY BLAISE
by PETER O'DONNELL
YOU CAN'T GO DOWN INTO COGGIE'S HOLE AFTER HER— YOU'LL NEVER COME UP OUT OF THAT VORTEX!
LET'S HOPE IT'S OVER-RATED.
LOOK, THIS IS ONLY A TWENTY-SEVEN POUND LINE!
THEN YOU'D BETTER BE GOOD WITH IT— AT LEAST I WON'T BE TRYING TO GET AWAY.
MODESTY!
OH, DEAR GOD..!
3439

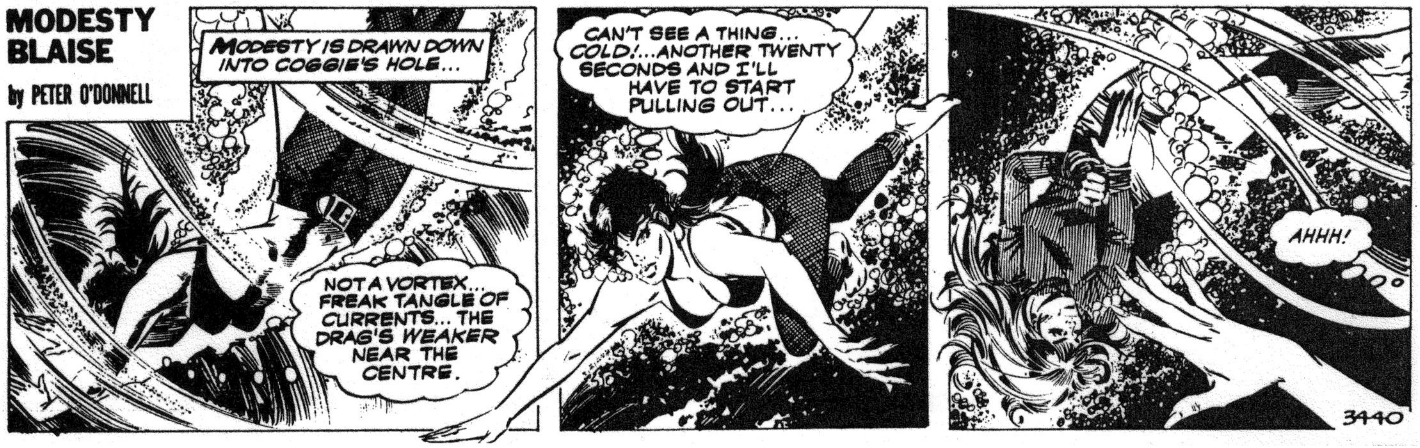
MODESTY BLAISE
by PETER O'DONNELL
MODESTY IS DRAWN DOWN INTO COGGIE'S HOLE...
NOT A VORTEX... FREAK TANGLE OF CURRENTS... THE DRAG'S WEAKER NEAR THE CENTRE.
CAN'T SEE A THING... COLD!...ANOTHER TWENTY SECONDS AND I'LL HAVE TO START PULLING OUT...
AHHH!
3440

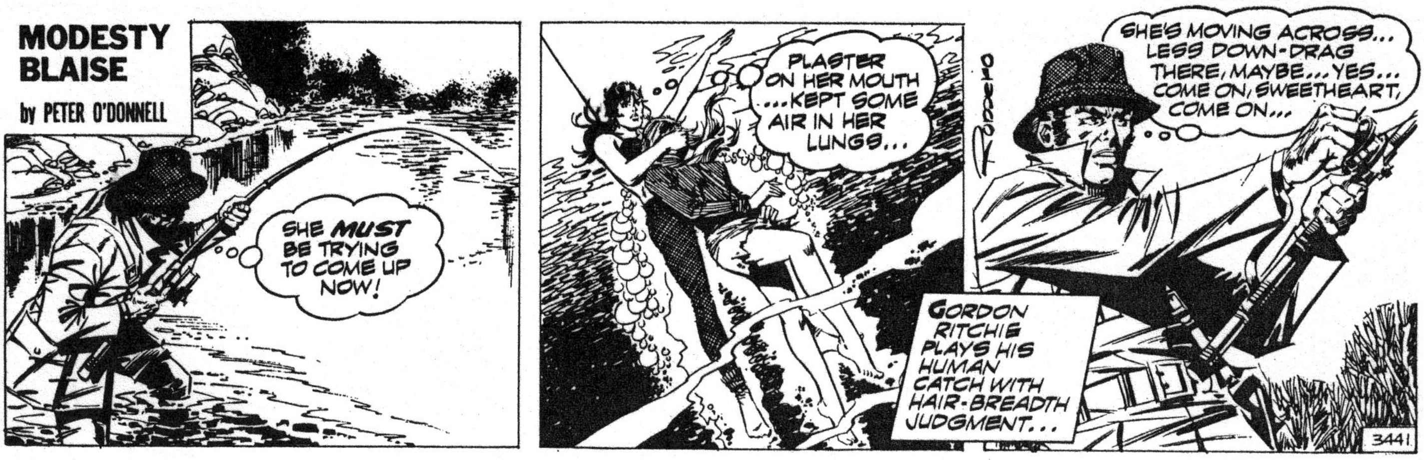
MODESTY BLAISE
by PETER O'DONNELL
SHE MUST BE TRYING TO COME UP NOW!
PLASTER ON HER MOUTH ...KEPT SOME AIR IN HER LUNGS...
SHE'S MOVING ACROSS... LESS DOWN-DRAG THERE, MAYBE... YES... COME ON, SWEETHEART, COME ON...
GORDON RITCHIE PLAYS HIS HUMAN CATCH WITH HAIR-BREADTH JUDGMENT...
3441

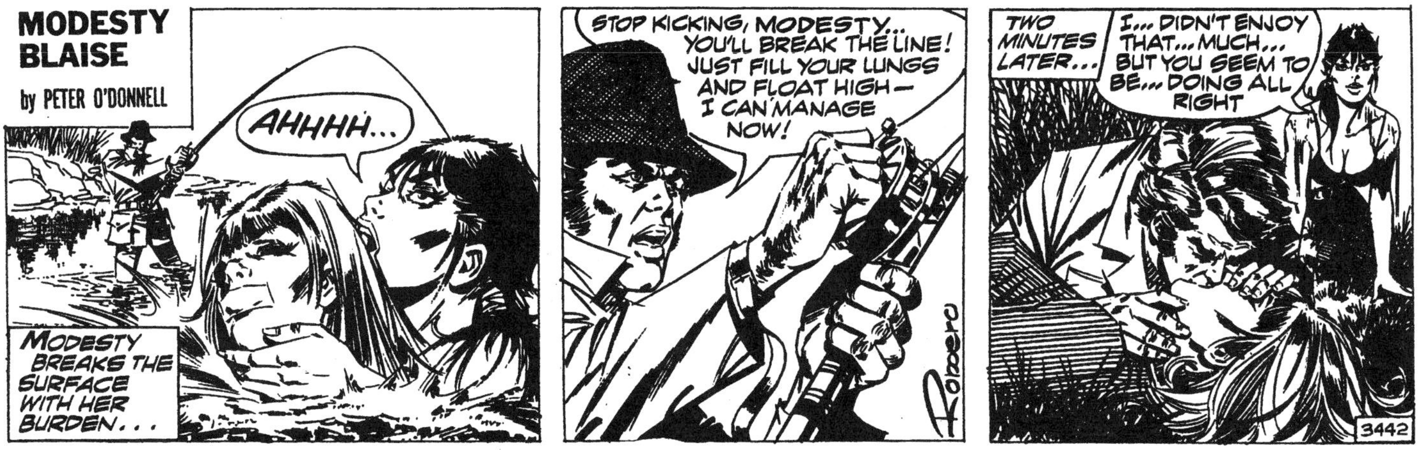
MODESTY BLAISE
by PETER O'DONNELL
AHHHH...
MODESTY BREAKS THE SURFACE WITH HER BURDEN...
STOP KICKING, MODESTY... YOU'LL BREAK THE LINE! JUST FILL YOUR LUNGS AND FLOAT HIGH— I CAN MANAGE NOW!
TWO MINUTES LATER...
I... DIDN'T ENJOY THAT... MUCH... BUT YOU SEEM TO BE... DOING ALL RIGHT
3442

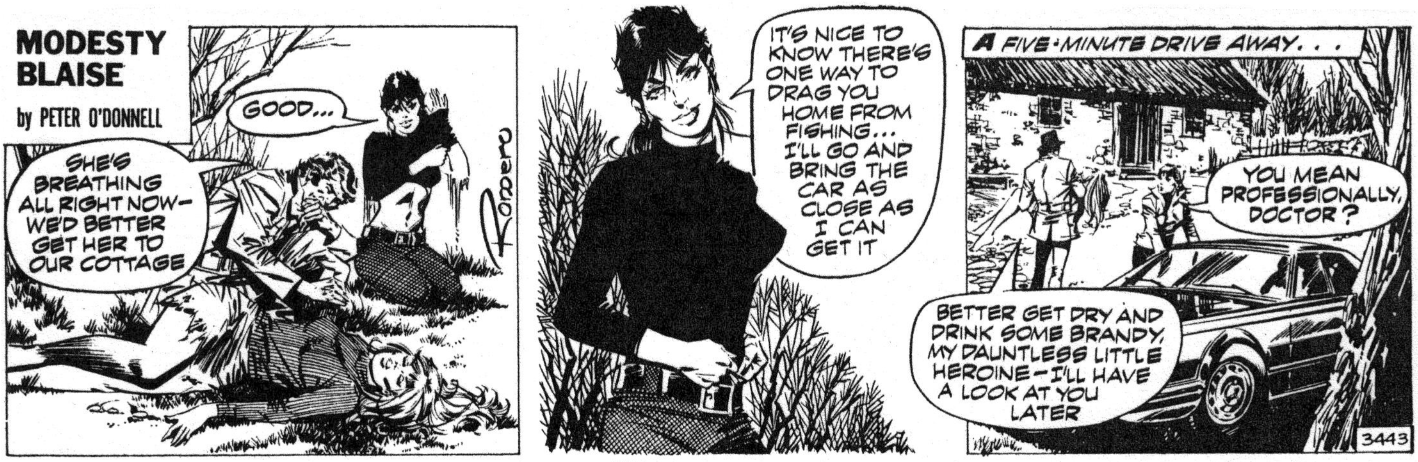
MODESTY BLAISE
by PETER O'DONNELL
GOOD...
SHE'S BREATHING ALL RIGHT NOW— WE'D BETTER GET HER TO OUR COTTAGE
IT'S NICE TO KNOW THERE'S ONE WAY TO DRAG YOU HOME FROM FISHING... I'LL GO AND BRING THE CAR AS CLOSE AS I CAN GET IT
A FIVE-MINUTE DRIVE AWAY...
BETTER GET DRY AND DRINK SOME BRANDY, MY DAUNTLESS LITTLE HEROINE— I'LL HAVE A LOOK AT YOU LATER
YOU MEAN PROFESSIONALLY, DOCTOR?
3443

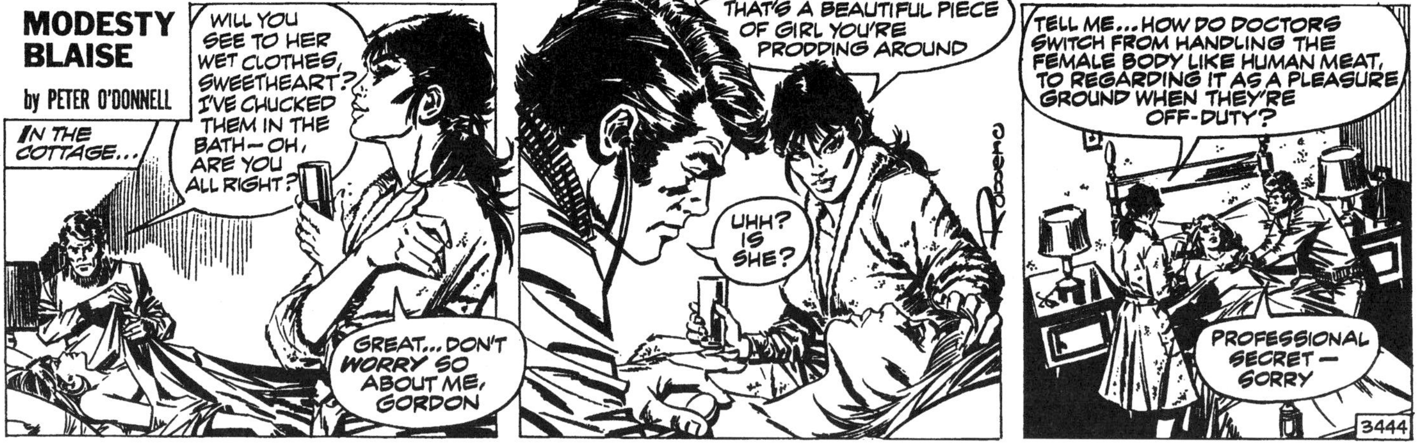
MODESTY BLAISE
by PETER O'DONNELL
IN THE COTTAGE...
WILL YOU SEE TO HER WET CLOTHES, SWEETHEART? I'VE CHUCKED THEM IN THE BATH— OH, ARE YOU ALL RIGHT?
GREAT... DON'T WORRY SO ABOUT ME, GORDON
THAT'S A BEAUTIFUL PIECE OF GIRL YOU'RE PRODDING AROUND
UHH? IS SHE?
TELL ME... HOW DO DOCTORS SWITCH FROM HANDLING THE FEMALE BODY LIKE HUMAN MEAT, TO REGARDING IT AS A PLEASURE GROUND WHEN THEY'RE OFF-DUTY?
PROFESSIONAL SECRET— SORRY
3444

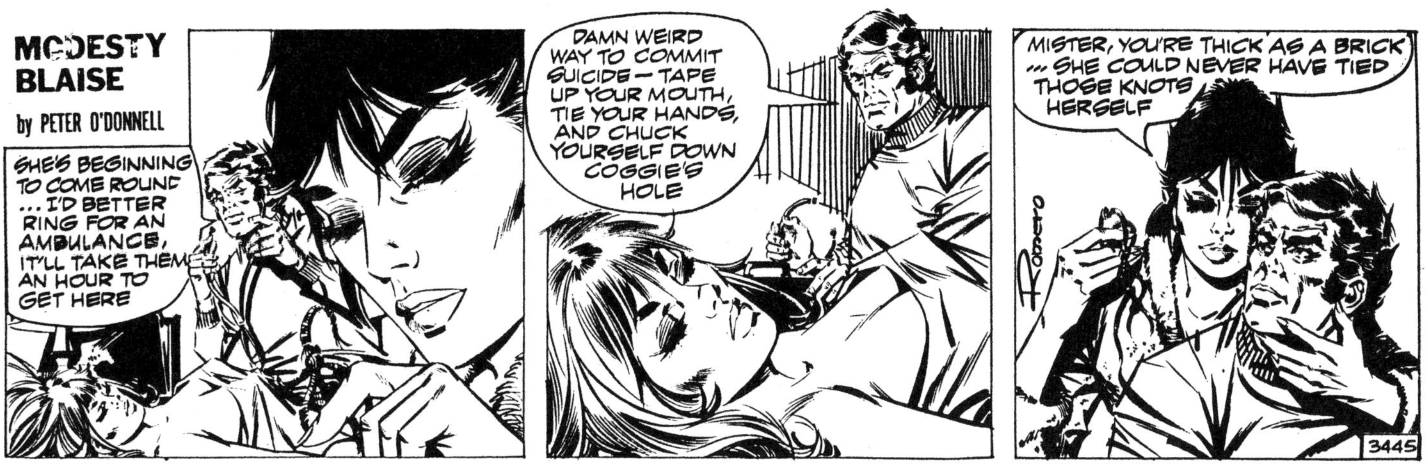
MODESTY BLAISE
by PETER O'DONNELL
SHE'S BEGINNING TO COME ROUND ... I'D BETTER RING FOR AN AMBULANCE, IT'LL TAKE THEM AN HOUR TO GET HERE
DAMN WEIRD WAY TO COMMIT SUICIDE — TAPE UP YOUR MOUTH, TIE YOUR HANDS, AND CHUCK YOURSELF DOWN COGGIE'S HOLE
MISTER, YOU'RE THICK AS A BRICK ... SHE COULD NEVER HAVE TIED THOSE KNOTS HERSELF
3445

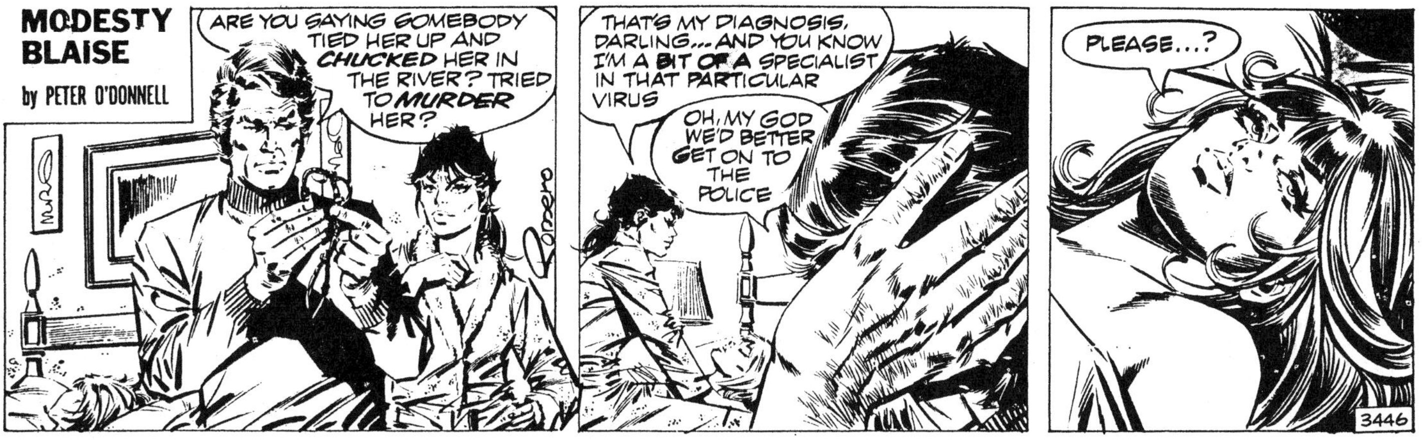
MODESTY BLAISE
by PETER O'DONNELL
ARE YOU SAYING SOMEBODY TIED HER UP AND CHUCKED HER IN THE RIVER? TRIED TO MURDER HER?
THAT'S MY DIAGNOSIS, DARLING... AND YOU KNOW I'M A BIT OF A SPECIALIST IN THAT PARTICULAR VIRUS
OH, MY GOD WE'D BETTER GET ON TO THE POLICE
PLEASE...?
3446

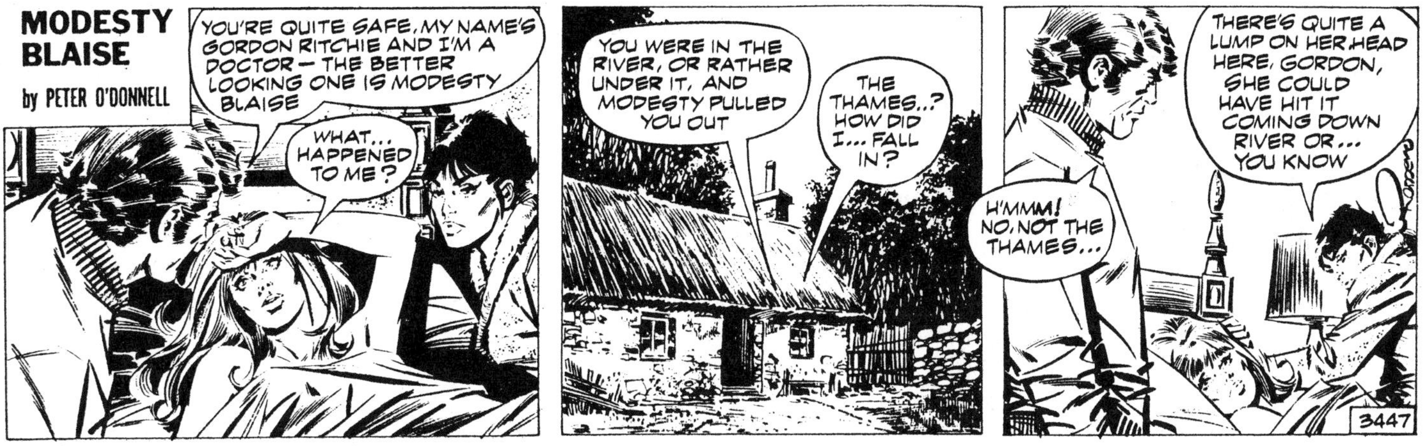
MODESTY BLAISE
by PETER O'DONNELL
YOU'RE QUITE SAFE, MY NAME'S GORDON RITCHIE AND I'M A DOCTOR — THE BETTER LOOKING ONE IS MODESTY BLAISE
WHAT... HAPPENED TO ME?
YOU WERE IN THE RIVER, OR RATHER UNDER IT, AND MODESTY PULLED YOU OUT
THE THAMES..? HOW DID I... FALL IN?
THERE'S QUITE A LUMP ON HER HEAD HERE, GORDON, SHE COULD HAVE HIT IT COMING DOWN RIVER OR... YOU KNOW
H'MMM! NO, NOT THE THAMES...
3447

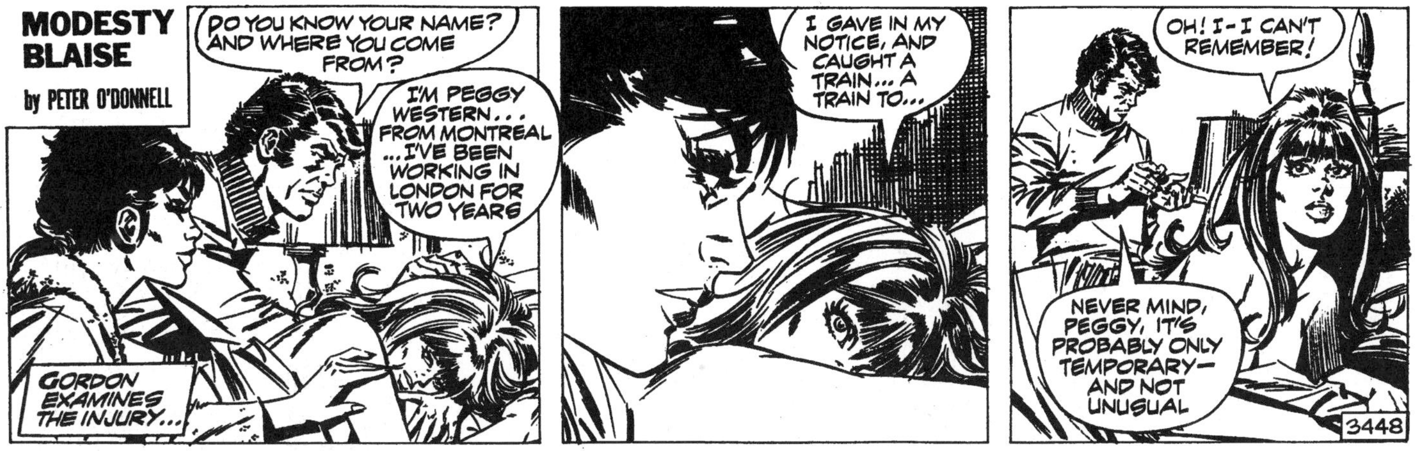
MODESTY BLAISE
by PETER O'DONNELL
DO YOU KNOW YOUR NAME? AND WHERE YOU COME FROM?
I'M PEGGY WESTERN... FROM MONTREAL ...I'VE BEEN WORKING IN LONDON FOR TWO YEARS
GORDON EXAMINES THE INJURY...
I GAVE IN MY NOTICE, AND CAUGHT A TRAIN... A TRAIN TO...
OH! I-I CAN'T REMEMBER!
NEVER MIND, PEGGY, IT'S PROBABLY ONLY TEMPORARY— AND NOT UNUSUAL
3448

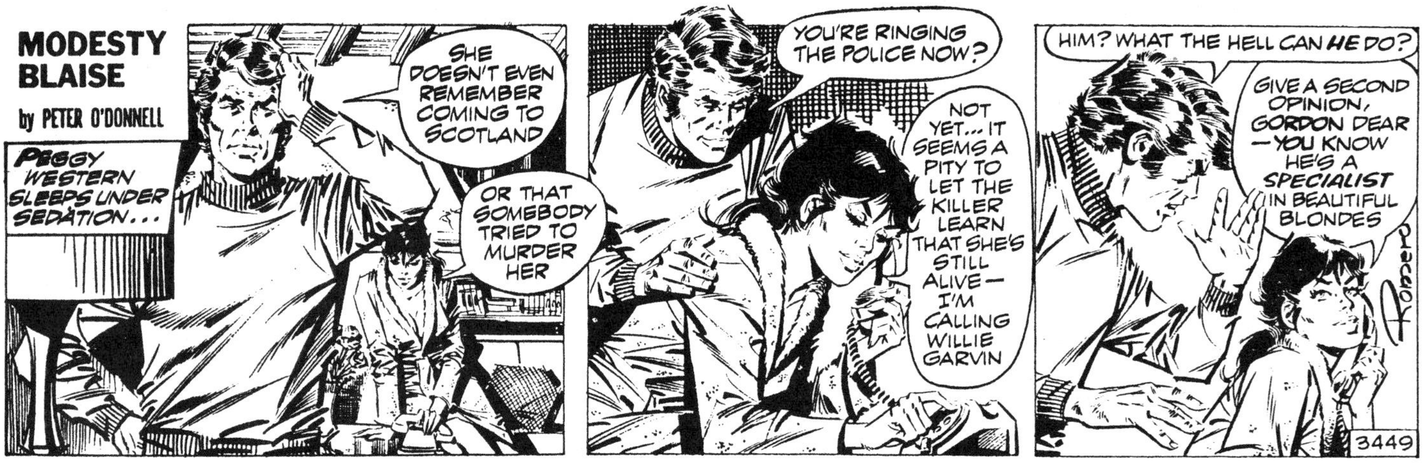
MODESTY BLAISE
by PETER O'DONNELL
PEGGY WESTERN SLEEPS UNDER SEDATION...
SHE DOESN'T EVEN REMEMBER COMING TO SCOTLAND
OR THAT SOMEBODY TRIED TO MURDER HER
YOU'RE RINGING THE POLICE NOW?
NOT YET... IT SEEMS A PITY TO LET THE KILLER LEARN THAT SHE'S STILL ALIVE— I'M CALLING WILLIE GARVIN
HIM? WHAT THE HELL CAN HE DO?
GIVE A SECOND OPINION, GORDON DEAR —YOU KNOW HE'S A SPECIALIST IN BEAUTIFUL BLONDES
3449

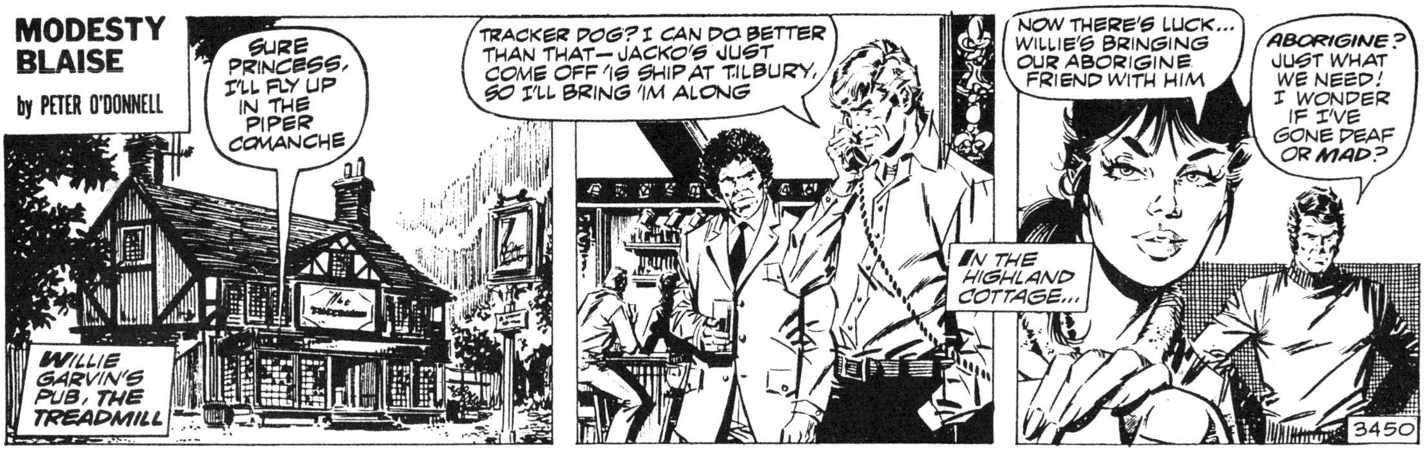
MODESTY BLAISE
by PETER O'DONNELL
SURE PRINCESS, I'LL FLY UP IN THE PIPER COMANCHE
WILLIE GARVIN'S PUB, THE TREADMILL
TRACKER DOG? I CAN DO BETTER THAN THAT— JACKO'S JUST COME OFF 'IS SHIP AT TILBURY, SO I'LL BRING 'IM ALONG
IN THE HIGHLAND COTTAGE...
NOW THERE'S LUCK... WILLIE'S BRINGING OUR ABORIGINE FRIEND WITH HIM
ABORIGINE? JUST WHAT WE NEED! I WONDER IF I'VE GONE DEAF OR MAD?
3450

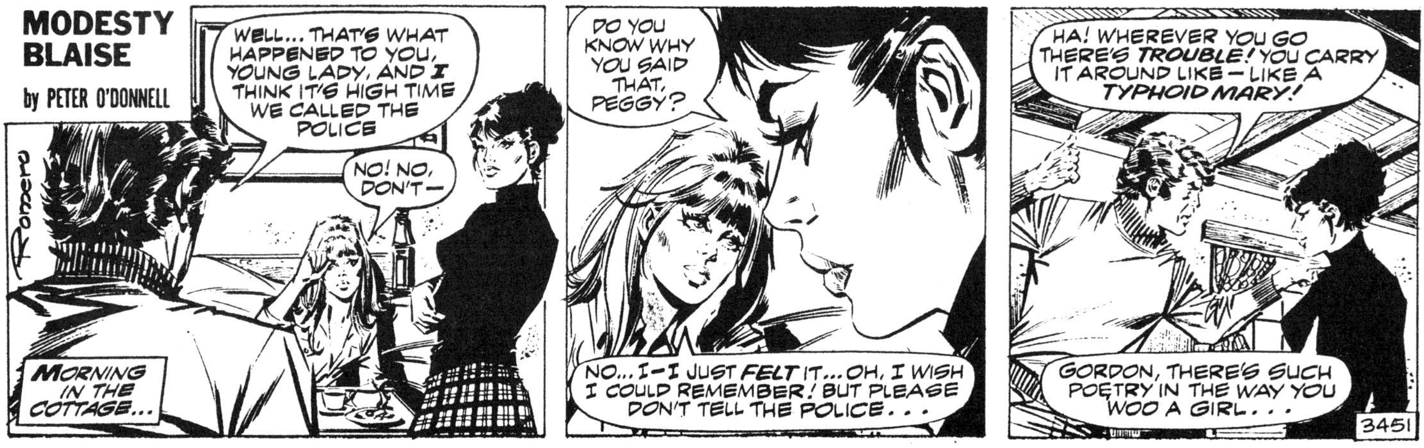
MODESTY BLAISE
by PETER O'DONNELL
WELL... THAT'S WHAT HAPPENED TO YOU, YOUNG LADY, AND I THINK IT'S HIGH TIME WE CALLED THE POLICE
NO! NO, DON'T—
MORNING IN THE COTTAGE...
DO YOU KNOW WHY YOU SAID THAT, PEGGY?
NO... I-I JUST FELT IT... OH, I WISH I COULD REMEMBER! BUT PLEASE DON'T TELL THE POLICE...
HA! WHEREVER YOU GO THERE'S TROUBLE! YOU CARRY IT AROUND LIKE—LIKE A TYPHOID MARY!
GORDON, THERE'S SUCH POETRY IN THE WAY YOU WOO A GIRL...
3451

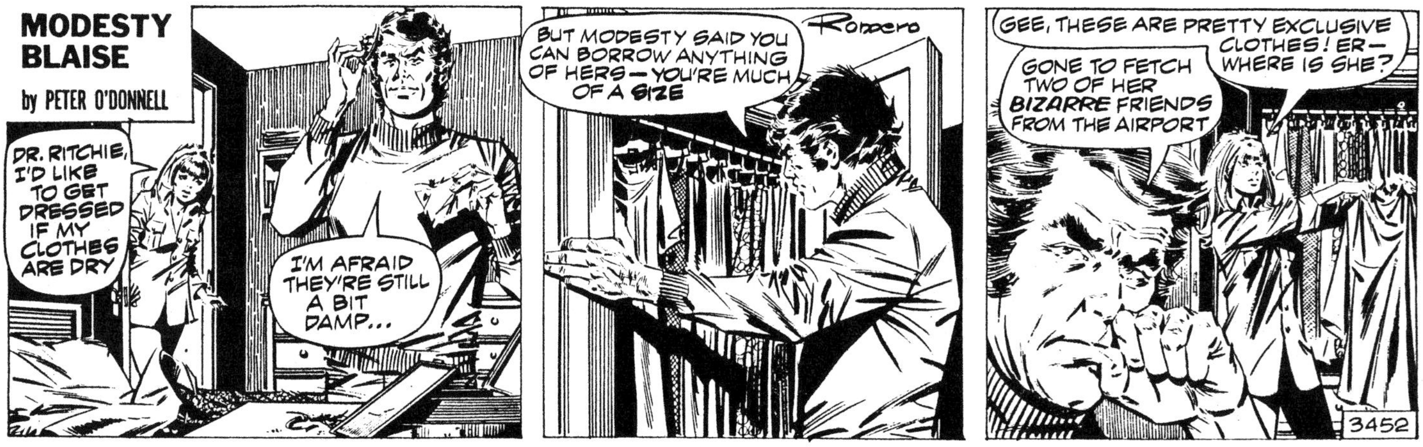
MODESTY BLAISE
by PETER O'DONNELL
DR. RITCHIE, I'D LIKE TO GET DRESSED IF MY CLOTHES ARE DRY
I'M AFRAID THEY'RE STILL A BIT DAMP...
BUT MODESTY SAID YOU CAN BORROW ANYTHING OF HERS—YOU'RE MUCH OF A SIZE
GEE, THESE ARE PRETTY EXCLUSIVE CLOTHES! ER— WHERE IS SHE?
GONE TO FETCH TWO OF HER BIZARRE FRIENDS FROM THE AIRPORT
3452

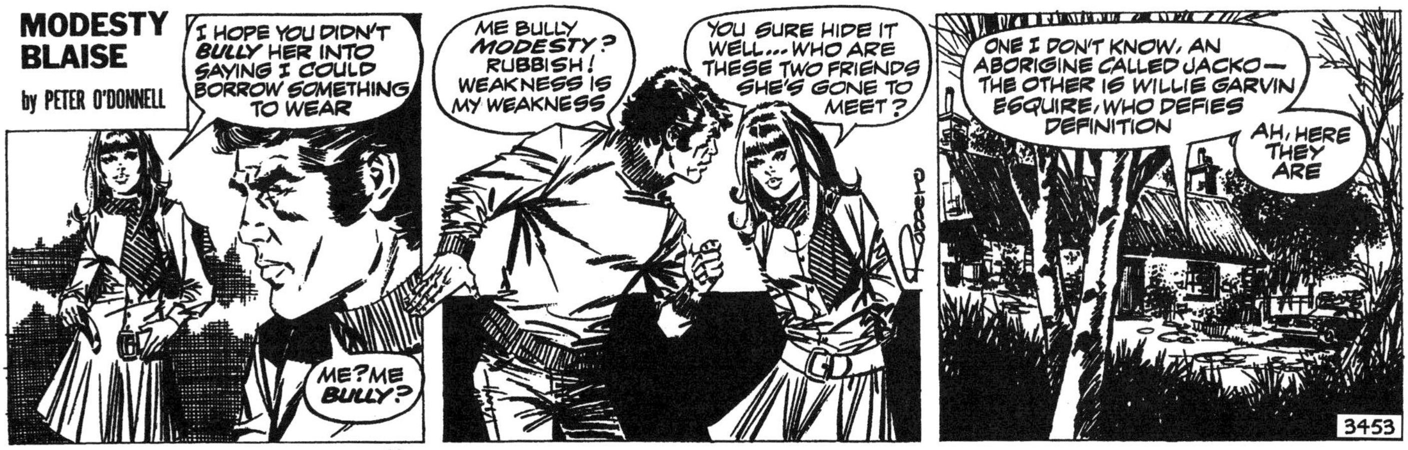
MODESTY BLAISE
by PETER O'DONNELL
I HOPE YOU DIDN'T BULLY HER INTO SAYING I COULD BORROW SOMETHING TO WEAR
ME? ME BULLY?
ME BULLY MODESTY? RUBBISH! WEAKNESS IS MY WEAKNESS
YOU SURE HIDE IT WELL... WHO ARE THESE TWO FRIENDS SHE'S GONE TO MEET?
ONE I DON'T KNOW, AN ABORIGINE CALLED JACKO — THE OTHER IS WILLIE GARVIN ESQUIRE, WHO DEFIES DEFINITION
AH, HERE THEY ARE
3453

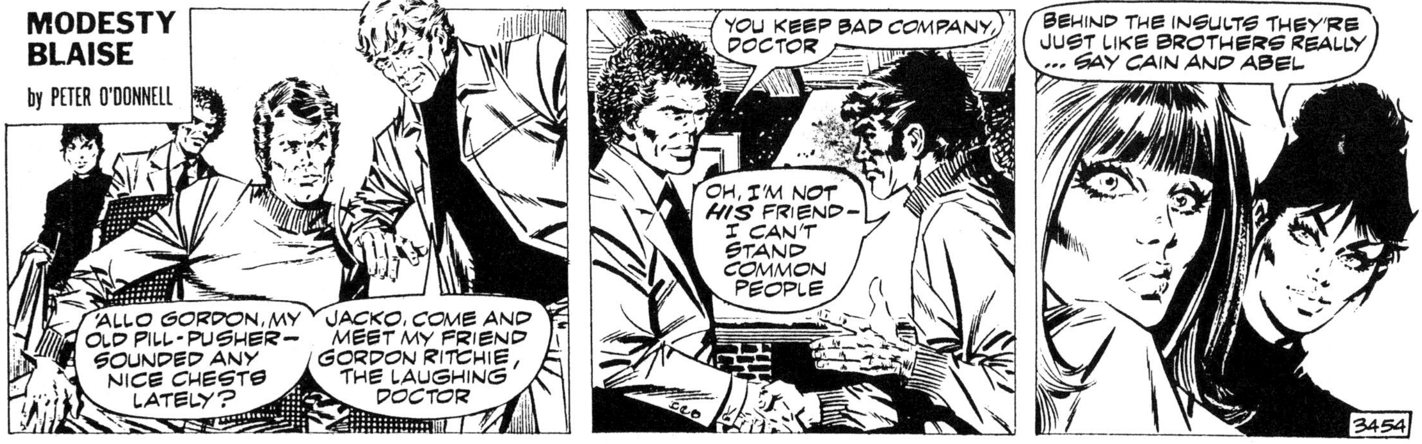
MODESTY BLAISE
by PETER O'DONNELL
'ALLO GORDON, MY OLD PILL-PUSHER — SOUNDED ANY NICE CHESTS LATELY?
JACKO, COME AND MEET MY FRIEND GORDON RITCHIE, THE LAUGHING DOCTOR
YOU KEEP BAD COMPANY, DOCTOR
OH, I'M NOT HIS FRIEND — I CAN'T STAND COMMON PEOPLE
BEHIND THE INSULTS THEY'RE JUST LIKE BROTHERS REALLY ... SAY CAIN AND ABEL
3454

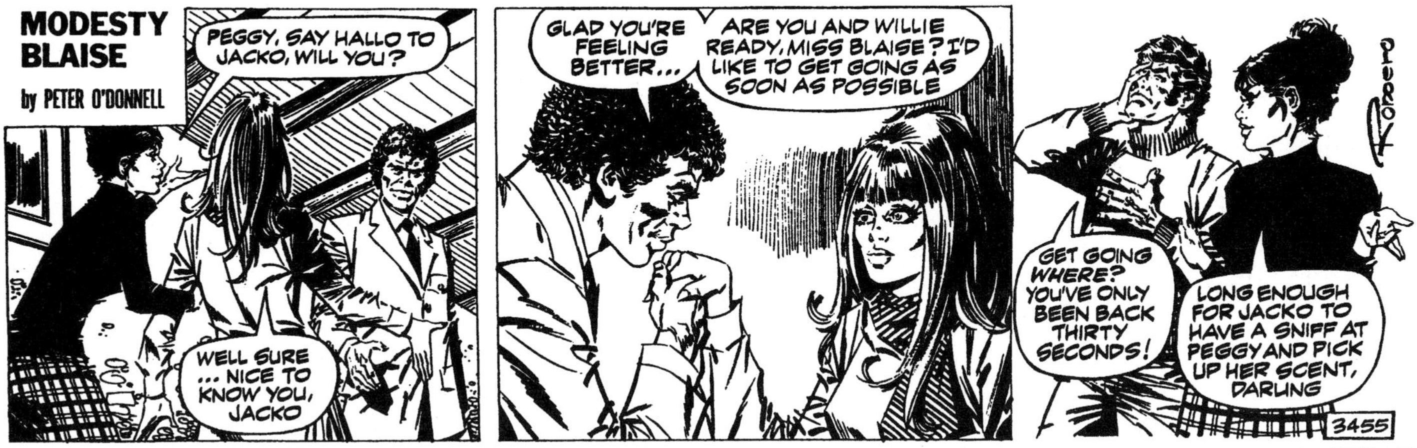
MODESTY BLAISE
by PETER O'DONNELL
PEGGY, SAY HALLO TO JACKO, WILL YOU?
WELL SURE ... NICE TO KNOW YOU, JACKO
GLAD YOU'RE FEELING BETTER...
ARE YOU AND WILLIE READY, MISS BLAISE? I'D LIKE TO GET GOING AS SOON AS POSSIBLE
GET GOING WHERE? YOU'VE ONLY BEEN BACK THIRTY SECONDS!
LONG ENOUGH FOR JACKO TO HAVE A SNIFF AT PEGGY AND PICK UP HER SCENT, DARLING
3455

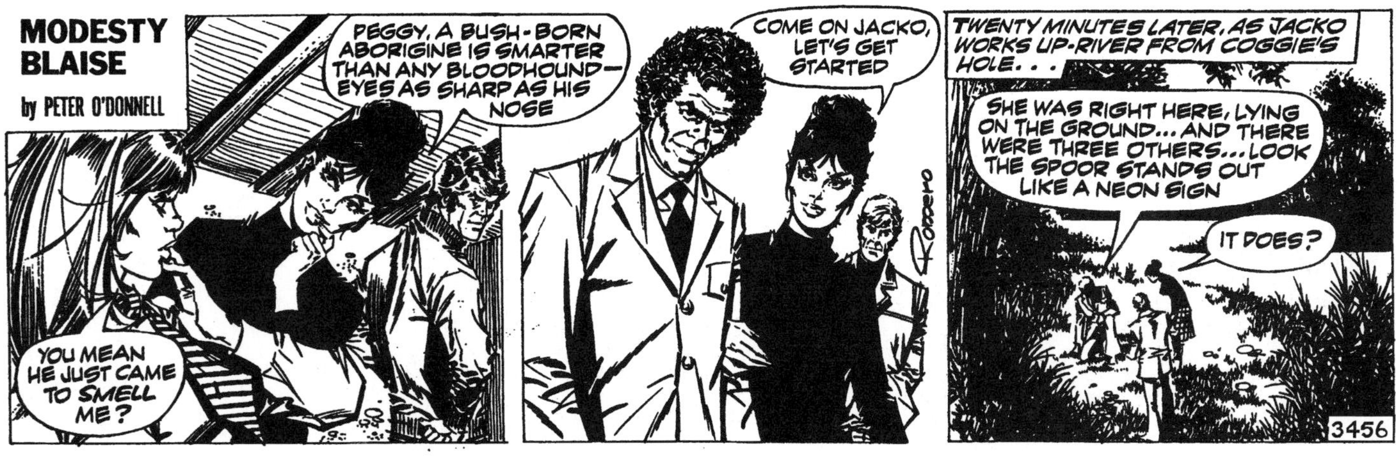
MODESTY BLAISE
by PETER O'DONNELL
PEGGY, A BUSH-BORN ABORIGINE IS SMARTER THAN ANY BLOODHOUND — EYES AS SHARP AS HIS NOSE
YOU MEAN HE JUST CAME TO SMELL ME?
COME ON JACKO, LET'S GET STARTED
TWENTY MINUTES LATER, AS JACKO WORKS UP-RIVER FROM COGGIE'S HOLE...
SHE WAS RIGHT HERE, LYING ON THE GROUND... AND THERE WERE THREE OTHERS... LOOK THE SPOOR STANDS OUT LIKE A NEON SIGN
IT DOES?
3456

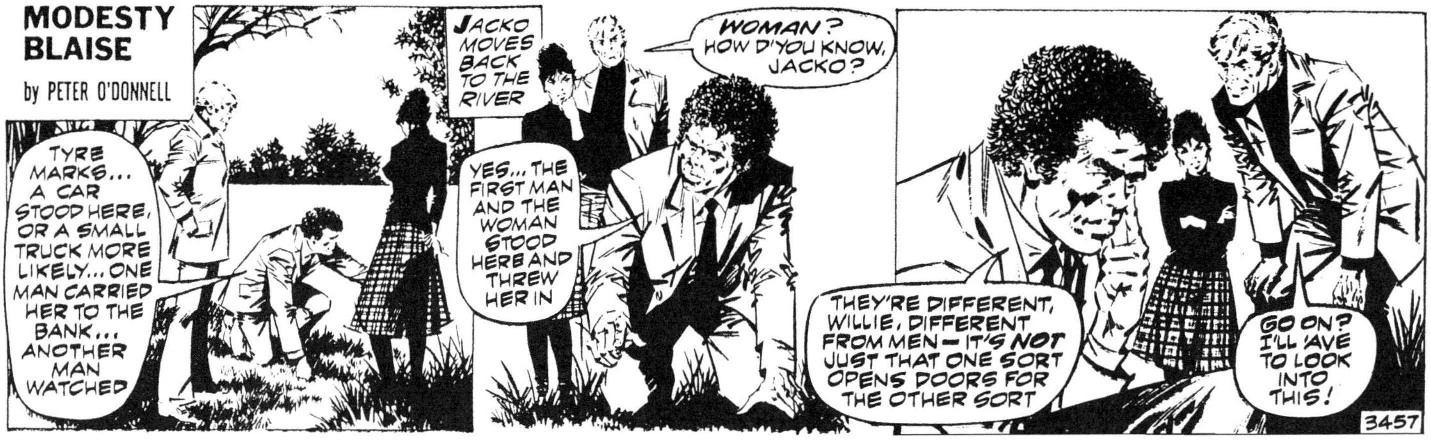
MODESTY BLAISE
by PETER O'DONNELL
TYRE MARKS... A CAR STOOD HERE, OR A SMALL TRUCK MORE LIKELY... ONE MAN CARRIED HER TO THE BANK... ANOTHER MAN WATCHED
JACKO MOVES BACK TO THE RIVER
WOMAN? HOW D'YOU KNOW, JACKO?
YES... THE FIRST MAN AND THE WOMAN STOOD HERE AND THREW HER IN
THEY'RE DIFFERENT, WILLIE, DIFFERENT FROM MEN — IT'S NOT JUST THAT ONE SORT OPENS DOORS FOR THE OTHER SORT
GO ON? I'LL 'AVE TO LOOK INTO THIS!
3457

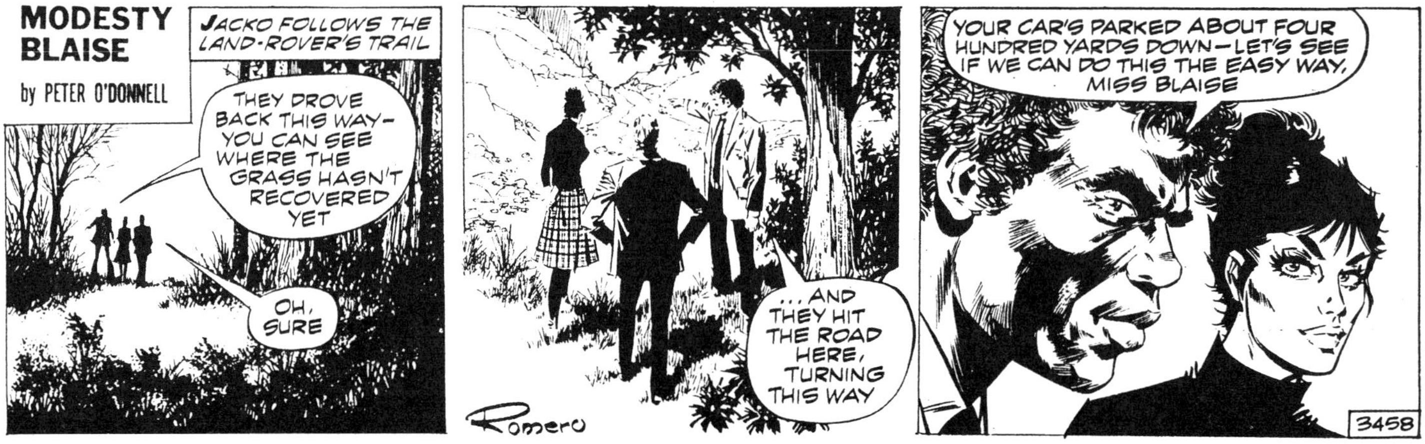
MODESTY BLAISE
by PETER O'DONNELL
JACKO FOLLOWS THE LAND-ROVER'S TRAIL
THEY DROVE BACK THIS WAY— YOU CAN SEE WHERE THE GRASS HASN'T RECOVERED YET
OH, SURE
... AND THEY HIT THE ROAD HERE, TURNING THIS WAY
Romero
YOUR CAR'S PARKED ABOUT FOUR HUNDRED YARDS DOWN—LET'S SEE IF WE CAN DO THIS THE EASY WAY, MISS BLAISE
3458

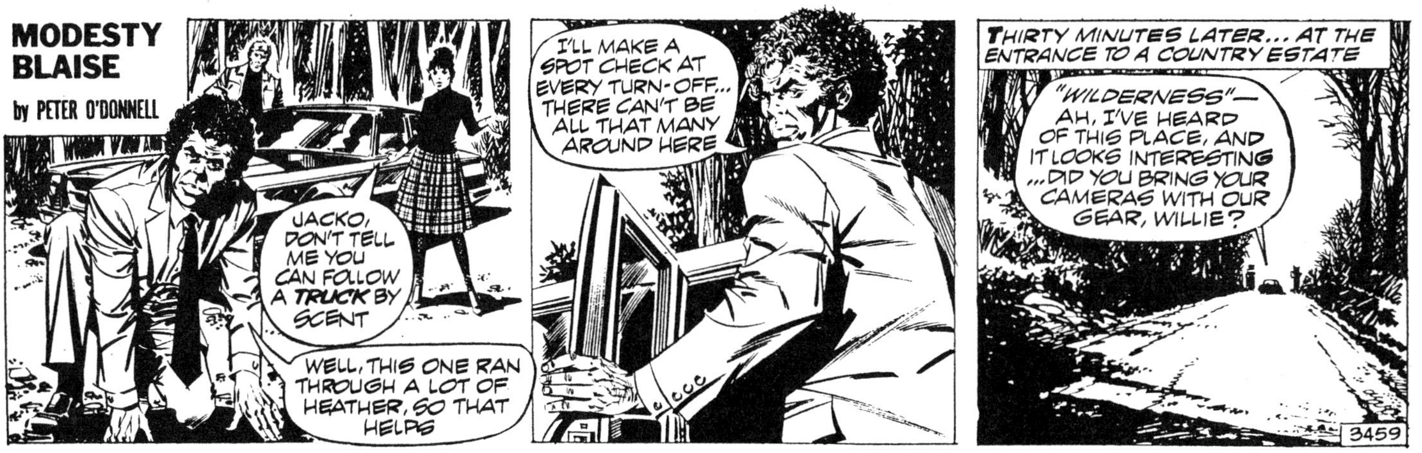
MODESTY BLAISE
by PETER O'DONNELL
JACKO, DON'T TELL ME YOU CAN FOLLOW A TRUCK BY SCENT
WELL, THIS ONE RAN THROUGH A LOT OF HEATHER, SO THAT HELPS
I'LL MAKE A SPOT CHECK AT EVERY TURN-OFF... THERE CAN'T BE ALL THAT MANY AROUND HERE
THIRTY MINUTES LATER... AT THE ENTRANCE TO A COUNTRY ESTATE
"WILDERNESS"— AH, I'VE HEARD OF THIS PLACE, AND IT LOOKS INTERESTING ...DID YOU BRING YOUR CAMERAS WITH OUR GEAR, WILLIE?
3459

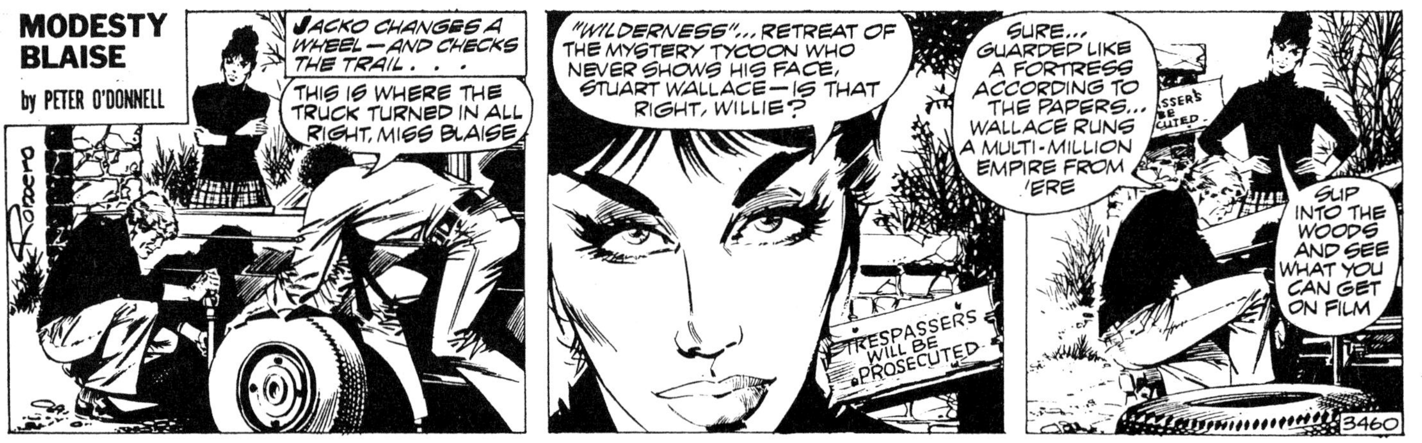
MODESTY BLAISE
by PETER O'DONNELL
JACKO CHANGES A WHEEL — AND CHECKS THE TRAIL. . .
THIS IS WHERE THE TRUCK TURNED IN ALL RIGHT, MISS BLAISE
"WILDERNESS"... RETREAT OF THE MYSTERY TYCOON WHO NEVER SHOWS HIS FACE, STUART WALLACE — IS THAT RIGHT, WILLIE?
TRESPASSERS WILL BE PROSECUTED
SURE... GUARDED LIKE A FORTRESS ACCORDING TO THE PAPERS... WALLACE RUNS A MULTI-MILLION EMPIRE FROM 'ERE
SLIP INTO THE WOODS AND SEE WHAT YOU CAN GET ON FILM
3460

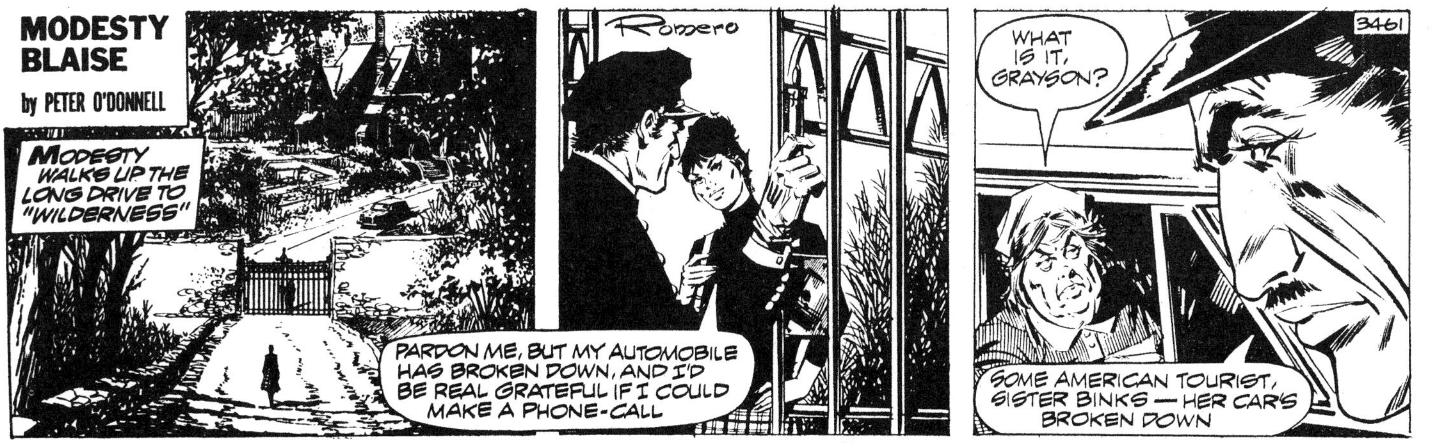
MODESTY BLAISE
by PETER O'DONNELL
MODESTY WALKS UP THE LONG DRIVE TO "WILDERNESS"
Romero
PARDON ME, BUT MY AUTOMOBILE HAS BROKEN DOWN, AND I'D BE REAL GRATEFUL IF I COULD MAKE A PHONE-CALL
3461
WHAT IS IT, GRAYSON?
SOME AMERICAN TOURIST, SISTER BINKS — HER CAR'S BROKEN DOWN

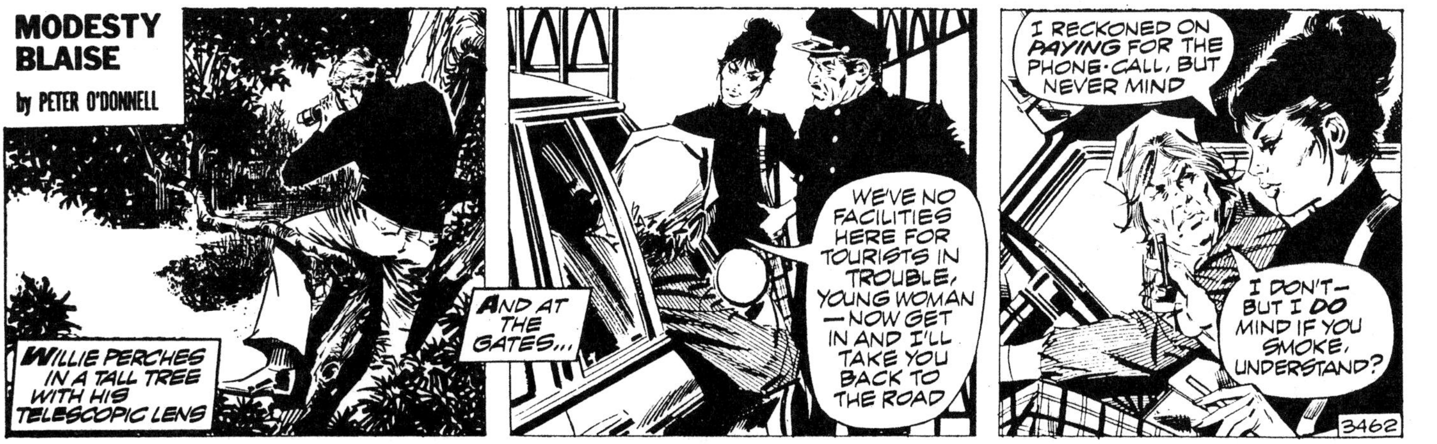
MODESTY BLAISE
by PETER O'DONNELL
WILLIE PERCHES IN A TALL TREE WITH HIS TELESCOPIC LENS
AND AT THE GATES...
WE'VE NO FACILITIES HERE FOR TOURISTS IN TROUBLE, YOUNG WOMAN — NOW GET IN AND I'LL TAKE YOU BACK TO THE ROAD
I RECKONED ON PAYING FOR THE PHONE-CALL, BUT NEVER MIND
I DON'T— BUT I DO MIND IF YOU SMOKE, UNDERSTAND?
3462

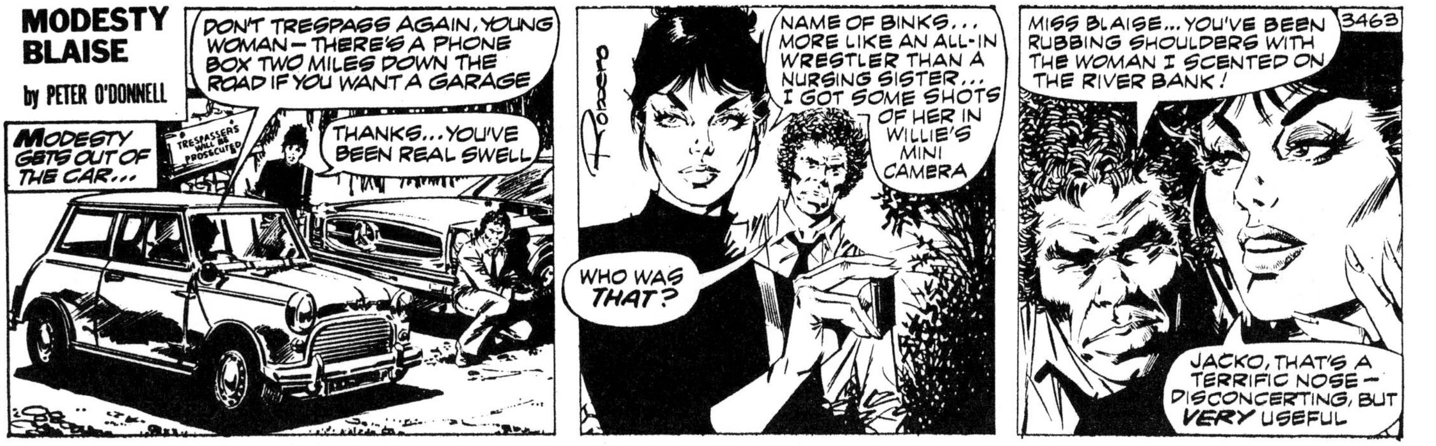
MODESTY BLAISE
by PETER O'DONNELL
MODESTY GETS OUT OF THE CAR...
DON'T TRESPASS AGAIN, YOUNG WOMAN — THERE'S A PHONE BOX TWO MILES DOWN THE ROAD IF YOU WANT A GARAGE
TRESPASSERS WILL BE PROSECUTED
THANKS... YOU'VE BEEN REAL SWELL
Romero
NAME OF BINKS... MORE LIKE AN ALL-IN WRESTLER THAN A NURSING SISTER... I GOT SOME SHOTS OF HER IN WILLIE'S MINI CAMERA
WHO WAS THAT?
3463
MISS BLAISE... YOU'VE BEEN RUBBING SHOULDERS WITH THE WOMAN I SCENTED ON THE RIVER BANK!
JACKO, THAT'S A TERRIFIC NOSE — DISCONCERTING, BUT VERY USEFUL

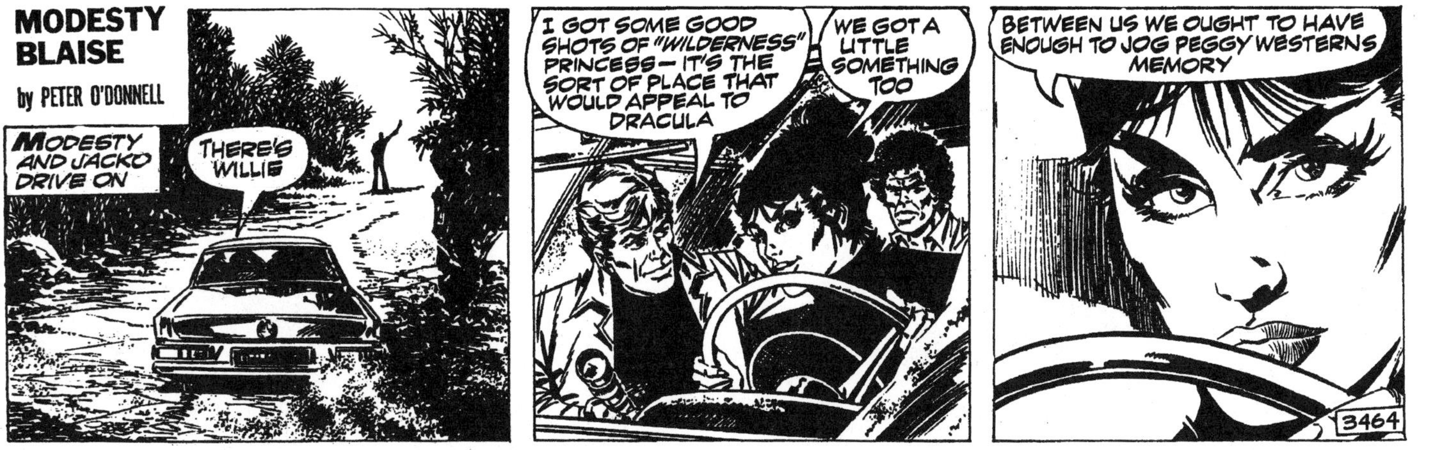
MODESTY BLAISE
by PETER O'DONNELL
MODESTY AND JACKO DRIVE ON
THERE'S WILLIE
I GOT SOME GOOD SHOTS OF "WILDERNESS" PRINCESS — IT'S THE SORT OF PLACE THAT WOULD APPEAL TO DRACULA
WE GOT A LITTLE SOMETHING TOO
BETWEEN US WE OUGHT TO HAVE ENOUGH TO JOG PEGGY WESTERNS MEMORY
3464

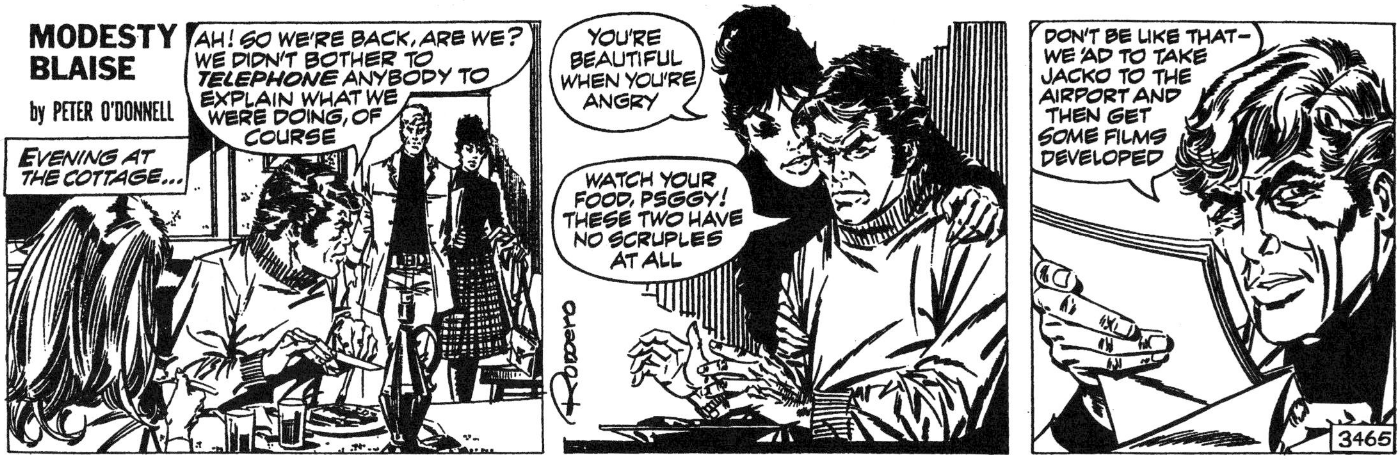
MODESTY BLAISE
by PETER O'DONNELL
EVENING AT THE COTTAGE...
AH! SO WE'RE BACK, ARE WE? WE DIDN'T BOTHER TO TELEPHONE ANYBODY TO EXPLAIN WHAT WE WERE DOING, OF COURSE
YOU'RE BEAUTIFUL WHEN YOU'RE ANGRY
WATCH YOUR FOOD, PEGGY! THESE TWO HAVE NO SCRUPLES AT ALL
DON'T BE LIKE THAT— WE 'AD TO TAKE JACKO TO THE AIRPORT AND THEN GET SOME FILMS DEVELOPED
Romero
3465

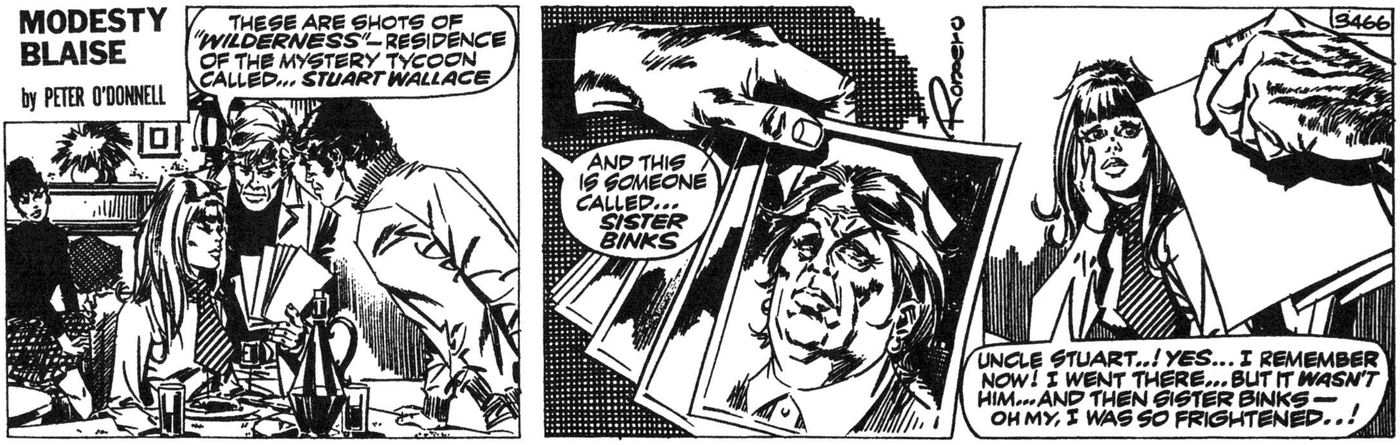
MODESTY BLAISE
by PETER O'DONNELL
THESE ARE SHOTS OF "WILDERNESS"—RESIDENCE OF THE MYSTERY TYCOON CALLED... STUART WALLACE
AND THIS IS SOMEONE CALLED... SISTER BINKS
Romero
3466
UNCLE STUART..! YES... I REMEMBER NOW! I WENT THERE... BUT IT WASN'T HIM... AND THEN SISTER BINKS — OH MY, I WAS SO FRIGHTENED..!

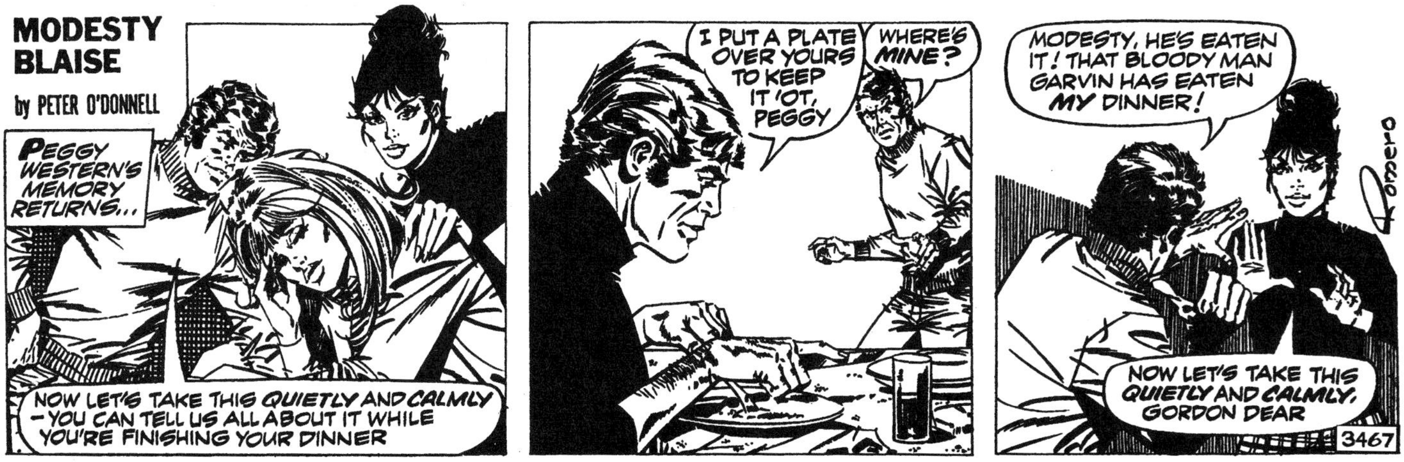
MODESTY BLAISE
by PETER O'DONNELL
PEGGY WESTERN'S MEMORY RETURNS...
NOW LET'S TAKE THIS QUIETLY AND CALMLY —YOU CAN TELL US ALL ABOUT IT WHILE YOU'RE FINISHING YOUR DINNER
I PUT A PLATE OVER YOURS TO KEEP IT 'OT, PEGGY
WHERE'S MINE?
MODESTY, HE'S EATEN IT! THAT BLOODY MAN GARVIN HAS EATEN MY DINNER!
Romero
NOW LET'S TAKE THIS QUIETLY AND CALMLY, GORDON DEAR
3467

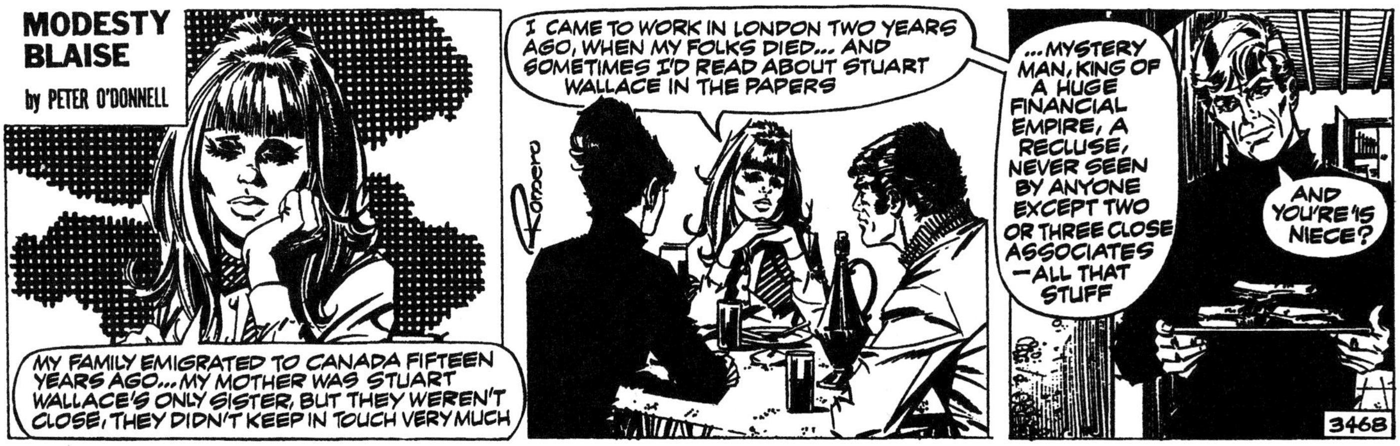
MODESTY BLAISE
by PETER O'DONNELL
MY FAMILY EMIGRATED TO CANADA FIFTEEN YEARS AGO... MY MOTHER WAS STUART WALLACE'S ONLY SISTER, BUT THEY WEREN'T CLOSE, THEY DIDN'T KEEP IN TOUCH VERY MUCH
I CAME TO WORK IN LONDON TWO YEARS AGO, WHEN MY FOLKS DIED... AND SOMETIMES I'D READ ABOUT STUART WALLACE IN THE PAPERS
Romero
...MYSTERY MAN, KING OF A HUGE FINANCIAL EMPIRE, A RECLUSE, NEVER SEEN BY ANYONE EXCEPT TWO OR THREE CLOSE ASSOCIATES —ALL THAT STUFF
AND YOU'RE 'IS NIECE?
3468

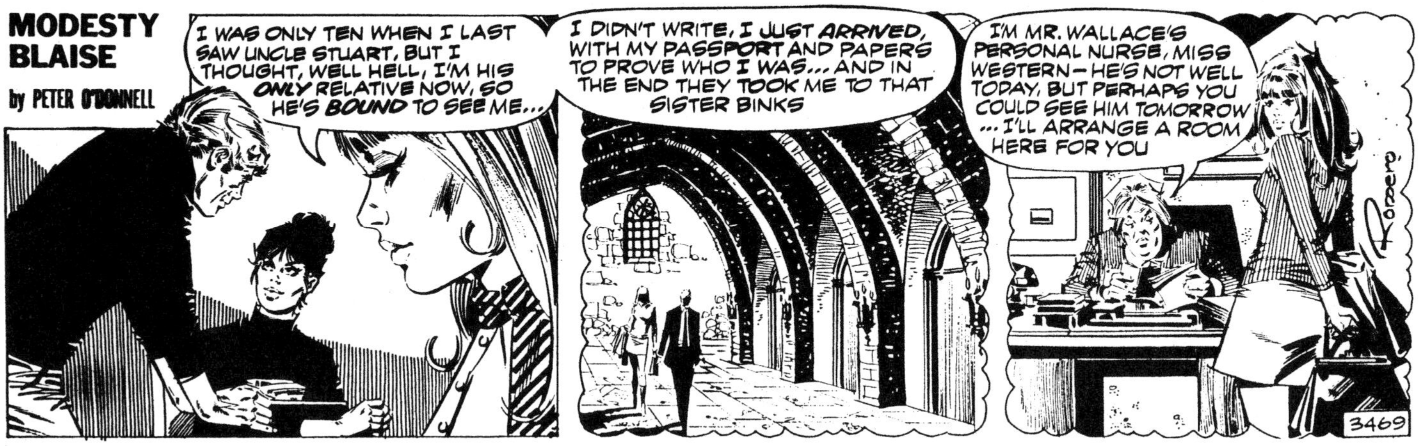
MODESTY BLAISE
by PETER O'DONNELL
I WAS ONLY TEN WHEN I LAST SAW UNCLE STUART, BUT I THOUGHT, WELL HELL, I'M HIS ONLY RELATIVE NOW, SO HE'S BOUND TO SEE ME...
I DIDN'T WRITE, I JUST ARRIVED, WITH MY PASSPORT AND PAPERS TO PROVE WHO I WAS... AND IN THE END THEY TOOK ME TO THAT SISTER BINKS
I'M MR. WALLACE'S PERSONAL NURSE, MISS WESTERN—HE'S NOT WELL TODAY, BUT PERHAPS YOU COULD SEE HIM TOMORROW ... I'LL ARRANGE A ROOM HERE FOR YOU
Romero
3469

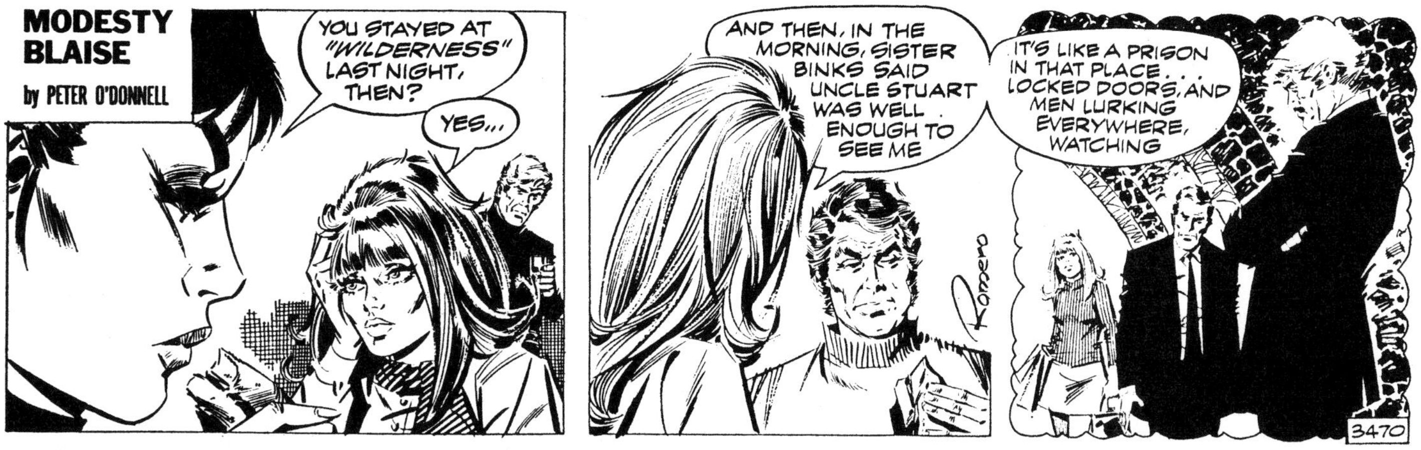
MODESTY BLAISE
by PETER O'DONNELL
YOU STAYED AT "WILDERNESS" LAST NIGHT, THEN?
YES...
AND THEN, IN THE MORNING, SISTER BINKS SAID UNCLE STUART WAS WELL ENOUGH TO SEE ME
Romero
IT'S LIKE A PRISON IN THAT PLACE . . . LOCKED DOORS, AND MEN LURKING EVERYWHERE, WATCHING
3470

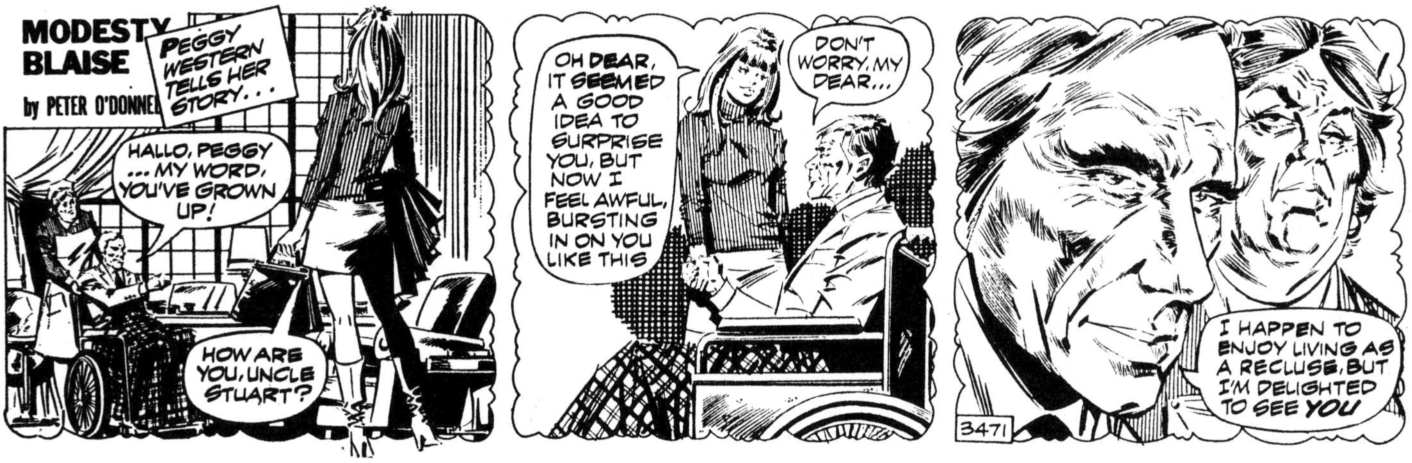
MODESTY BLAISE
by PETER O'DONNELL
PEGGY WESTERN TELLS HER STORY . . .
HALLO, PEGGY ... MY WORD, YOU'VE GROWN UP!
HOW ARE YOU, UNCLE STUART?
OH DEAR, IT SEEMED A GOOD IDEA TO SURPRISE YOU, BUT NOW I FEEL AWFUL, BURSTING IN ON YOU LIKE THIS
DON'T WORRY, MY DEAR...
I HAPPEN TO ENJOY LIVING AS A RECLUSE, BUT I'M DELIGHTED TO SEE YOU
3471

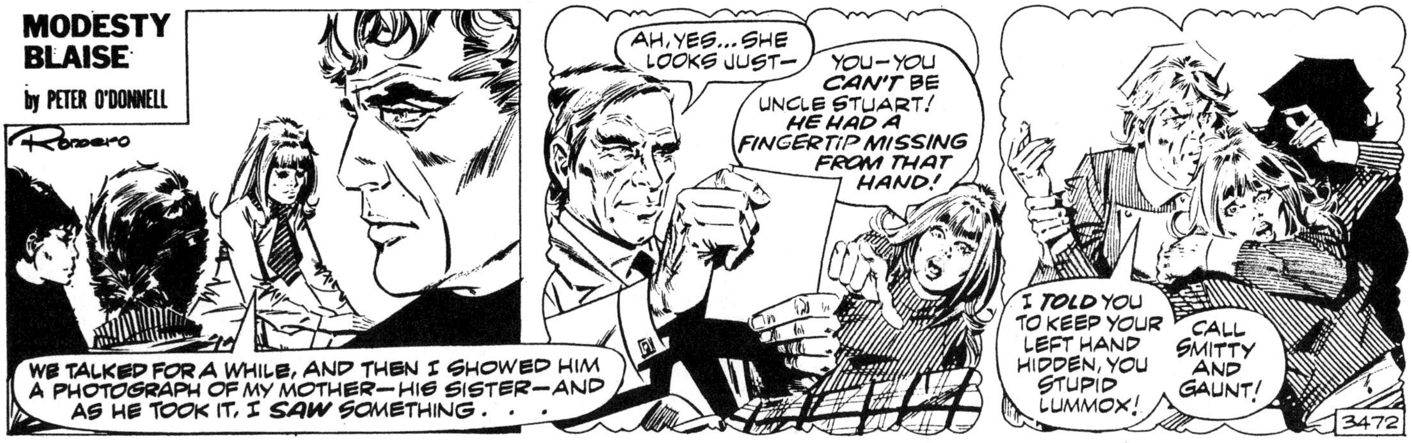
MODESTY BLAISE
by PETER O'DONNELL
Romero
WE TALKED FOR A WHILE, AND THEN I SHOWED HIM A PHOTOGRAPH OF MY MOTHER—HIS SISTER—AND AS HE TOOK IT, I SAW SOMETHING . . .
AH, YES... SHE LOOKS JUST—
YOU—YOU CAN'T BE UNCLE STUART! HE HAD A FINGERTIP MISSING FROM THAT HAND!
I TOLD YOU TO KEEP YOUR LEFT HAND HIDDEN, YOU STUPID LUMMOX!
CALL SMITTY AND GAUNT!
3472

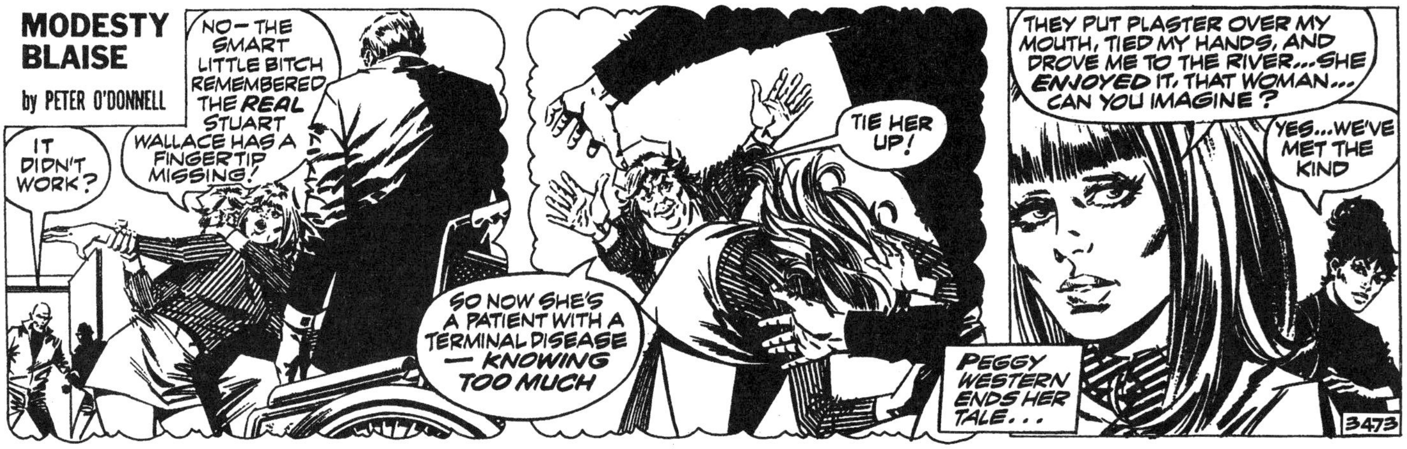
MODESTY BLAISE
by PETER O'DONNELL
IT DIDN'T WORK?
NO– THE SMART LITTLE BITCH REMEMBERED THE REAL STUART WALLACE HAS A FINGERTIP MISSING!
TIE HER UP!
SO NOW SHE'S A PATIENT WITH A TERMINAL DISEASE — KNOWING TOO MUCH
THEY PUT PLASTER OVER MY MOUTH, TIED MY HANDS, AND DROVE ME TO THE RIVER... SHE ENJOYED IT, THAT WOMAN... CAN YOU IMAGINE?
YES... WE'VE MET THE KIND
PEGGY WESTERN ENDS HER TALE...
3473

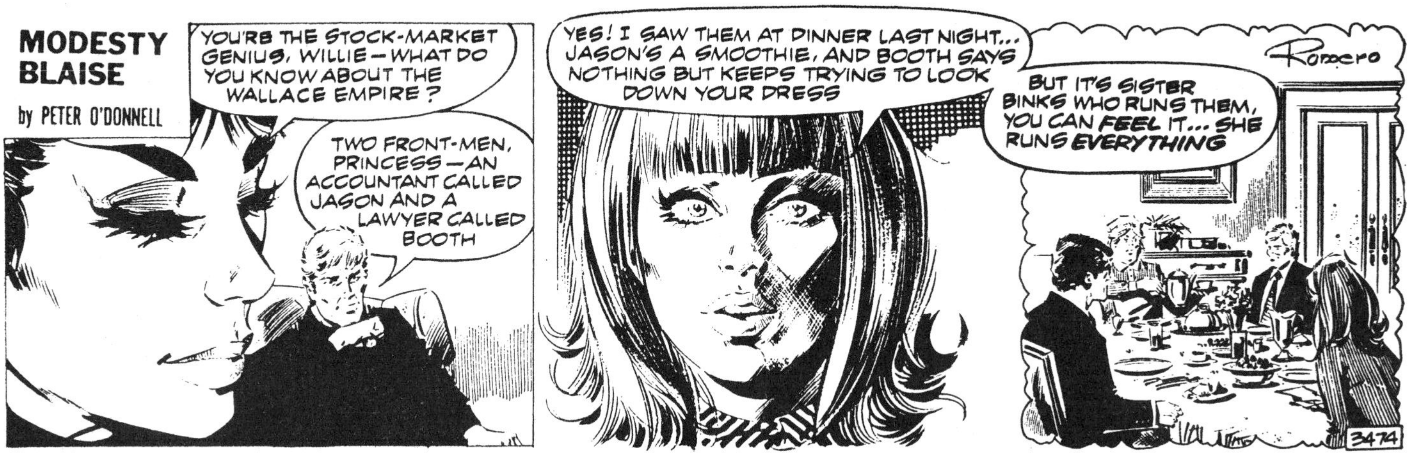
MODESTY BLAISE
by PETER O'DONNELL
YOU'RE THE STOCK-MARKET GENIUS, WILLIE — WHAT DO YOU KNOW ABOUT THE WALLACE EMPIRE?
TWO FRONT-MEN, PRINCESS — AN ACCOUNTANT CALLED JASON AND A LAWYER CALLED BOOTH
YES! I SAW THEM AT DINNER LAST NIGHT... JASON'S A SMOOTHIE, AND BOOTH SAYS NOTHING BUT KEEPS TRYING TO LOOK DOWN YOUR DRESS
Romero
BUT IT'S SISTER BINKS WHO RUNS THEM, YOU CAN FEEL IT... SHE RUNS EVERYTHING
3474

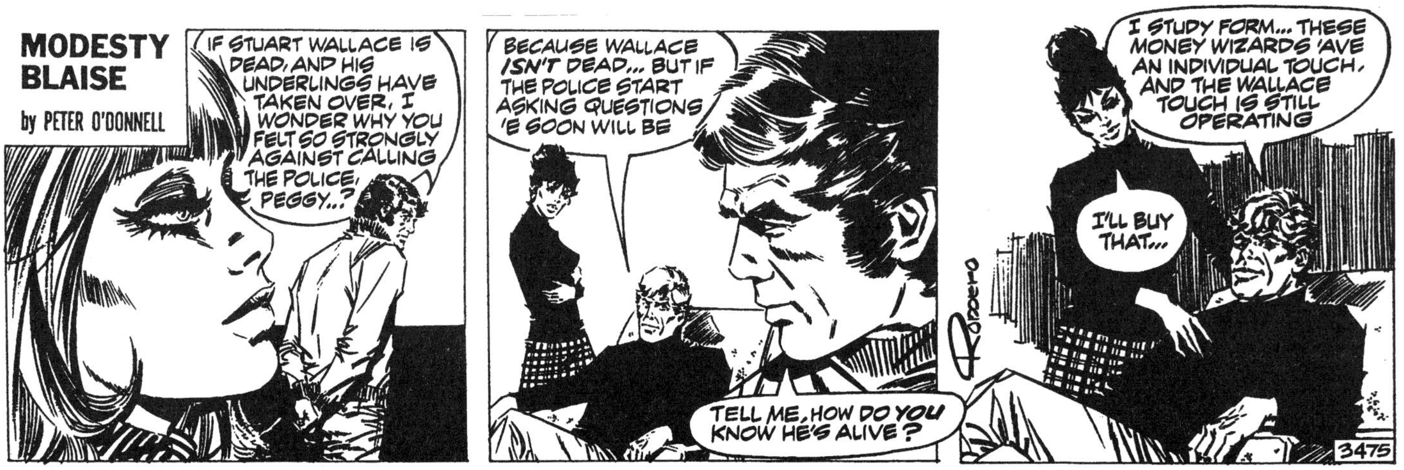
MODESTY BLAISE
by PETER O'DONNELL
IF STUART WALLACE IS DEAD, AND HIS UNDERLINGS HAVE TAKEN OVER, I WONDER WHY YOU FELT SO STRONGLY AGAINST CALLING THE POLICE, PEGGY..?
BECAUSE WALLACE ISN'T DEAD... BUT IF THE POLICE START ASKING QUESTIONS 'E SOON WILL BE
TELL ME, HOW DO YOU KNOW HE'S ALIVE?
Romero
I STUDY FORM... THESE MONEY WIZARDS 'AVE AN INDIVIDUAL TOUCH, AND THE WALLACE TOUCH IS STILL OPERATING
I'LL BUY THAT...
3475

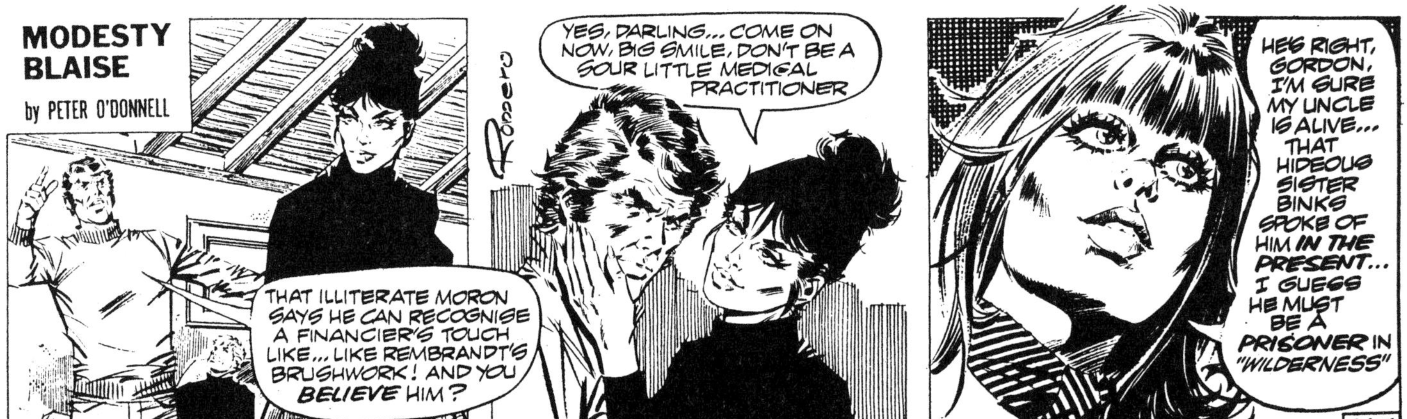
MODESTY BLAISE
by PETER O'DONNELL
THAT ILLITERATE MORON SAYS HE CAN RECOGNISE A FINANCIER'S TOUCH LIKE... LIKE REMBRANDT'S BRUSHWORK! AND YOU BELIEVE HIM?
Romero
YES, DARLING... COME ON NOW, BIG SMILE, DON'T BE A SOUR LITTLE MEDICAL PRACTITIONER
HE'S RIGHT, GORDON, I'M SURE MY UNCLE IS ALIVE... THAT HIDEOUS SISTER BINKS SPOKE OF HIM IN THE PRESENT... I GUESS HE MUST BE A PRISONER IN "WILDERNESS"
3476

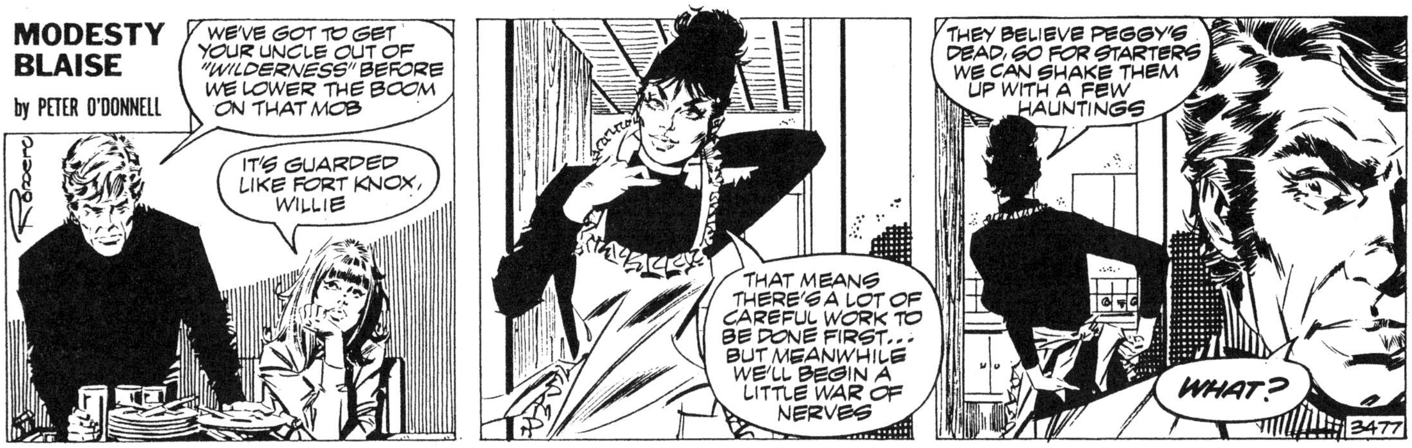
MODESTY BLAISE
by PETER O'DONNELL
WE'VE GOT TO GET YOUR UNCLE OUT OF "WILDERNESS" BEFORE WE LOWER THE BOOM ON THAT MOB
IT'S GUARDED LIKE FORT KNOX, WILLIE
THAT MEANS THERE'S A LOT OF CAREFUL WORK TO BE DONE FIRST... BUT MEANWHILE WE'LL BEGIN A LITTLE WAR OF NERVES
THEY BELIEVE PEGGY'S DEAD, SO FOR STARTERS WE CAN SHAKE THEM UP WITH A FEW HAUNTINGS
WHAT?
3477

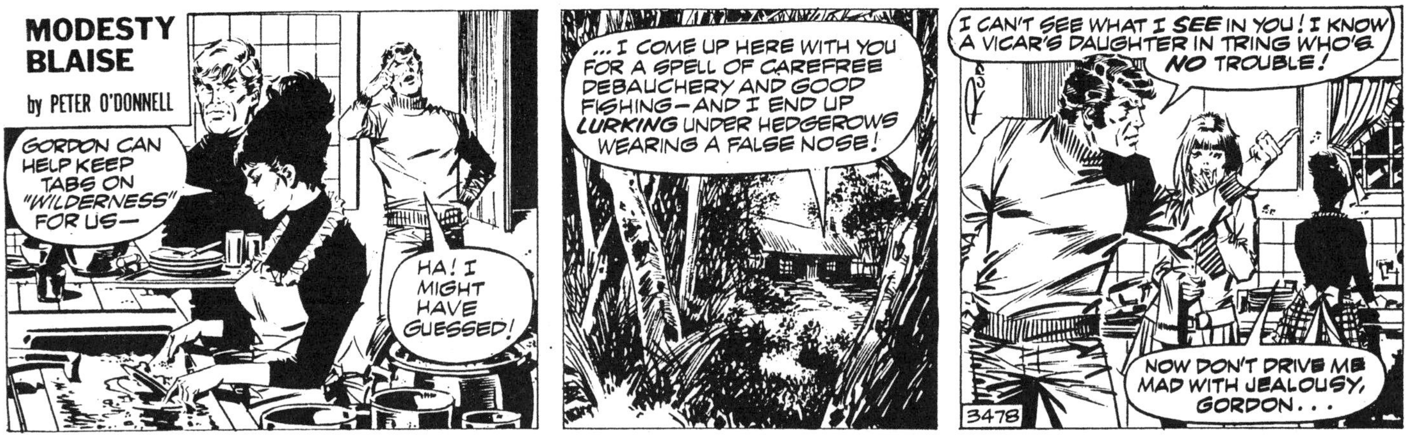
MODESTY BLAISE
by PETER O'DONNELL
GORDON CAN HELP KEEP TABS ON "WILDERNESS" FOR US—
HA! I MIGHT HAVE GUESSED!
...I COME UP HERE WITH YOU FOR A SPELL OF CAREFREE DEBAUCHERY AND GOOD FISHING—AND I END UP LURKING UNDER HEDGEROWS WEARING A FALSE NOSE!
I CAN'T SEE WHAT I SEE IN YOU! I KNOW A VICAR'S DAUGHTER IN TRING WHO'S NO TROUBLE!
NOW DON'T DRIVE ME MAD WITH JEALOUSY, GORDON...
3478

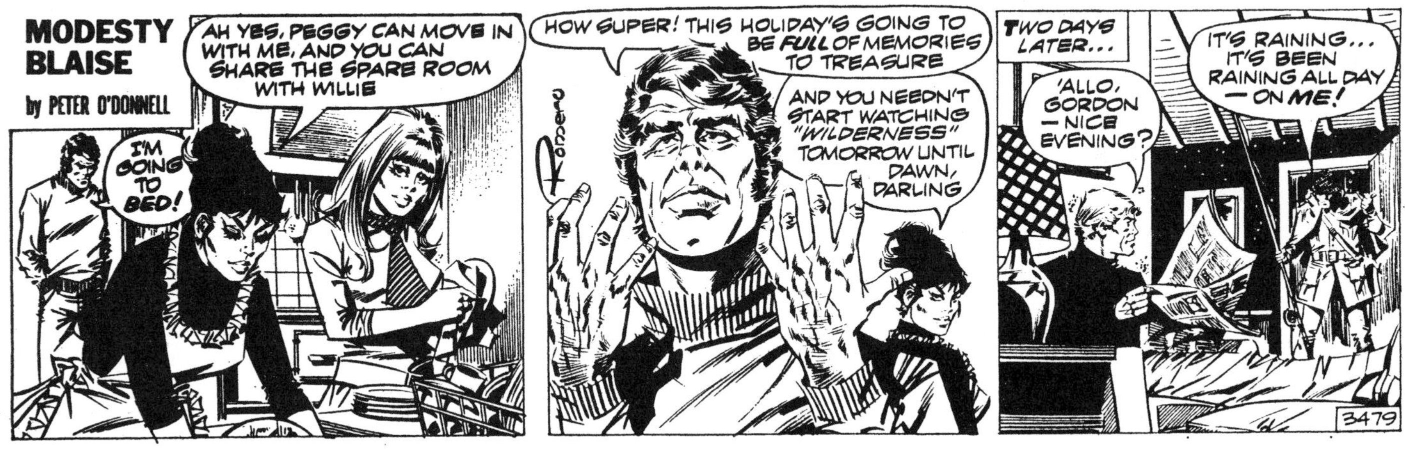
MODESTY BLAISE
by PETER O'DONNELL
AH YES, PEGGY CAN MOVE IN WITH ME, AND YOU CAN SHARE THE SPARE ROOM WITH WILLIE
I'M GOING TO BED!
HOW SUPER! THIS HOLIDAY'S GOING TO BE FULL OF MEMORIES TO TREASURE
AND YOU NEEDN'T START WATCHING "WILDERNESS" TOMORROW UNTIL DAWN, DARLING
TWO DAYS LATER...
'ALLO, GORDON — NICE EVENING?
IT'S RAINING... IT'S BEEN RAINING ALL DAY — ON ME!
3479

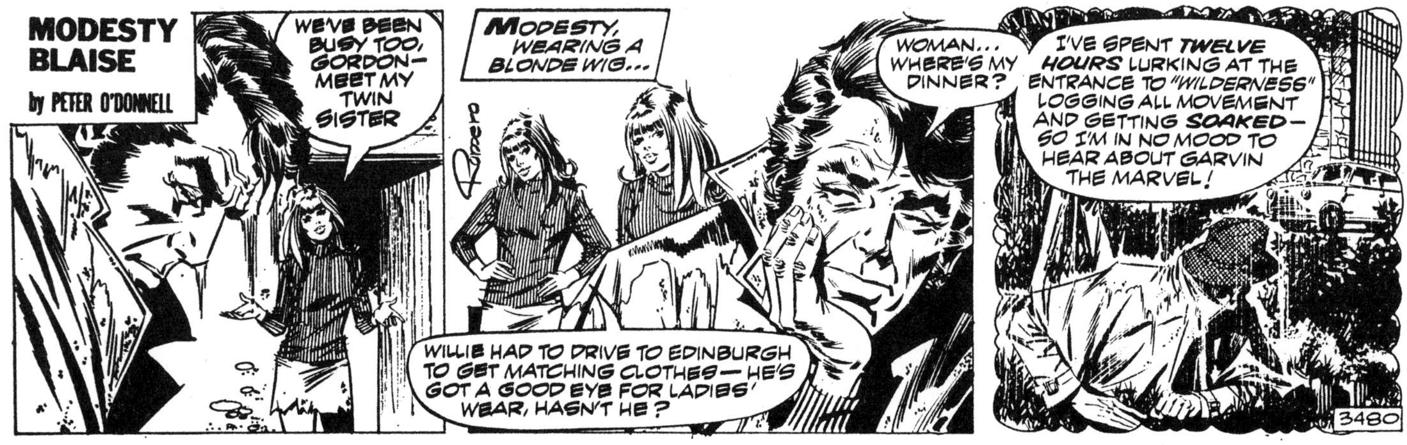
MODESTY BLAISE
by PETER O'DONNELL
WE'VE BEEN BUSY TOO, GORDON— MEET MY TWIN SISTER
MODESTY, WEARING A BLONDE WIG...
WILLIE HAD TO DRIVE TO EDINBURGH TO GET MATCHING CLOTHES—HE'S GOT A GOOD EYE FOR LADIES' WEAR, HASN'T HE?
WOMAN... WHERE'S MY DINNER?
I'VE SPENT TWELVE HOURS LURKING AT THE ENTRANCE TO "WILDERNESS" LOGGING ALL MOVEMENT AND GETTING SOAKED— SO I'M IN NO MOOD TO HEAR ABOUT GARVIN THE MARVEL!
3480

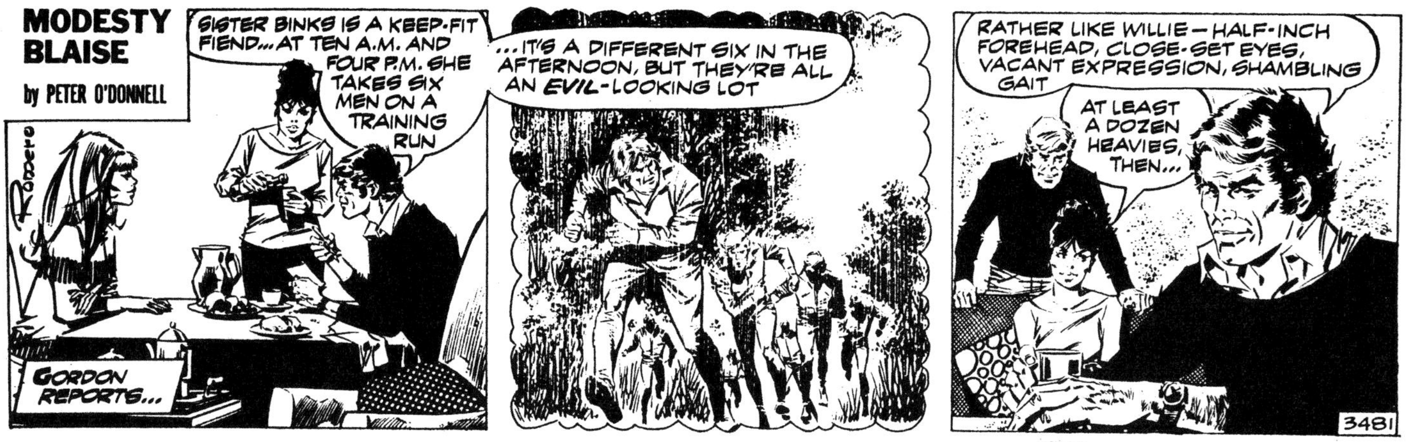
MODESTY BLAISE
by PETER O'DONNELL
GORDON REPORTS...
SISTER BINKS IS A KEEP-FIT FIEND... AT TEN A.M. AND FOUR P.M. SHE TAKES SIX MEN ON A TRAINING RUN
... IT'S A DIFFERENT SIX IN THE AFTERNOON, BUT THEY'RE ALL AN EVIL-LOOKING LOT
RATHER LIKE WILLIE — HALF-INCH FOREHEAD, CLOSE-SET EYES, VACANT EXPRESSION, SHAMBLING GAIT
AT LEAST A DOZEN HEAVIES, THEN...
3481

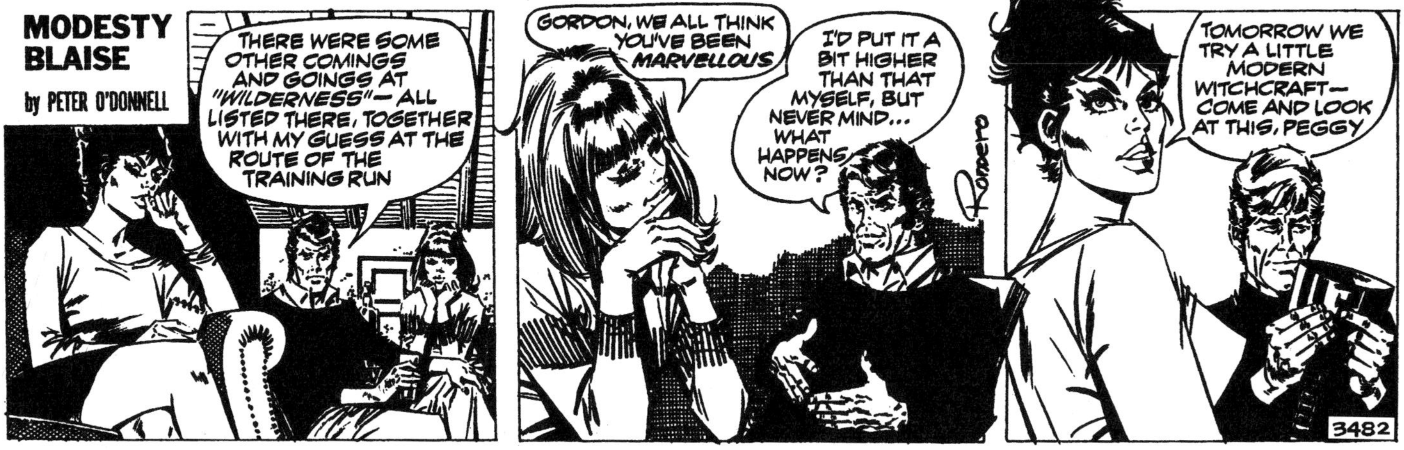
MODESTY BLAISE
by PETER O'DONNELL
THERE WERE SOME OTHER COMINGS AND GOINGS AT "WILDERNESS" — ALL LISTED THERE, TOGETHER WITH MY GUESS AT THE ROUTE OF THE TRAINING RUN
GORDON, WE ALL THINK YOU'VE BEEN MARVELLOUS
I'D PUT IT A BIT HIGHER THAN THAT MYSELF, BUT NEVER MIND... WHAT HAPPENS NOW?
TOMORROW WE TRY A LITTLE MODERN WITCHCRAFT — COME AND LOOK AT THIS, PEGGY
3482

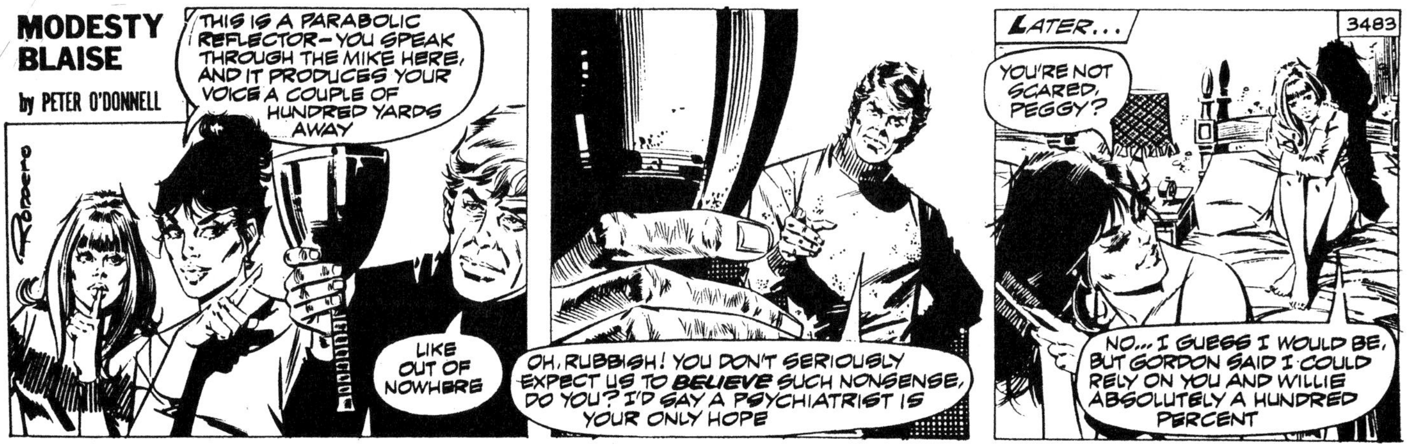
MODESTY BLAISE
by PETER O'DONNELL
THIS IS A PARABOLIC REFLECTOR — YOU SPEAK THROUGH THE MIKE HERE, AND IT PRODUCES YOUR VOICE A COUPLE OF HUNDRED YARDS AWAY
LIKE OUT OF NOWHERE
OH, RUBBISH! YOU DON'T SERIOUSLY EXPECT US TO BELIEVE SUCH NONSENSE, DO YOU? I'D SAY A PSYCHIATRIST IS YOUR ONLY HOPE
LATER...
3483
YOU'RE NOT SCARED, PEGGY?
NO... I GUESS I WOULD BE, BUT GORDON SAID I COULD RELY ON YOU AND WILLIE ABSOLUTELY A HUNDRED PERCENT

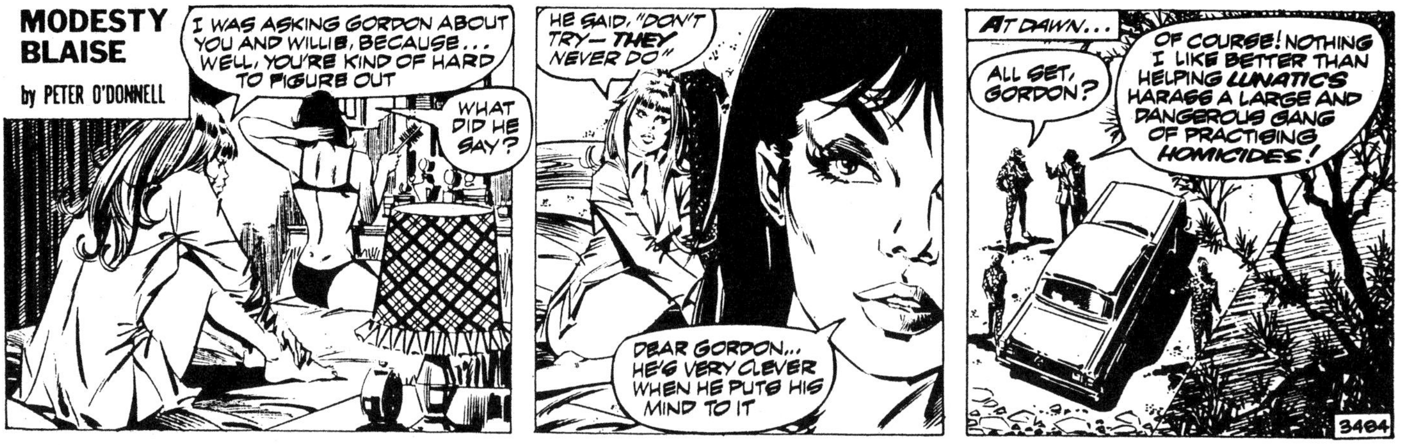
MODESTY BLAISE
by PETER O'DONNELL
I WAS ASKING GORDON ABOUT YOU AND WILLIE, BECAUSE... WELL, YOU'RE KIND OF HARD TO FIGURE OUT
WHAT DID HE SAY?
HE SAID, "DON'T TRY — THEY NEVER DO"
DEAR GORDON... HE'S VERY CLEVER WHEN HE PUTS HIS MIND TO IT
AT DAWN...
ALL SET, GORDON?
OF COURSE! NOTHING I LIKE BETTER THAN HELPING LUNATICS HARASS A LARGE AND DANGEROUS GANG OF PRACTISING HOMICIDES!
3484

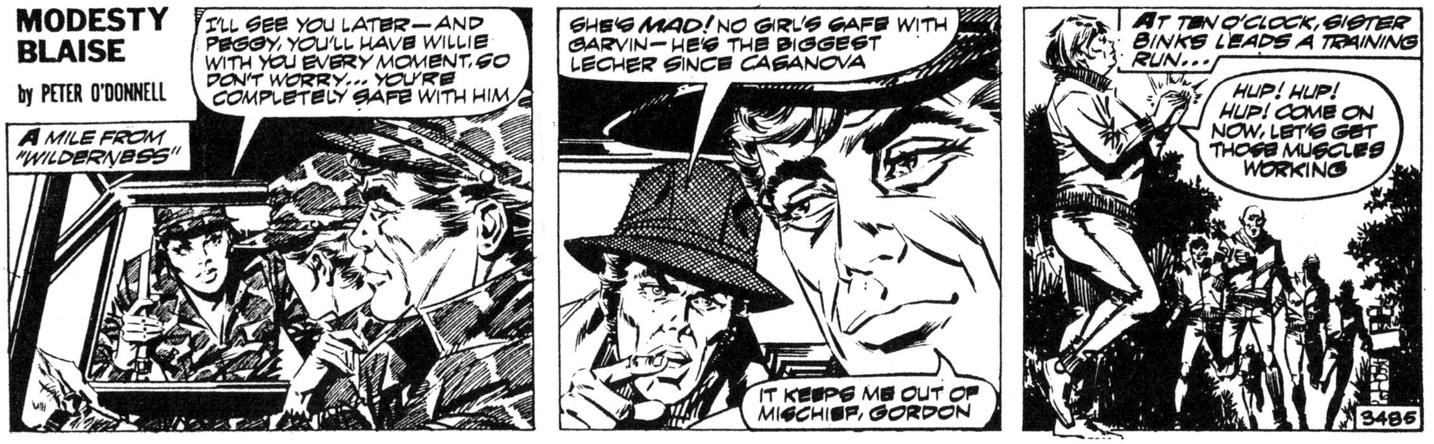
MODESTY BLAISE
by PETER O'DONNELL
A MILE FROM "WILDERNESS"
I'LL SEE YOU LATER—AND PEGGY, YOU'LL HAVE WILLIE WITH YOU EVERY MOMENT, SO DON'T WORRY... YOU'RE COMPLETELY SAFE WITH HIM
SHE'S MAD! NO GIRL'S SAFE WITH GARVIN—HE'S THE BIGGEST LECHER SINCE CASANOVA
IT KEEPS ME OUT OF MISCHIEF, GORDON
AT TEN O'CLOCK, SISTER BINKS LEADS A TRAINING RUN...
HUP! HUP! HUP! COME ON NOW, LET'S GET THOSE MUSCLES WORKING
3485

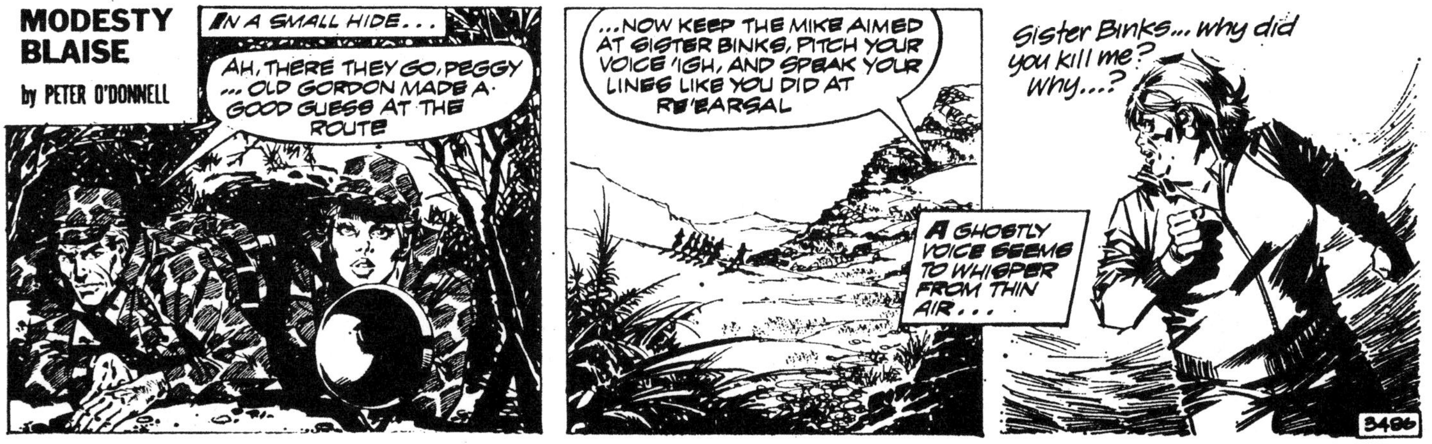
MODESTY BLAISE
by PETER O'DONNELL
IN A SMALL HIDE...
AH, THERE THEY GO, PEGGY ... OLD GORDON MADE A GOOD GUESS AT THE ROUTE
...NOW KEEP THE MIKE AIMED AT SISTER BINKS, PITCH YOUR VOICE 'IGH, AND SPEAK YOUR LINES LIKE YOU DID AT RE'EARSAL
A GHOSTLY VOICE SEEMS TO WHISPER FROM THIN AIR...
Sister Binks... why did you kill me? Why...?
3486

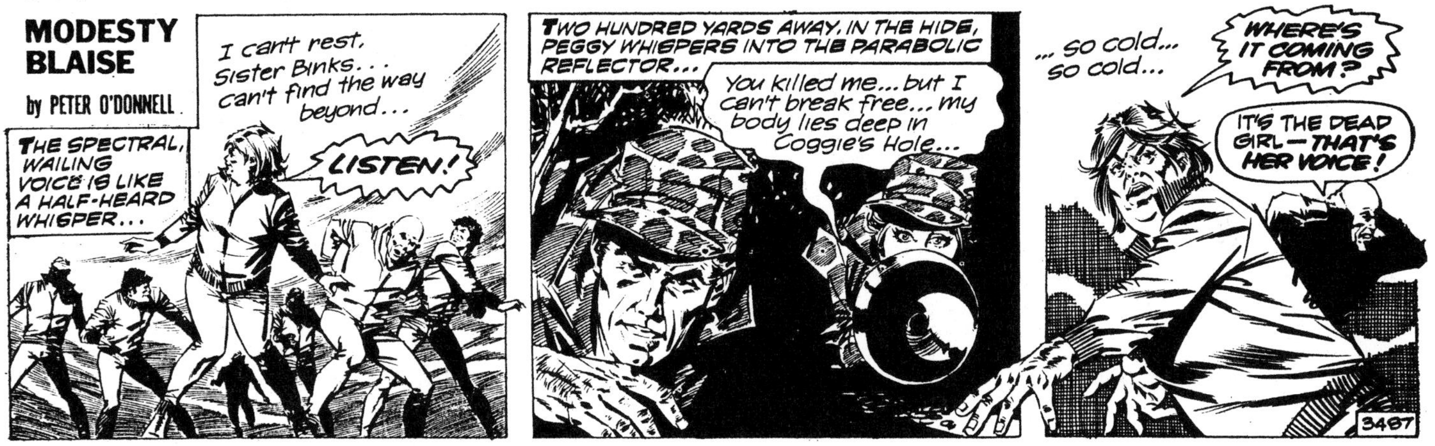
MODESTY BLAISE
by PETER O'DONNELL
I can't rest, Sister Binks... can't find the way beyond...
THE SPECTRAL, WAILING VOICE IS LIKE A HALF-HEARD WHISPER...
LISTEN!
TWO HUNDRED YARDS AWAY, IN THE HIDE, PEGGY WHISPERS INTO THE PARABOLIC REFLECTOR...
You killed me... but I can't break free... my body lies deep in Coggie's Hole...
... so cold... so cold...
WHERE'S IT COMING FROM?
IT'S THE DEAD GIRL—THAT'S HER VOICE!
3487

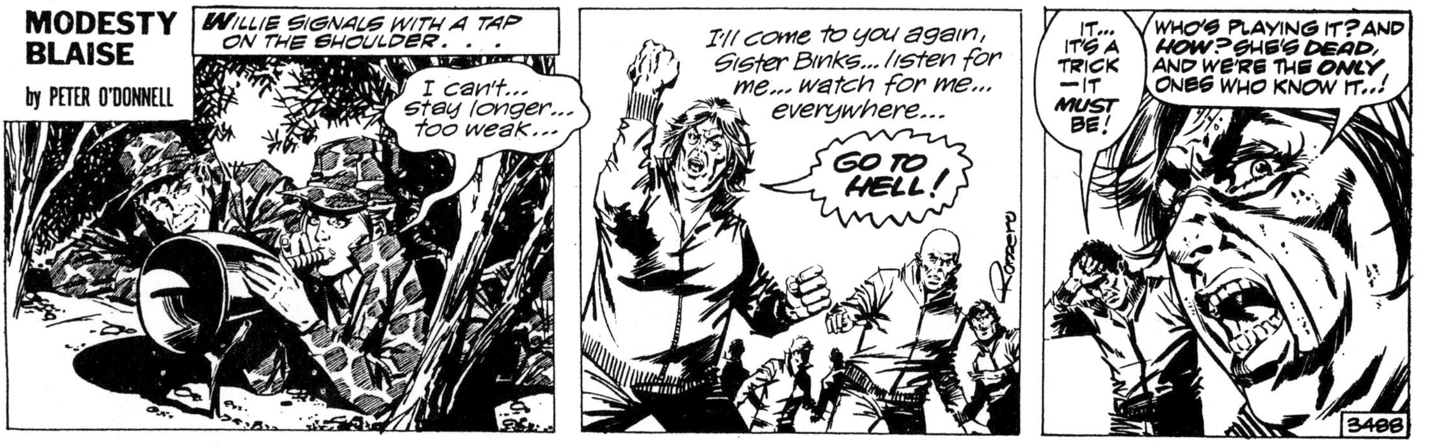
MODESTY BLAISE
by PETER O'DONNELL
WILLIE SIGNALS WITH A TAP ON THE SHOULDER...
I can't... stay longer... too weak...
I'll come to you again, Sister Binks... listen for me... watch for me... everywhere...
GO TO HELL!
IT... IT'S A TRICK —IT MUST BE!
WHO'S PLAYING IT? AND HOW? SHE'S DEAD, AND WE'RE THE ONLY ONES WHO KNOW IT...!
3488

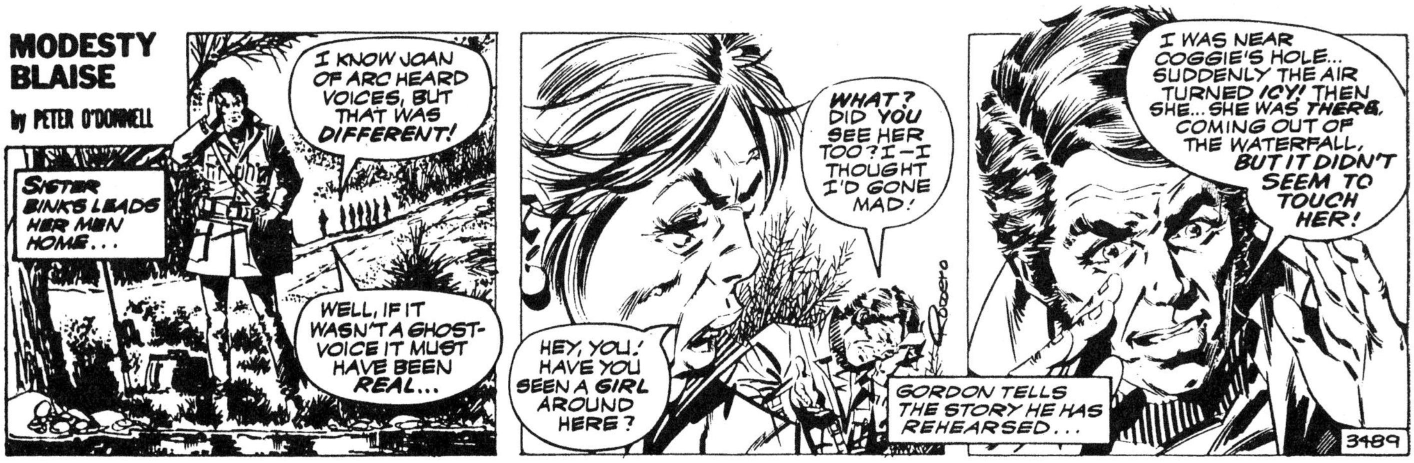
MODESTY BLAISE
by PETER O'DONNELL
SISTER BINKS LEADS HER MEN HOME...
I KNOW JOAN OF ARC HEARD VOICES, BUT THAT WAS DIFFERENT!
WELL, IF IT WASN'T A GHOST-VOICE IT MUST HAVE BEEN REAL...
HEY, YOU! HAVE YOU SEEN A GIRL AROUND HERE?
WHAT? DID YOU SEE HER TOO? I–I THOUGHT I'D GONE MAD!
GORDON TELLS THE STORY HE HAS REHEARSED...
I WAS NEAR COGGIE'S HOLE... SUDDENLY THE AIR TURNED ICY! THEN SHE... SHE WAS THERE, COMING OUT OF THE WATERFALL, BUT IT DIDN'T SEEM TO TOUCH HER!
3489

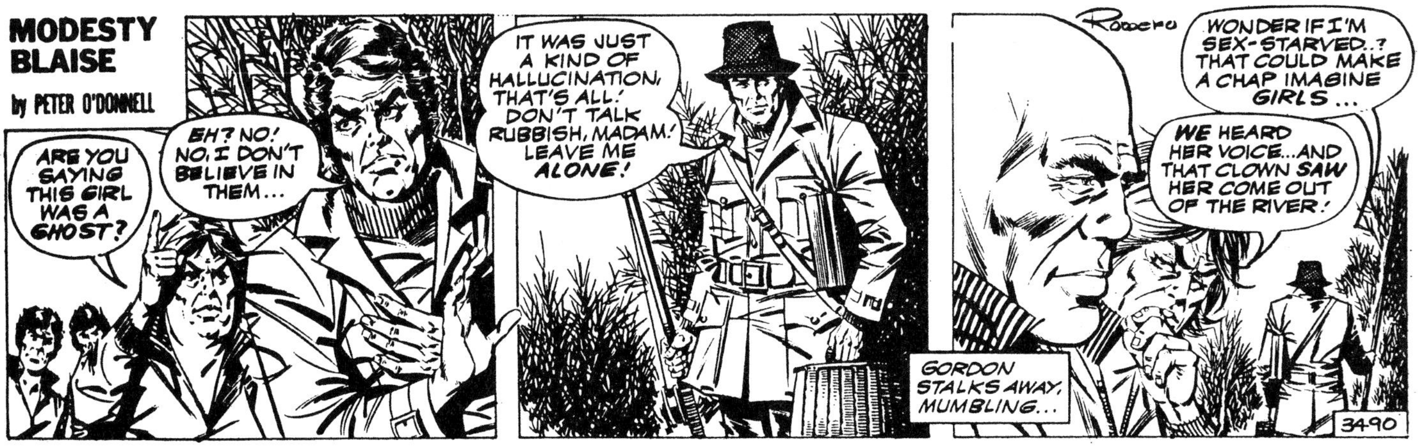
MODESTY BLAISE
by PETER O'DONNELL
ARE YOU SAYING THIS GIRL WAS A GHOST?
EH? NO! NO, I DON'T BELIEVE IN THEM...
IT WAS JUST A KIND OF HALLUCINATION, THAT'S ALL! DON'T TALK RUBBISH, MADAM! LEAVE ME ALONE!
GORDON STALKS AWAY, MUMBLING...
WONDER IF I'M SEX-STARVED..? THAT COULD MAKE A CHAP IMAGINE GIRLS...
WE HEARD HER VOICE... AND THAT CLOWN SAW HER COME OUT OF THE RIVER!
3490

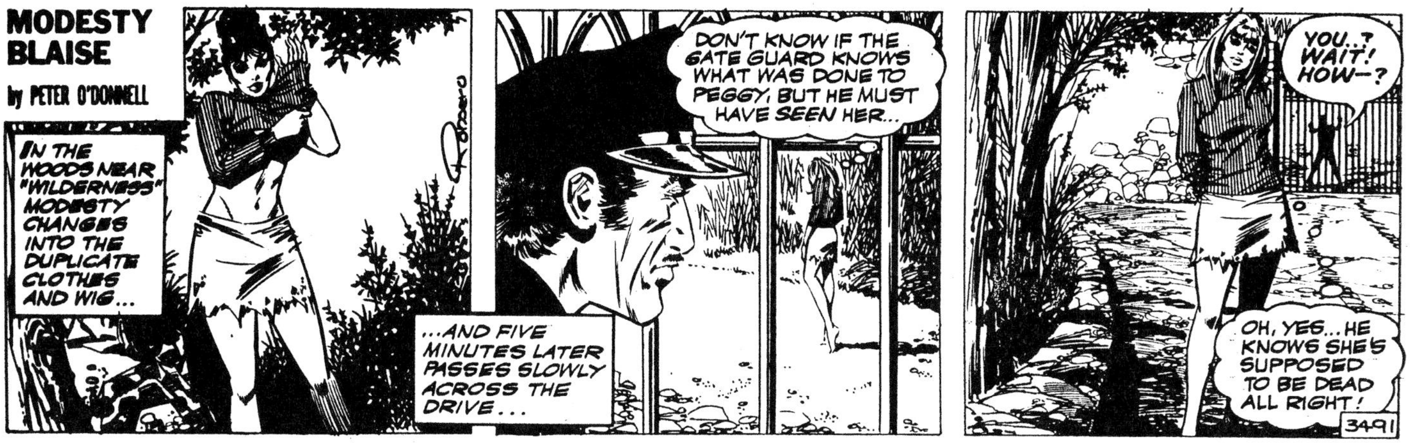
MODESTY BLAISE
by PETER O'DONNELL
IN THE WOODS NEAR "WILDERNESS" MODESTY CHANGES INTO THE DUPLICATE CLOTHES AND WIG...
...AND FIVE MINUTES LATER PASSES SLOWLY ACROSS THE DRIVE...
DON'T KNOW IF THE GATE GUARD KNOWS WHAT WAS DONE TO PEGGY, BUT HE MUST HAVE SEEN HER...
YOU..? WAIT! HOW–?
OH, YES... HE KNOWS SHE'S SUPPOSED TO BE DEAD ALL RIGHT!
3491

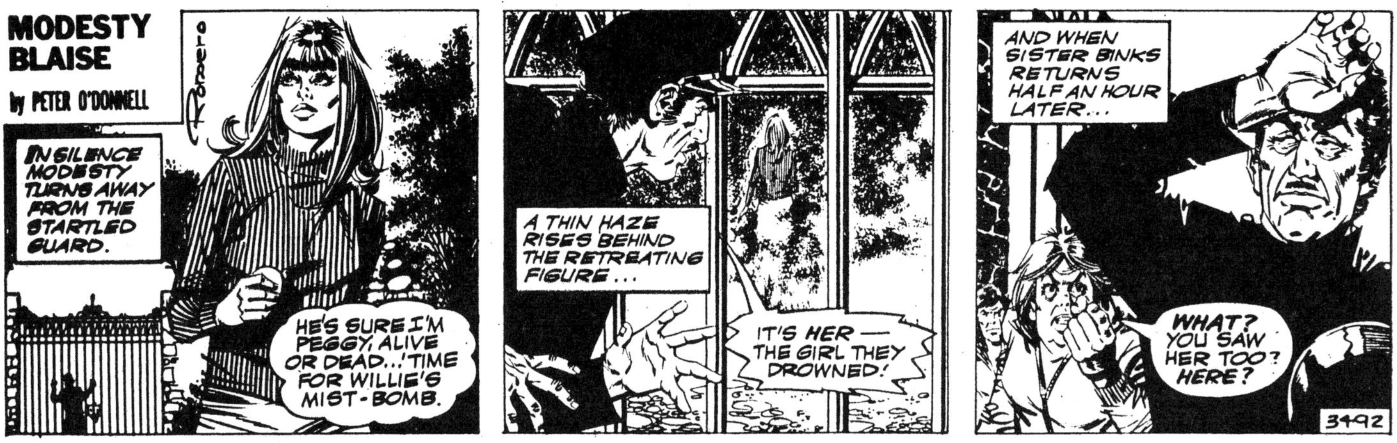
MODESTY BLAISE
by PETER O'DONNELL
IN SILENCE MODESTY TURNS AWAY FROM THE STARTLED GUARD.
HE'S SURE I'M PEGGY, ALIVE OR DEAD...TIME FOR WILLIE'S MIST-BOMB.
A THIN HAZE RISES BEHIND THE RETREATING FIGURE...
IT'S HER — THE GIRL THEY DROWNED!
AND WHEN SISTER BINKS RETURNS HALF AN HOUR LATER...
WHAT? YOU SAW HER TOO? HERE?
3492

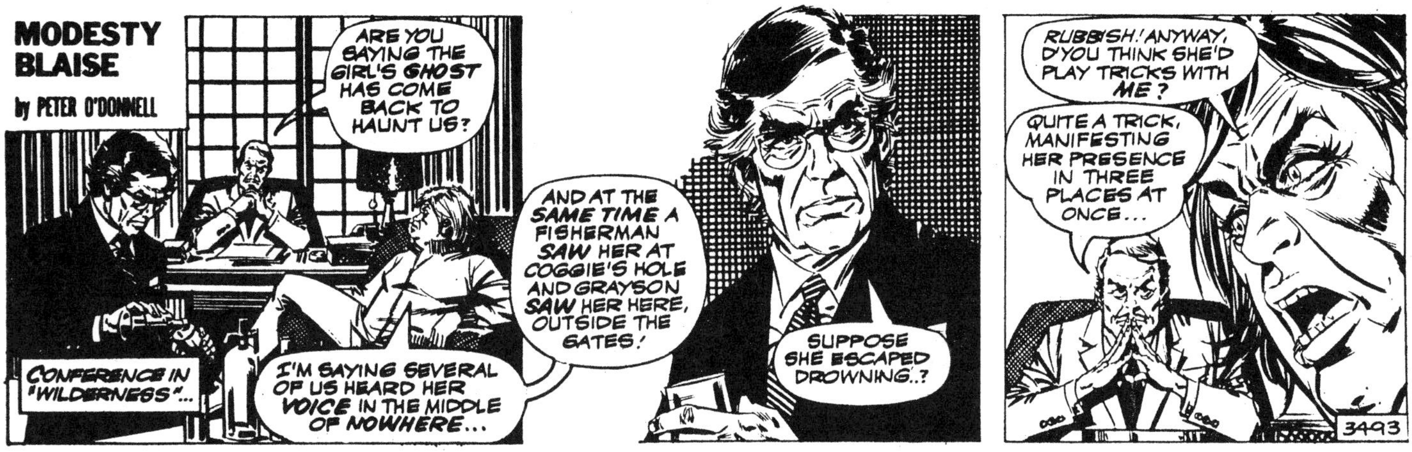
MODESTY BLAISE
by PETER O'DONNELL
CONFERENCE IN "WILDERNESS"...
ARE YOU SAYING THE GIRL'S GHOST HAS COME BACK TO HAUNT US?
I'M SAYING SEVERAL OF US HEARD HER VOICE IN THE MIDDLE OF NOWHERE...
AND AT THE SAME TIME A FISHERMAN SAW HER AT COGGIE'S HOLE AND GRAYSON SAW HER HERE, OUTSIDE THE GATES!
SUPPOSE SHE ESCAPED DROWNING..?
RUBBISH! ANYWAY, D'YOU THINK SHE'D PLAY TRICKS WITH ME?
QUITE A TRICK, MANIFESTING HER PRESENCE IN THREE PLACES AT ONCE...
3493

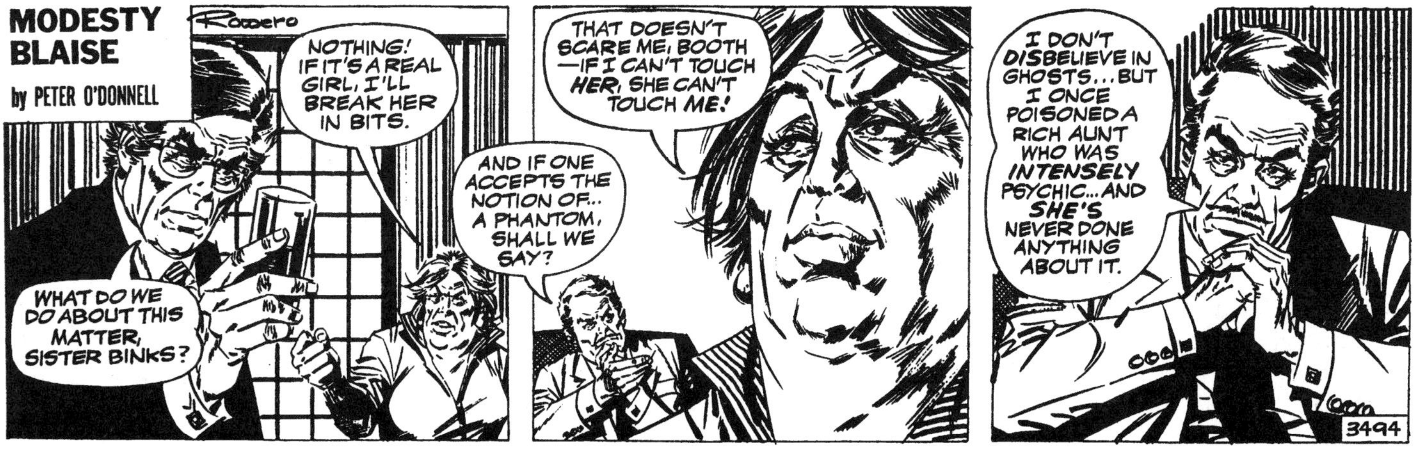
MODESTY BLAISE
by PETER O'DONNELL
Romero
WHAT DO WE DO ABOUT THIS MATTER, SISTER BINKS?
NOTHING! IF IT'S A REAL GIRL, I'LL BREAK HER IN BITS.
AND IF ONE ACCEPTS THE NOTION OF... A PHANTOM, SHALL WE SAY?
THAT DOESN'T SCARE ME, BOOTH —IF I CAN'T TOUCH HER, SHE CAN'T TOUCH ME!
I DON'T DISBELIEVE IN GHOSTS... BUT I ONCE POISONED A RICH AUNT WHO WAS INTENSELY PSYCHIC...AND SHE'S NEVER DONE ANYTHING ABOUT IT.
3494

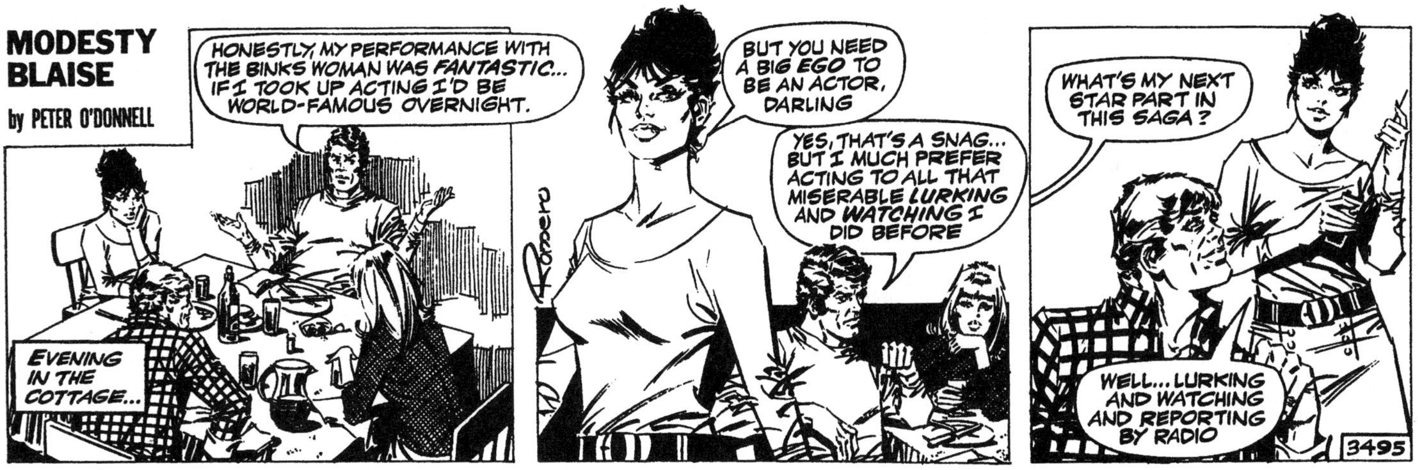
MODESTY BLAISE
by PETER O'DONNELL
EVENING IN THE COTTAGE...
HONESTLY, MY PERFORMANCE WITH THE BINKS WOMAN WAS FANTASTIC... IF I TOOK UP ACTING I'D BE WORLD-FAMOUS OVERNIGHT.
Romero
BUT YOU NEED A BIG EGO TO BE AN ACTOR, DARLING
YES, THAT'S A SNAG... BUT I MUCH PREFER ACTING TO ALL THAT MISERABLE LURKING AND WATCHING I DID BEFORE
WHAT'S MY NEXT STAR PART IN THIS SAGA?
WELL... LURKING AND WATCHING AND REPORTING BY RADIO
3495

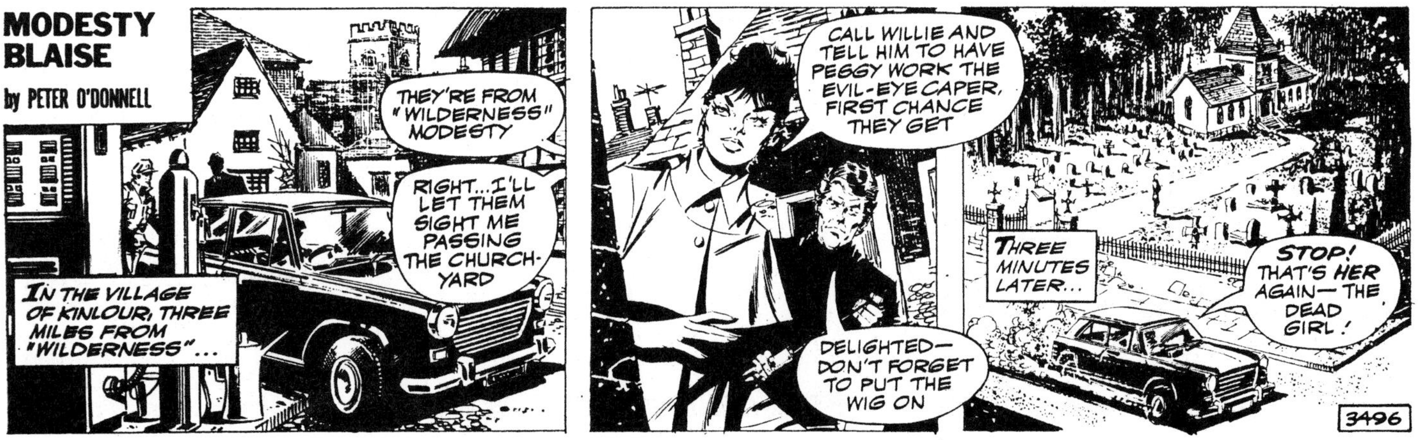
MODESTY BLAISE
by PETER O'DONNELL
IN THE VILLAGE OF KINLOUR, THREE MILES FROM "WILDERNESS"...
THEY'RE FROM "WILDERNESS" MODESTY
RIGHT...I'LL LET THEM SIGHT ME PASSING THE CHURCH-YARD
CALL WILLIE AND TELL HIM TO HAVE PEGGY WORK THE EVIL-EYE CAPER, FIRST CHANCE THEY GET
DELIGHTED— DON'T FORGET TO PUT THE WIG ON
THREE MINUTES LATER...
STOP! THAT'S HER AGAIN— THE DEAD GIRL!
3496

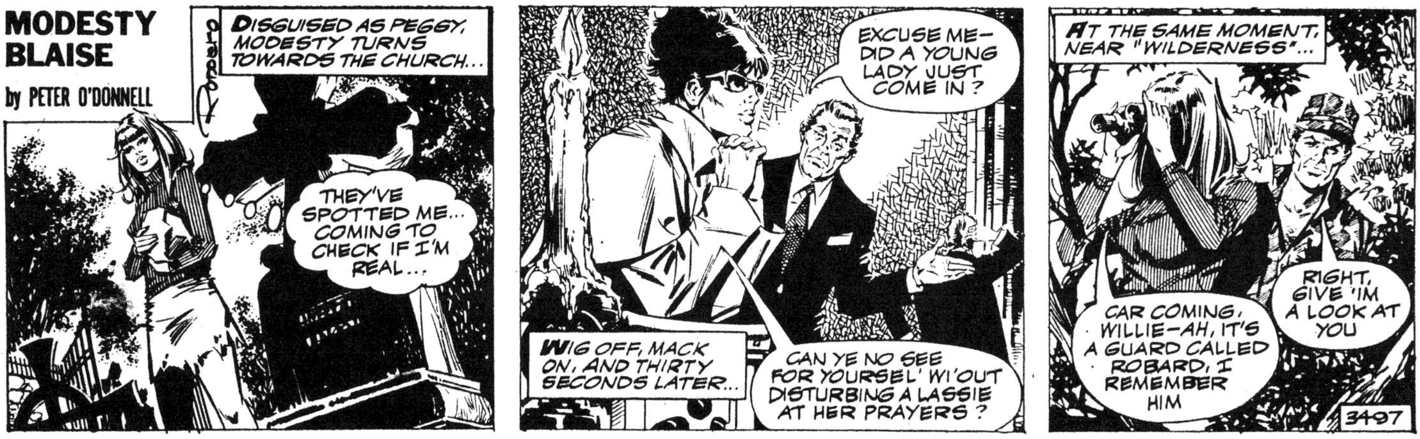
MODESTY BLAISE
by PETER O'DONNELL
DISGUISED AS PEGGY, MODESTY TURNS TOWARDS THE CHURCH...
THEY'VE SPOTTED ME... COMING TO CHECK IF I'M REAL...
WIG OFF, MACK ON, AND THIRTY SECONDS LATER...
EXCUSE ME- DID A YOUNG LADY JUST COME IN?
CAN YE NO SEE FOR YOURSEL' WI'OUT DISTURBING A LASSIE AT HER PRAYERS?
AT THE SAME MOMENT, NEAR "WILDERNESS"...
CAR COMING, WILLIE—AH, IT'S A GUARD CALLED ROBARD, I REMEMBER HIM
RIGHT, GIVE 'IM A LOOK AT YOU
3497

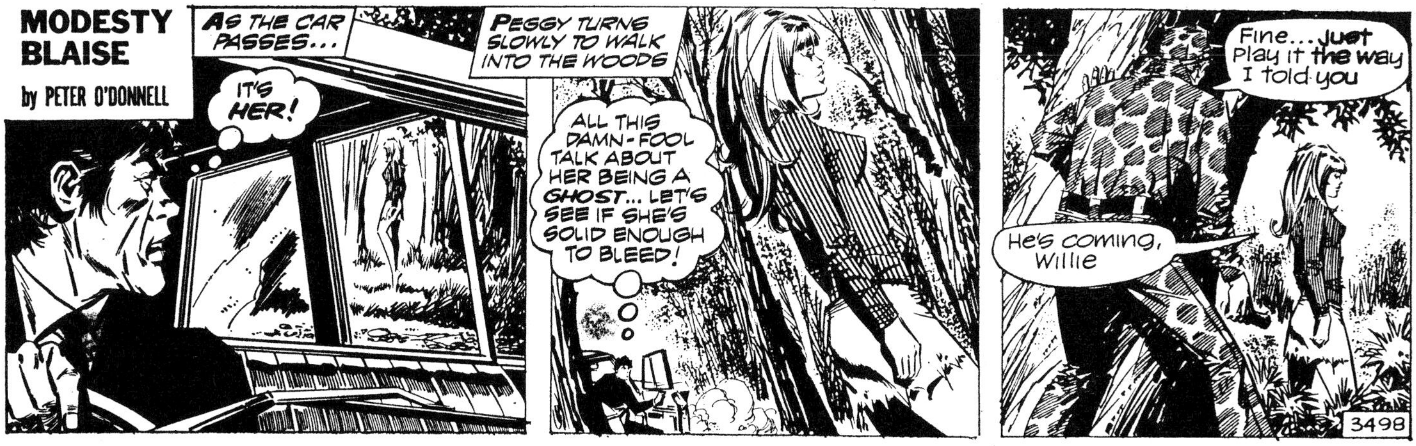
MODESTY BLAISE
by PETER O'DONNELL
AS THE CAR PASSES...
IT'S HER!
PEGGY TURNS SLOWLY TO WALK INTO THE WOODS
ALL THIS DAMN-FOOL TALK ABOUT HER BEING A GHOST... LET'S SEE IF SHE'S SOLID ENOUGH TO BLEED!
Fine... just play it the way I told you
He's coming, Willie
3498

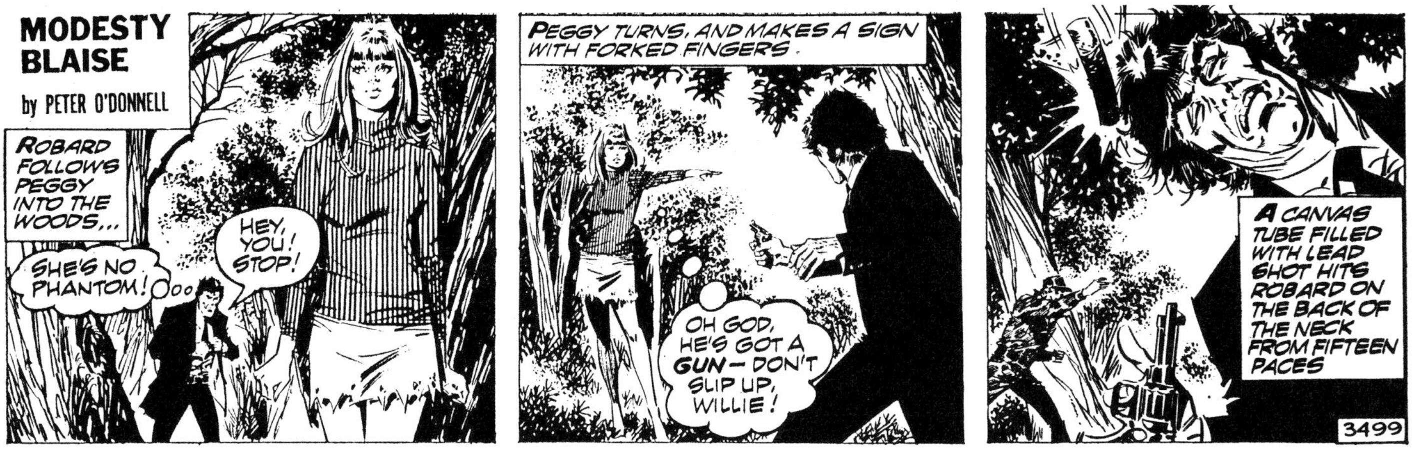
MODESTY BLAISE
by PETER O'DONNELL
ROBARD FOLLOWS PEGGY INTO THE WOODS...
SHE'S NO PHANTOM!
HEY, YOU! STOP!
PEGGY TURNS, AND MAKES A SIGN WITH FORKED FINGERS.
OH GOD, HE'S GOT A GUN— DON'T SLIP UP, WILLIE!
A CANVAS TUBE FILLED WITH LEAD SHOT HITS ROBARD ON THE BACK OF THE NECK FROM FIFTEEN PACES
3499

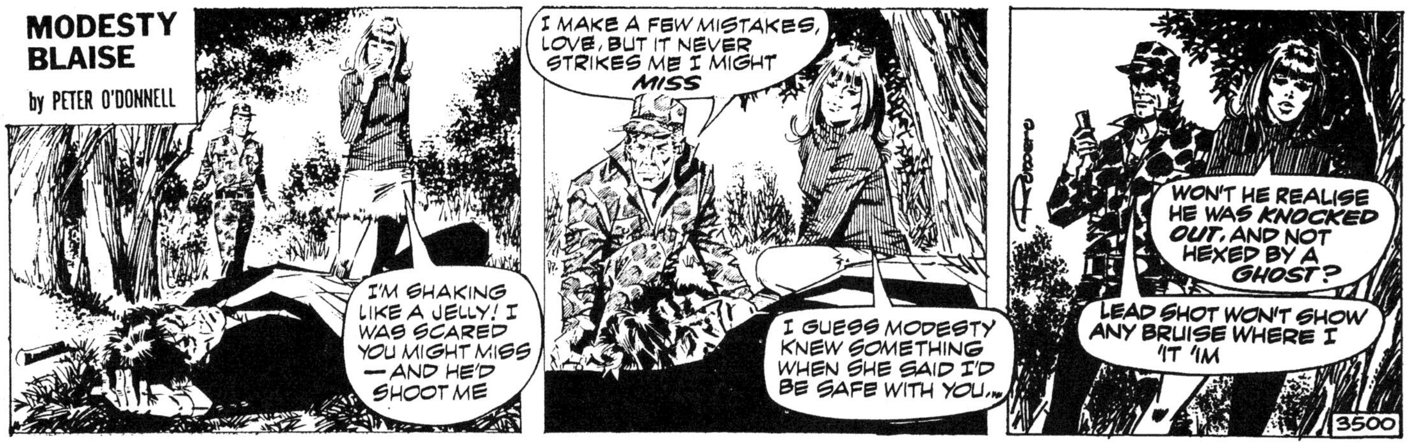
MODESTY BLAISE
by PETER O'DONNELL
I'M SHAKING LIKE A JELLY! I WAS SCARED YOU MIGHT MISS —AND HE'D SHOOT ME
I MAKE A FEW MISTAKES, LOVE, BUT IT NEVER STRIKES ME I MIGHT MISS
I GUESS MODESTY KNEW SOMETHING WHEN SHE SAID I'D BE SAFE WITH YOU...
WON'T HE REALISE HE WAS KNOCKED OUT, AND NOT HEXED BY A GHOST?
LEAD SHOT WON'T SHOW ANY BRUISE WHERE I 'IT 'IM
3500

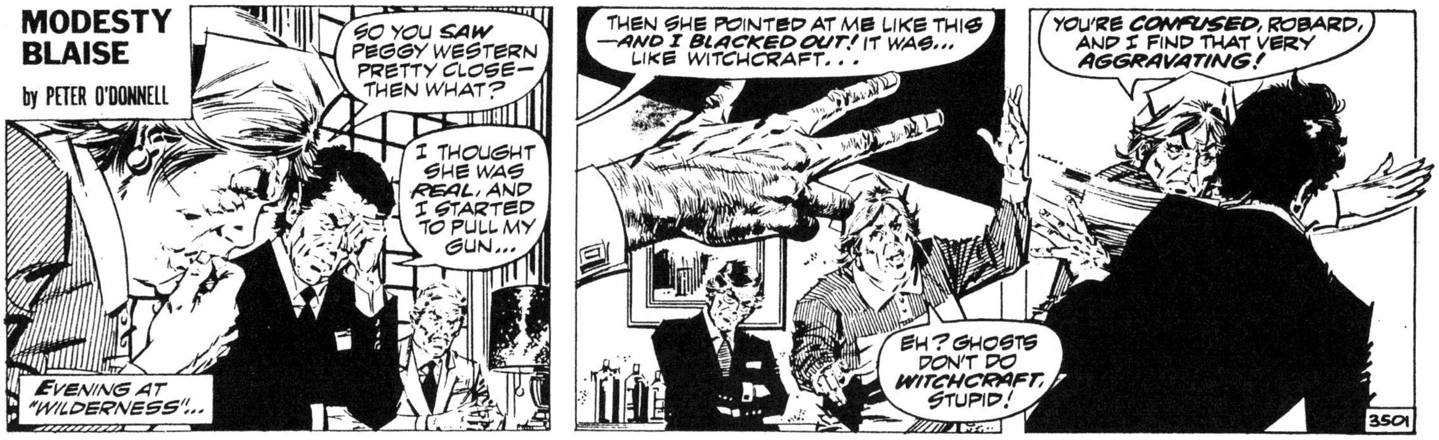
MODESTY BLAISE
by PETER O'DONNELL
EVENING AT "WILDERNESS"...
SO YOU SAW PEGGY WESTERN PRETTY CLOSE—THEN WHAT?
I THOUGHT SHE WAS REAL, AND I STARTED TO PULL MY GUN...
THEN SHE POINTED AT ME LIKE THIS —AND I BLACKED OUT! IT WAS... LIKE WITCHCRAFT...
YOU'RE CONFUSED, ROBARD, AND I FIND THAT VERY AGGRAVATING!
EH? GHOSTS DON'T DO WITCHCRAFT, STUPID!
3501

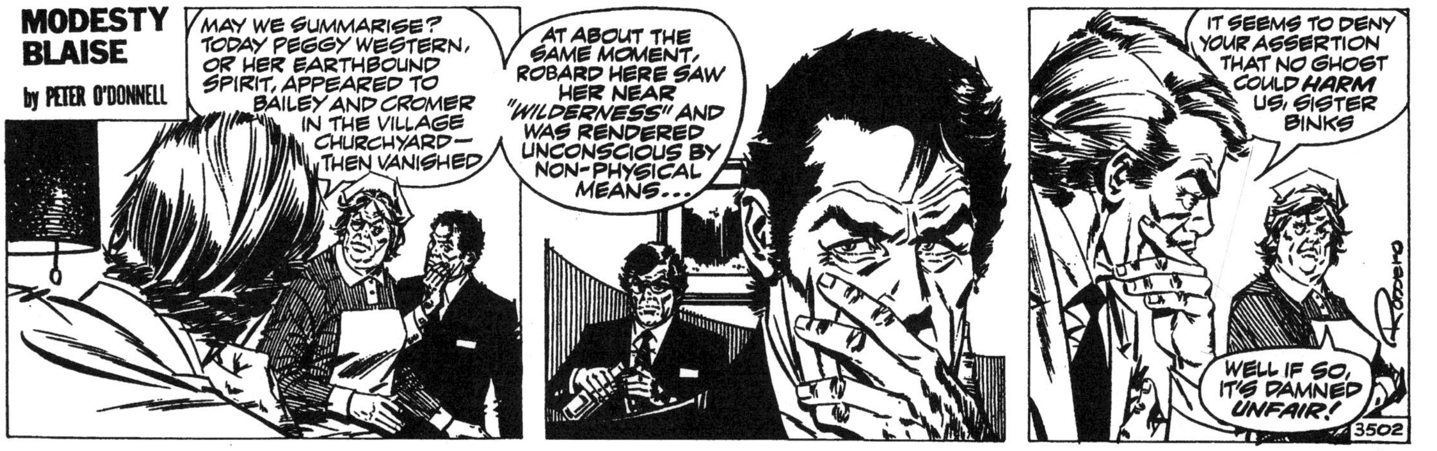
MODESTY BLAISE
by PETER O'DONNELL
MAY WE SUMMARISE? TODAY PEGGY WESTERN, OR HER EARTHBOUND SPIRIT, APPEARED TO BAILEY AND CROMER IN THE VILLAGE CHURCHYARD—THEN VANISHED
AT ABOUT THE SAME MOMENT, ROBARD HERE SAW HER NEAR "WILDERNESS" AND WAS RENDERED UNCONSCIOUS BY NON-PHYSICAL MEANS...
IT SEEMS TO DENY YOUR ASSERTION THAT NO GHOST COULD HARM US, SISTER BINKS
WELL IF SO, IT'S DAMNED UNFAIR!
3502

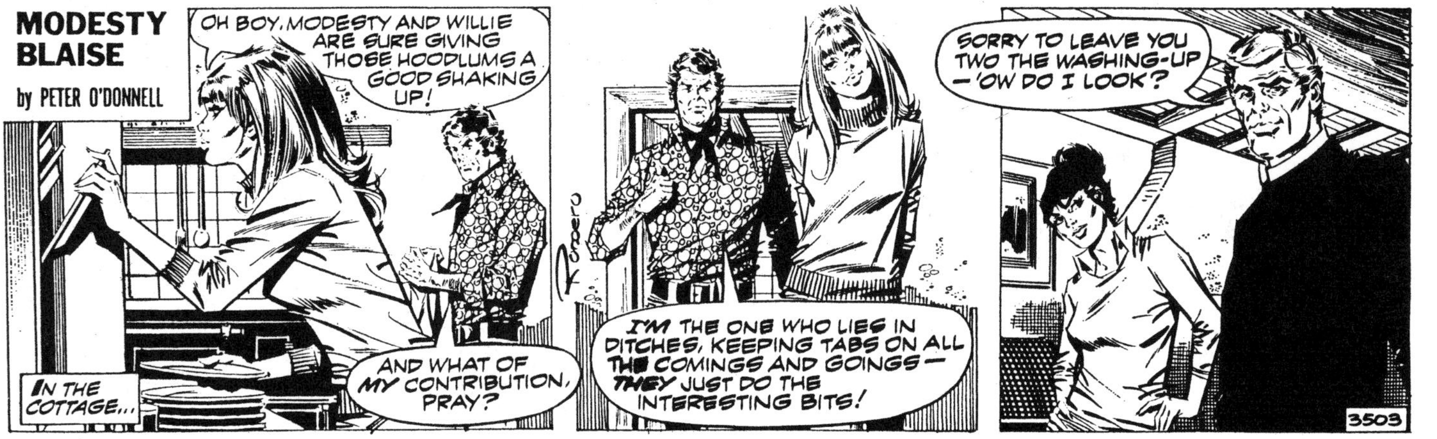
MODESTY BLAISE
by PETER O'DONNELL
IN THE COTTAGE...
OH BOY, MODESTY AND WILLIE ARE SURE GIVING THOSE HOODLUMS A GOOD SHAKING UP!
AND WHAT OF MY CONTRIBUTION, PRAY?
I'M THE ONE WHO LIES IN DITCHES, KEEPING TABS ON ALL THE COMINGS AND GOINGS—THEY JUST DO THE INTERESTING BITS!
SORRY TO LEAVE YOU TWO THE WASHING-UP —'OW DO I LOOK?
3503

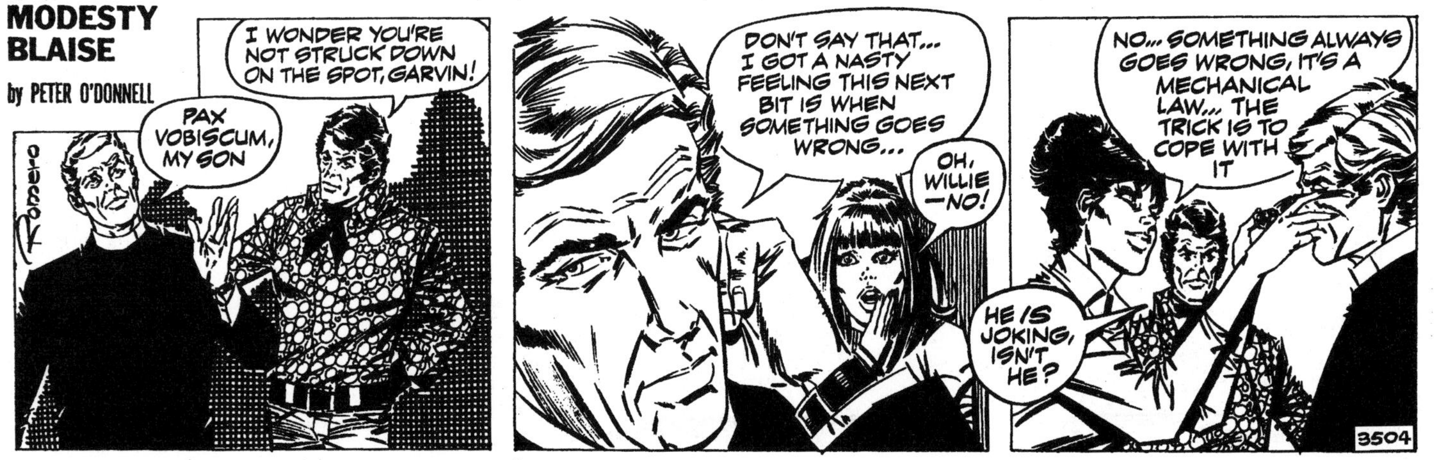
MODESTY BLAISE
by PETER O'DONNELL
I WONDER YOU'RE NOT STRUCK DOWN ON THE SPOT, GARVIN!
PAX VOBISCUM, MY SON
DON'T SAY THAT... I GOT A NASTY FEELING THIS NEXT BIT IS WHEN SOMETHING GOES WRONG...
OH, WILLIE —NO!
NO... SOMETHING ALWAYS GOES WRONG, IT'S A MECHANICAL LAW... THE TRICK IS TO COPE WITH IT
HE IS JOKING, ISN'T HE?
3504

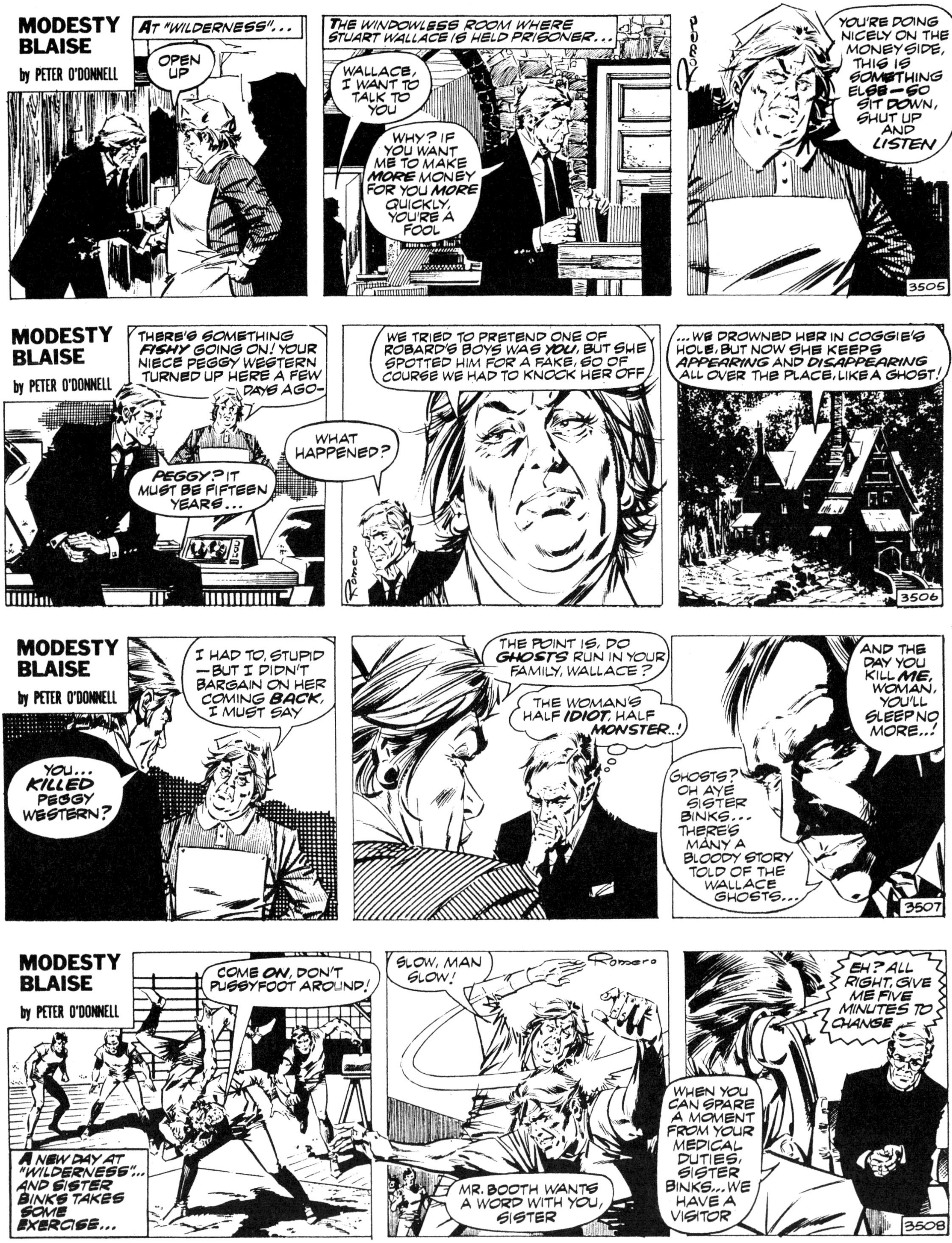
MODESTY BLAISE
by PETER O'DONNELL
AT "WILDERNESS"...
OPEN UP
THE WINDOWLESS ROOM WHERE STUART WALLACE IS HELD PRISONER...
WALLACE, I WANT TO TALK TO YOU
WHY? IF YOU WANT ME TO MAKE MORE MONEY FOR YOU MORE QUICKLY, YOU'RE A FOOL
YOU'RE DOING NICELY ON THE MONEY SIDE, THIS IS SOMETHING ELSE — SO SIT DOWN, SHUT UP AND LISTEN
3505
MODESTY BLAISE
by PETER O'DONNELL
THERE'S SOMETHING FISHY GOING ON! YOUR NIECE PEGGY WESTERN TURNED UP HERE A FEW DAYS AGO—
PEGGY? IT MUST BE FIFTEEN YEARS...
WE TRIED TO PRETEND ONE OF ROBARD'S BOYS WAS YOU, BUT SHE SPOTTED HIM FOR A FAKE, SO OF COURSE WE HAD TO KNOCK HER OFF
WHAT HAPPENED?
...WE DROWNED HER IN COGGIE'S HOLE, BUT NOW SHE KEEPS APPEARING AND DISAPPEARING ALL OVER THE PLACE, LIKE A GHOST!
3506
MODESTY BLAISE
by PETER O'DONNELL
YOU... KILLED PEGGY WESTERN?
I HAD TO, STUPID — BUT I DIDN'T BARGAIN ON HER COMING BACK, I MUST SAY
THE POINT IS, DO GHOSTS RUN IN YOUR FAMILY, WALLACE?
THE WOMAN'S HALF IDIOT, HALF MONSTER..!
GHOSTS? OH AYE SISTER BINKS... THERE'S MANY A BLOODY STORY TOLD OF THE WALLACE GHOSTS...
AND THE DAY YOU KILL ME, WOMAN, YOU'LL SLEEP NO MORE..!
3507
MODESTY BLAISE
by PETER O'DONNELL
COME ON, DON'T PUSSYFOOT AROUND!
A NEW DAY AT "WILDERNESS"... AND SISTER BINKS TAKES SOME EXERCISE...
SLOW, MAN SLOW!
Romero
MR. BOOTH WANTS A WORD WITH YOU, SISTER
EH? ALL RIGHT, GIVE ME FIVE MINUTES TO CHANGE
WHEN YOU CAN SPARE A MOMENT FROM YOUR MEDICAL DUTIES, SISTER BINKS... WE HAVE A VISITOR
3508

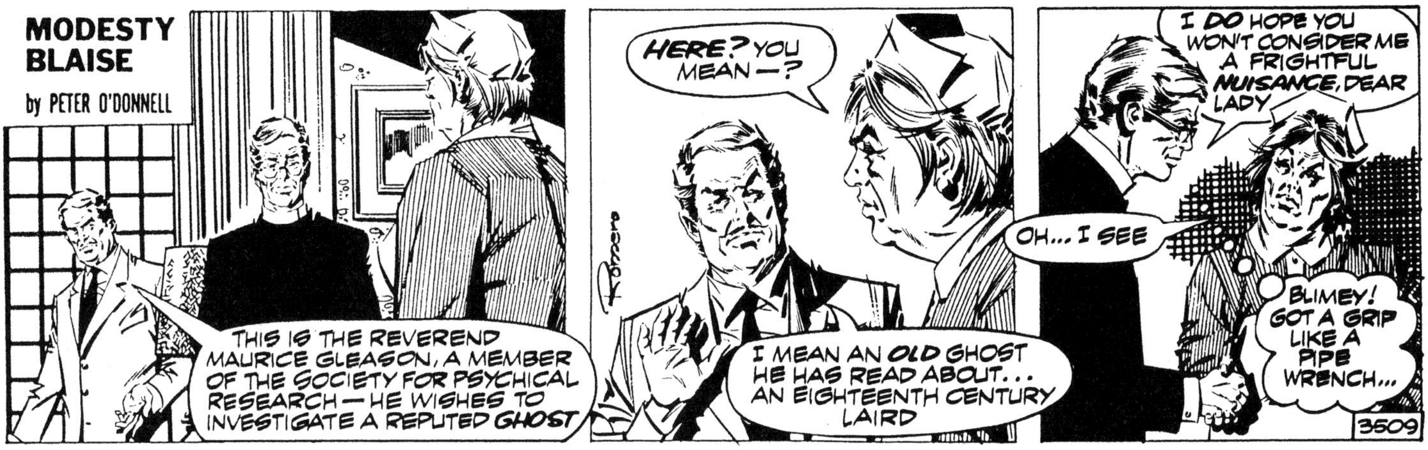
MODESTY BLAISE
by PETER O'DONNELL
THIS IS THE REVEREND MAURICE GLEASON, A MEMBER OF THE SOCIETY FOR PSYCHICAL RESEARCH — HE WISHES TO INVESTIGATE A REPUTED GHOST
HERE? YOU MEAN —?
I MEAN AN OLD GHOST HE HAS READ ABOUT... AN EIGHTEENTH CENTURY LAIRD
I DO HOPE YOU WON'T CONSIDER ME A FRIGHTFUL NUISANCE, DEAR LADY
OH... I SEE
BLIMEY! GOT A GRIP LIKE A PIPE WRENCH...
3509

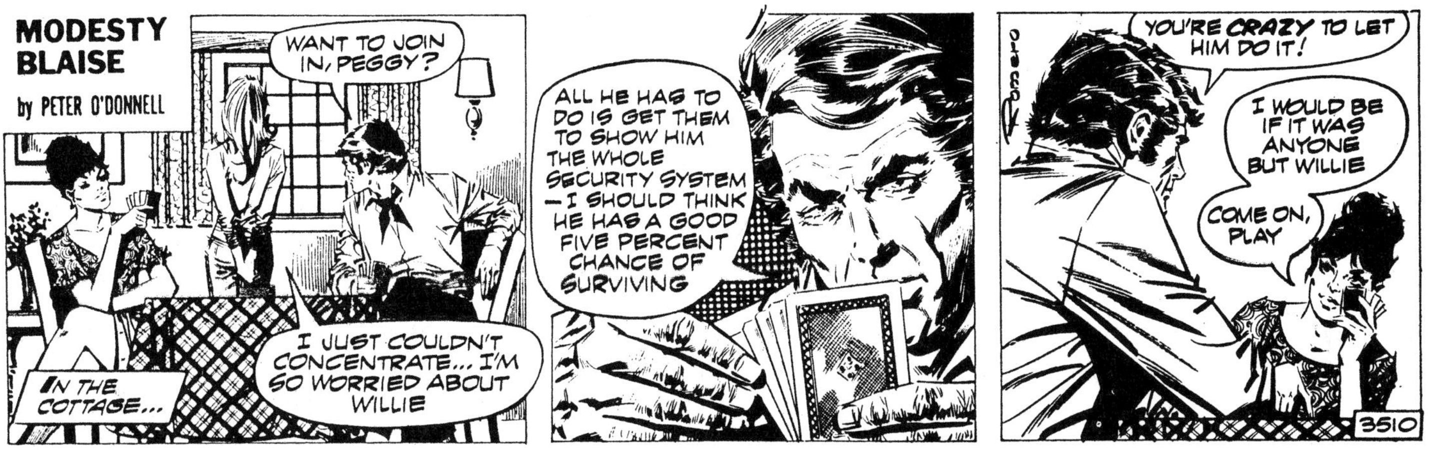
MODESTY BLAISE
by PETER O'DONNELL
IN THE COTTAGE...
WANT TO JOIN IN, PEGGY?
I JUST COULDN'T CONCENTRATE... I'M SO WORRIED ABOUT WILLIE
ALL HE HAS TO DO IS GET THEM TO SHOW HIM THE WHOLE SECURITY SYSTEM — I SHOULD THINK HE HAS A GOOD FIVE PERCENT CHANCE OF SURVIVING
YOU'RE CRAZY TO LET HIM DO IT!
I WOULD BE IF IT WAS ANYONE BUT WILLIE
COME ON, PLAY
3510

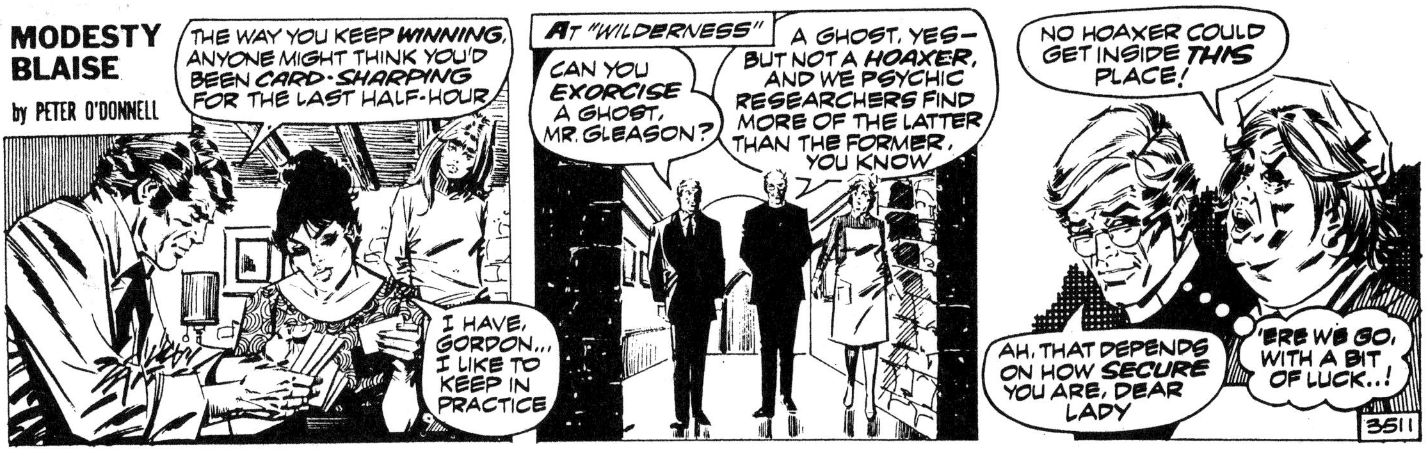
MODESTY BLAISE
by PETER O'DONNELL
THE WAY YOU KEEP WINNING, ANYONE MIGHT THINK YOU'D BEEN CARD-SHARPING FOR THE LAST HALF-HOUR
I HAVE, GORDON... I LIKE TO KEEP IN PRACTICE
AT "WILDERNESS"
CAN YOU EXORCISE A GHOST, MR. GLEASON?
A GHOST, YES— BUT NOT A HOAXER, AND WE PSYCHIC RESEARCHERS FIND MORE OF THE LATTER THAN THE FORMER, YOU KNOW
NO HOAXER COULD GET INSIDE THIS PLACE!
AH, THAT DEPENDS ON HOW SECURE YOU ARE, DEAR LADY
'ERE WE GO, WITH A BIT OF LUCK..!
3511

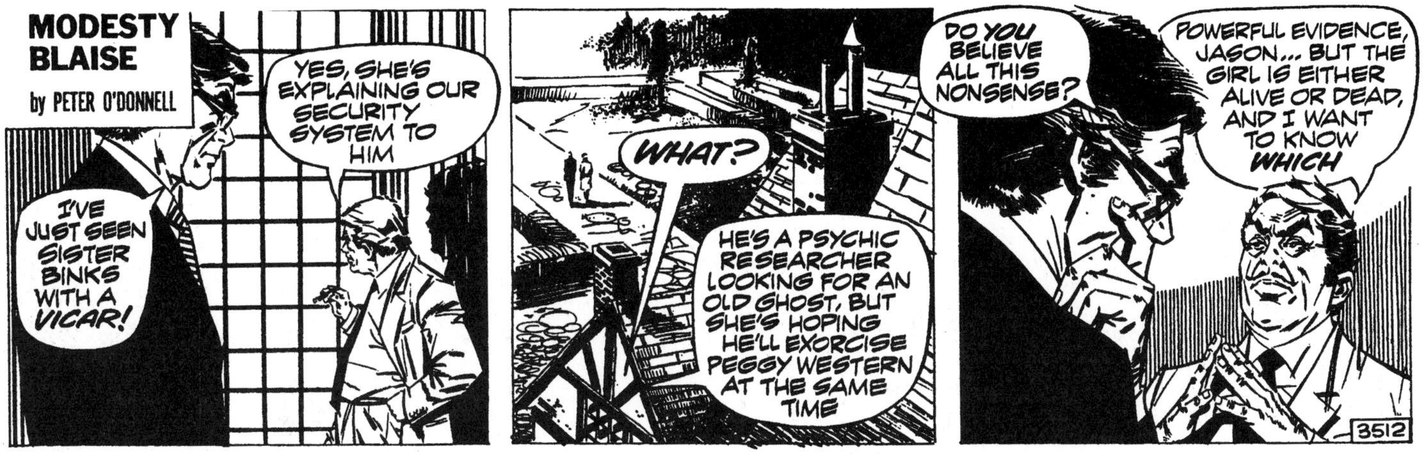
MODESTY BLAISE
by PETER O'DONNELL
I'VE JUST SEEN SISTER BINKS WITH A VICAR!
YES, SHE'S EXPLAINING OUR SECURITY SYSTEM TO HIM
WHAT?
HE'S A PSYCHIC RESEARCHER LOOKING FOR AN OLD GHOST, BUT SHE'S HOPING HE'LL EXORCISE PEGGY WESTERN AT THE SAME TIME
DO YOU BELIEVE ALL THIS NONSENSE?
POWERFUL EVIDENCE, JASON... BUT THE GIRL IS EITHER ALIVE OR DEAD, AND I WANT TO KNOW WHICH
3512

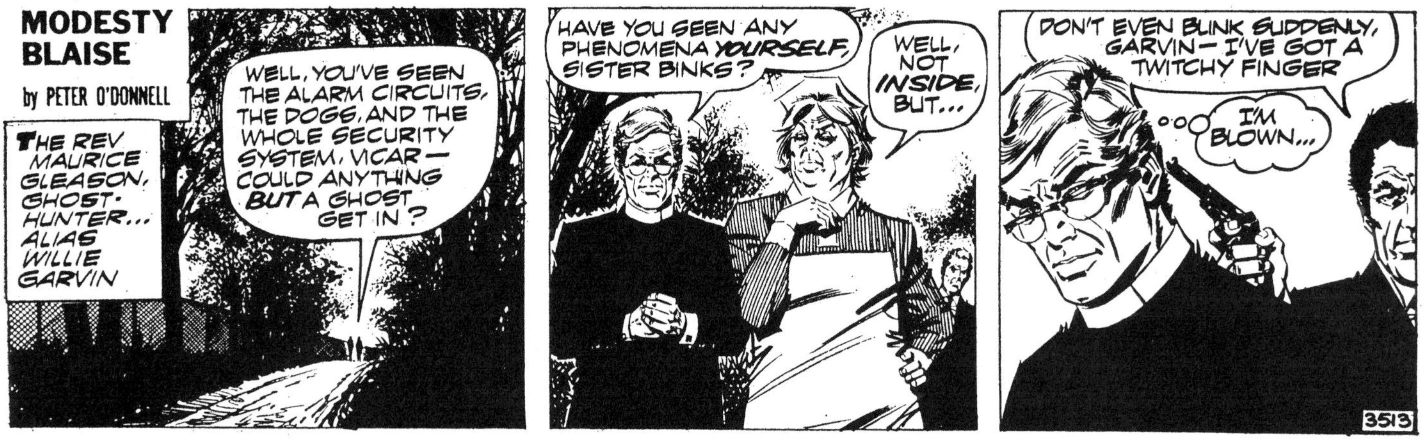
MODESTY BLAISE
by PETER O'DONNELL
THE REV MAURICE GLEASON, GHOST-HUNTER... ALIAS WILLIE GARVIN
WELL, YOU'VE SEEN THE ALARM CIRCUITS, THE DOGS, AND THE WHOLE SECURITY SYSTEM, VICAR — COULD ANYTHING BUT A GHOST GET IN?
HAVE YOU SEEN ANY PHENOMENA YOURSELF, SISTER BINKS?
WELL, NOT INSIDE, BUT...
DON'T EVEN BLINK SUDDENLY, GARVIN — I'VE GOT A TWITCHY FINGER
I'M BLOWN...
3513

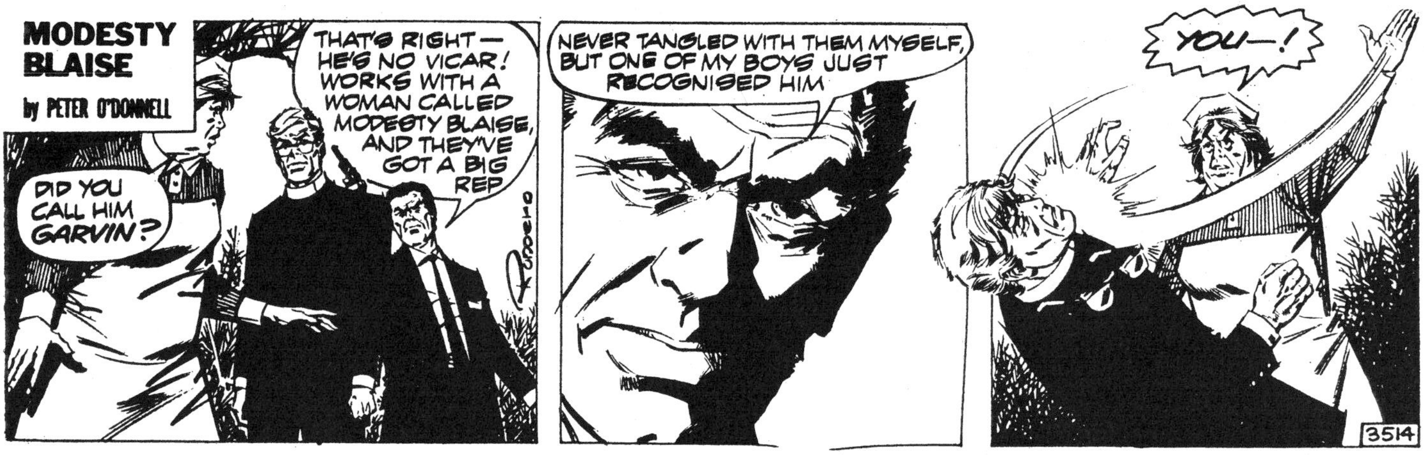
MODESTY BLAISE
by PETER O'DONNELL
DID YOU CALL HIM GARVIN?
THAT'S RIGHT — HE'S NO VICAR! WORKS WITH A WOMAN CALLED MODESTY BLAISE, AND THEY'VE GOT A BIG REP
NEVER TANGLED WITH THEM MYSELF, BUT ONE OF MY BOYS JUST RECOGNISED HIM
YOU—!
3514

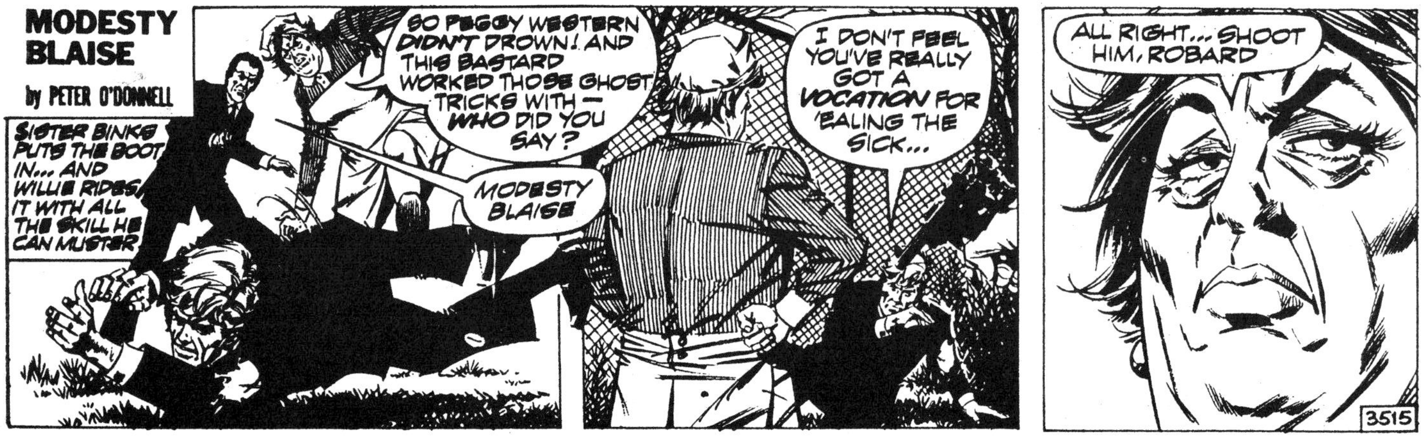
MODESTY BLAISE
by PETER O'DONNELL
SISTER BINKS PUTS THE BOOT IN... AND WILLIE RIDES IT WITH ALL THE SKILL HE CAN MUSTER
SO PEGGY WESTERN DIDN'T DROWN! AND THIS BASTARD WORKED THOSE GHOST TRICKS WITH — WHO DID YOU SAY?
MODESTY BLAISE
I DON'T FEEL YOU'VE REALLY GOT A VOCATION FOR 'EALING THE SICK...
ALL RIGHT... SHOOT HIM, ROBARD
3515

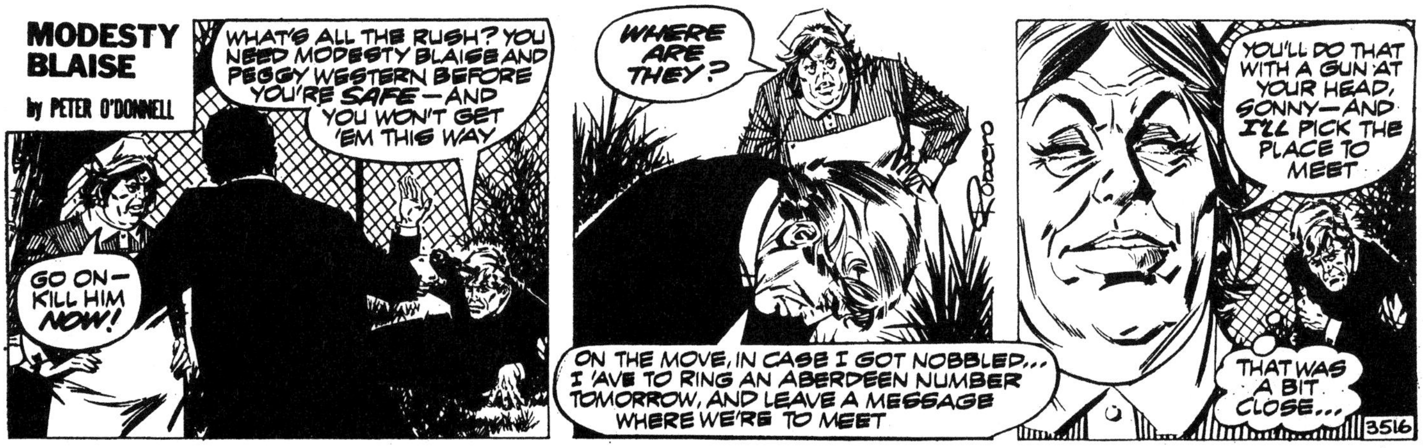
MODESTY BLAISE
by PETER O'DONNELL
WHAT'S ALL THE RUSH? YOU NEED MODESTY BLAISE AND PEGGY WESTERN BEFORE YOU'RE SAFE — AND YOU WON'T GET 'EM THIS WAY
GO ON — KILL HIM NOW!
WHERE ARE THEY?
ON THE MOVE, IN CASE I GOT NOBBLED... I 'AVE TO RING AN ABERDEEN NUMBER TOMORROW, AND LEAVE A MESSAGE WHERE WE'RE TO MEET
YOU'LL DO THAT WITH A GUN AT YOUR HEAD, SONNY — AND I'LL PICK THE PLACE TO MEET
THAT WAS A BIT CLOSE...
3516

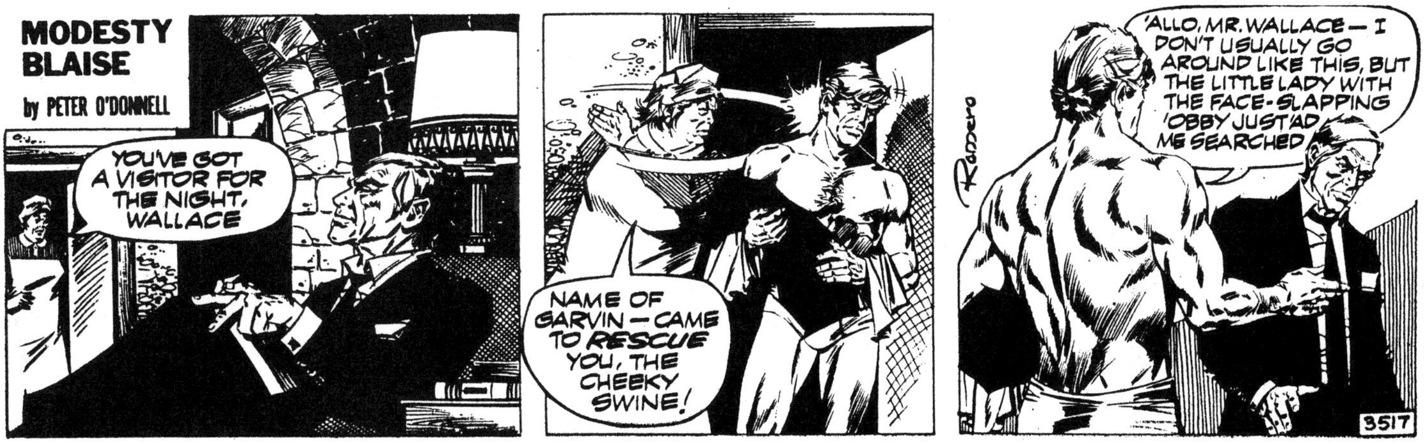
MODESTY BLAISE
by PETER O'DONNELL
YOU'VE GOT A VISITOR FOR THE NIGHT, WALLACE
NAME OF GARVIN — CAME TO RESCUE YOU, THE CHEEKY SWINE!
'ALLO, MR. WALLACE — I DON'T USUALLY GO AROUND LIKE THIS, BUT THE LITTLE LADY WITH THE FACE-SLAPPING 'OBBY JUST 'AD ME SEARCHED
3517

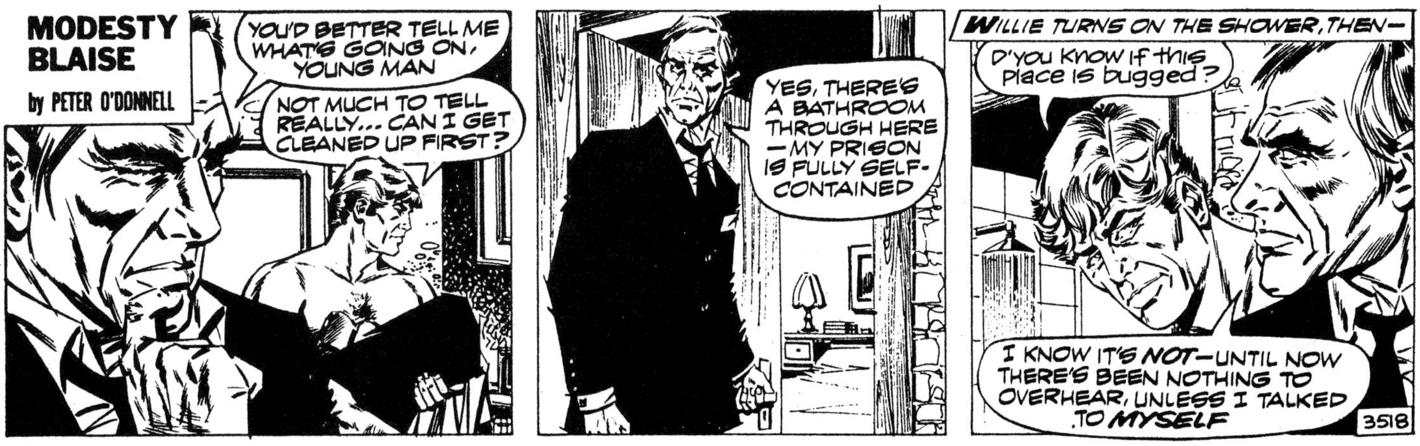
MODESTY BLAISE
by PETER O'DONNELL
YOU'D BETTER TELL ME WHAT'S GOING ON, YOUNG MAN
NOT MUCH TO TELL REALLY... CAN I GET CLEANED UP FIRST?
YES, THERE'S A BATHROOM THROUGH HERE — MY PRISON IS FULLY SELF-CONTAINED
WILLIE TURNS ON THE SHOWER, THEN—
D'you know if this place is bugged?
I KNOW IT'S NOT — UNTIL NOW THERE'S BEEN NOTHING TO OVERHEAR, UNLESS I TALKED TO MYSELF
3518

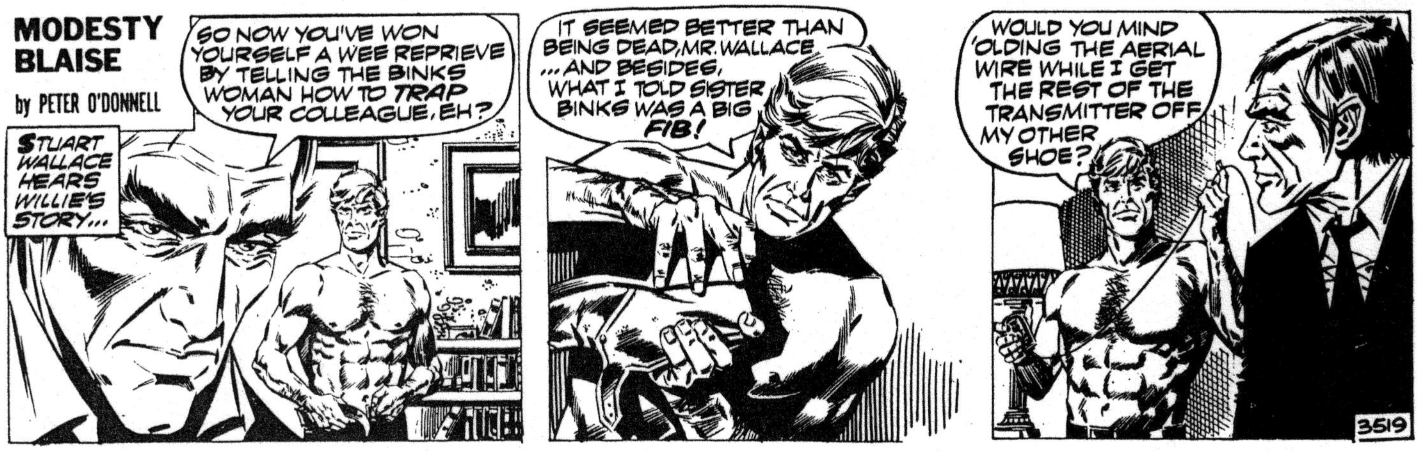
MODESTY BLAISE
by PETER O'DONNELL
STUART WALLACE HEARS WILLIE'S STORY...
SO NOW YOU'VE WON YOURSELF A WEE REPRIEVE BY TELLING THE BINKS WOMAN HOW TO TRAP YOUR COLLEAGUE, EH?
IT SEEMED BETTER THAN BEING DEAD, MR. WALLACE ...AND BESIDES, WHAT I TOLD SISTER BINKS WAS A BIG FIB!
WOULD YOU MIND 'OLDING THE AERIAL WIRE WHILE I GET THE REST OF THE TRANSMITTER OFF MY OTHER SHOE?
3519

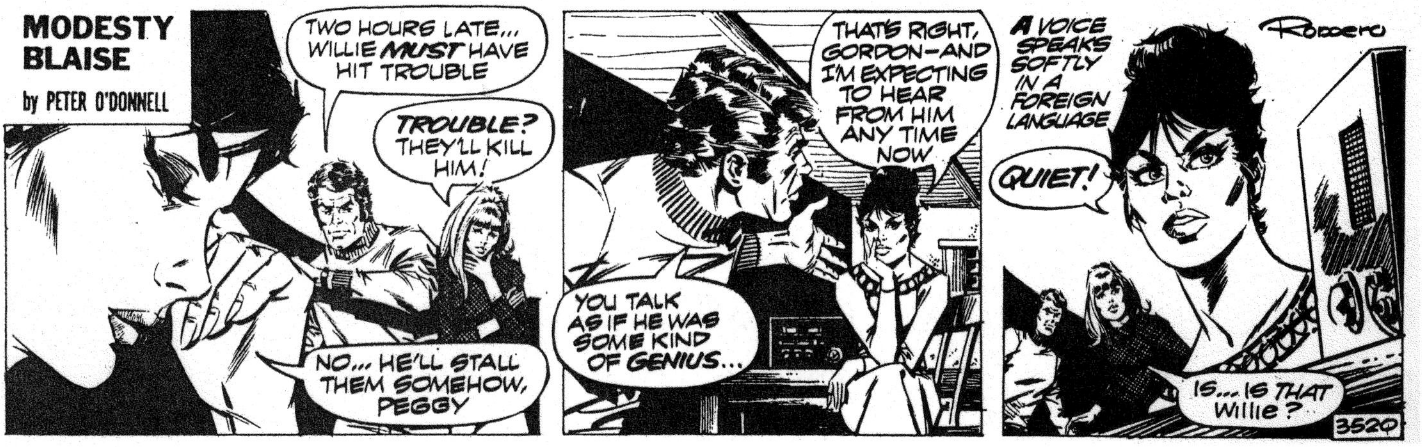
MODESTY BLAISE
by PETER O'DONNELL
TWO HOURS LATE... WILLIE MUST HAVE HIT TROUBLE
TROUBLE? THEY'LL KILL HIM!
NO... HE'LL STALL THEM SOMEHOW, PEGGY
THAT'S RIGHT, GORDON — AND I'M EXPECTING TO HEAR FROM HIM ANY TIME NOW
YOU TALK AS IF HE WAS SOME KIND OF GENIUS...
A VOICE SPEAKS SOFTLY IN A FOREIGN LANGUAGE
QUIET!
IS... IS THAT Willie?
3520

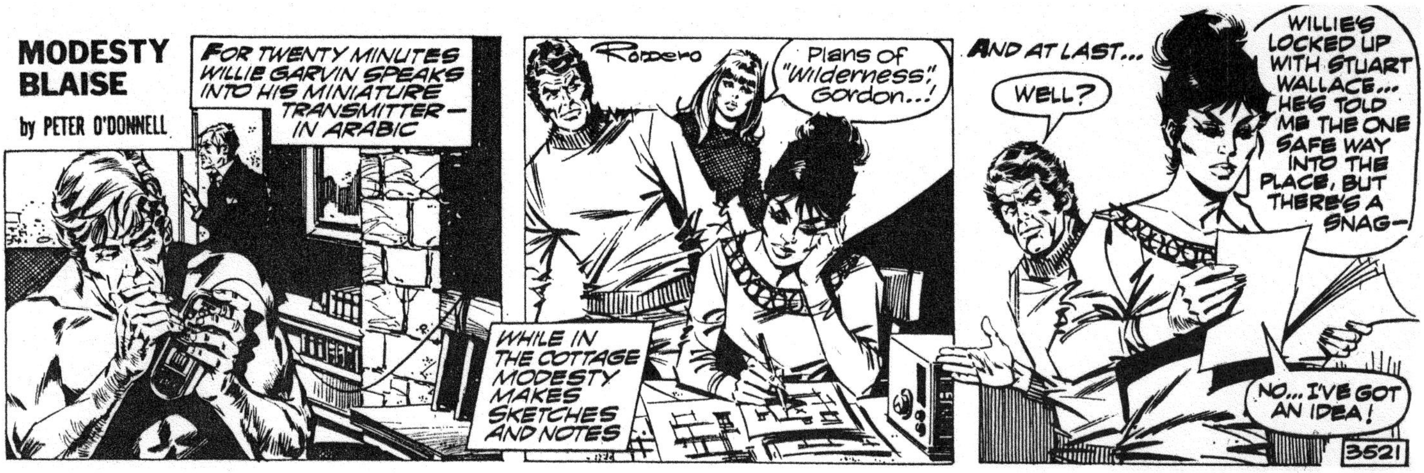
MODESTY BLAISE
by PETER O'DONNELL
FOR TWENTY MINUTES WILLIE GARVIN SPEAKS INTO HIS MINIATURE TRANSMITTER — IN ARABIC
Plans of "Wilderness," Gordon...!
WHILE IN THE COTTAGE MODESTY MAKES SKETCHES AND NOTES
AND AT LAST...
WELL?
WILLIE'S LOCKED UP WITH STUART WALLACE... HE'S TOLD ME THE ONE SAFE WAY INTO THE PLACE, BUT THERE'S A SNAG—
NO... I'VE GOT AN IDEA!
3521

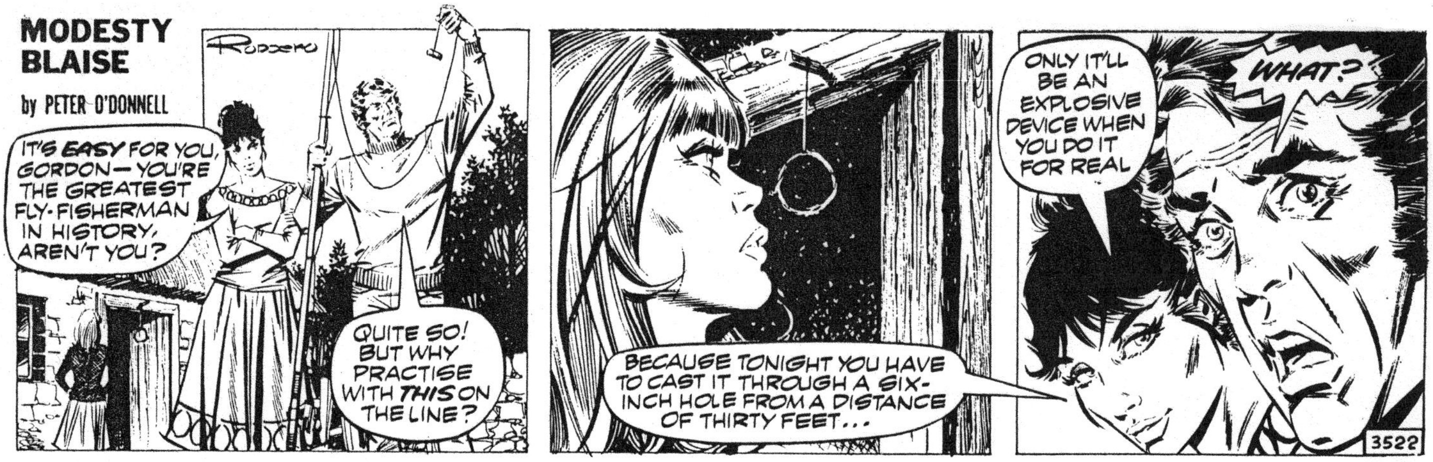
MODESTY BLAISE
by PETER O'DONNELL
IT'S EASY FOR YOU, GORDON — YOU'RE THE GREATEST FLY-FISHERMAN IN HISTORY, AREN'T YOU?
QUITE SO! BUT WHY PRACTISE WITH THIS ON THE LINE?
BECAUSE TONIGHT YOU HAVE TO CAST IT THROUGH A SIX-INCH HOLE FROM A DISTANCE OF THIRTY FEET...
ONLY IT'LL BE AN EXPLOSIVE DEVICE WHEN YOU DO IT FOR REAL
WHAT?
3522

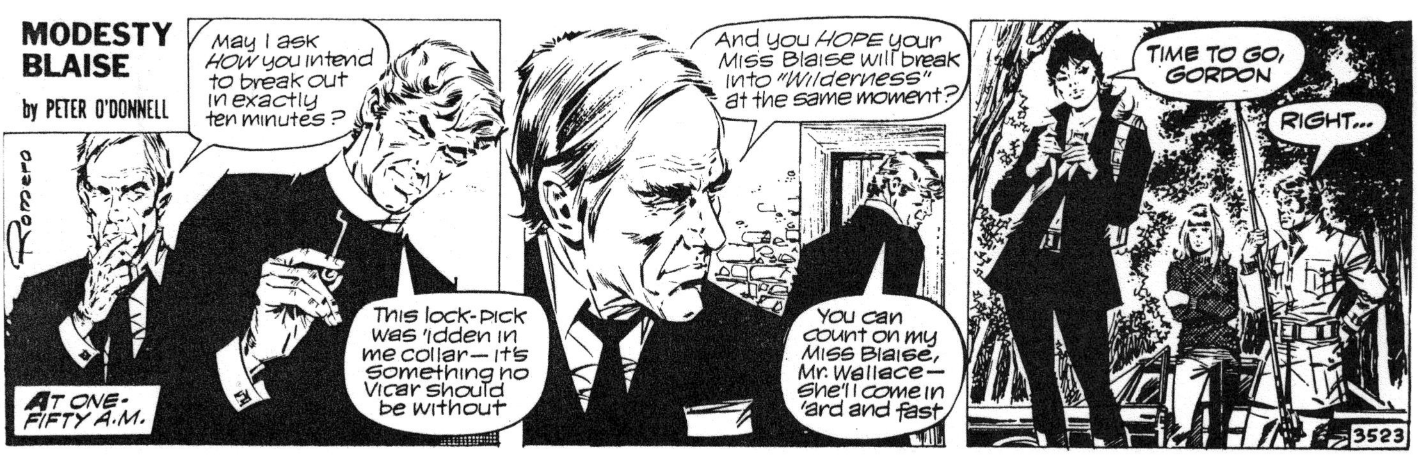
MODESTY BLAISE
by PETER O'DONNELL
May I ask HOW you intend to break out in exactly ten minutes?
This lock-pick was 'idden in me collar — it's something no Vicar should be without
AT ONE-FIFTY A.M.
And you HOPE your Miss Blaise will break into "Wilderness" at the same moment?
You can count on my Miss Blaise, Mr. Wallace — she'll come in 'ard and fast
TIME TO GO, GORDON
RIGHT...
3523

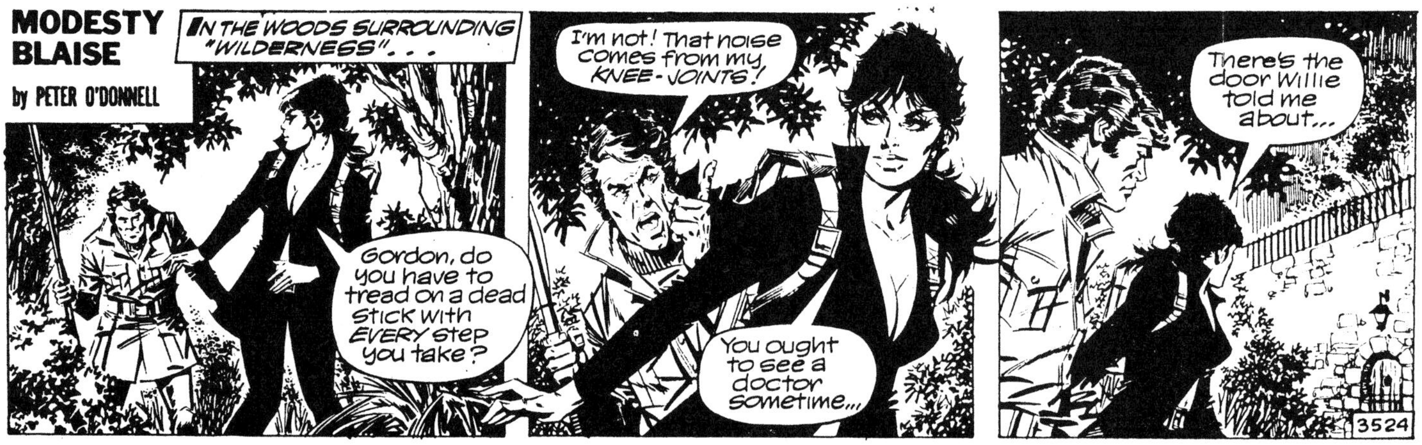
MODESTY BLAISE
by PETER O'DONNELL
IN THE WOODS SURROUNDING "WILDERNESS"...
Gordon, do you have to tread on a dead stick with EVERY step you take?
I'm not! That noise comes from my KNEE-JOINTS!
You ought to see a doctor sometime...
There's the door Willie told me about...
3524

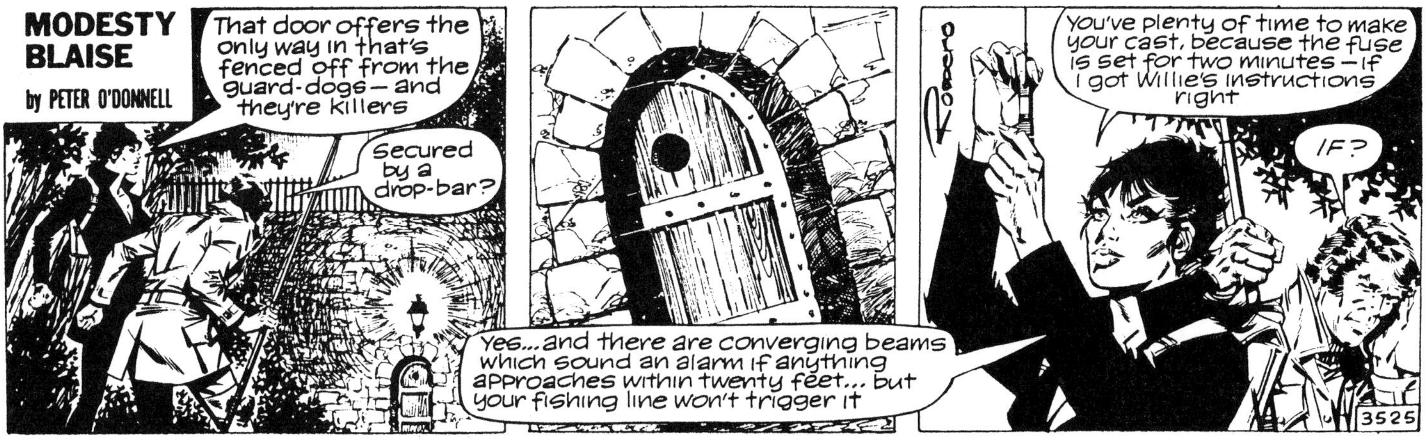
MODESTY BLAISE
by PETER O'DONNELL
That door offers the only way in that's fenced off from the guard-dogs — and they're killers
Secured by a drop-bar?
Yes... and there are converging beams which sound an alarm if anything approaches within twenty feet... but your fishing line won't trigger it
You've plenty of time to make your cast, because the fuse is set for two minutes — if I got Willie's instructions right
IF?
3525

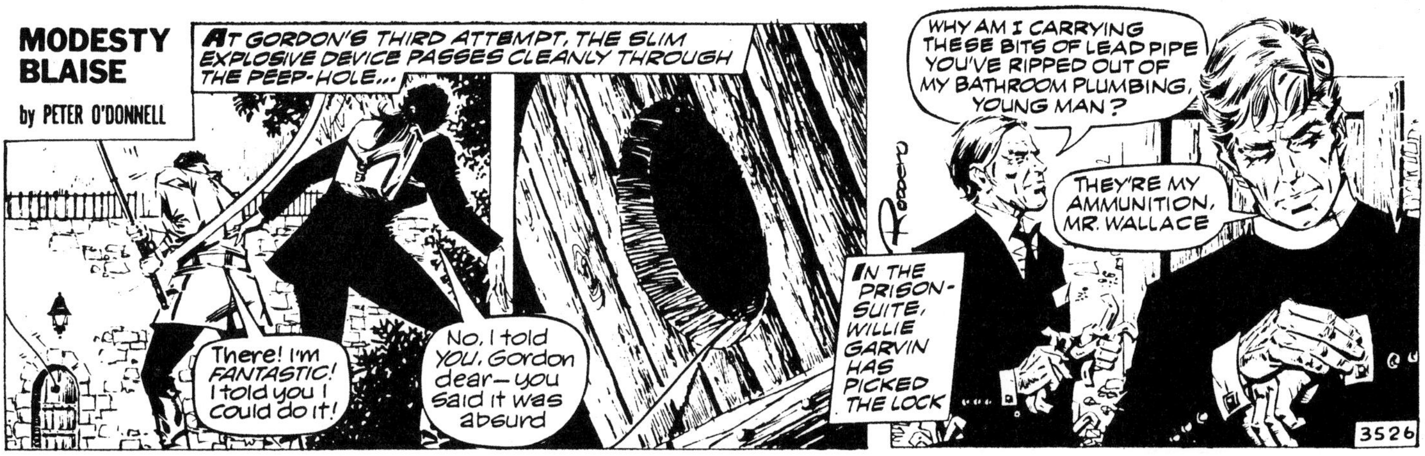
MODESTY BLAISE
by PETER O'DONNELL
AT GORDON'S THIRD ATTEMPT, THE SLIM EXPLOSIVE DEVICE PASSES CLEANLY THROUGH THE PEEP-HOLE...
There! I'm FANTASTIC! I told you I could do it!
No, I told YOU, Gordon dear — you said it was absurd
IN THE PRISON-SUITE, WILLIE GARVIN HAS PICKED THE LOCK
WHY AM I CARRYING THESE BITS OF LEAD PIPE YOU'VE RIPPED OUT OF MY BATHROOM PLUMBING, YOUNG MAN?
THEY'RE MY AMMUNITION, MR. WALLACE
3526

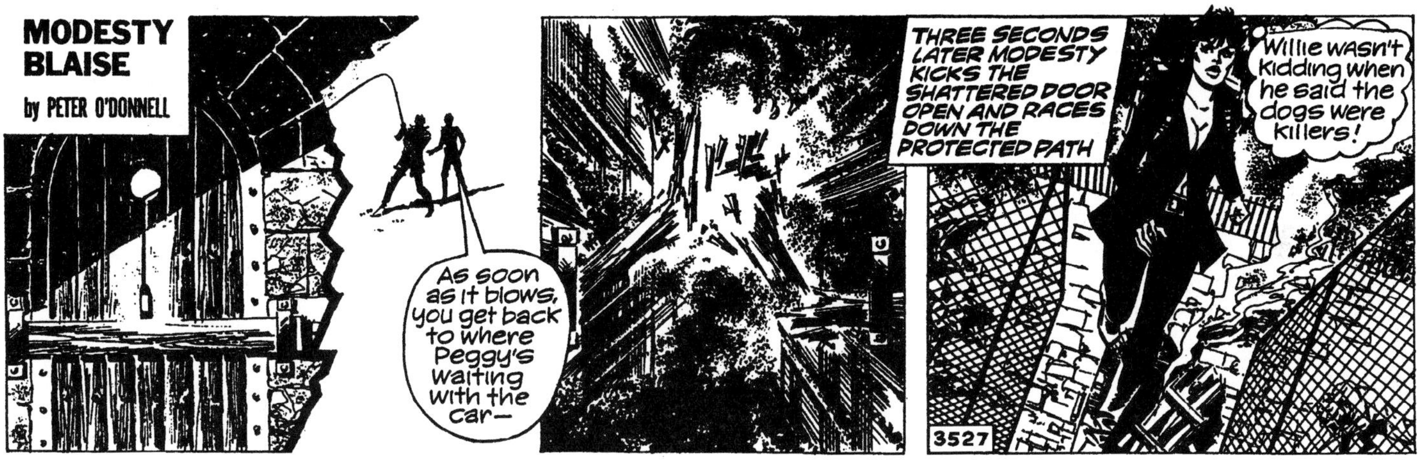
MODESTY BLAISE
by PETER O'DONNELL
As soon as it blows, you get back to where Peggy's waiting with the car—
THREE SECONDS LATER MODESTY KICKS THE SHATTERED DOOR OPEN AND RACES DOWN THE PROTECTED PATH
Willie wasn't kidding when he said the dogs were killers!
3527

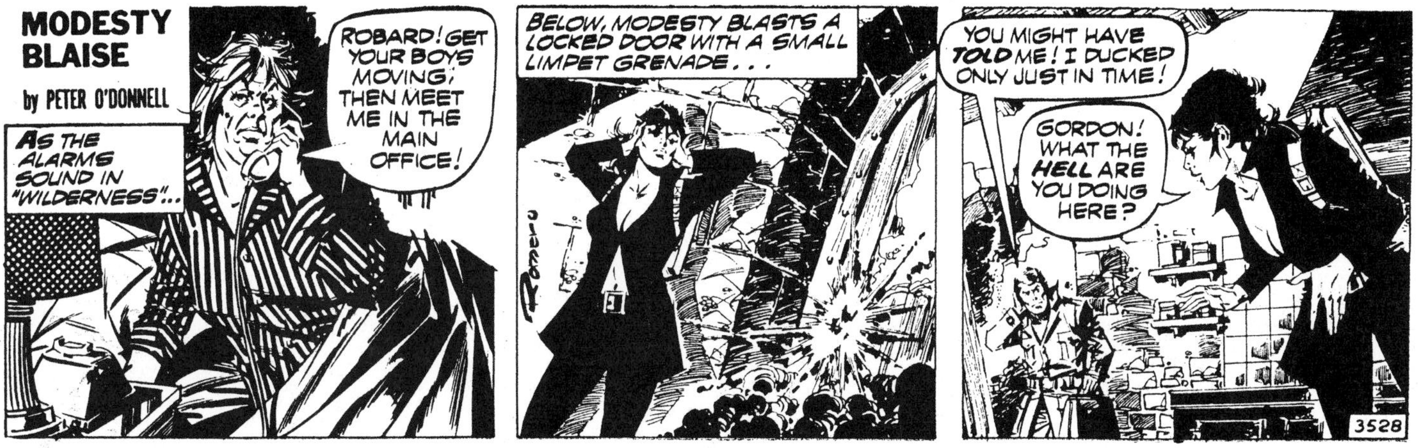
MODESTY BLAISE
by PETER O'DONNELL
AS THE ALARMS SOUND IN "WILDERNESS"...
ROBARD! GET YOUR BOYS MOVING; THEN MEET ME IN THE MAIN OFFICE!
BELOW, MODESTY BLASTS A LOCKED DOOR WITH A SMALL LIMPET GRENADE...
YOU MIGHT HAVE TOLD ME! I DUCKED ONLY JUST IN TIME!
GORDON! WHAT THE HELL ARE YOU DOING HERE?
3528

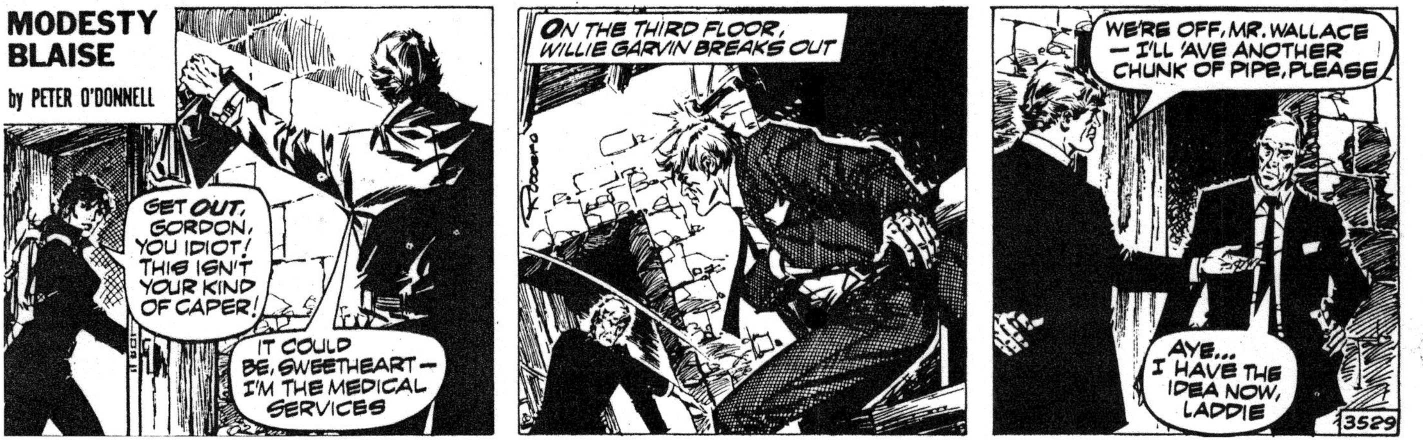
MODESTY BLAISE
by PETER O'DONNELL
GET OUT, GORDON, YOU IDIOT! THIS ISN'T YOUR KIND OF CAPER!
IT COULD BE, SWEETHEART—I'M THE MEDICAL SERVICES
ON THE THIRD FLOOR, WILLIE GARVIN BREAKS OUT
WE'RE OFF, MR. WALLACE —I'LL 'AVE ANOTHER CHUNK OF PIPE, PLEASE
AYE... I HAVE THE IDEA NOW, LADDIE
3529

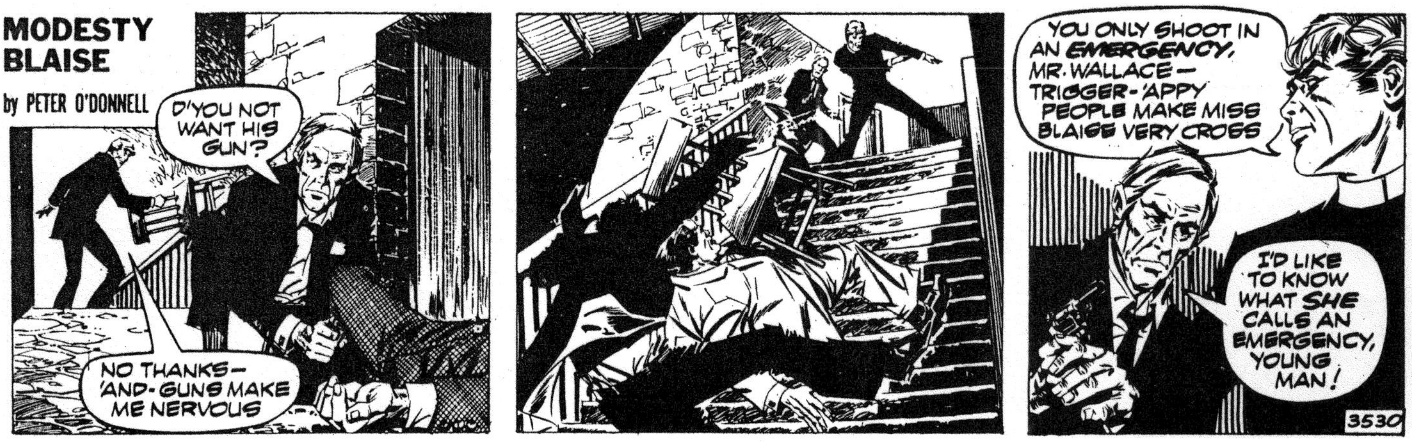
MODESTY BLAISE
by PETER O'DONNELL
D'YOU NOT WANT HIS GUN?
NO THANKS— 'AND-GUNS MAKE ME NERVOUS
YOU ONLY SHOOT IN AN EMERGENCY, MR. WALLACE— TRIGGER-'APPY PEOPLE MAKE MISS BLAISE VERY CROSS
I'D LIKE TO KNOW WHAT SHE CALLS AN EMERGENCY, YOUNG MAN!
3530

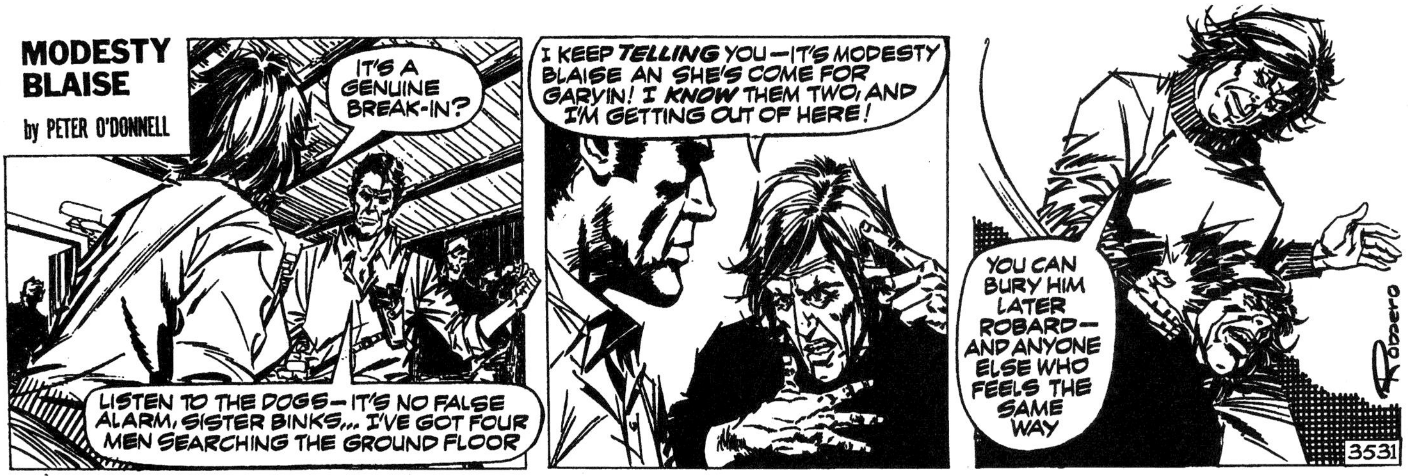
MODESTY BLAISE
by PETER O'DONNELL
IT'S A GENUINE BREAK-IN?
LISTEN TO THE DOGS—IT'S NO FALSE ALARM, SISTER BINKS... I'VE GOT FOUR MEN SEARCHING THE GROUND FLOOR
I KEEP TELLING YOU—IT'S MODESTY BLAISE AN SHE'S COME FOR GARVIN! I KNOW THEM TWO; AND I'M GETTING OUT OF HERE!
YOU CAN BURY HIM LATER ROBARD— AND ANYONE ELSE WHO FEELS THE SAME WAY
3531

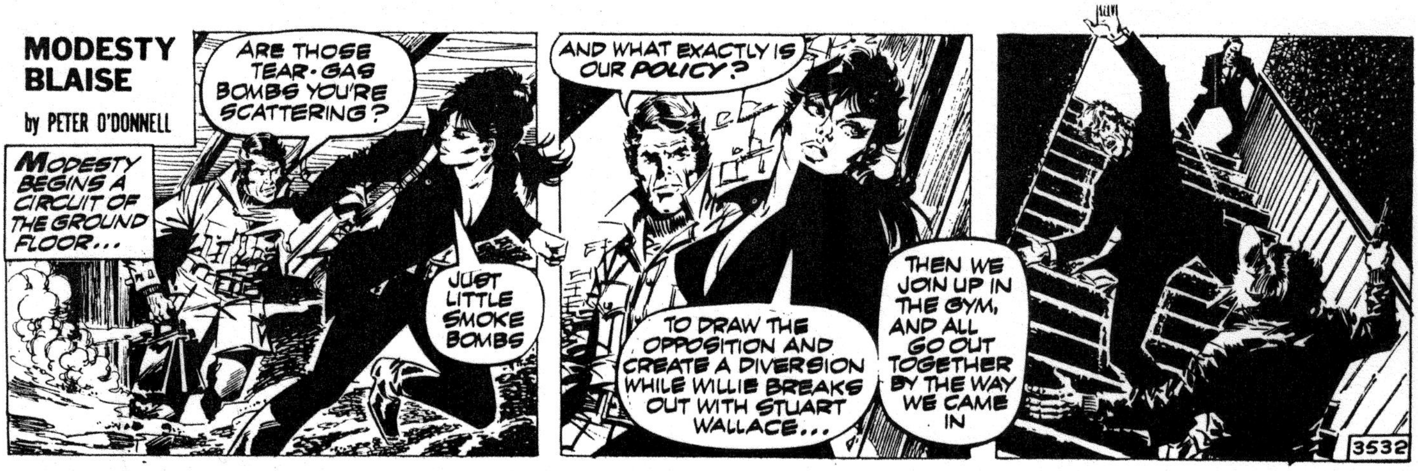
MODESTY BLAISE
by PETER O'DONNELL
MODESTY BEGINS A CIRCUIT OF THE GROUND FLOOR...
ARE THOSE TEAR-GAS BOMBS YOU'RE SCATTERING?
JUST LITTLE SMOKE BOMBS
AND WHAT EXACTLY IS OUR POLICY?
TO DRAW THE OPPOSITION AND CREATE A DIVERSION WHILE WILLIE BREAKS OUT WITH STUART WALLACE...
THEN WE JOIN UP IN THE GYM, AND ALL GO OUT TOGETHER BY THE WAY WE CAME IN
3532

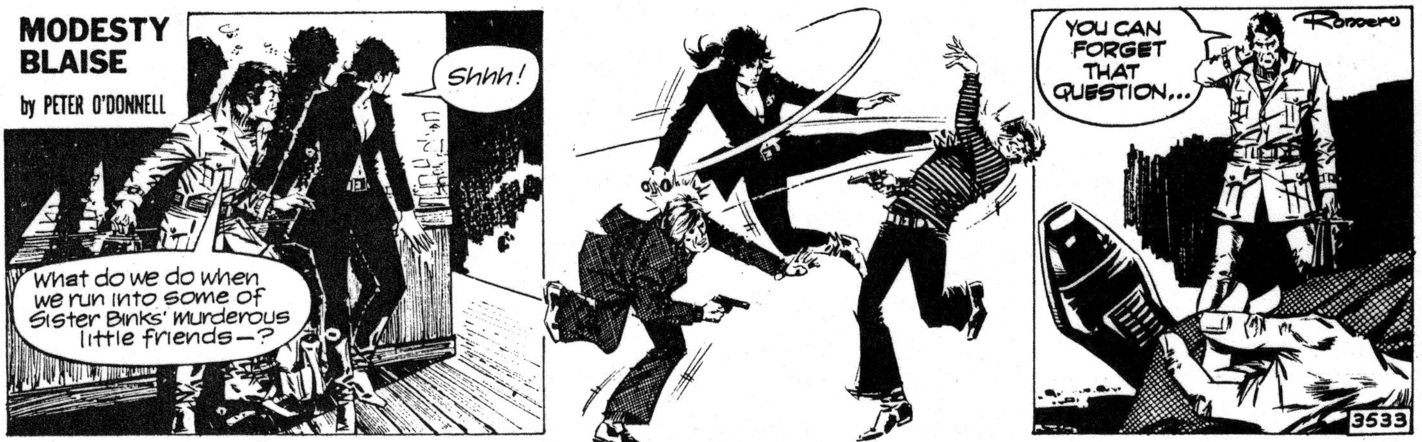

MODESTY BLAISE
by PETER O'DONNELL
Shhh!
What do we do when we run into some of Sister Binks' murderous little friends—?
YOU CAN FORGET THAT QUESTION,...
Romero
3533

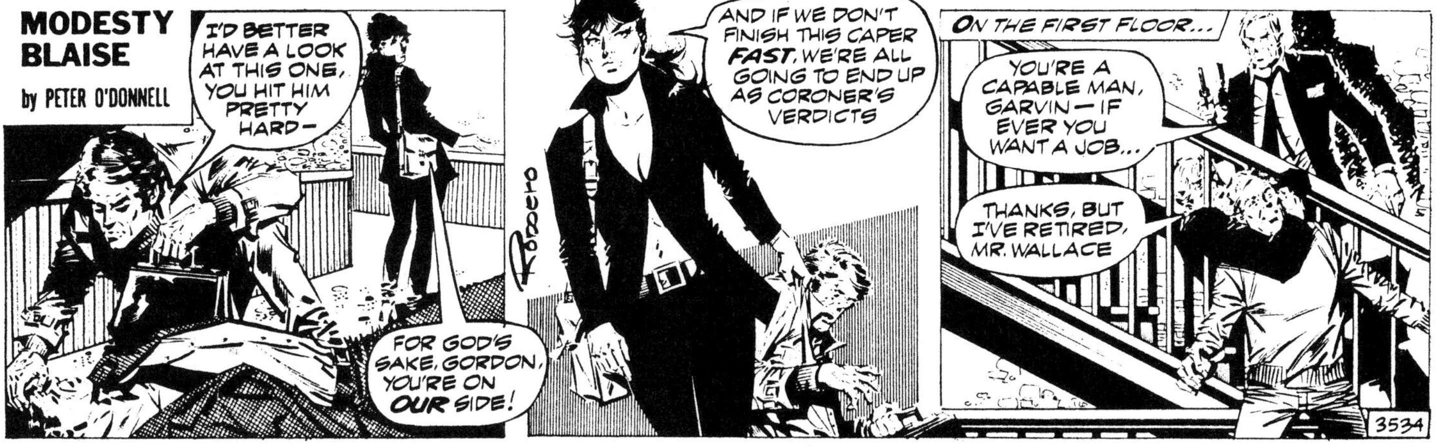

MODESTY BLAISE
by PETER O'DONNELL
I'D BETTER HAVE A LOOK AT THIS ONE, YOU HIT HIM PRETTY HARD—
FOR GOD'S SAKE, GORDON, YOU'RE ON OUR SIDE!
AND IF WE DON'T FINISH THIS CAPER FAST, WE'RE ALL GOING TO END UP AS CORONER'S VERDICTS
Romero
ON THE FIRST FLOOR...
YOU'RE A CAPABLE MAN, GARVIN—IF EVER YOU WANT A JOB...
THANKS, BUT I'VE RETIRED, MR. WALLACE
3534

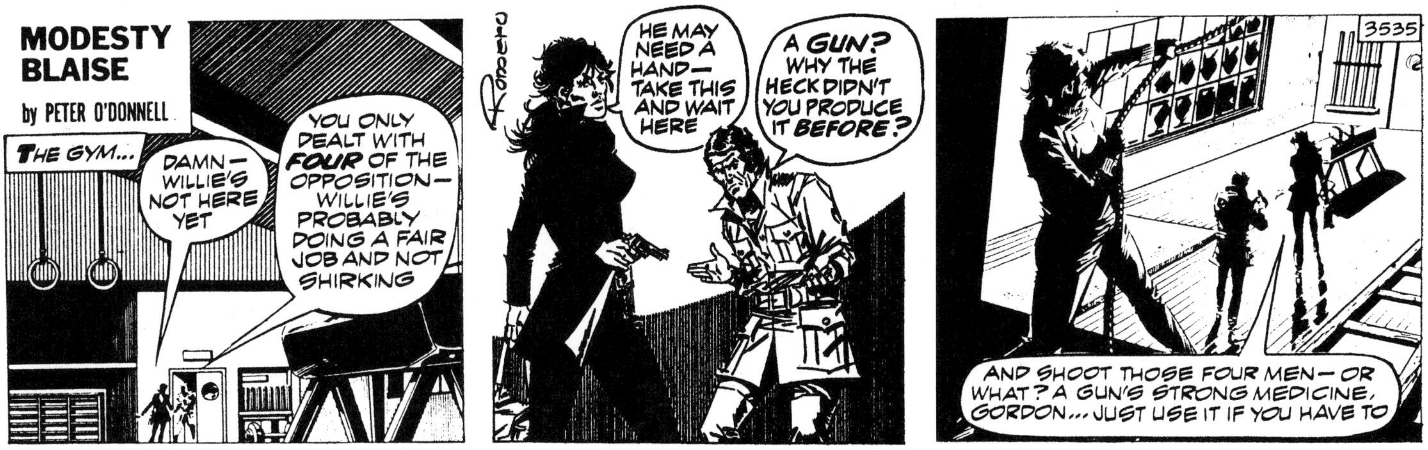

MODESTY BLAISE
by PETER O'DONNELL
THE GYM...
DAMN—WILLIE'S NOT HERE YET
YOU ONLY DEALT WITH FOUR OF THE OPPOSITION—WILLIE'S PROBABLY DOING A FAIR JOB AND NOT SHIRKING
Romero
HE MAY NEED A HAND—TAKE THIS AND WAIT HERE
A GUN? WHY THE HECK DIDN'T YOU PRODUCE IT BEFORE?
3535
AND SHOOT THOSE FOUR MEN—OR WHAT? A GUN'S STRONG MEDICINE, GORDON... JUST USE IT IF YOU HAVE TO

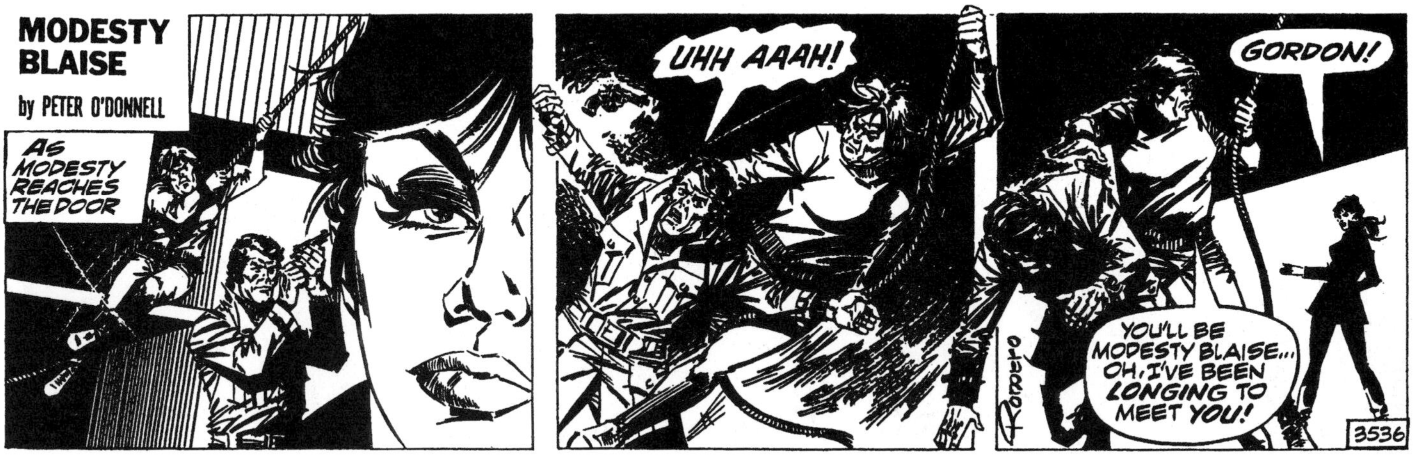

MODESTY BLAISE
by PETER O'DONNELL
AS MODESTY REACHES THE DOOR
UHH AAAH!
GORDON!
YOU'LL BE MODESTY BLAISE... OH, I'VE BEEN LONGING TO MEET YOU!
Romero
3536

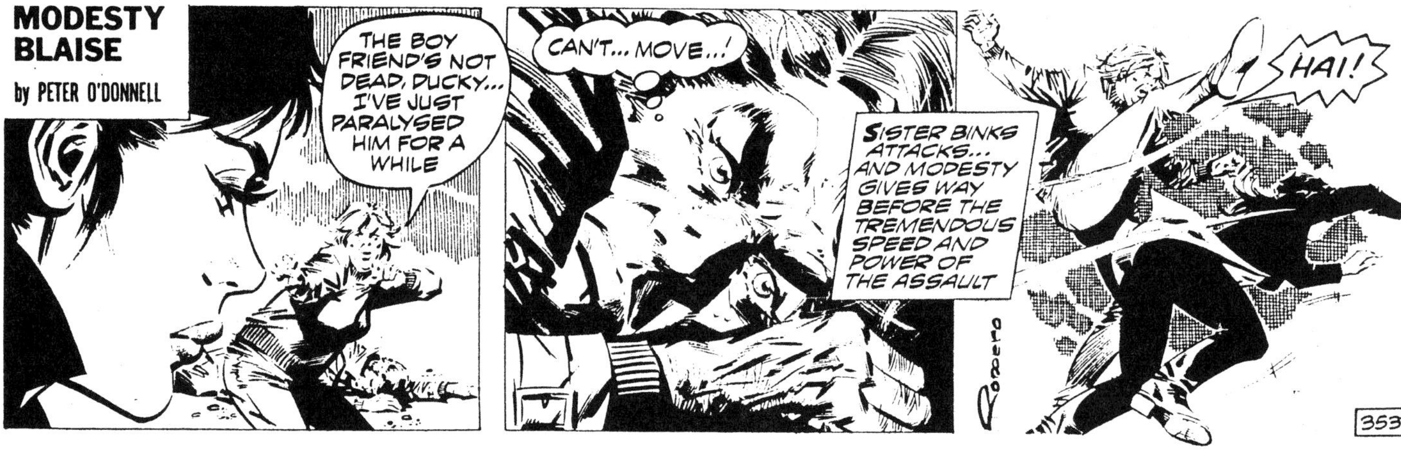
MODESTY BLAISE
by PETER O'DONNELL
THE BOY FRIEND'S NOT DEAD, DUCKY... I'VE JUST PARALYSED HIM FOR A WHILE
CAN'T... MOVE...!
SISTER BINKS ATTACKS... AND MODESTY GIVES WAY BEFORE THE TREMENDOUS SPEED AND POWER OF THE ASSAULT
HAI!
Romero
3537

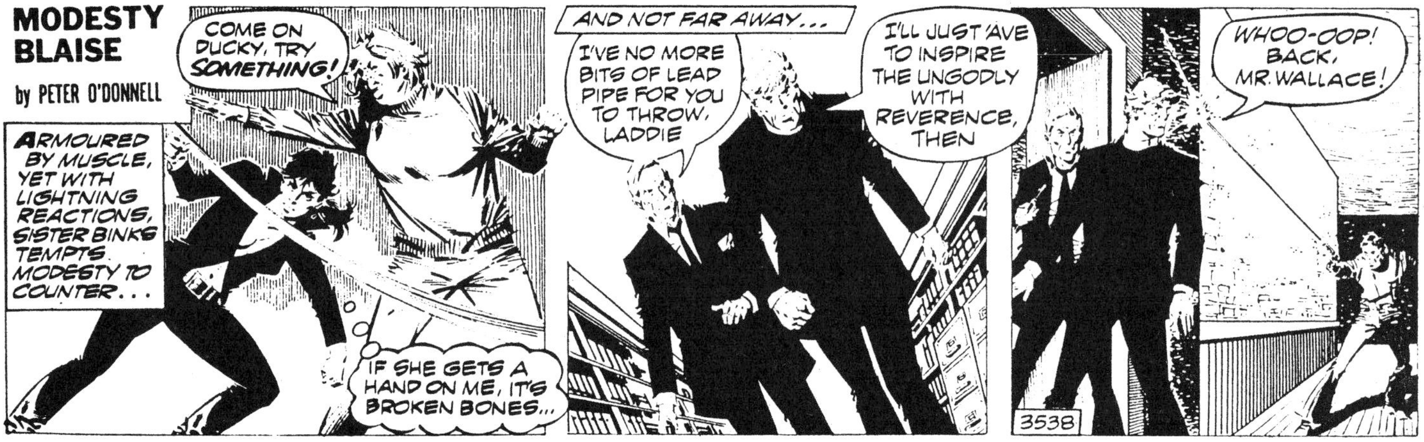
MODESTY BLAISE
by PETER O'DONNELL
COME ON DUCKY, TRY SOMETHING!
ARMOURED BY MUSCLE, YET WITH LIGHTNING REACTIONS, SISTER BINKS TEMPTS MODESTY TO COUNTER...
IF SHE GETS A HAND ON ME, IT'S BROKEN BONES...
AND NOT FAR AWAY...
I'VE NO MORE BITS OF LEAD PIPE FOR YOU TO THROW, LADDIE
I'LL JUST 'AVE TO INSPIRE THE UNGODLY WITH REVERENCE, THEN
3538
WHOO-OOP! BACK, MR. WALLACE!

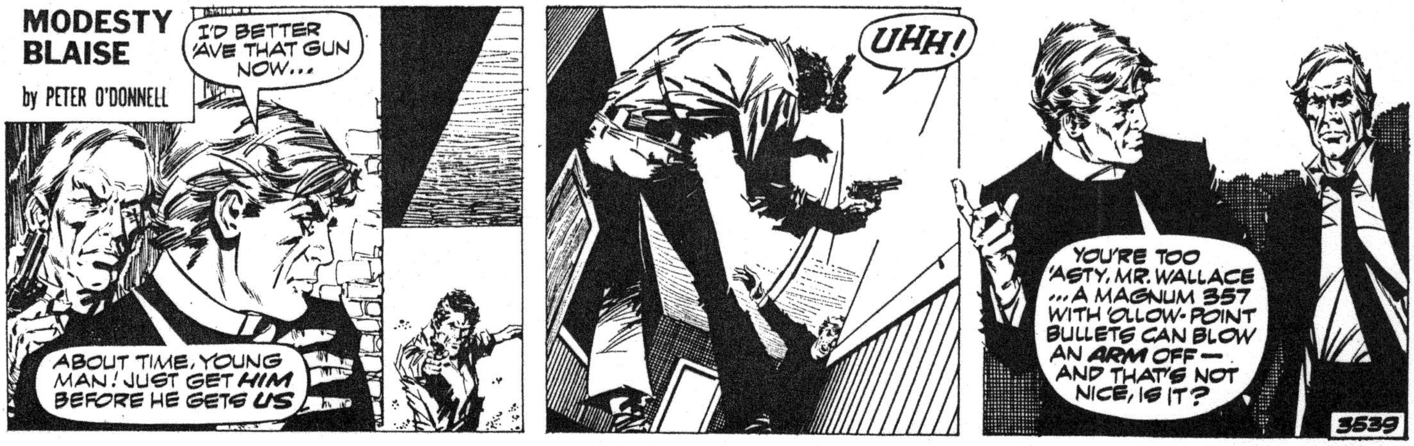
MODESTY BLAISE
by PETER O'DONNELL
I'D BETTER 'AVE THAT GUN NOW...
ABOUT TIME, YOUNG MAN! JUST GET HIM BEFORE HE GETS US
UHH!
YOU'RE TOO 'ASTY, MR. WALLACE ...A MAGNUM 357 WITH 'OLLOW-POINT BULLETS CAN BLOW AN ARM OFF— AND THAT'S NOT NICE, IS IT?
3539

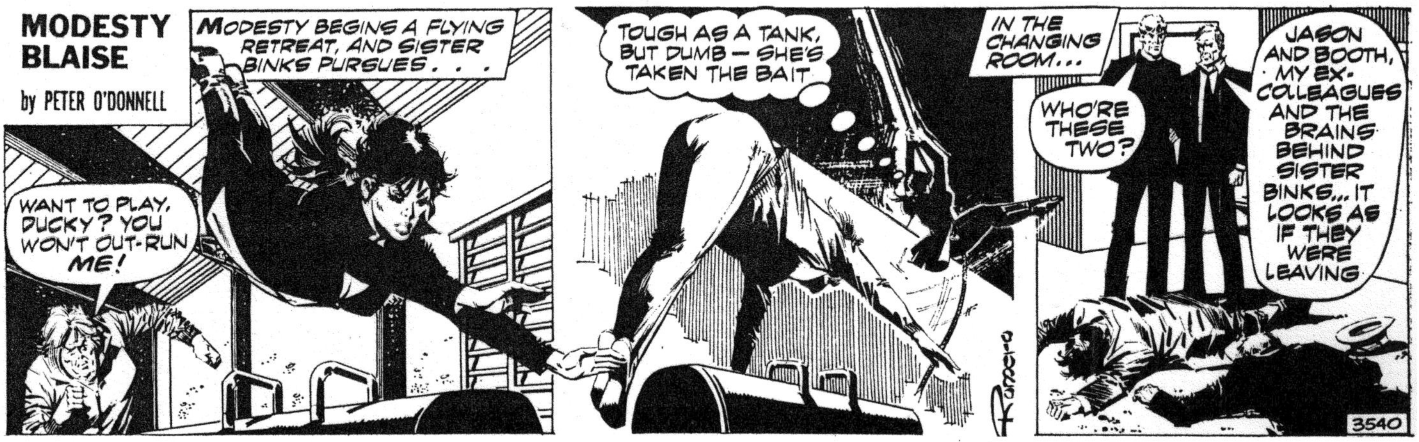
MODESTY BLAISE
by PETER O'DONNELL
MODESTY BEGINS A FLYING RETREAT, AND SISTER BINKS PURSUES...
WANT TO PLAY, DUCKY? YOU WON'T OUT-RUN ME!
TOUGH AS A TANK, BUT DUMB — SHE'S TAKEN THE BAIT
Romero
IN THE CHANGING ROOM...
WHO'RE THESE TWO?
JASON AND BOOTH, MY EX-COLLEAGUES AND THE BRAINS BEHIND SISTER BINKS... IT LOOKS AS IF THEY WERE LEAVING
3540

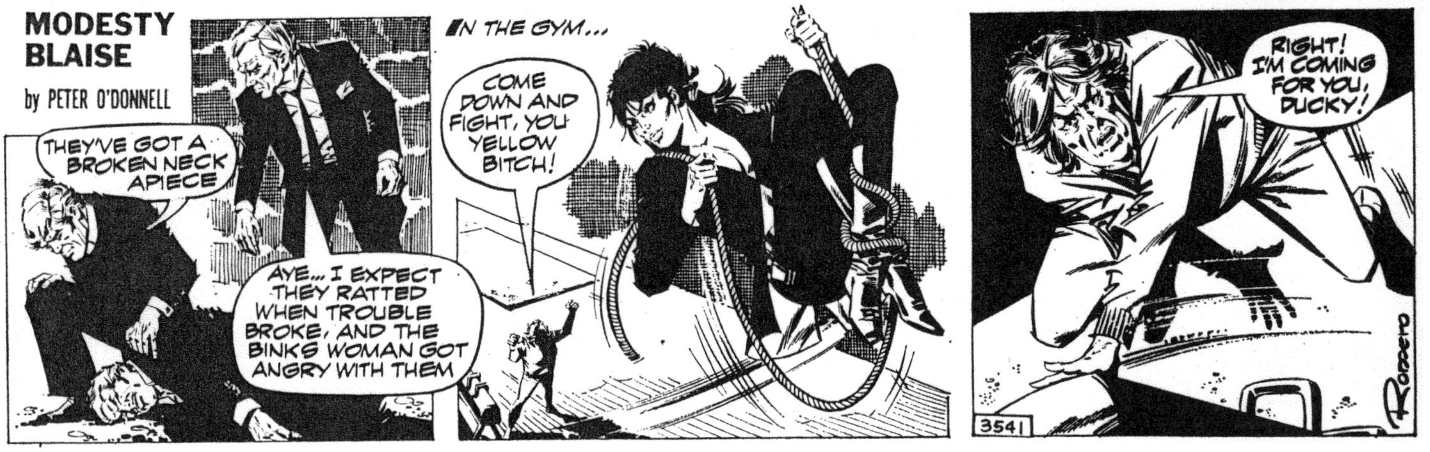
MODESTY BLAISE
by PETER O'DONNELL
THEY'VE GOT A BROKEN NECK APIECE
AYE... I EXPECT THEY RATTED WHEN TROUBLE BROKE, AND THE BINKS WOMAN GOT ANGRY WITH THEM
IN THE GYM...
COME DOWN AND FIGHT, YOU YELLOW BITCH!
RIGHT! I'M COMING FOR YOU, DUCKY!
Romero
3541

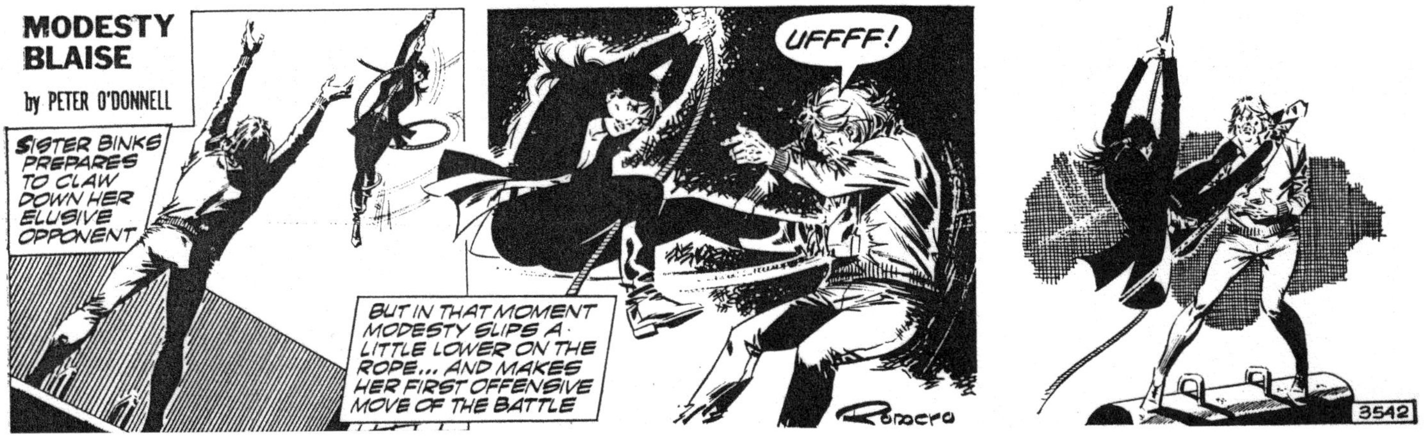
MODESTY BLAISE
by PETER O'DONNELL
SISTER BINKS PREPARES TO CLAW DOWN HER ELUSIVE OPPONENT
UFFFF!
BUT IN THAT MOMENT MODESTY SLIPS A LITTLE LOWER ON THE ROPE... AND MAKES HER FIRST OFFENSIVE MOVE OF THE BATTLE
Romero
3542

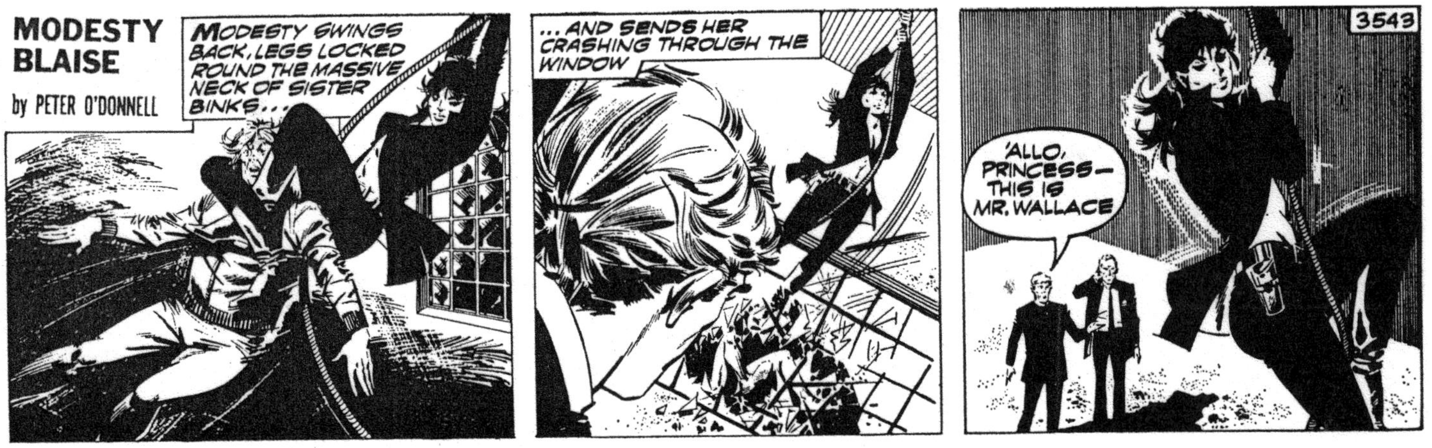
MODESTY BLAISE
by PETER O'DONNELL
MODESTY SWINGS BACK, LEGS LOCKED ROUND THE MASSIVE NECK OF SISTER BINKS...
...AND SENDS HER CRASHING THROUGH THE WINDOW
3543
'ALLO, PRINCESS—THIS IS MR. WALLACE

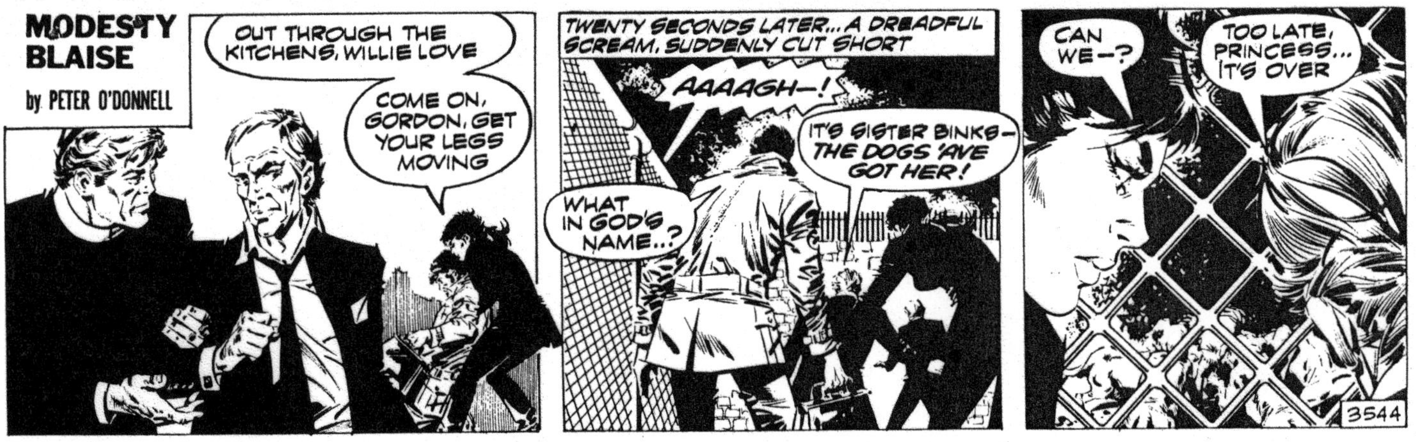
MODESTY BLAISE
by PETER O'DONNELL
OUT THROUGH THE KITCHENS, WILLIE LOVE
COME ON, GORDON, GET YOUR LEGS MOVING
TWENTY SECONDS LATER... A DREADFUL SCREAM, SUDDENLY CUT SHORT
AAAAGH—!
IT'S SISTER BINKS—THE DOGS 'AVE GOT HER!
WHAT IN GOD'S NAME...?
CAN WE—?
TOO LATE, PRINCESS... IT'S OVER
3544

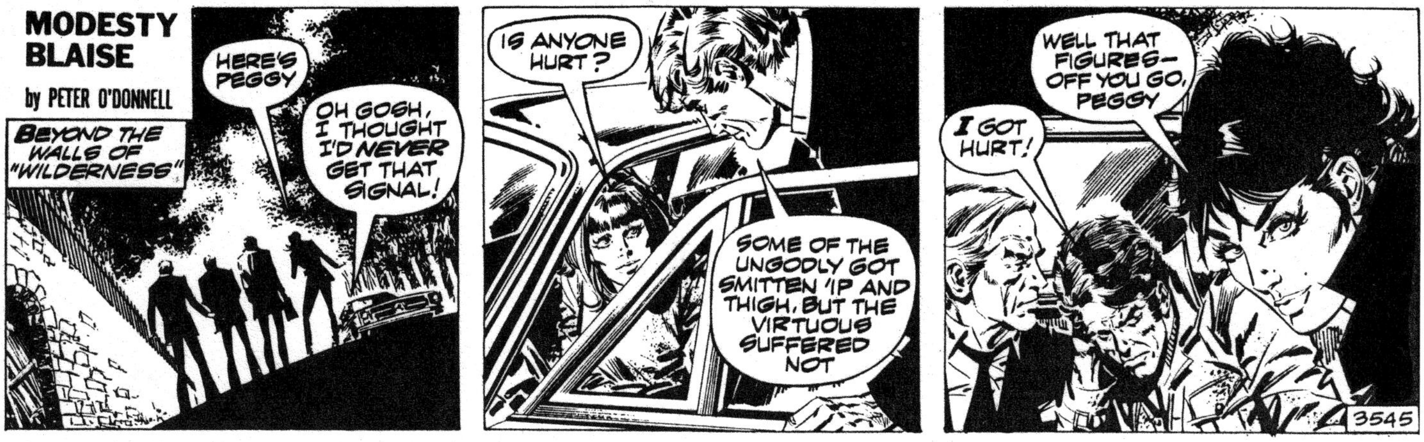
MODESTY BLAISE
by PETER O'DONNELL
BEYOND THE WALLS OF "WILDERNESS"
HERE'S PEGGY
OH GOSH, I THOUGHT I'D NEVER GET THAT SIGNAL!
IS ANYONE HURT?
SOME OF THE UNGODLY GOT SMITTEN 'IP AND THIGH, BUT THE VIRTUOUS SUFFERED NOT
I GOT HURT!
WELL THAT FIGURES— OFF YOU GO, PEGGY
3545

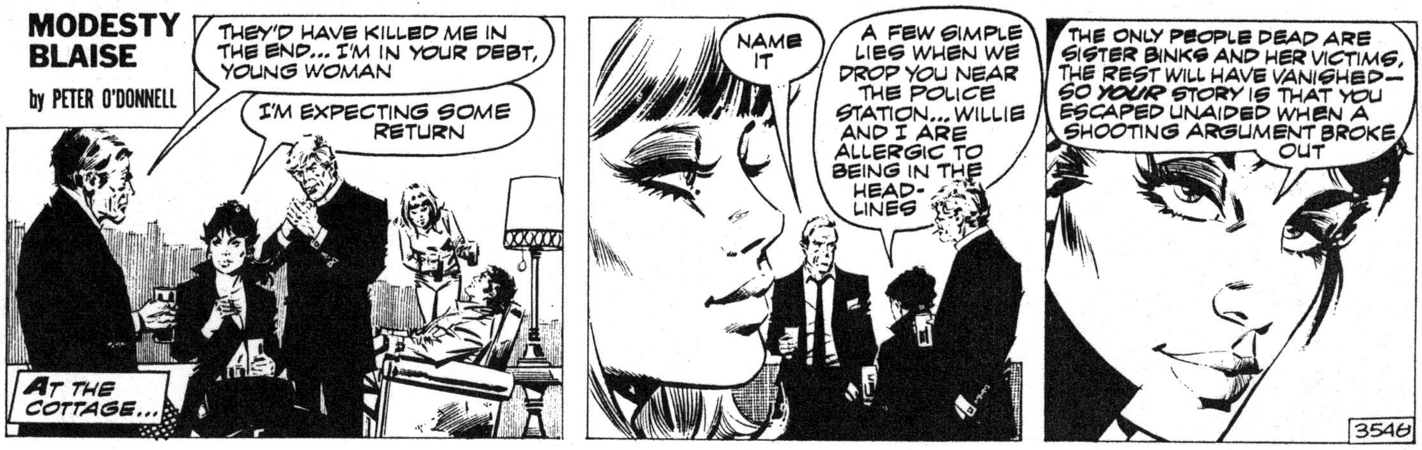
MODESTY BLAISE
by PETER O'DONNELL
AT THE COTTAGE...
THEY'D HAVE KILLED ME IN THE END... I'M IN YOUR DEBT, YOUNG WOMAN
I'M EXPECTING SOME RETURN
NAME IT
A FEW SIMPLE LIES WHEN WE DROP YOU NEAR THE POLICE STATION... WILLIE AND I ARE ALLERGIC TO BEING IN THE HEAD-LINES
THE ONLY PEOPLE DEAD ARE SISTER BINKS AND HER VICTIMS, THE REST WILL HAVE VANISHED— SO YOUR STORY IS THAT YOU ESCAPED UNAIDED WHEN A SHOOTING ARGUMENT BROKE OUT
3546

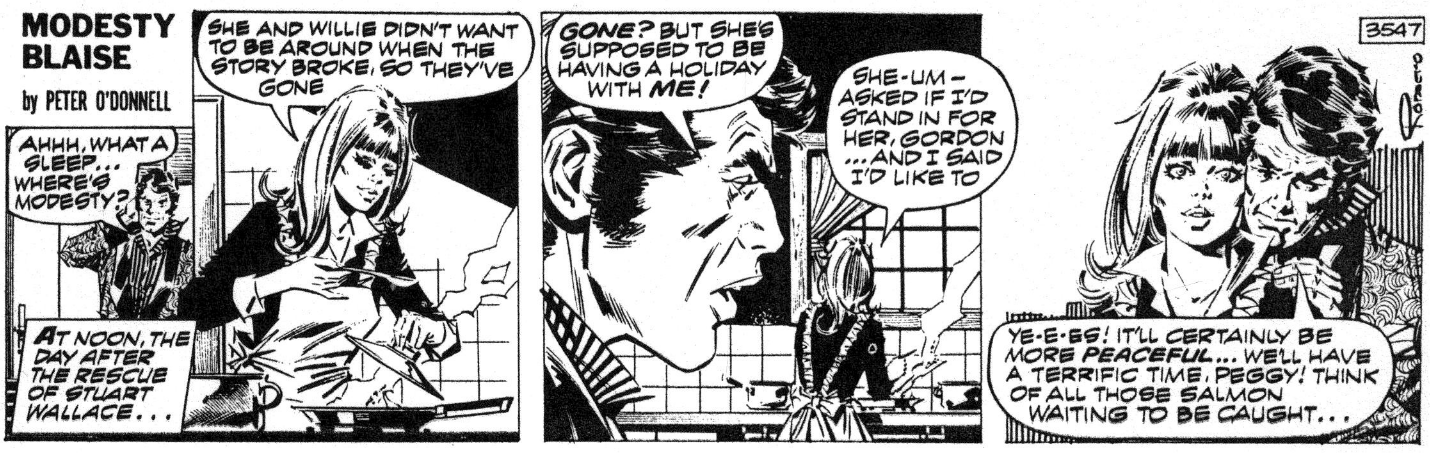
MODESTY BLAISE
by PETER O'DONNELL
AHHH, WHAT A SLEEP... WHERE'S MODESTY?
AT NOON, THE DAY AFTER THE RESCUE OF STUART WALLACE...
SHE AND WILLIE DIDN'T WANT TO BE AROUND WHEN THE STORY BROKE, SO THEY'VE GONE
GONE? BUT SHE'S SUPPOSED TO BE HAVING A HOLIDAY WITH ME!
SHE-UM- ASKED IF I'D STAND IN FOR HER, GORDON ... AND I SAID I'D LIKE TO
3547
YE-E-ES! IT'LL CERTAINLY BE MORE PEACEFUL... WE'LL HAVE A TERRIFIC TIME, PEGGY! THINK OF ALL THOSE SALMON WAITING TO BE CAUGHT...

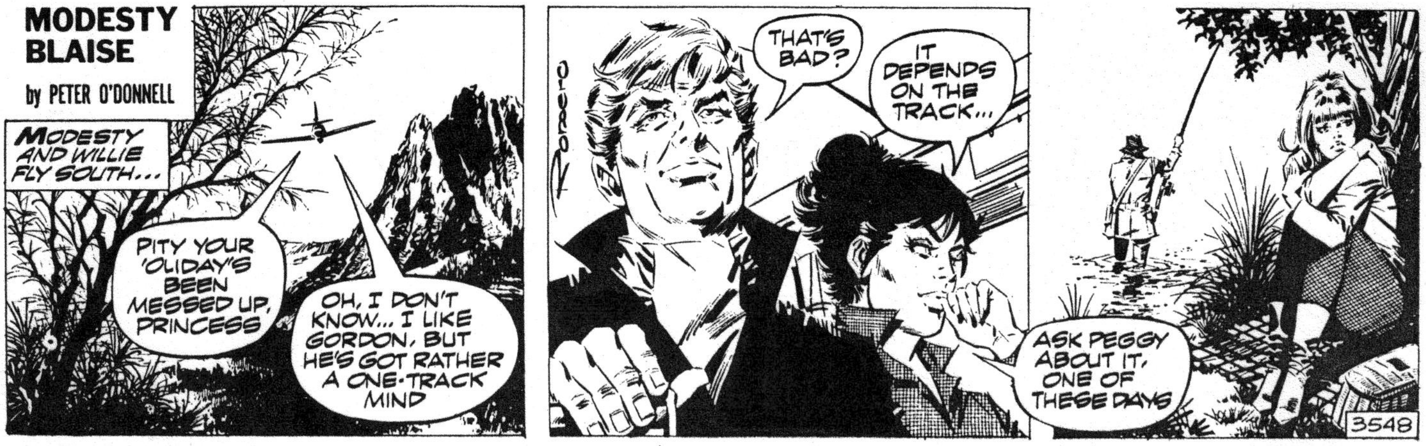
MODESTY BLAISE
by PETER O'DONNELL
MODESTY AND WILLIE FLY SOUTH...
PITY YOUR 'OLIDAY'S BEEN MESSED UP, PRINCESS
OH, I DON'T KNOW... I LIKE GORDON, BUT HE'S GOT RATHER A ONE-TRACK MIND
THAT'S BAD?
IT DEPENDS ON THE TRACK...
ASK PEGGY ABOUT IT, ONE OF THESE DAYS
3548

CRY WOLF

I'm sometimes asked how I think up ideas for stories. That's an easy question. The answer is, I don't know. I just browse around in a general way expecting something to click, and usually it does. A tiny germ of an idea emerges from something I've seen or heard or imagined, and I know it can grow into a story. If nothing clicks after a few days I set myself a challenge of some sort. I might think up a dramatic title and then work out a story to fit it. I recall that one of my favourite stories emerged from the title 'The Girl From the Future'. That was quite a challenge.

'Cry Wolf' started from a different challenge. In my office I have a globe of the Earth. I gave it a spin, jabbed a finger at it to make it stop, and found I'd picked Lapland as the location for the next story. Since I knew almost nothing about Lapland I had to do some research on it, and spent a couple of days at the London Library (this was in the days before you could do it all on the Internet) and I discovered a wealth of truly fascinating material.

There's a danger of being carried away by this, because it's all so interesting that you feel you just have to pass it on, but if you try to do that you'll end up with something more like a travel brochure than a story, and that's not what I'm here for. I can only use what fits into the storyline, and keep that pretty brief too. For example, I only use two frames to tell what Lapland farmers do when wolves attack their reindeer herds. I bet you'll never guess!

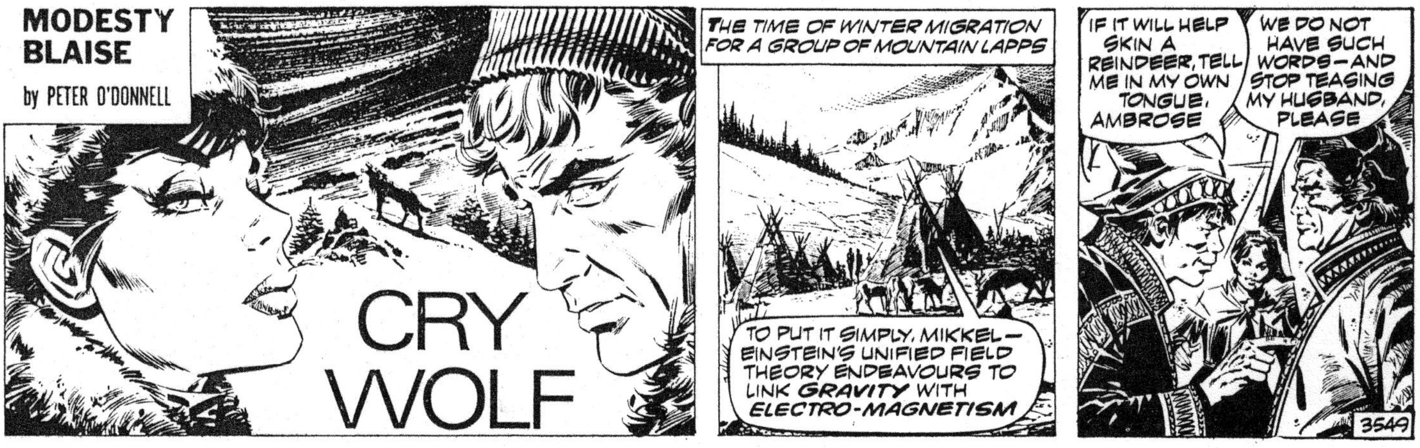
MODESTY BLAISE
by PETER O'DONNELL
CRY WOLF
THE TIME OF WINTER MIGRATION FOR A GROUP OF MOUNTAIN LAPPS
TO PUT IT SIMPLY, MIKKEL— EINSTEIN'S UNIFIED FIELD THEORY ENDEAVOURS TO LINK GRAVITY WITH ELECTRO-MAGNETISM
IF IT WILL HELP SKIN A REINDEER, TELL ME IN MY OWN TONGUE, AMBROSE
WE DO NOT HAVE SUCH WORDS—AND STOP TEASING MY HUSBAND, PLEASE
3549

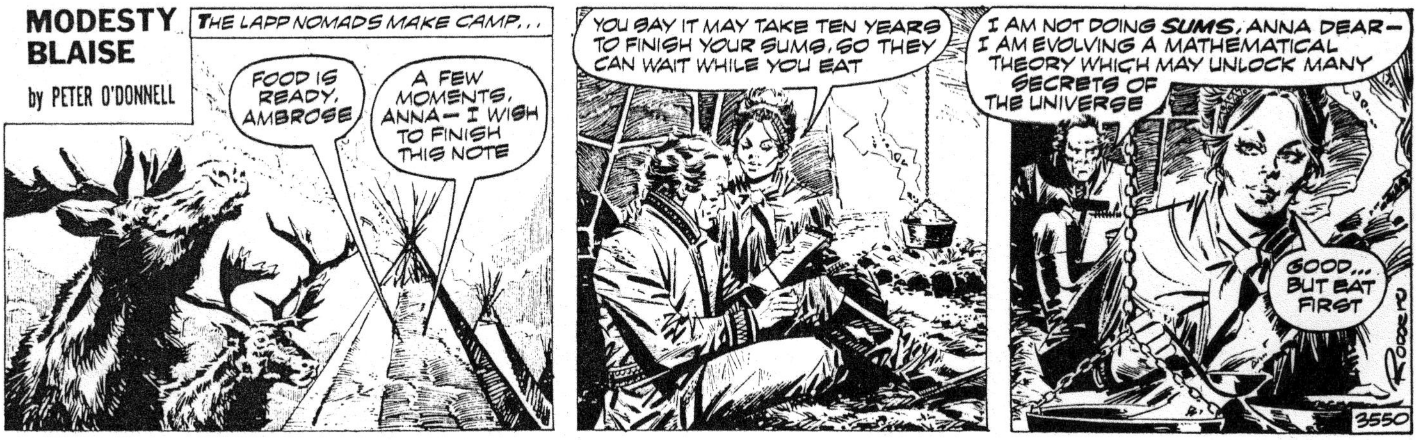
MODESTY BLAISE
by PETER O'DONNELL
THE LAPP NOMADS MAKE CAMP...
FOOD IS READY, AMBROSE
A FEW MOMENTS, ANNA—I WISH TO FINISH THIS NOTE
YOU SAY IT MAY TAKE TEN YEARS TO FINISH YOUR SUMS, SO THEY CAN WAIT WHILE YOU EAT
I AM NOT DOING SUMS, ANNA DEAR—I AM EVOLVING A MATHEMATICAL THEORY WHICH MAY UNLOCK MANY SECRETS OF THE UNIVERSE
GOOD... BUT EAT FIRST
3550

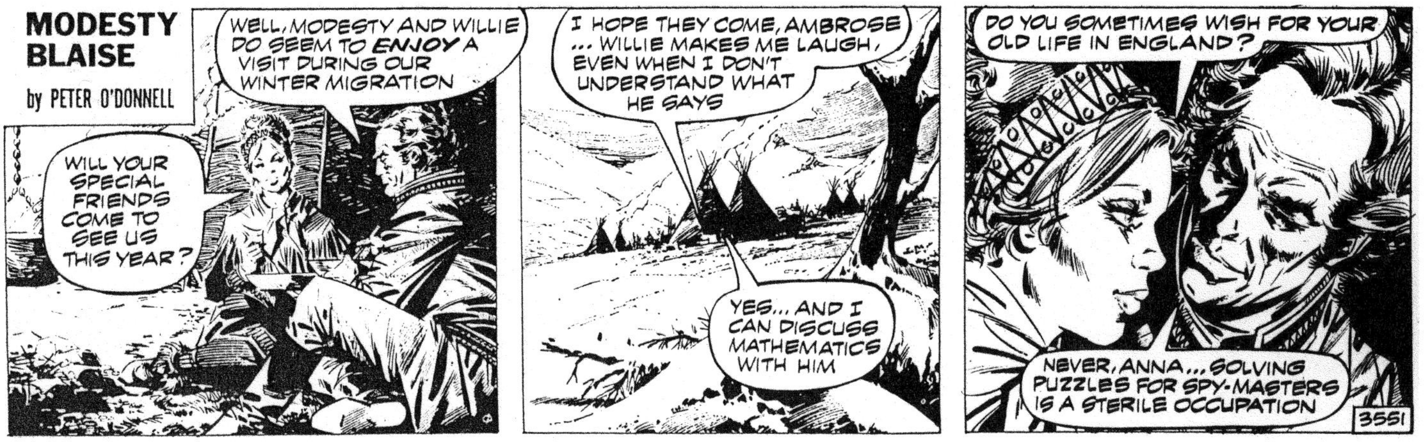
MODESTY BLAISE
by PETER O'DONNELL
WILL YOUR SPECIAL FRIENDS COME TO SEE US THIS YEAR?
WELL, MODESTY AND WILLIE DO SEEM TO ENJOY A VISIT DURING OUR WINTER MIGRATION
I HOPE THEY COME, AMBROSE ... WILLIE MAKES ME LAUGH, EVEN WHEN I DON'T UNDERSTAND WHAT HE SAYS
YES... AND I CAN DISCUSS MATHEMATICS WITH HIM
DO YOU SOMETIMES WISH FOR YOUR OLD LIFE IN ENGLAND?
NEVER, ANNA... SOLVING PUZZLES FOR SPY-MASTERS IS A STERILE OCCUPATION
3551

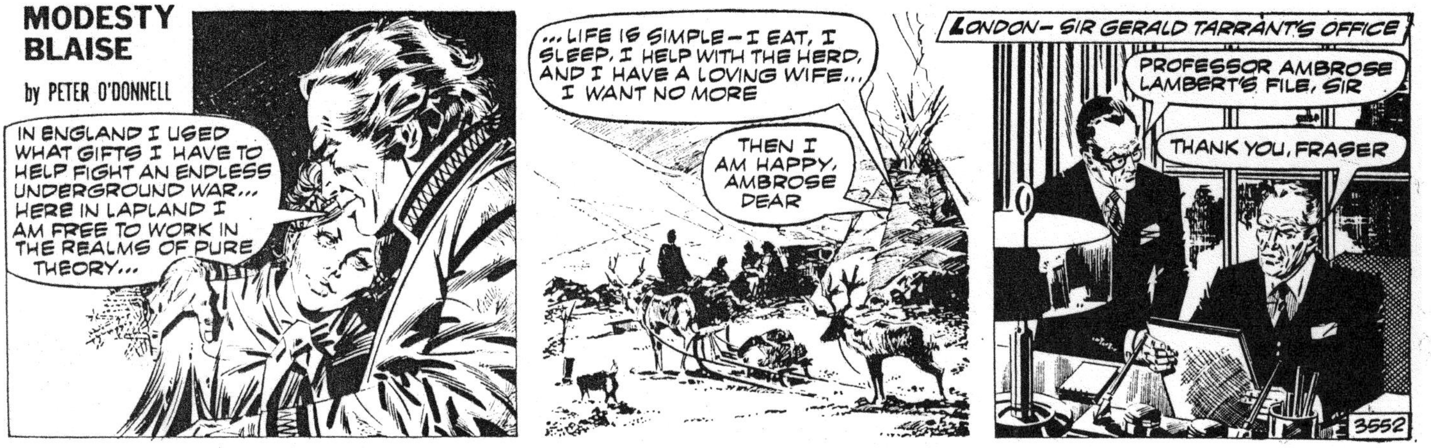
MODESTY BLAISE
by PETER O'DONNELL
IN ENGLAND I USED WHAT GIFTS I HAVE TO HELP FIGHT AN ENDLESS UNDERGROUND WAR... HERE IN LAPLAND I AM FREE TO WORK IN THE REALMS OF PURE THEORY...
... LIFE IS SIMPLE—I EAT, I SLEEP, I HELP WITH THE HERD, AND I HAVE A LOVING WIFE... I WANT NO MORE
THEN I AM HAPPY, AMBROSE DEAR
LONDON—SIR GERALD TARRANT'S OFFICE
PROFESSOR AMBROSE LAMBERT'S FILE, SIR
THANK YOU, FRASER
3552

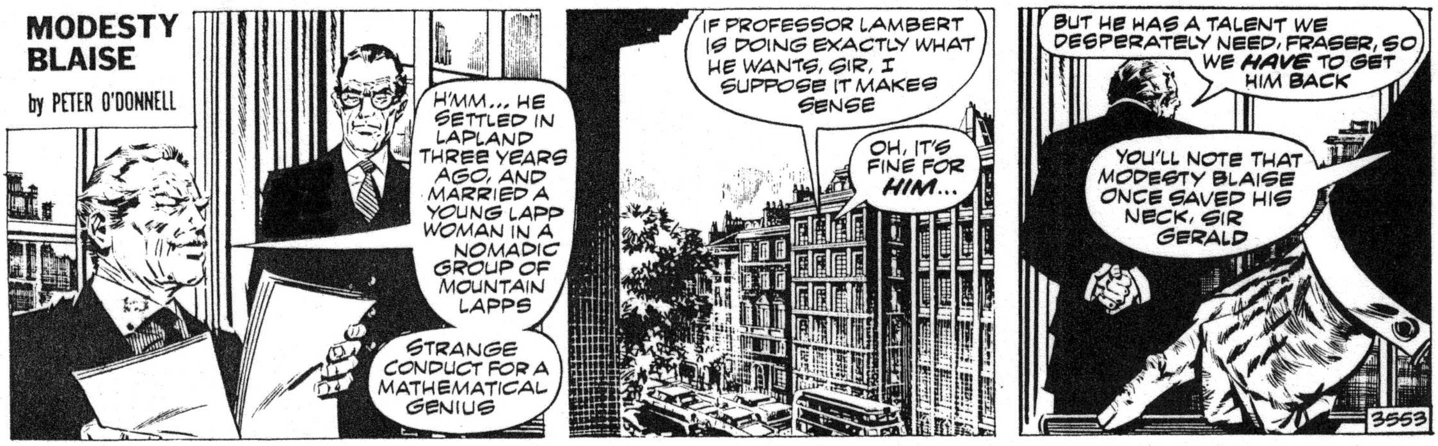
MODESTY BLAISE
by PETER O'DONNELL
H'MM... HE SETTLED IN LAPLAND THREE YEARS AGO, AND MARRIED A YOUNG LAPP WOMAN IN A NOMADIC GROUP OF MOUNTAIN LAPPS
STRANGE CONDUCT FOR A MATHEMATICAL GENIUS
IF PROFESSOR LAMBERT IS DOING EXACTLY WHAT HE WANTS, SIR, I SUPPOSE IT MAKES SENSE
OH, IT'S FINE FOR *HIM*...
BUT HE HAS A TALENT WE DESPERATELY NEED, FRASER, SO WE *HAVE* TO GET HIM BACK
YOU'LL NOTE THAT MODESTY BLAISE ONCE SAVED HIS NECK, SIR GERALD
3553

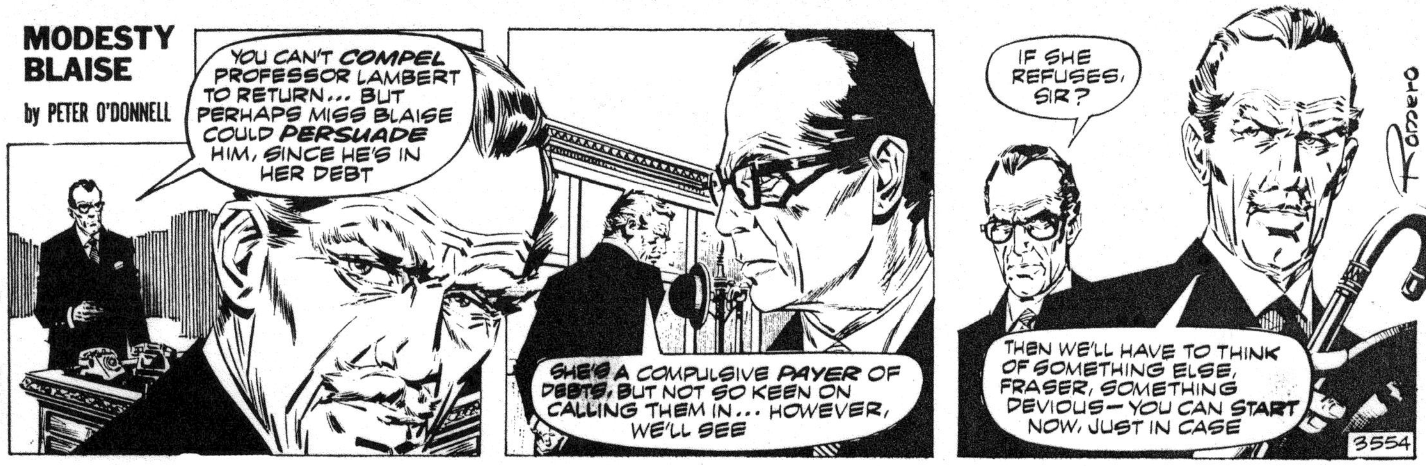
MODESTY BLAISE
by PETER O'DONNELL
YOU CAN'T *COMPEL* PROFESSOR LAMBERT TO RETURN... BUT PERHAPS MISS BLAISE COULD *PERSUADE* HIM, SINCE HE'S IN HER DEBT
SHE'S A COMPULSIVE *PAYER* OF DEBTS, BUT NOT SO KEEN ON CALLING THEM IN... HOWEVER, WE'LL SEE
IF SHE REFUSES, SIR?
THEN WE'LL HAVE TO THINK OF SOMETHING ELSE, FRASER, SOMETHING DEVIOUS—YOU CAN *START* NOW, JUST IN CASE
Romero
3554

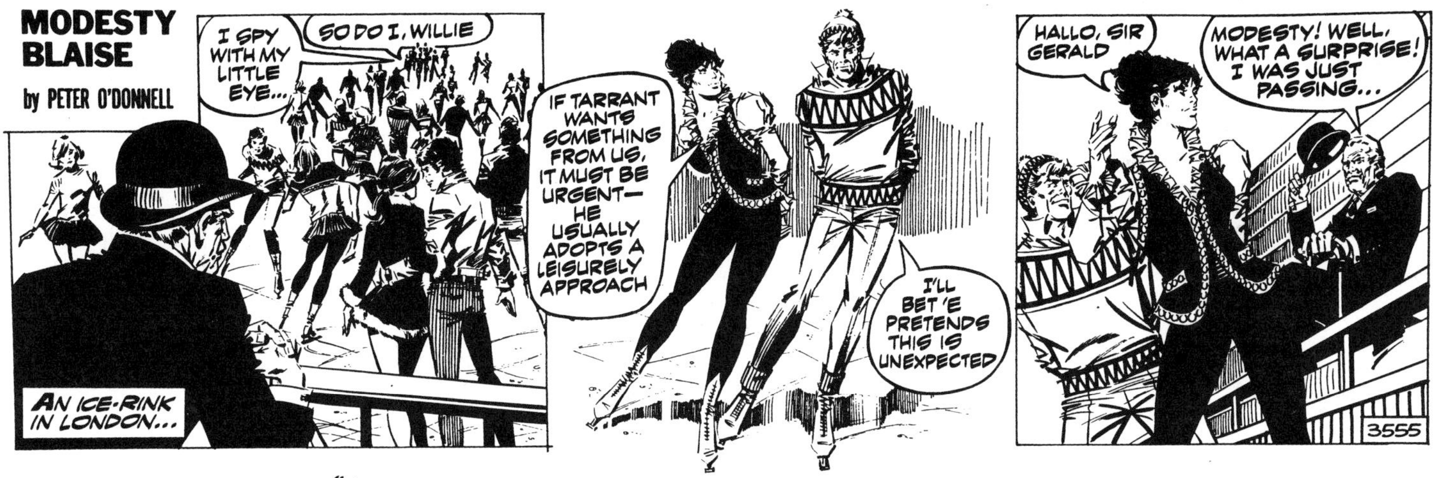
MODESTY BLAISE
by PETER O'DONNELL
I SPY WITH MY LITTLE EYE...
SO DO I, WILLIE
AN ICE-RINK IN LONDON...
IF TARRANT WANTS SOMETHING FROM US, IT MUST BE URGENT—HE USUALLY ADOPTS A LEISURELY APPROACH
I'LL BET 'E PRETENDS THIS IS UNEXPECTED
HALLO, SIR GERALD
MODESTY! WELL, WHAT A SURPRISE! I WAS JUST PASSING...
3555

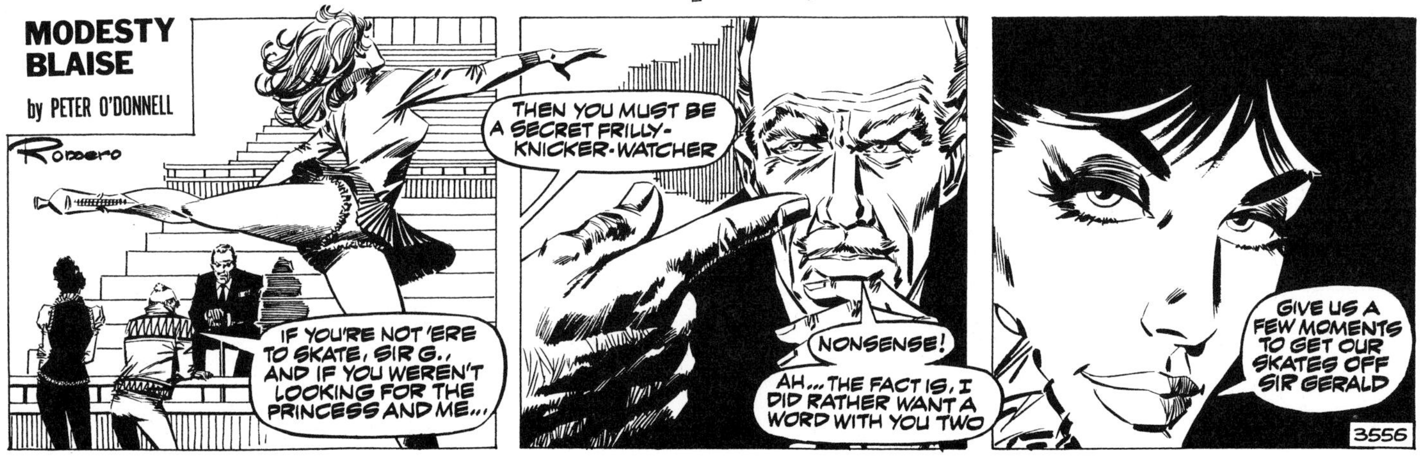
MODESTY BLAISE
by PETER O'DONNELL
Romero
IF YOU'RE NOT 'ERE TO SKATE, SIR G., AND IF YOU WEREN'T LOOKING FOR THE PRINCESS AND ME...
THEN YOU MUST BE A SECRET FRILLY-KNICKER-WATCHER
NONSENSE!
AH... THE FACT IS, I DID RATHER WANT A WORD WITH YOU TWO
GIVE US A FEW MOMENTS TO GET OUR SKATES OFF SIR GERALD
3556

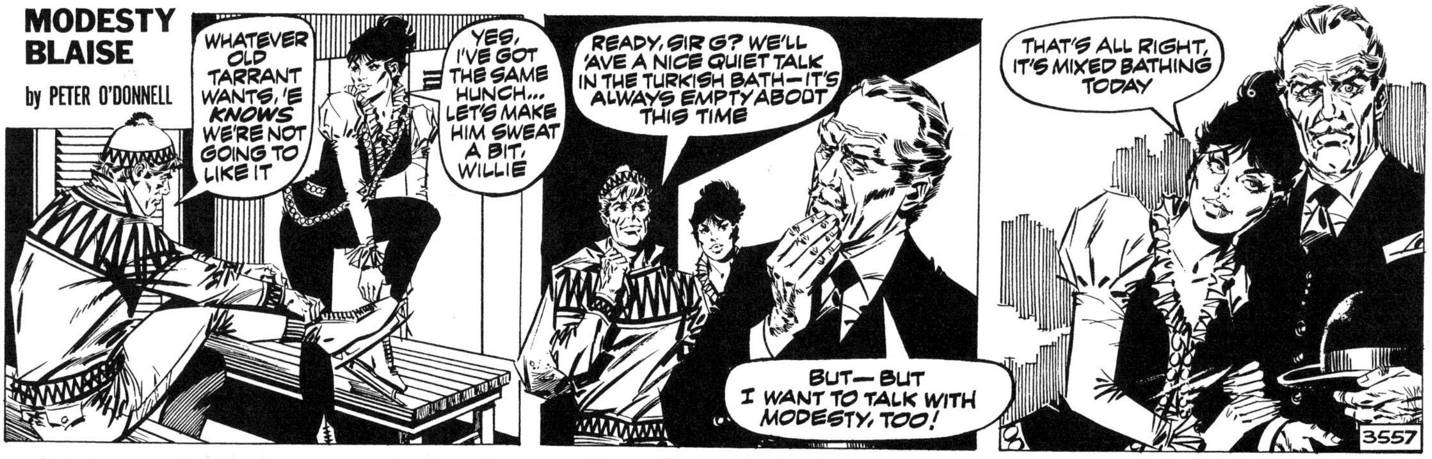
MODESTY BLAISE
by PETER O'DONNELL
WHATEVER OLD TARRANT WANTS, 'E KNOWS WE'RE NOT GOING TO LIKE IT
YES, I'VE GOT THE SAME HUNCH... LET'S MAKE HIM SWEAT A BIT, WILLIE
READY, SIR G? WE'LL 'AVE A NICE QUIET TALK IN THE TURKISH BATH—IT'S ALWAYS EMPTY ABOUT THIS TIME
BUT—BUT I WANT TO TALK WITH MODESTY, TOO!
THAT'S ALL RIGHT, IT'S MIXED BATHING TODAY
3557

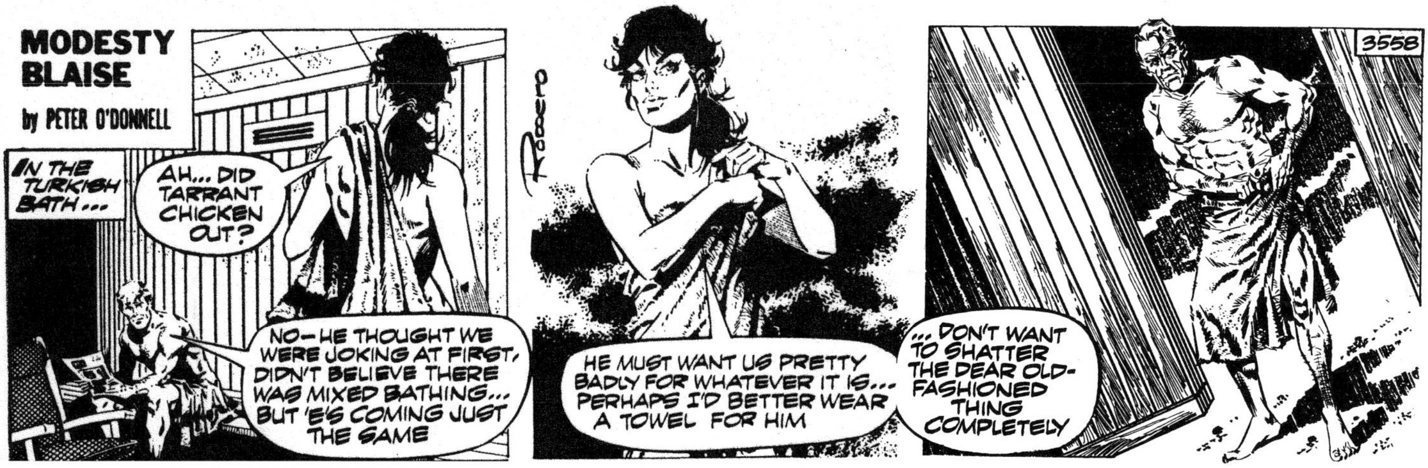
MODESTY BLAISE
by PETER O'DONNELL
IN THE TURKISH BATH...
AH... DID TARRANT CHICKEN OUT?
NO—HE THOUGHT WE WERE JOKING AT FIRST, DIDN'T BELIEVE THERE WAS MIXED BATHING... BUT 'E'S COMING JUST THE SAME
HE MUST WANT US PRETTY BADLY FOR WHATEVER IT IS... PERHAPS I'D BETTER WEAR A TOWEL FOR HIM
...DON'T WANT TO SHATTER THE DEAR OLD-FASHIONED THING COMPLETELY
3558

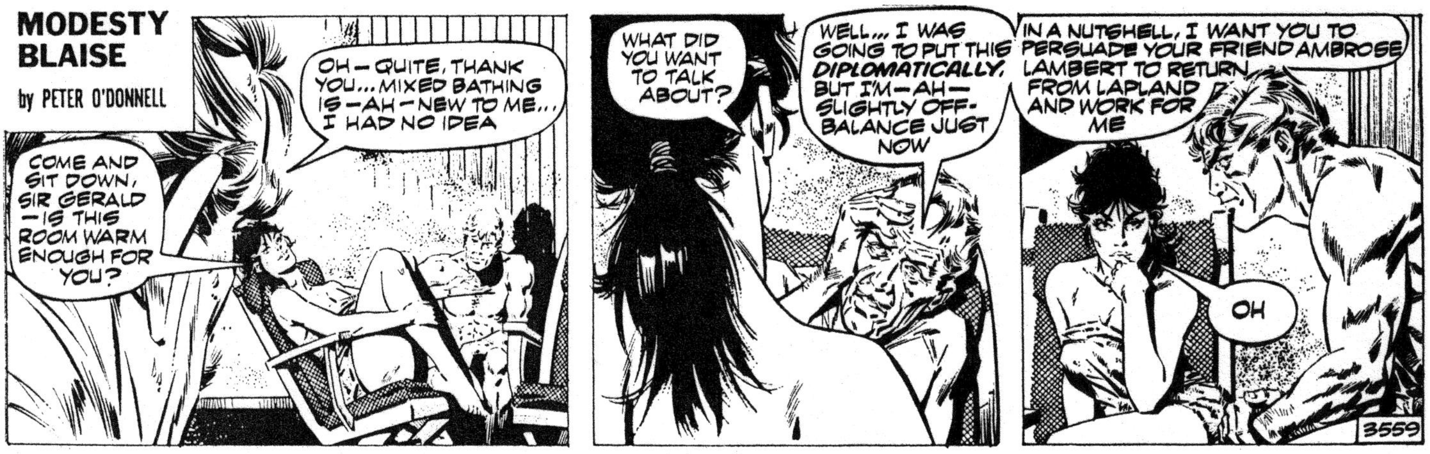
MODESTY BLAISE
by PETER O'DONNELL
COME AND SIT DOWN, SIR GERALD—IS THIS ROOM WARM ENOUGH FOR YOU?
OH—QUITE, THANK YOU... MIXED BATHING IS—AH—NEW TO ME... I HAD NO IDEA
WHAT DID YOU WANT TO TALK ABOUT?
WELL... I WAS GOING TO PUT THIS DIPLOMATICALLY, BUT I'M—AH—SLIGHTLY OFF-BALANCE JUST NOW
IN A NUTSHELL, I WANT YOU TO PERSUADE YOUR FRIEND AMBROSE LAMBERT TO RETURN FROM LAPLAND AND WORK FOR ME
OH
3559

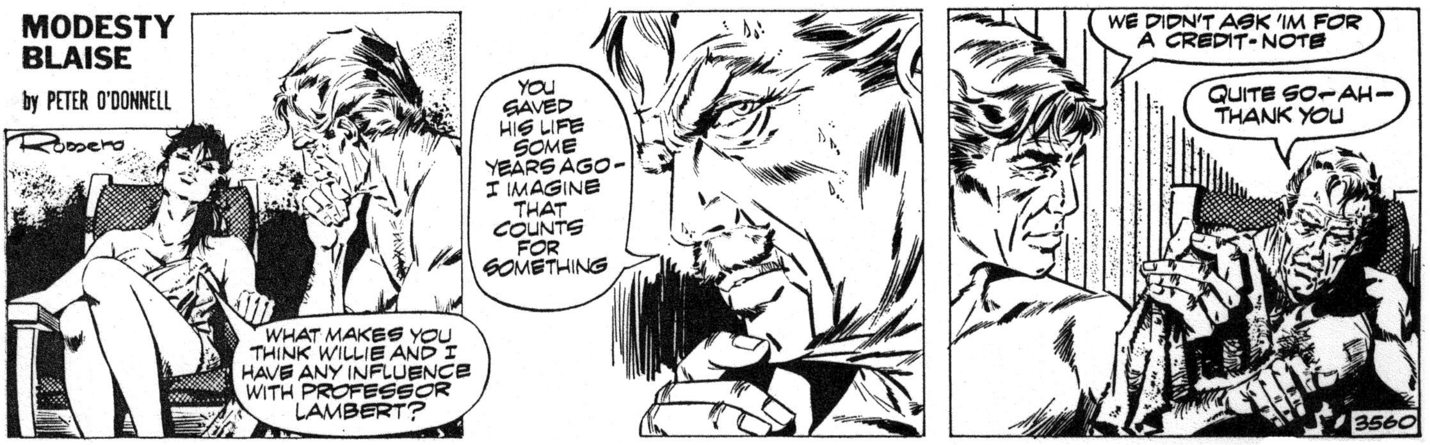
MODESTY BLAISE
by PETER O'DONNELL
WHAT MAKES YOU THINK WILLIE AND I HAVE ANY INFLUENCE WITH PROFESSOR LAMBERT?
YOU SAVED HIS LIFE SOME YEARS AGO—I IMAGINE THAT COUNTS FOR SOMETHING
WE DIDN'T ASK 'IM FOR A CREDIT-NOTE
QUITE SO—AH—THANK YOU
3560

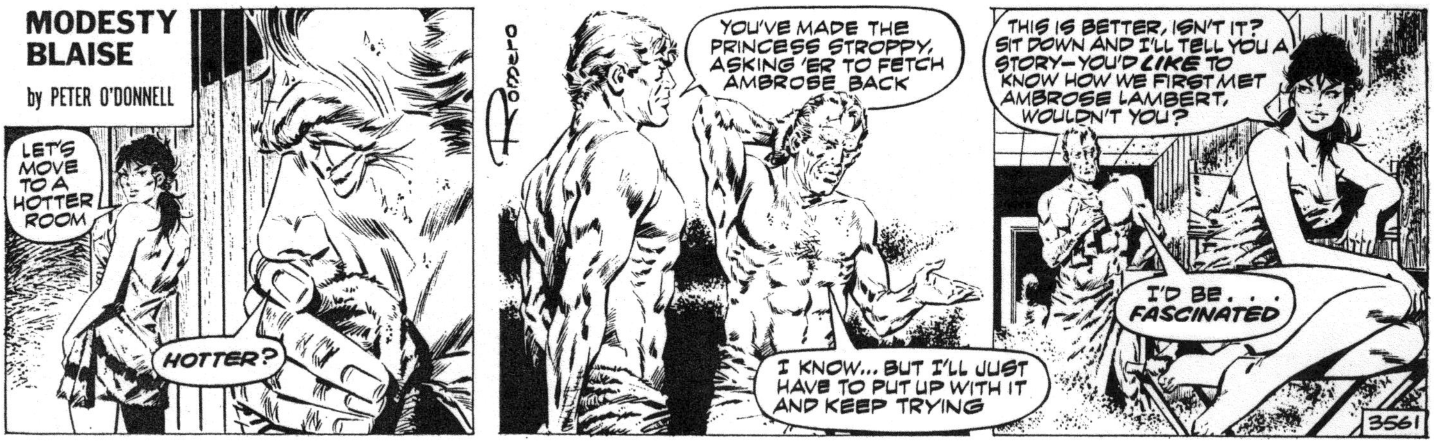
MODESTY BLAISE
by PETER O'DONNELL
LET'S MOVE TO A HOTTER ROOM
HOTTER?
YOU'VE MADE THE PRINCESS STROPPY, ASKING 'ER TO FETCH AMBROSE BACK
I KNOW... BUT I'LL JUST HAVE TO PUT UP WITH IT AND KEEP TRYING
THIS IS BETTER, ISN'T IT? SIT DOWN AND I'LL TELL YOU A STORY—YOU'D LIKE TO KNOW HOW WE FIRST MET AMBROSE LAMBERT, WOULDN'T YOU?
I'D BE . . . FASCINATED
3561

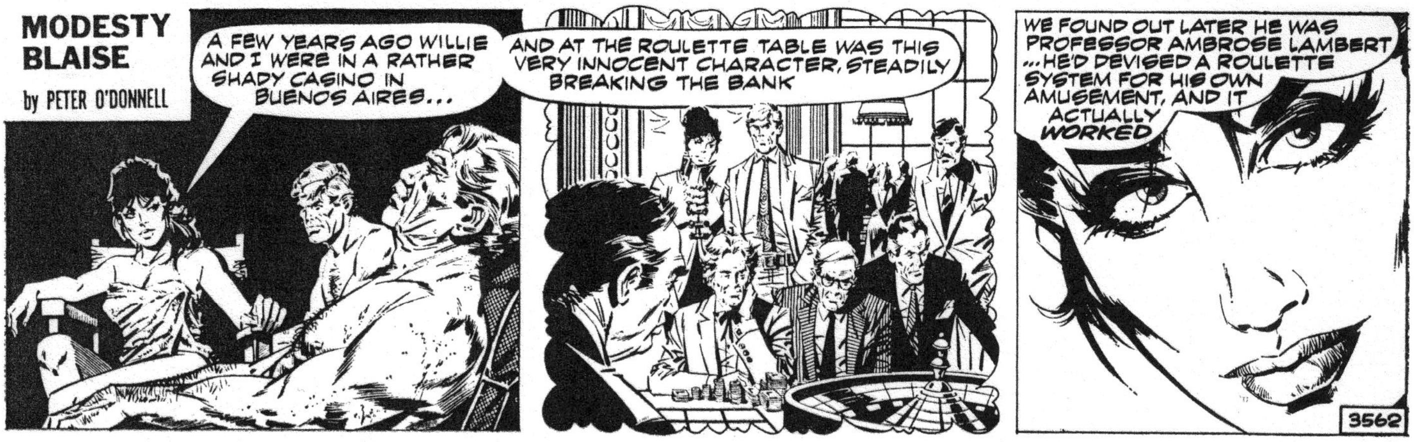
MODESTY BLAISE
by PETER O'DONNELL
A FEW YEARS AGO WILLIE AND I WERE IN A RATHER SHADY CASINO IN BUENOS AIRES...
AND AT THE ROULETTE TABLE WAS THIS VERY INNOCENT CHARACTER, STEADILY BREAKING THE BANK
WE FOUND OUT LATER HE WAS PROFESSOR AMBROSE LAMBERT ...HE'D DEVISED A ROULETTE SYSTEM FOR HIS OWN AMUSEMENT, AND IT ACTUALLY WORKED
3562

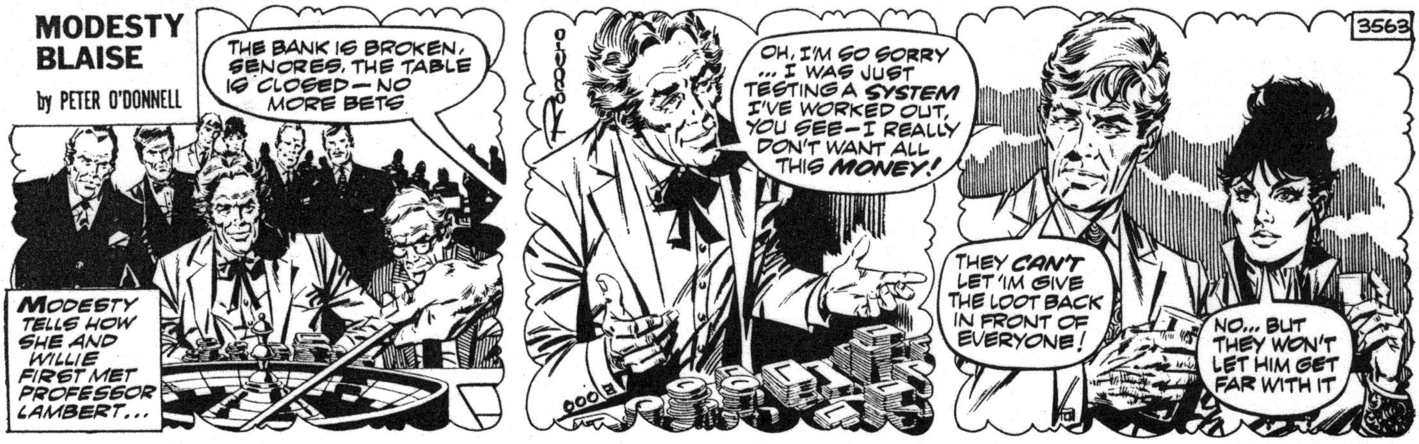
MODESTY BLAISE
by PETER O'DONNELL
THE BANK IS BROKEN, SENORES. THE TABLE IS CLOSED—NO MORE BETS
MODESTY TELLS HOW SHE AND WILLIE FIRST MET PROFESSOR LAMBERT...
OH, I'M SO SORRY ... I WAS JUST TESTING A SYSTEM I'VE WORKED OUT, YOU SEE—I REALLY DON'T WANT ALL THIS MONEY!
3563
THEY CAN'T LET 'IM GIVE THE LOOT BACK IN FRONT OF EVERYONE!
NO... BUT THEY WON'T LET HIM GET FAR WITH IT

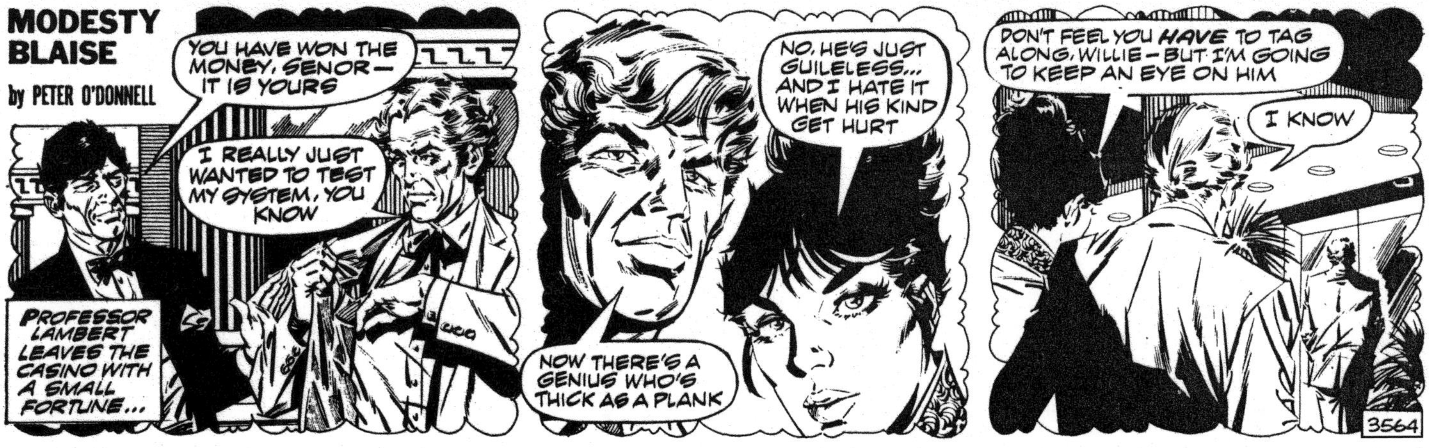
MODESTY BLAISE
by PETER O'DONNELL
YOU HAVE WON THE MONEY, SENOR—IT IS YOURS
I REALLY JUST WANTED TO TEST MY SYSTEM, YOU KNOW
PROFESSOR LAMBERT LEAVES THE CASINO WITH A SMALL FORTUNE...
NO, HE'S JUST GUILELESS... AND I HATE IT WHEN HIS KIND GET HURT
NOW THERE'S A GENIUS WHO'S THICK AS A PLANK
DON'T FEEL YOU HAVE TO TAG ALONG, WILLIE—BUT I'M GOING TO KEEP AN EYE ON HIM
I KNOW
3564

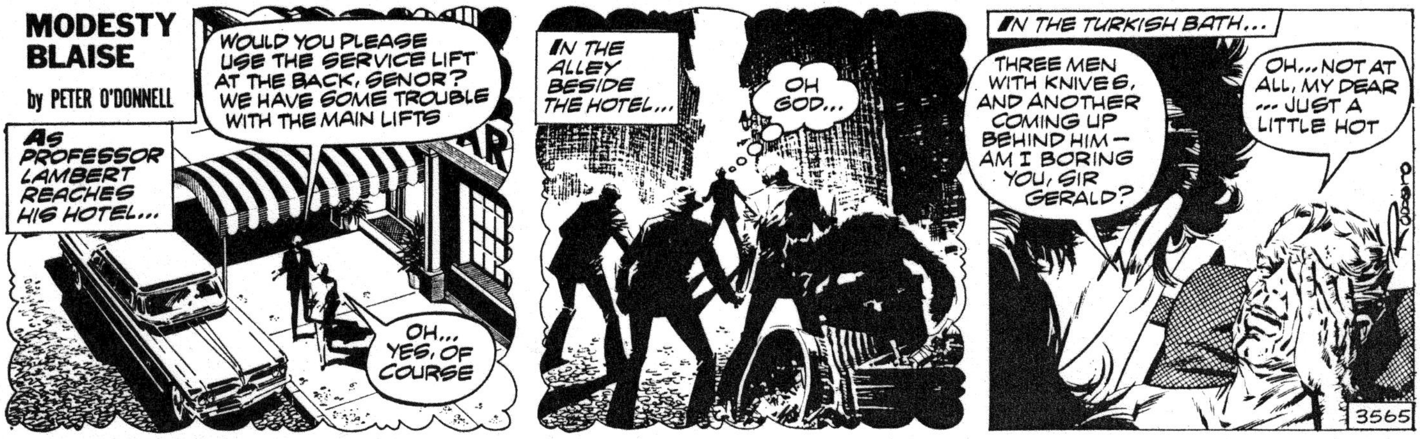
MODESTY BLAISE
by PETER O'DONNELL
AS PROFESSOR LAMBERT REACHES HIS HOTEL...
WOULD YOU PLEASE USE THE SERVICE LIFT AT THE BACK, SENOR? WE HAVE SOME TROUBLE WITH THE MAIN LIFTS
OH... YES, OF COURSE
IN THE ALLEY BESIDE THE HOTEL...
OH GOD...
IN THE TURKISH BATH...
THREE MEN WITH KNIVES, AND ANOTHER COMING UP BEHIND HIM — AM I BORING YOU, SIR GERALD?
OH... NOT AT ALL, MY DEAR ... JUST A LITTLE HOT
3565

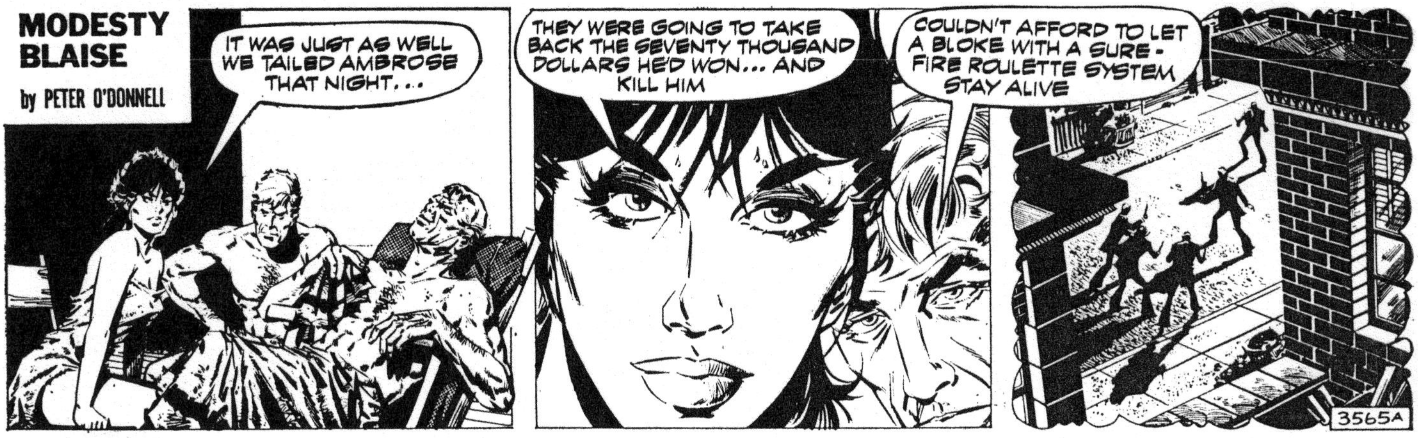
MODESTY BLAISE
by PETER O'DONNELL
IT WAS JUST AS WELL WE TAILED AMBROSE THAT NIGHT...
THEY WERE GOING TO TAKE BACK THE SEVENTY THOUSAND DOLLARS HE'D WON... AND KILL HIM
COULDN'T AFFORD TO LET A BLOKE WITH A SURE-FIRE ROULETTE SYSTEM STAY ALIVE
3565A

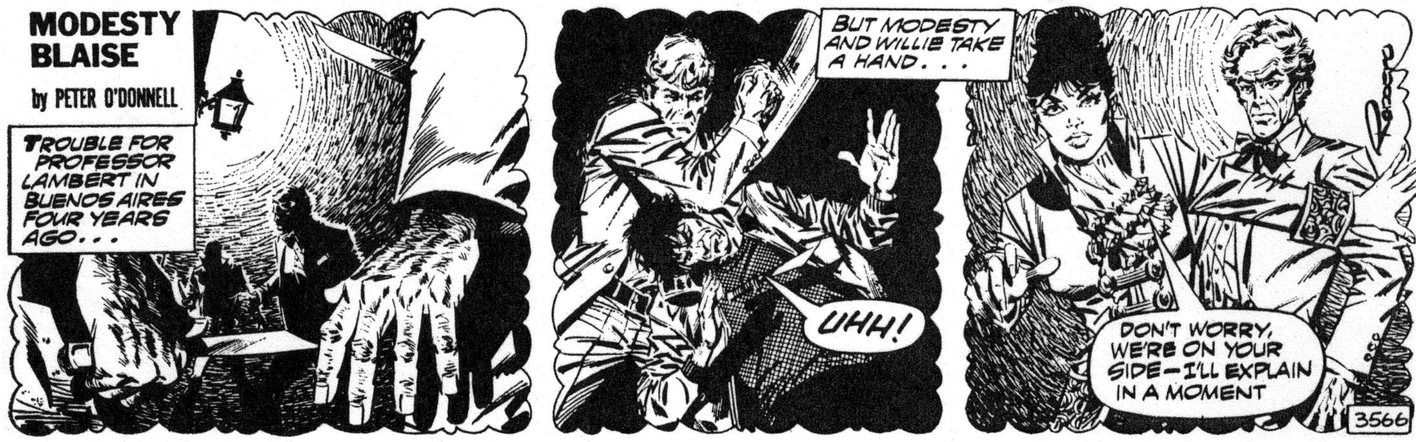
MODESTY BLAISE
by PETER O'DONNELL
TROUBLE FOR PROFESSOR LAMBERT IN BUENOS AIRES FOUR YEARS AGO...
BUT MODESTY AND WILLIE TAKE A HAND...
UHH!
DON'T WORRY, WE'RE ON YOUR SIDE — I'LL EXPLAIN IN A MOMENT
3566

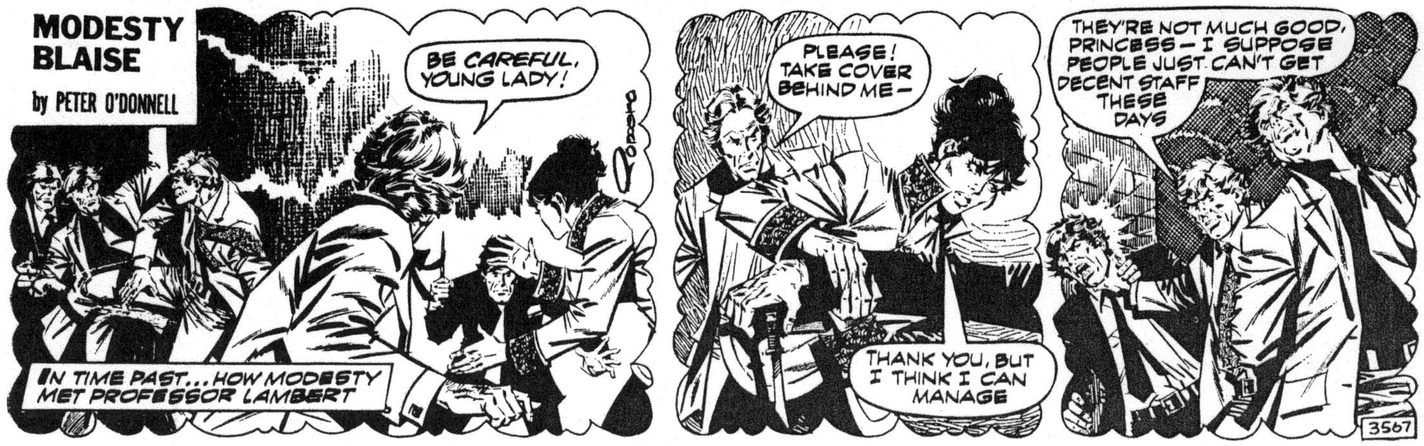
MODESTY BLAISE
by PETER O'DONNELL
BE CAREFUL, YOUNG LADY!
IN TIME PAST... HOW MODESTY MET PROFESSOR LAMBERT
PLEASE! TAKE COVER BEHIND ME —
THANK YOU, BUT I THINK I CAN MANAGE
THEY'RE NOT MUCH GOOD, PRINCESS — I SUPPOSE PEOPLE JUST CAN'T GET DECENT STAFF THESE DAYS
3567

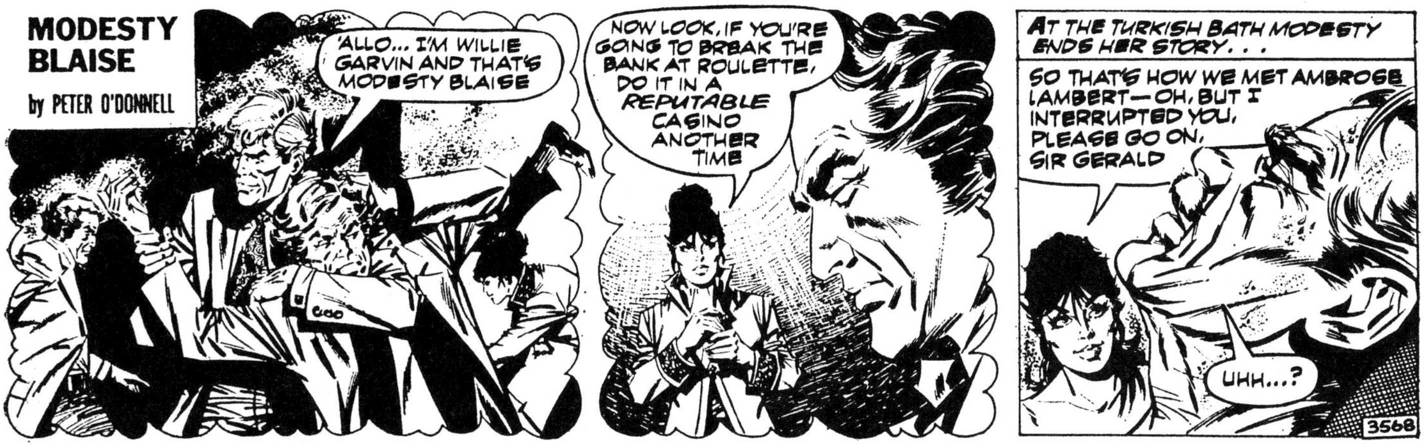
MODESTY BLAISE
by PETER O'DONNELL
'ALLO... I'M WILLIE GARVIN AND THAT'S MODESTY BLAISE
NOW LOOK, IF YOU'RE GOING TO BREAK THE BANK AT ROULETTE, DO IT IN A REPUTABLE CASINO ANOTHER TIME
AT THE TURKISH BATH MODESTY ENDS HER STORY . . .
SO THAT'S HOW WE MET AMBROSE LAMBERT—OH, BUT I INTERRUPTED YOU, PLEASE GO ON, SIR GERALD
UHH...?
3568

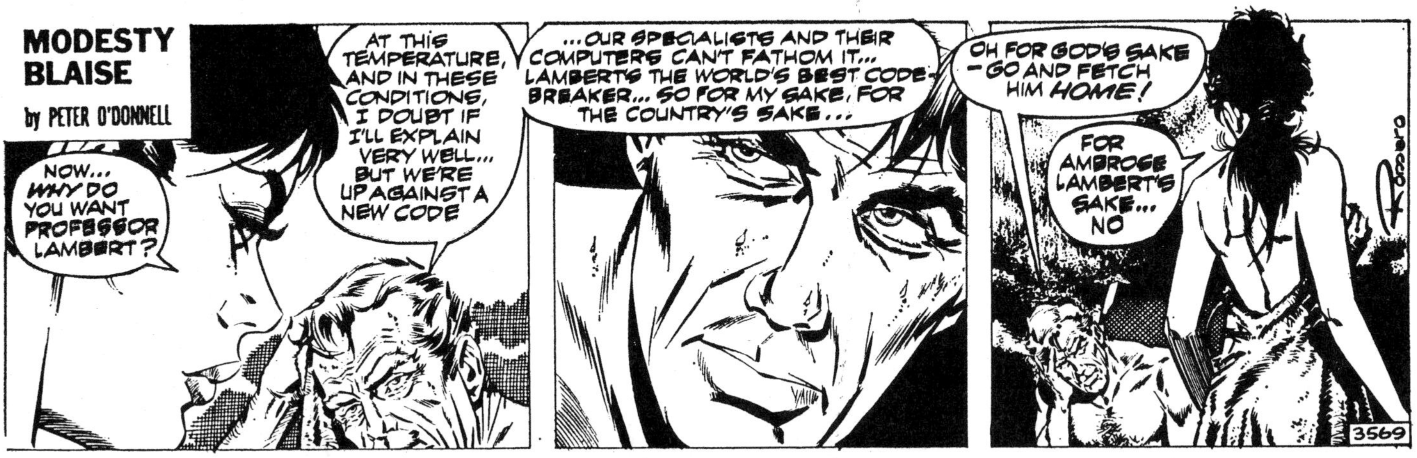
MODESTY BLAISE
by PETER O'DONNELL
NOW... WHY DO YOU WANT PROFESSOR LAMBERT?
AT THIS TEMPERATURE, AND IN THESE CONDITIONS, I DOUBT IF I'LL EXPLAIN VERY WELL... BUT WE'RE UP AGAINST A NEW CODE
...OUR SPECIALISTS AND THEIR COMPUTERS CAN'T FATHOM IT... LAMBERT'S THE WORLD'S BEST CODE-BREAKER... SO FOR MY SAKE, FOR THE COUNTRY'S SAKE...
OH FOR GOD'S SAKE —GO AND FETCH HIM HOME!
FOR AMBROSE LAMBERT'S SAKE... NO
3569

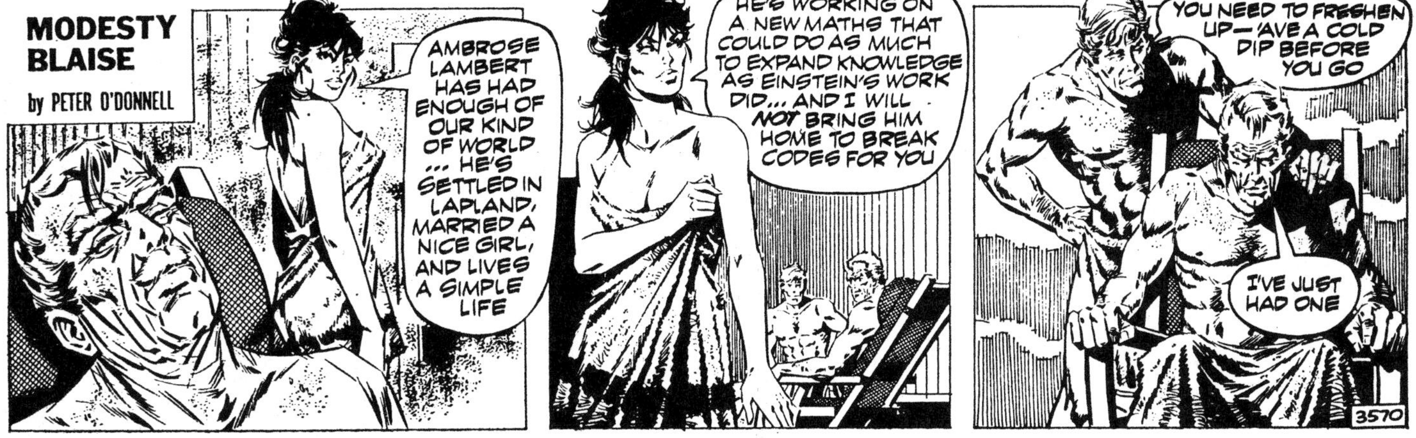
MODESTY BLAISE
by PETER O'DONNELL
AMBROSE LAMBERT HAS HAD ENOUGH OF OUR KIND OF WORLD ... HE'S SETTLED IN LAPLAND, MARRIED A NICE GIRL, AND LIVES A SIMPLE LIFE
HE'S WORKING ON A NEW MATHS THAT COULD DO AS MUCH TO EXPAND KNOWLEDGE AS EINSTEIN'S WORK DID... AND I WILL NOT BRING HIM HOME TO BREAK CODES FOR YOU
YOU NEED TO FRESHEN UP—'AVE A COLD DIP BEFORE YOU GO
I'VE JUST HAD ONE
3570

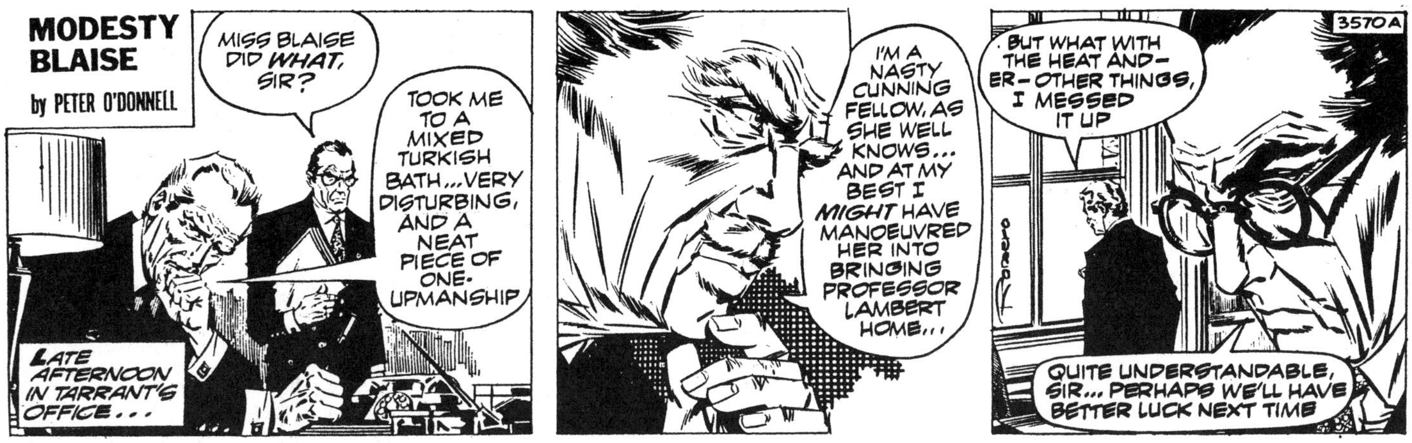
MODESTY BLAISE
by PETER O'DONNELL
MISS BLAISE DID WHAT, SIR?
TOOK ME TO A MIXED TURKISH BATH... VERY DISTURBING, AND A NEAT PIECE OF ONE-UPMANSHIP
LATE AFTERNOON IN TARRANT'S OFFICE . . .
I'M A NASTY CUNNING FELLOW, AS SHE WELL KNOWS... AND AT MY BEST I MIGHT HAVE MANOEUVRED HER INTO BRINGING PROFESSOR LAMBERT HOME...
3570 A
BUT WHAT WITH THE HEAT AND— ER— OTHER THINGS, I MESSED IT UP
QUITE UNDERSTANDABLE, SIR... PERHAPS WE'LL HAVE BETTER LUCK NEXT TIME

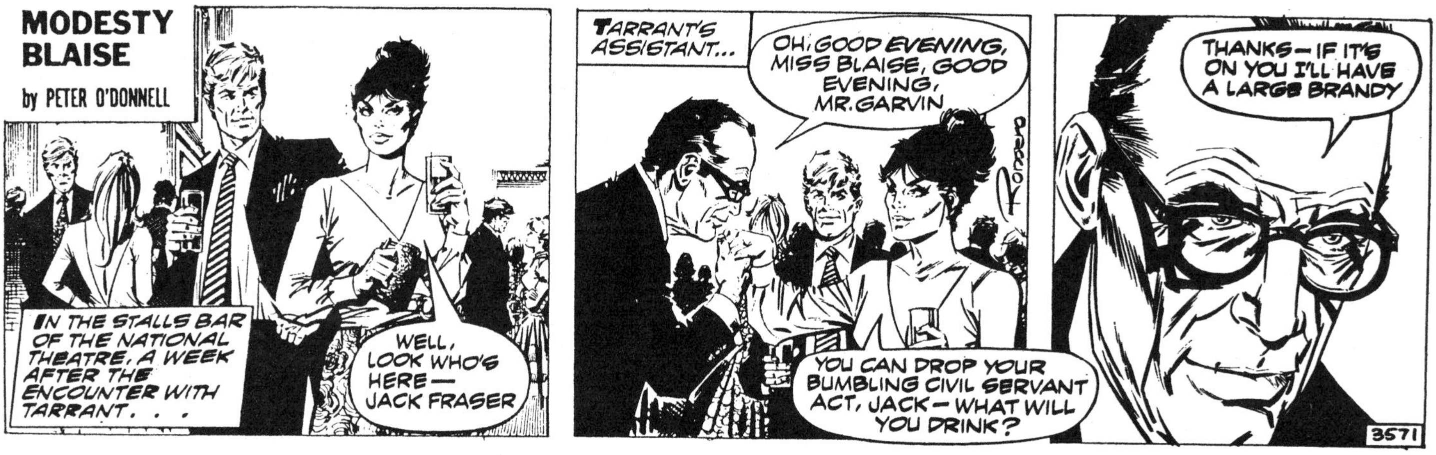
MODESTY BLAISE
by PETER O'DONNELL
IN THE STALLS BAR OF THE NATIONAL THEATRE, A WEEK AFTER THE ENCOUNTER WITH TARRANT . . .
WELL, LOOK WHO'S HERE— JACK FRASER
TARRANT'S ASSISTANT...
OH, GOOD EVENING, MISS BLAISE, GOOD EVENING, MR. GARVIN
YOU CAN DROP YOUR BUMBLING CIVIL SERVANT ACT, JACK—WHAT WILL YOU DRINK?
THANKS—IF IT'S ON YOU I'LL HAVE A LARGE BRANDY
3571

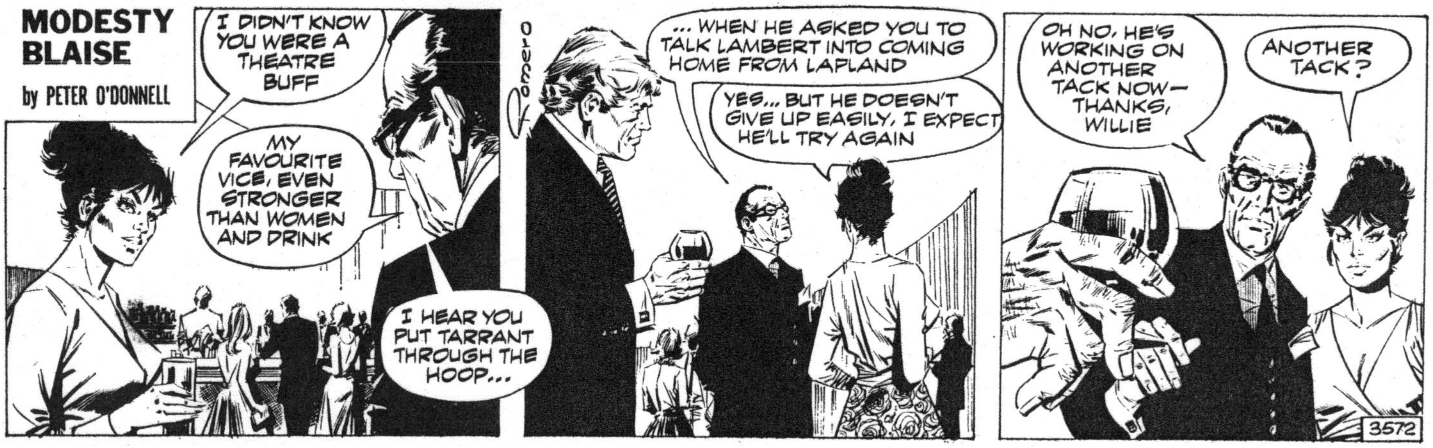
MODESTY BLAISE
by PETER O'DONNELL
I DIDN'T KNOW YOU WERE A THEATRE BUFF
MY FAVOURITE VICE, EVEN STRONGER THAN WOMEN AND DRINK
I HEAR YOU PUT TARRANT THROUGH THE HOOP...
... WHEN HE ASKED YOU TO TALK LAMBERT INTO COMING HOME FROM LAPLAND
YES... BUT HE DOESN'T GIVE UP EASILY, I EXPECT HE'LL TRY AGAIN
OH NO, HE'S WORKING ON ANOTHER TACK NOW— THANKS, WILLIE
ANOTHER TACK?
3572

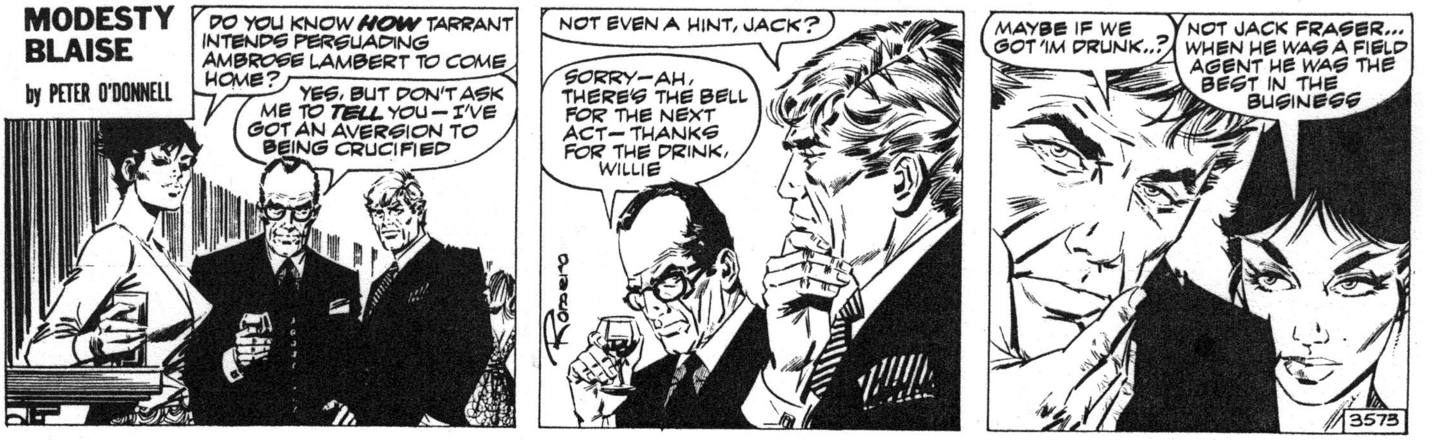
MODESTY BLAISE
by PETER O'DONNELL
DO YOU KNOW HOW TARRANT INTENDS PERSUADING AMBROSE LAMBERT TO COME HOME?
YES, BUT DON'T ASK ME TO TELL YOU—I'VE GOT AN AVERSION TO BEING CRUCIFIED
NOT EVEN A HINT, JACK?
SORRY—AH, THERE'S THE BELL FOR THE NEXT ACT—THANKS FOR THE DRINK, WILLIE
MAYBE IF WE GOT 'IM DRUNK..?
NOT JACK FRASER... WHEN HE WAS A FIELD AGENT HE WAS THE BEST IN THE BUSINESS
3573

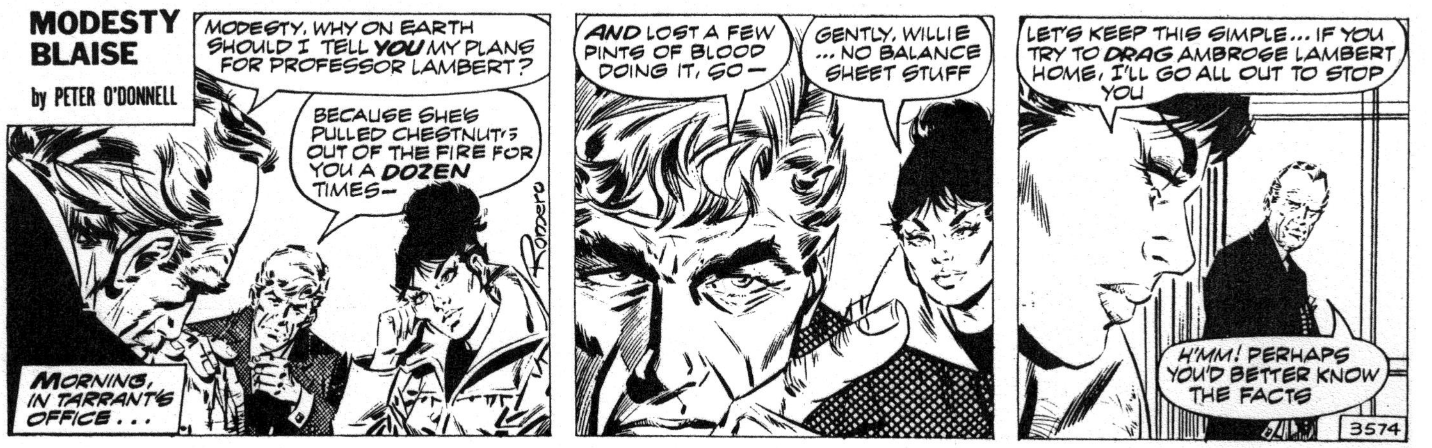
MODESTY BLAISE
by PETER O'DONNELL
MORNING, IN TARRANT'S OFFICE . . .
MODESTY, WHY ON EARTH SHOULD I TELL YOU MY PLANS FOR PROFESSOR LAMBERT?
BECAUSE SHE'S PULLED CHESTNUTS OUT OF THE FIRE FOR YOU A DOZEN TIMES—
AND LOST A FEW PINTS OF BLOOD DOING IT, SO—
GENTLY, WILLIE ... NO BALANCE SHEET STUFF
LET'S KEEP THIS SIMPLE... IF YOU TRY TO DRAG AMBROSE LAMBERT HOME, I'LL GO ALL OUT TO STOP YOU
H'MM! PERHAPS YOU'D BETTER KNOW THE FACTS
3574

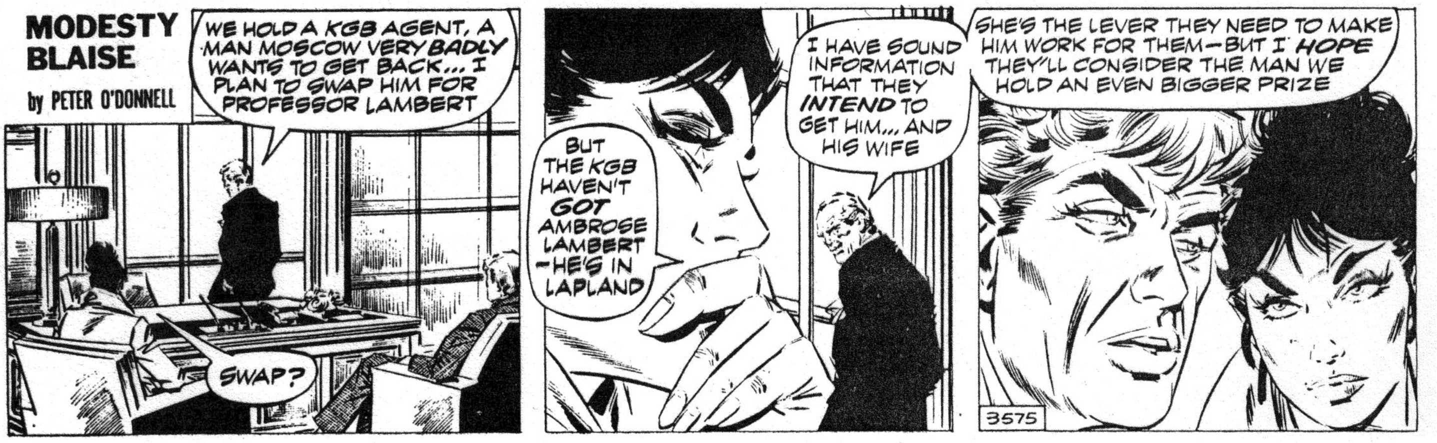
MODESTY BLAISE
by PETER O'DONNELL
WE HOLD A KGB AGENT, A MAN MOSCOW VERY BADLY WANTS TO GET BACK... I PLAN TO SWAP HIM FOR PROFESSOR LAMBERT
SWAP?
BUT THE KGB HAVEN'T GOT AMBROSE LAMBERT—HE'S IN LAPLAND
I HAVE SOUND INFORMATION THAT THEY INTEND TO GET HIM... AND HIS WIFE
SHE'S THE LEVER THEY NEED TO MAKE HIM WORK FOR THEM—BUT I HOPE THEY'LL CONSIDER THE MAN WE HOLD AN EVEN BIGGER PRIZE
3575

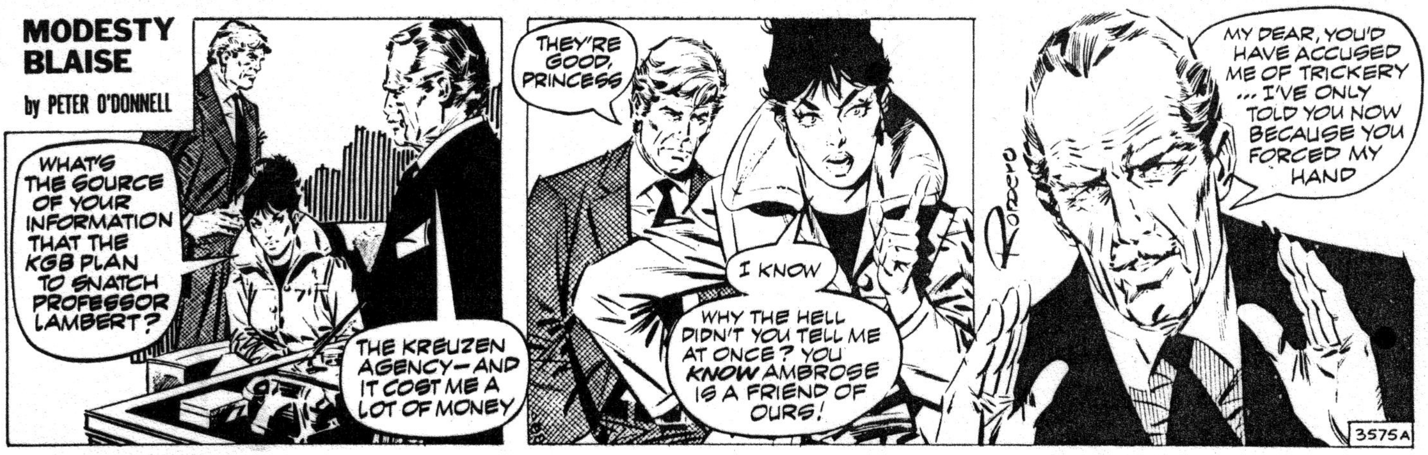
MODESTY BLAISE
by PETER O'DONNELL
WHAT'S THE SOURCE OF YOUR INFORMATION THAT THE KGB PLAN TO SNATCH PROFESSOR LAMBERT?
THE KREUZEN AGENCY—AND IT COST ME A LOT OF MONEY
THEY'RE GOOD, PRINCESS
I KNOW
WHY THE HELL DIDN'T YOU TELL ME AT ONCE? YOU KNOW AMBROSE IS A FRIEND OF OURS!
MY DEAR, YOU'D HAVE ACCUSED ME OF TRICKERY ... I'VE ONLY TOLD YOU NOW BECAUSE YOU FORCED MY HAND
3575A

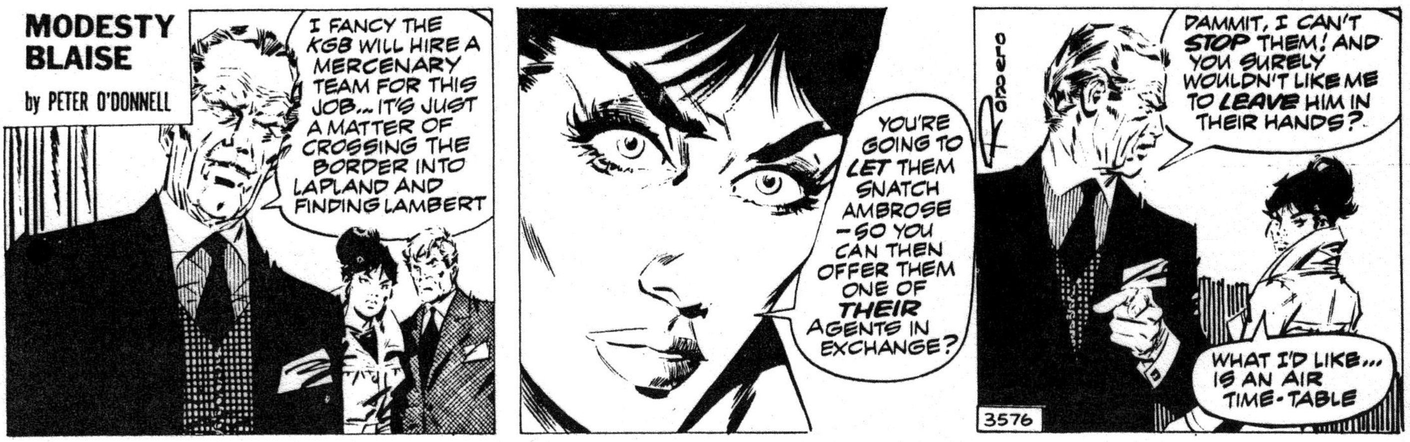
MODESTY BLAISE
by PETER O'DONNELL
I FANCY THE KGB WILL HIRE A MERCENARY TEAM FOR THIS JOB... IT'S JUST A MATTER OF CROSSING THE BORDER INTO LAPLAND AND FINDING LAMBERT
YOU'RE GOING TO LET THEM SNATCH AMBROSE —SO YOU CAN THEN OFFER THEM ONE OF THEIR AGENTS IN EXCHANGE?
DAMMIT, I CAN'T STOP THEM! AND YOU SURELY WOULDN'T LIKE ME TO LEAVE HIM IN THEIR HANDS?
WHAT I'D LIKE... IS AN AIR TIME-TABLE
3576

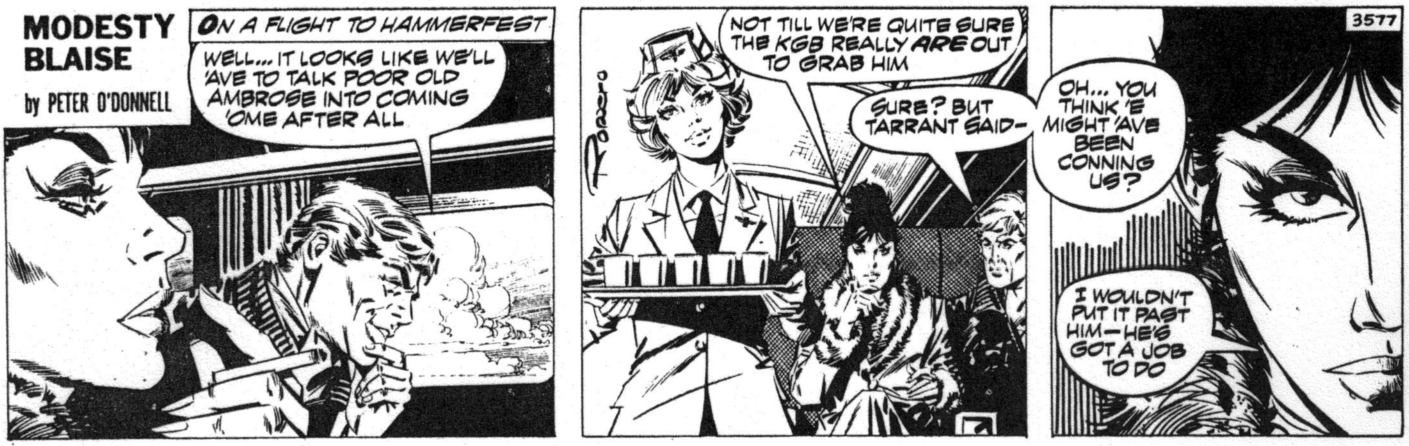
MODESTY BLAISE
by PETER O'DONNELL
ON A FLIGHT TO HAMMERFEST
WELL... IT LOOKS LIKE WE'LL 'AVE TO TALK POOR OLD AMBROSE INTO COMING 'OME AFTER ALL
NOT TILL WE'RE QUITE SURE THE KGB REALLY ARE OUT TO GRAB HIM
SURE? BUT TARRANT SAID—
3577
OH... YOU THINK 'E MIGHT 'AVE BEEN CONNING US?
I WOULDN'T PUT IT PAST HIM—HE'S GOT A JOB TO DO

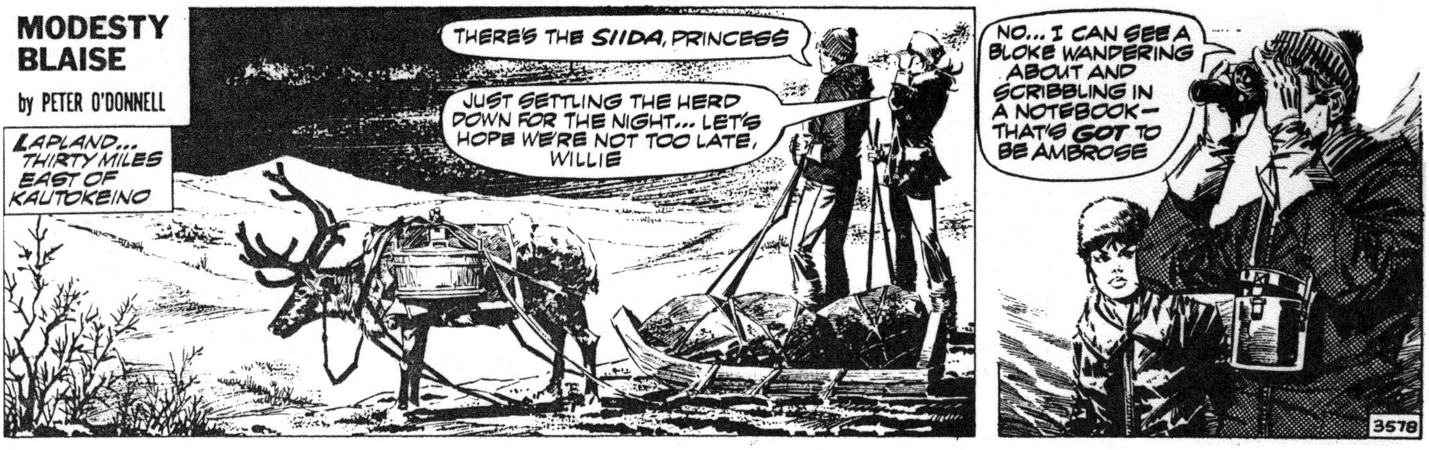
MODESTY BLAISE
by PETER O'DONNELL
LAPLAND... THIRTY MILES EAST OF KAUTOKEINO
THERE'S THE SIIDA, PRINCESS
JUST SETTLING THE HERD DOWN FOR THE NIGHT... LET'S HOPE WE'RE NOT TOO LATE, WILLIE
NO... I CAN SEE A BLOKE WANDERING ABOUT AND SCRIBBLING IN A NOTEBOOK— THAT'S GOT TO BE AMBROSE
3578

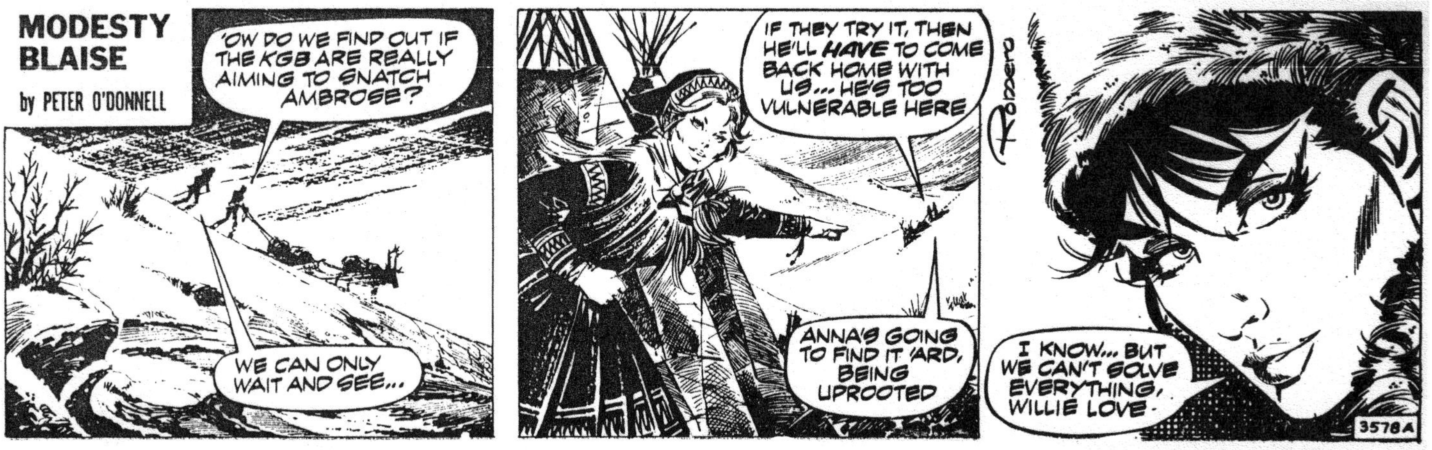
MODESTY BLAISE
by PETER O'DONNELL
'OW DO WE FIND OUT IF THE KGB ARE REALLY AIMING TO SNATCH AMBROSE?
WE CAN ONLY WAIT AND SEE...
IF THEY TRY IT, THEN HE'LL HAVE TO COME BACK HOME WITH US... HE'S TOO VULNERABLE HERE
ANNA'S GOING TO FIND IT 'ARD, BEING UPROOTED
I KNOW... BUT WE CAN'T SOLVE EVERYTHING, WILLIE LOVE
3578A

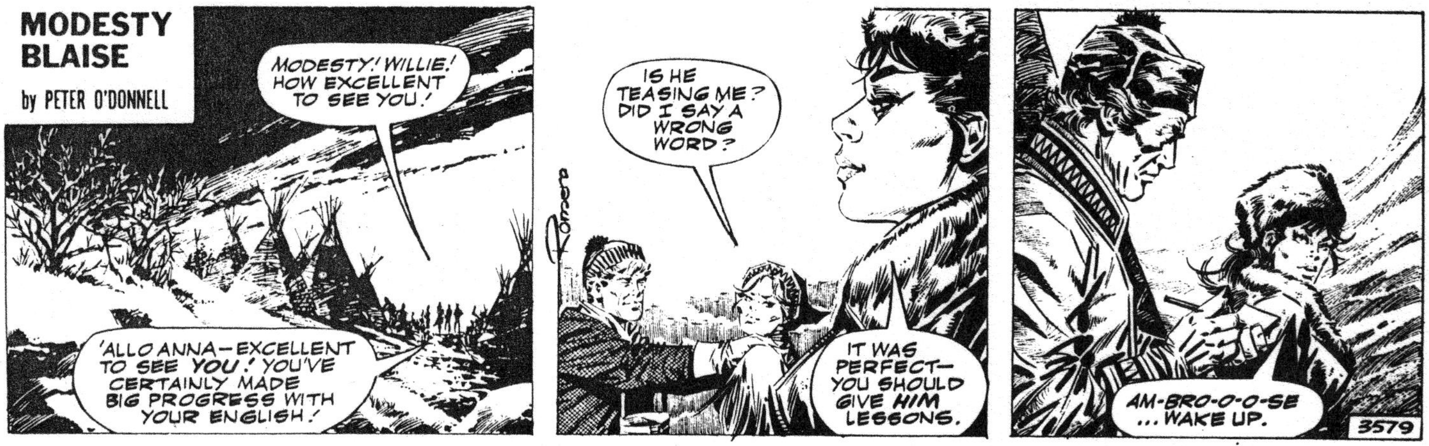
MODESTY BLAISE
by PETER O'DONNELL
MODESTY! WILLIE! HOW EXCELLENT TO SEE YOU!
'ALLO ANNA—EXCELLENT TO SEE YOU! YOU'VE CERTAINLY MADE BIG PROGRESS WITH YOUR ENGLISH!
IS HE TEASING ME? DID I SAY A WRONG WORD?
IT WAS PERFECT— YOU SHOULD GIVE HIM LESSONS.
AM-BRO-O-O-SE ... WAKE UP.
3579

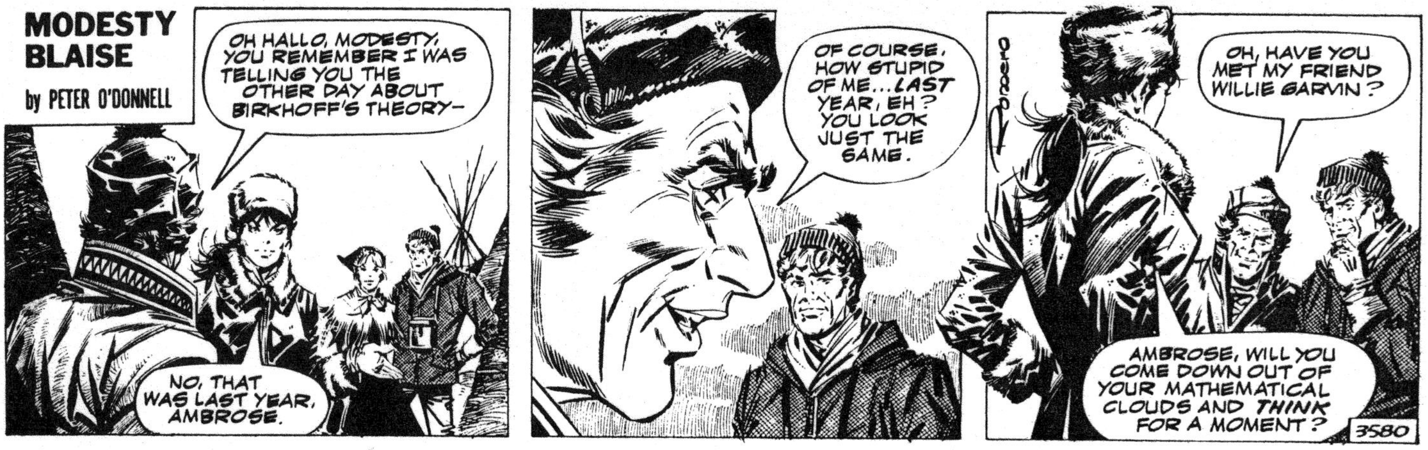
MODESTY BLAISE
by PETER O'DONNELL
OH HALLO, MODESTY, YOU REMEMBER I WAS TELLING YOU THE OTHER DAY ABOUT BIRKHOFF'S THEORY—
NO, THAT WAS LAST YEAR, AMBROSE.
OF COURSE, HOW STUPID OF ME... LAST YEAR, EH? YOU LOOK JUST THE SAME.
OH, HAVE YOU MET MY FRIEND WILLIE GARVIN?
AMBROSE, WILL YOU COME DOWN OUT OF YOUR MATHEMATICAL CLOUDS AND THINK FOR A MOMENT?
3580

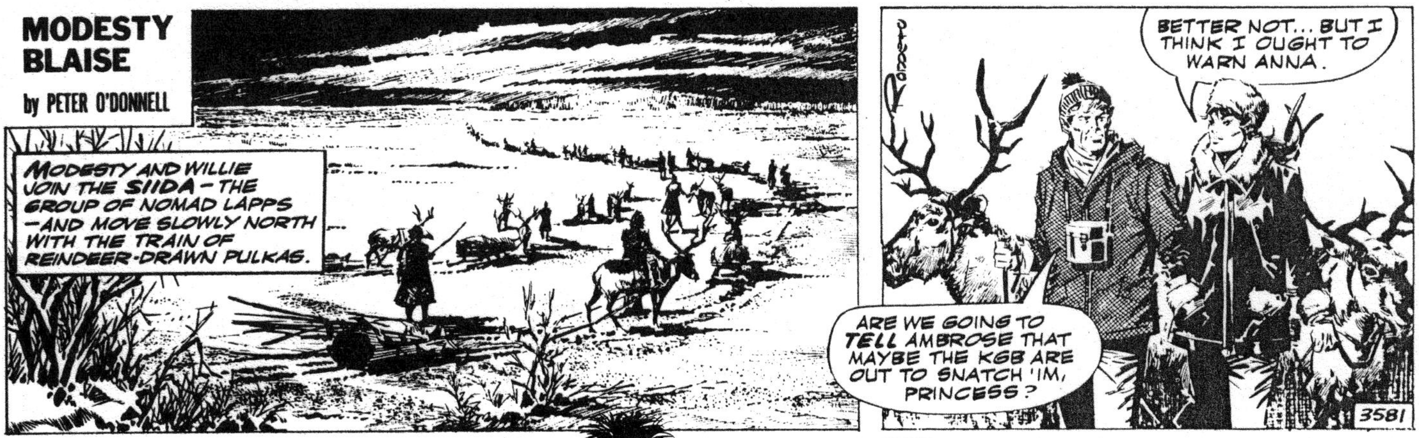
MODESTY BLAISE
by PETER O'DONNELL
MODESTY AND WILLIE JOIN THE SIIDA – THE GROUP OF NOMAD LAPPS – AND MOVE SLOWLY NORTH WITH THE TRAIN OF REINDEER-DRAWN PULKAS.
BETTER NOT... BUT I THINK I OUGHT TO WARN ANNA.
ARE WE GOING TO TELL AMBROSE THAT MAYBE THE KGB ARE OUT TO SNATCH 'IM, PRINCESS?
3581

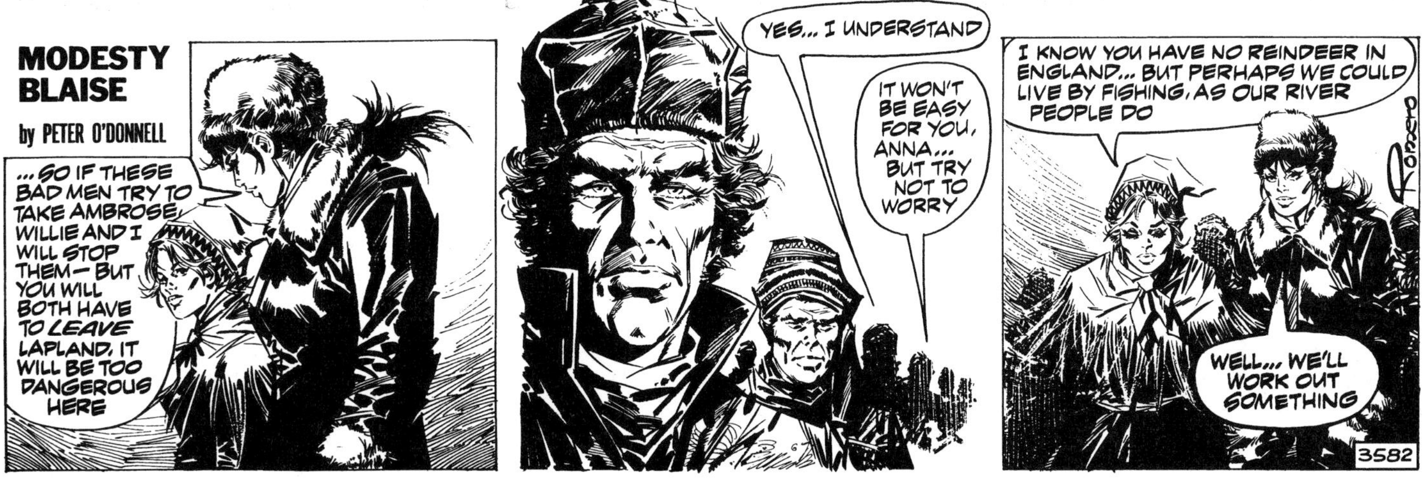
MODESTY BLAISE
by PETER O'DONNELL
...SO IF THESE BAD MEN TRY TO TAKE AMBROSE, WILLIE AND I WILL STOP THEM – BUT YOU WILL BOTH HAVE TO LEAVE LAPLAND. IT WILL BE TOO DANGEROUS HERE
YES... I UNDERSTAND
IT WON'T BE EASY FOR YOU, ANNA... BUT TRY NOT TO WORRY
I KNOW YOU HAVE NO REINDEER IN ENGLAND... BUT PERHAPS WE COULD LIVE BY FISHING, AS OUR RIVER PEOPLE DO
WELL... WE'LL WORK OUT SOMETHING
3582

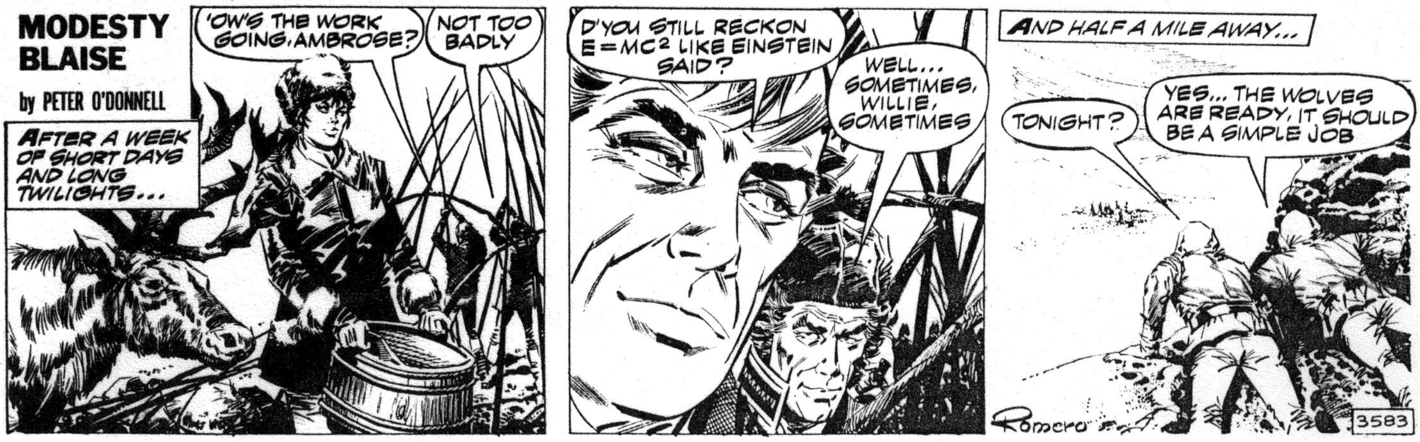
MODESTY BLAISE
by PETER O'DONNELL
AFTER A WEEK OF SHORT DAYS AND LONG TWILIGHTS...
'OW'S THE WORK GOING, AMBROSE?
NOT TOO BADLY
D'YOU STILL RECKON E=MC² LIKE EINSTEIN SAID?
WELL... SOMETIMES, WILLIE, SOMETIMES
AND HALF A MILE AWAY...
TONIGHT?
YES... THE WOLVES ARE READY. IT SHOULD BE A SIMPLE JOB
Romero
3583

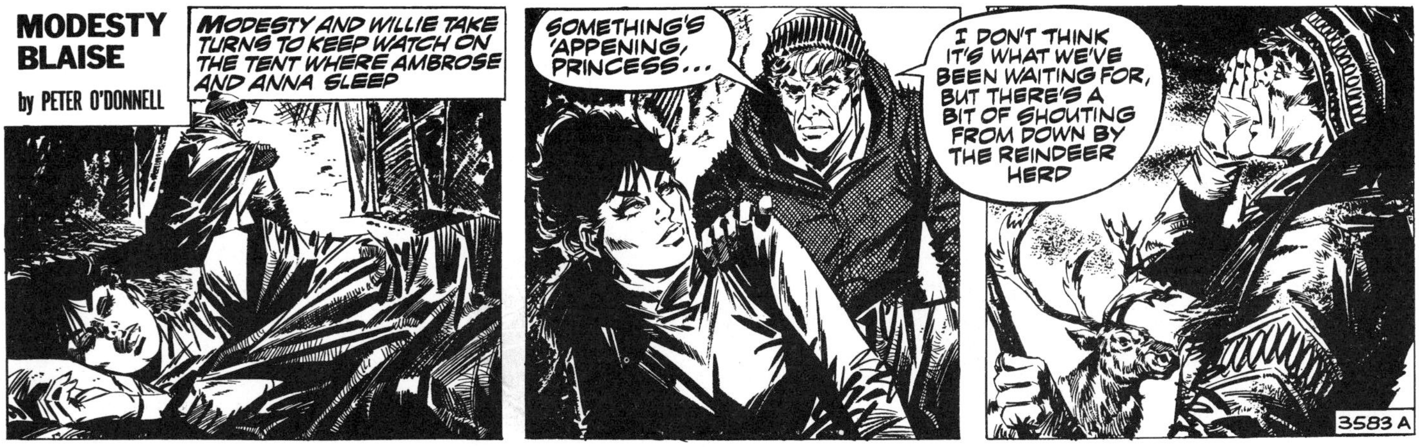
MODESTY BLAISE
by PETER O'DONNELL
MODESTY AND WILLIE TAKE TURNS TO KEEP WATCH ON THE TENT WHERE AMBROSE AND ANNA SLEEP
SOMETHING'S 'APPENING, PRINCESS...
I DON'T THINK IT'S WHAT WE'VE BEEN WAITING FOR, BUT THERE'S A BIT OF SHOUTING FROM DOWN BY THE REINDEER HERD
3583 A

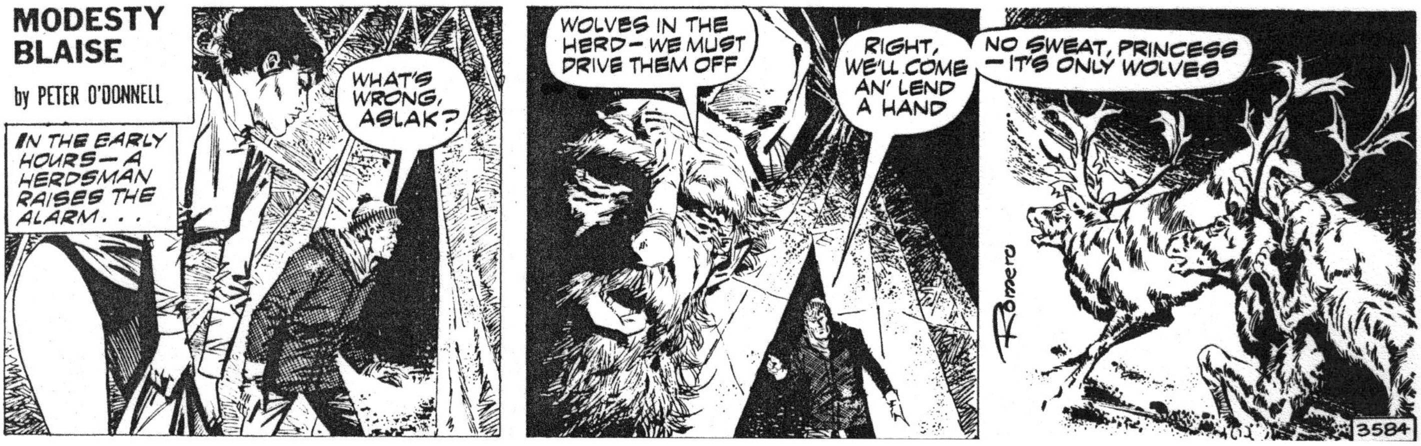
MODESTY BLAISE
by PETER O'DONNELL
IN THE EARLY HOURS— A HERDSMAN RAISES THE ALARM . . .
WHAT'S WRONG, ASLAK?
WOLVES IN THE HERD— WE MUST DRIVE THEM OFF
RIGHT, WE'LL COME AN' LEND A HAND
NO SWEAT, PRINCESS —IT'S ONLY WOLVES
3584

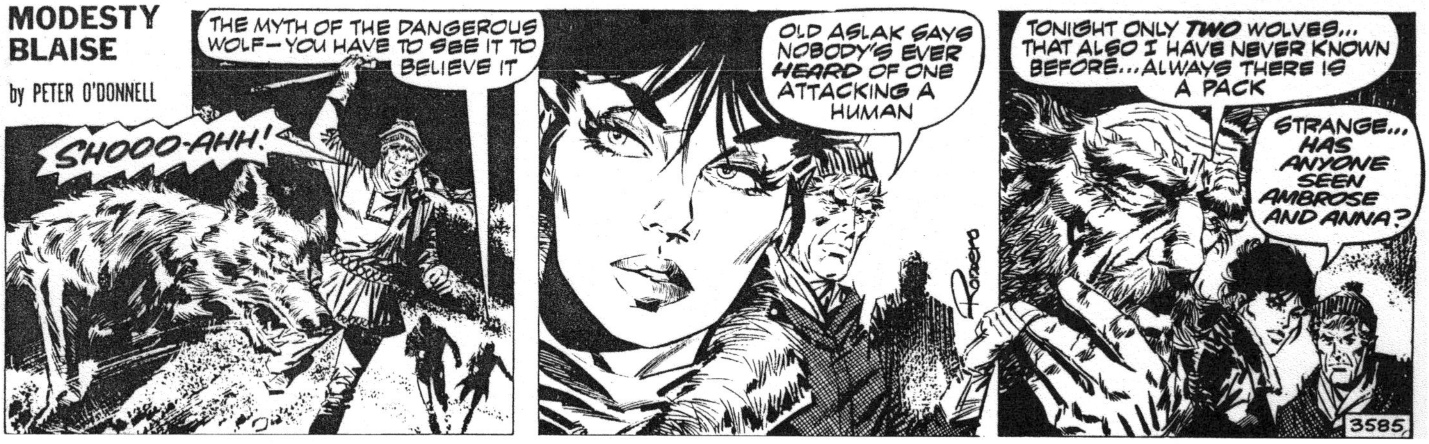
MODESTY BLAISE
by PETER O'DONNELL
THE MYTH OF THE DANGEROUS WOLF— YOU HAVE TO SEE IT TO BELIEVE IT
SHOOO-AHH!
OLD ASLAK SAYS NOBODY'S EVER HEARD OF ONE ATTACKING A HUMAN
TONIGHT ONLY TWO WOLVES... THAT ALSO I HAVE NEVER KNOWN BEFORE... ALWAYS THERE IS A PACK
STRANGE... HAS ANYONE SEEN AMBROSE AND ANNA?
3585

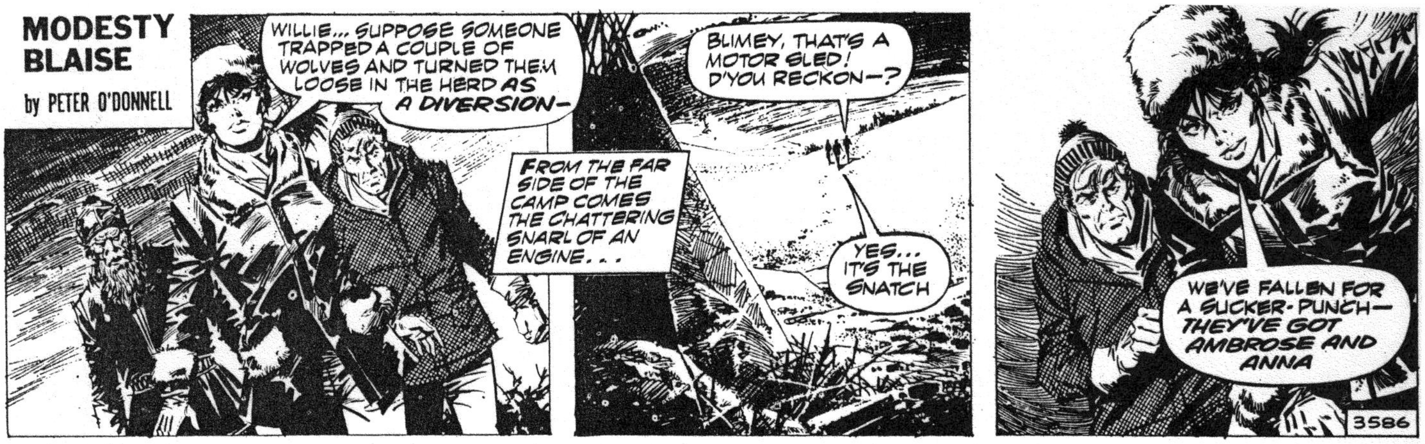
MODESTY BLAISE
by PETER O'DONNELL
WILLIE... SUPPOSE SOMEONE TRAPPED A COUPLE OF WOLVES AND TURNED THEM LOOSE IN THE HERD AS A DIVERSION—
FROM THE FAR SIDE OF THE CAMP COMES THE CHATTERING SNARL OF AN ENGINE . . .
BLIMEY, THAT'S A MOTOR SLED! D'YOU RECKON—?
YES... IT'S THE SNATCH
WE'VE FALLEN FOR A SUCKER-PUNCH— THEY'VE GOT AMBROSE AND ANNA
3586

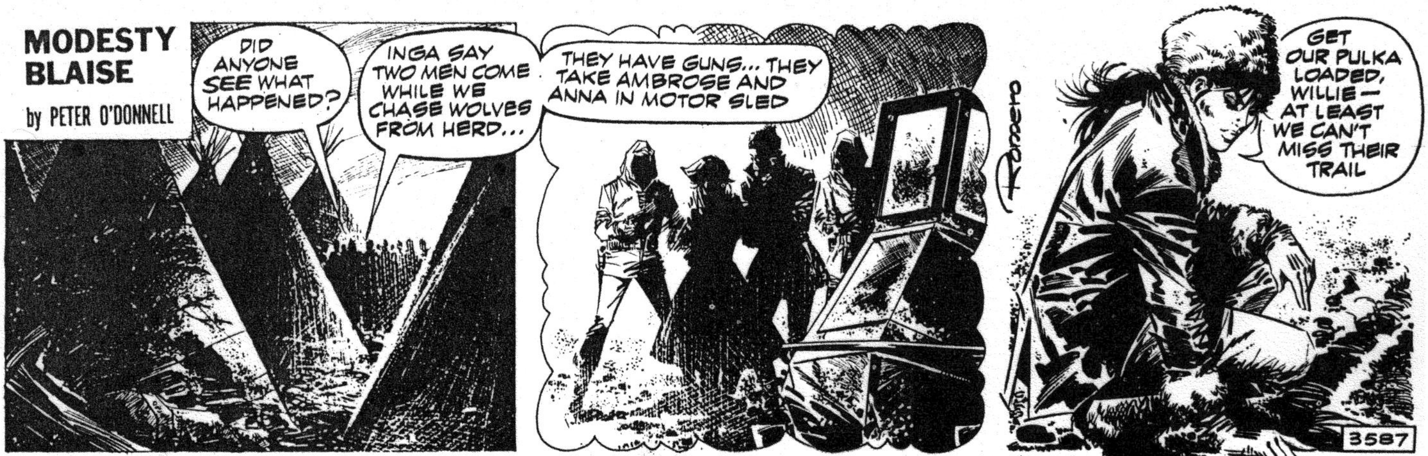
MODESTY BLAISE
by PETER O'DONNELL
DID ANYONE SEE WHAT HAPPENED?
INGA SAY TWO MEN COME WHILE WE CHASE WOLVES FROM HERD...
THEY HAVE GUNS... THEY TAKE AMBROSE AND ANNA IN MOTOR SLED
GET OUR PULKA LOADED, WILLIE— AT LEAST WE CAN'T MISS THEIR TRAIL
3587

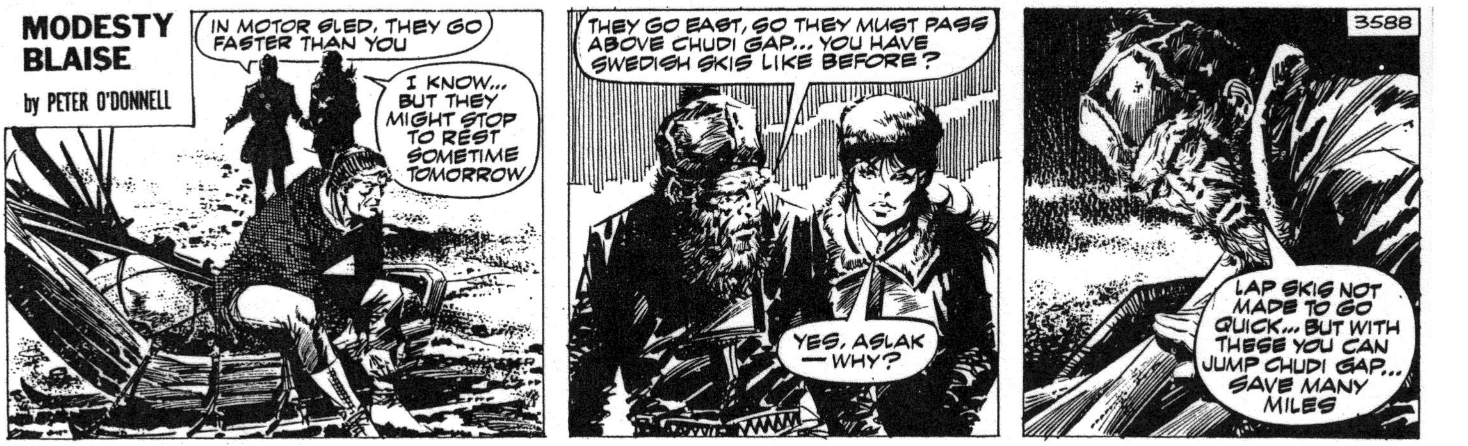
MODESTY BLAISE
by PETER O'DONNELL
IN MOTOR SLED, THEY GO FASTER THAN YOU
I KNOW... BUT THEY MIGHT STOP TO REST SOMETIME TOMORROW
THEY GO EAST, SO THEY MUST PASS ABOVE CHUDI GAP... YOU HAVE SWEDISH SKIS LIKE BEFORE?
YES, ASLAK —WHY?
3588
LAP SKIS NOT MADE TO GO QUICK... BUT WITH THESE YOU CAN JUMP CHUDI GAP... SAVE MANY MILES

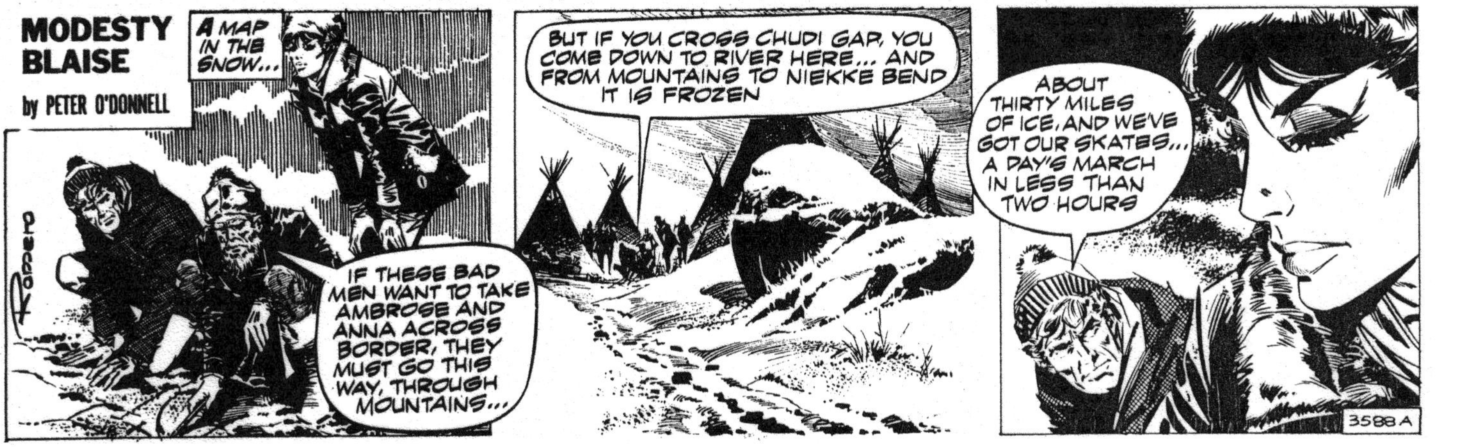
MODESTY BLAISE
by PETER O'DONNELL
A MAP IN THE SNOW...
IF THESE BAD MEN WANT TO TAKE AMBROSE AND ANNA ACROSS BORDER, THEY MUST GO THIS WAY, THROUGH MOUNTAINS...
BUT IF YOU CROSS CHUDI GAP, YOU COME DOWN TO RIVER HERE... AND FROM MOUNTAINS TO NIEKKE BEND IT IS FROZEN
ABOUT THIRTY MILES OF ICE, AND WE'VE GOT OUR SKATES... A DAY'S MARCH IN LESS THAN TWO HOURS
3588 A

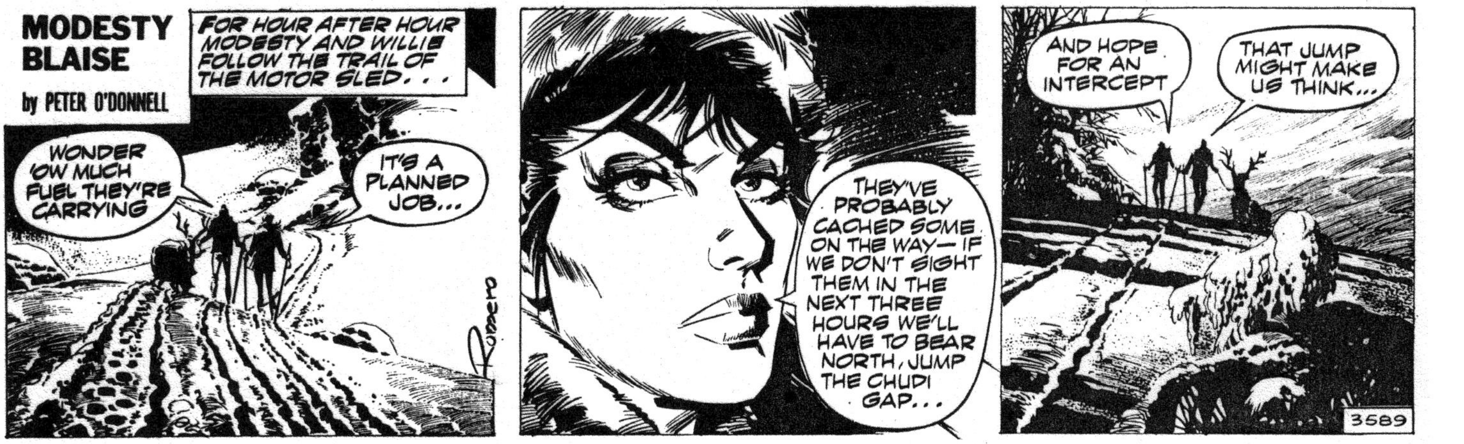
MODESTY BLAISE
by PETER O'DONNELL
FOR HOUR AFTER HOUR MODESTY AND WILLIE FOLLOW THE TRAIL OF THE MOTOR SLED...
WONDER 'OW MUCH FUEL THEY'RE CARRYING
IT'S A PLANNED JOB...
THEY'VE PROBABLY CACHED SOME ON THE WAY— IF WE DON'T SIGHT THEM IN THE NEXT THREE HOURS WE'LL HAVE TO BEAR NORTH, JUMP THE CHUDI GAP...
AND HOPE FOR AN INTERCEPT
THAT JUMP MIGHT MAKE US THINK...
3589

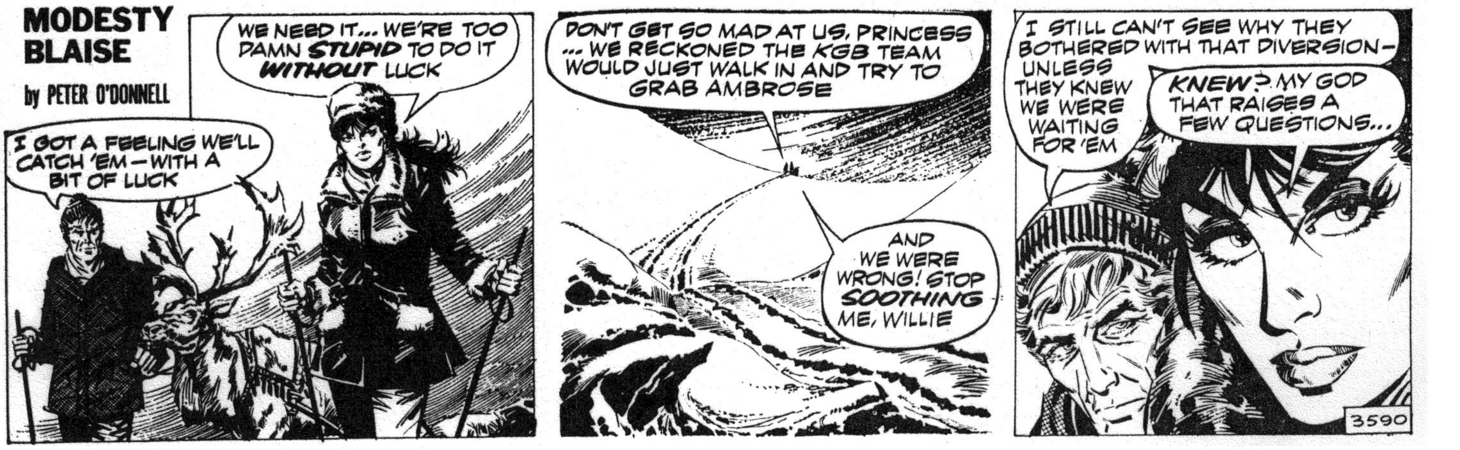
MODESTY BLAISE
by PETER O'DONNELL
I GOT A FEELING WE'LL CATCH 'EM — WITH A BIT OF LUCK
WE NEED IT... WE'RE TOO DAMN STUPID TO DO IT WITHOUT LUCK
DON'T GET SO MAD AT US, PRINCESS... WE RECKONED THE KGB TEAM WOULD JUST WALK IN AND TRY TO GRAB AMBROSE
AND WE WERE WRONG! STOP SOOTHING ME, WILLIE
I STILL CAN'T SEE WHY THEY BOTHERED WITH THAT DIVERSION— UNLESS THEY KNEW WE WERE WAITING FOR 'EM
KNEW? MY GOD THAT RAISES A FEW QUESTIONS...
3590

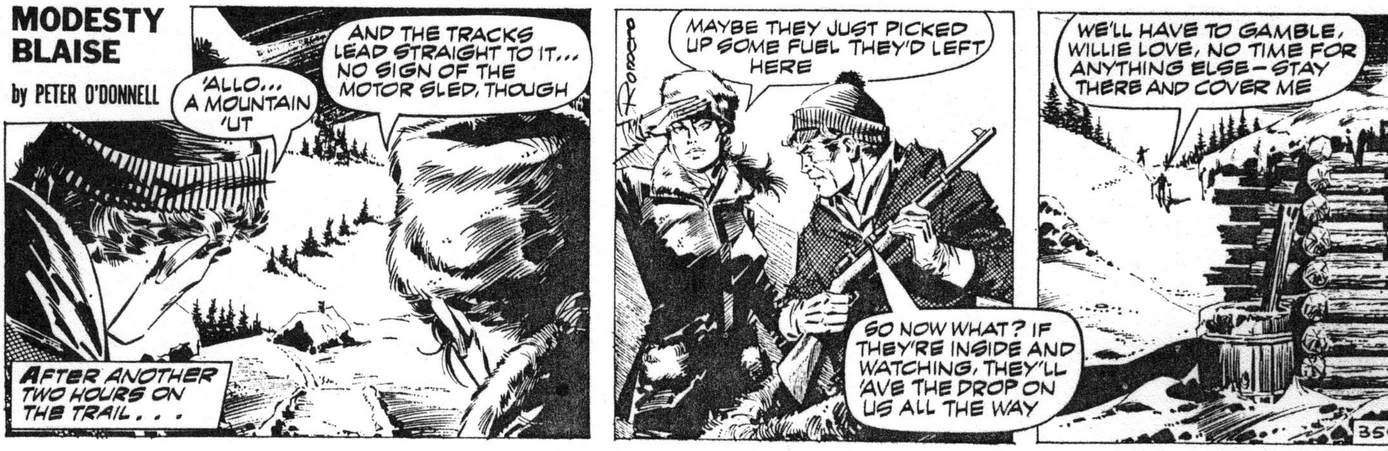
MODESTY BLAISE
by PETER O'DONNELL
AFTER ANOTHER TWO HOURS ON THE TRAIL . . .
'ALLO... A MOUNTAIN 'UT
AND THE TRACKS LEAD STRAIGHT TO IT... NO SIGN OF THE MOTOR SLED, THOUGH
MAYBE THEY JUST PICKED UP SOME FUEL THEY'D LEFT HERE
SO NOW WHAT? IF THEY'RE INSIDE AND WATCHING, THEY'LL 'AVE THE DROP ON US ALL THE WAY
WE'LL HAVE TO GAMBLE, WILLIE LOVE, NO TIME FOR ANYTHING ELSE—STAY THERE AND COVER ME
3591

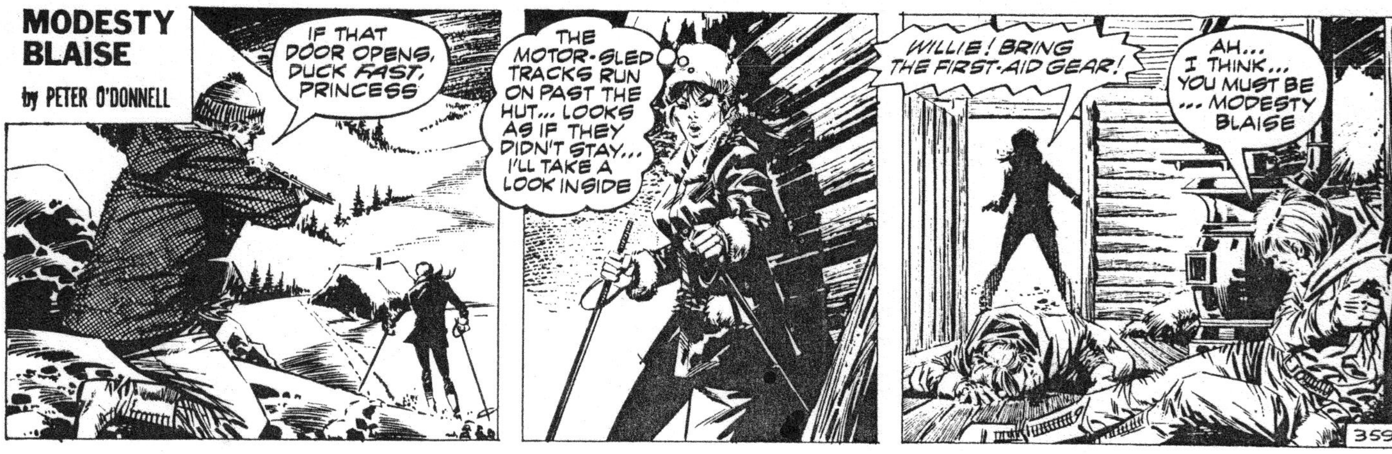
MODESTY BLAISE
by PETER O'DONNELL
IF THAT DOOR OPENS, DUCK FAST, PRINCESS
THE MOTOR-SLED TRACKS RUN ON PAST THE HUT... LOOKS AS IF THEY DIDN'T STAY... I'LL TAKE A LOOK INSIDE
WILLIE! BRING THE FIRST-AID GEAR!
AH... I THINK... YOU MUST BE ... MODESTY BLAISE
3592

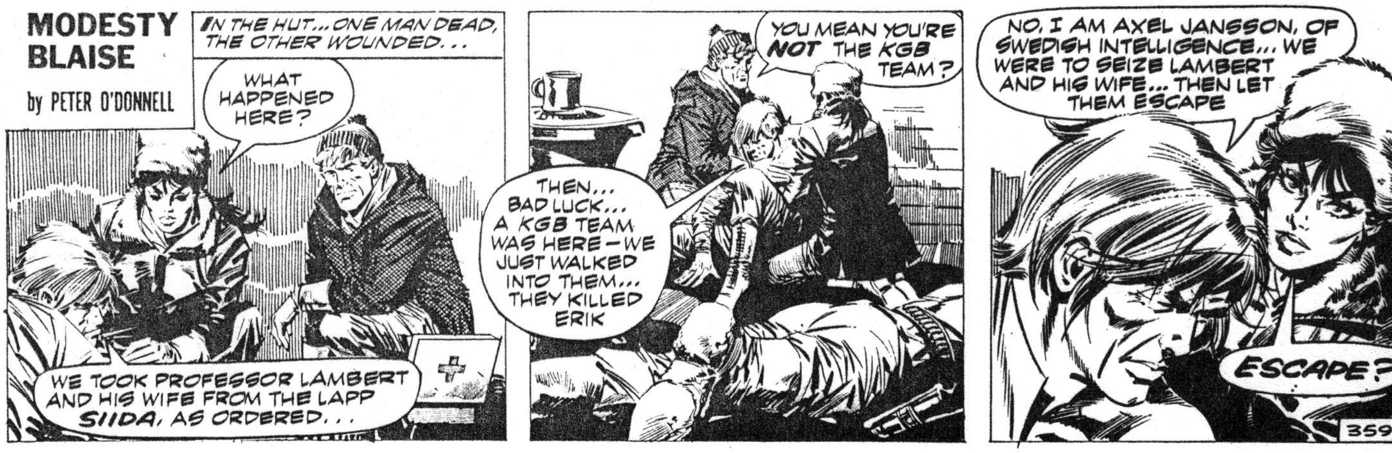
MODESTY BLAISE
by PETER O'DONNELL
IN THE HUT... ONE MAN DEAD, THE OTHER WOUNDED...
WHAT HAPPENED HERE?
WE TOOK PROFESSOR LAMBERT AND HIS WIFE FROM THE LAPP SIIDA, AS ORDERED...
THEN... BAD LUCK... A KGB TEAM WAS HERE—WE JUST WALKED INTO THEM... THEY KILLED ERIK
YOU MEAN YOU'RE NOT THE KGB TEAM?
NO, I AM AXEL JANSSON, OF SWEDISH INTELLIGENCE... WE WERE TO SEIZE LAMBERT AND HIS WIFE... THEN LET THEM ESCAPE
ESCAPE?
3593

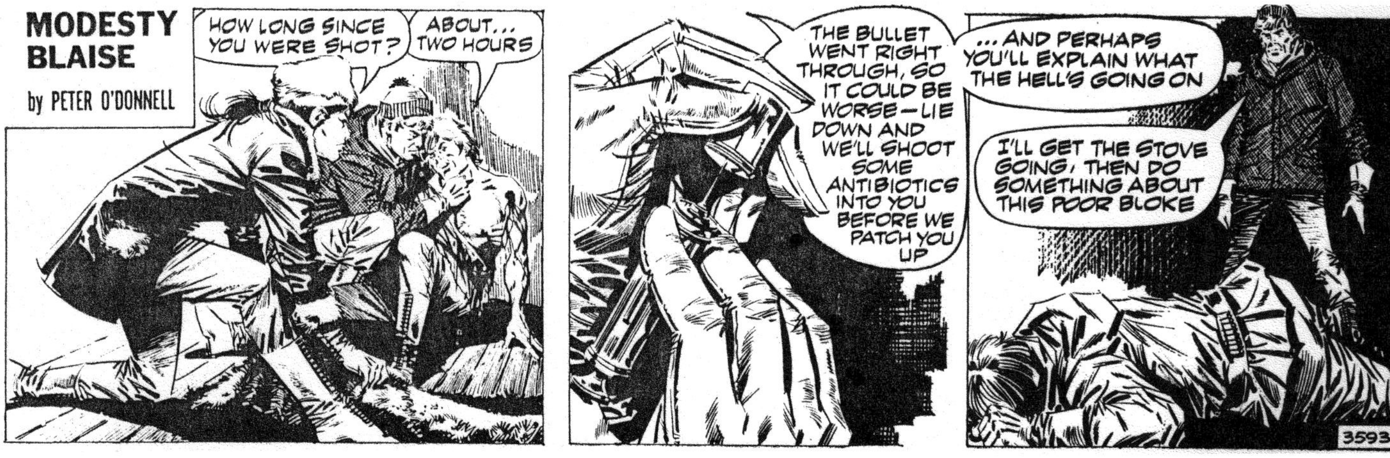
MODESTY BLAISE
by PETER O'DONNELL
HOW LONG SINCE YOU WERE SHOT?
ABOUT... TWO HOURS
THE BULLET WENT RIGHT THROUGH, SO IT COULD BE WORSE—LIE DOWN AND WE'LL SHOOT SOME ANTIBIOTICS INTO YOU BEFORE WE PATCH YOU UP
... AND PERHAPS YOU'LL EXPLAIN WHAT THE HELL'S GOING ON
I'LL GET THE STOVE GOING, THEN DO SOMETHING ABOUT THIS POOR BLOKE
3593A

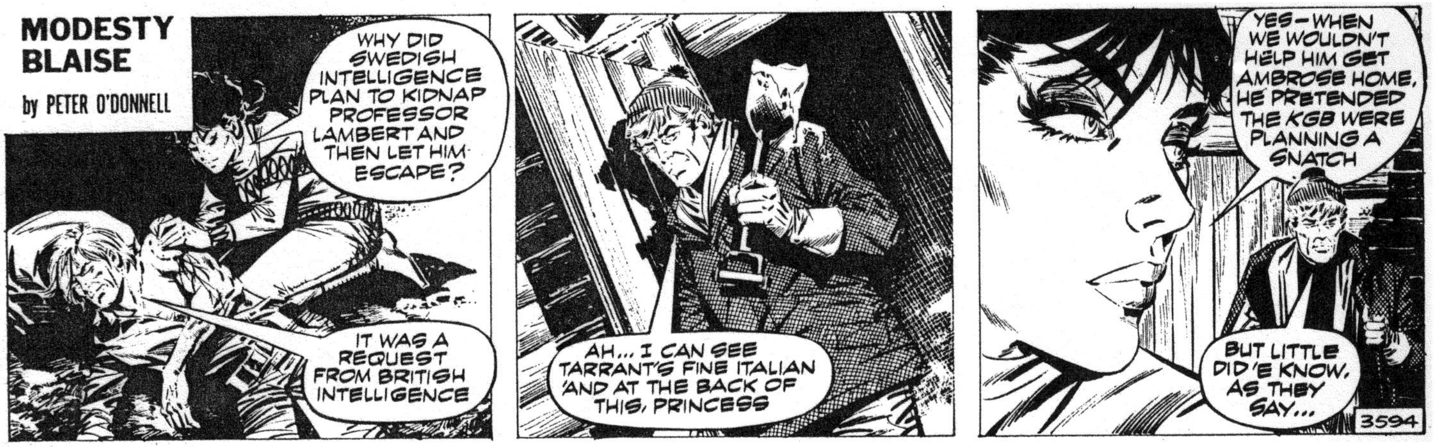
MODESTY BLAISE
by PETER O'DONNELL
WHY DID SWEDISH INTELLIGENCE PLAN TO KIDNAP PROFESSOR LAMBERT AND THEN LET HIM ESCAPE?
IT WAS A REQUEST FROM BRITISH INTELLIGENCE
AH... I CAN SEE TARRANT'S FINE ITALIAN 'AND AT THE BACK OF THIS, PRINCESS
YES—WHEN WE WOULDN'T HELP HIM GET AMBROSE HOME, HE PRETENDED THE KGB WERE PLANNING A SNATCH
BUT LITTLE DID 'E KNOW, AS THEY SAY...
3594

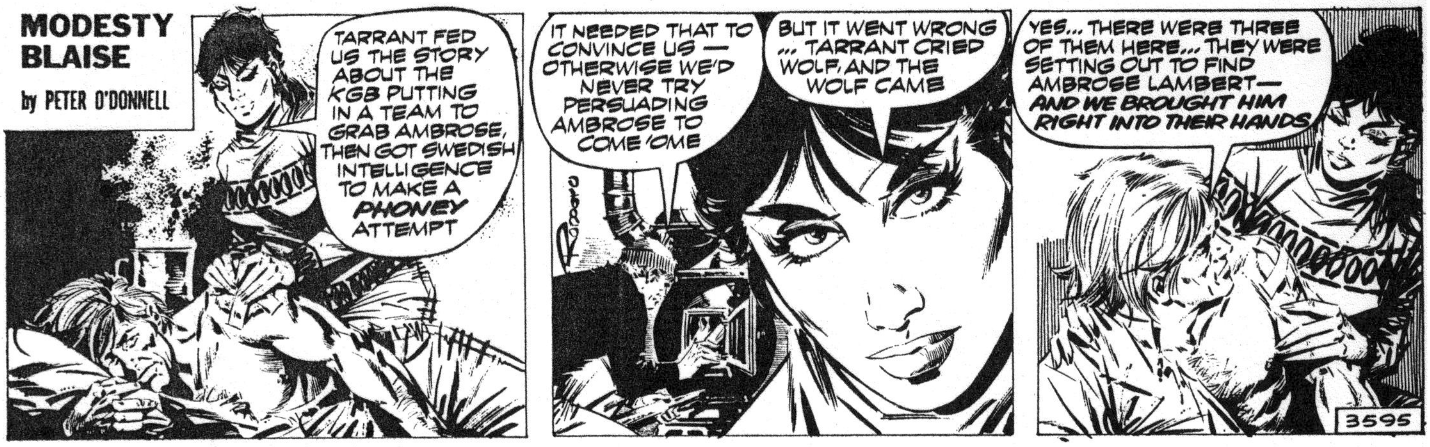
MODESTY BLAISE
by PETER O'DONNELL
TARRANT FED US THE STORY ABOUT THE KGB PUTTING IN A TEAM TO GRAB AMBROSE, THEN GOT SWEDISH INTELLIGENCE TO MAKE A PHONEY ATTEMPT
IT NEEDED THAT TO CONVINCE US — OTHERWISE WE'D NEVER TRY PERSUADING AMBROSE TO COME 'OME
BUT IT WENT WRONG ... TARRANT CRIED WOLF, AND THE WOLF CAME
YES... THERE WERE THREE OF THEM HERE... THEY WERE SETTING OUT TO FIND AMBROSE LAMBERT— AND WE BROUGHT HIM RIGHT INTO THEIR HANDS
3595

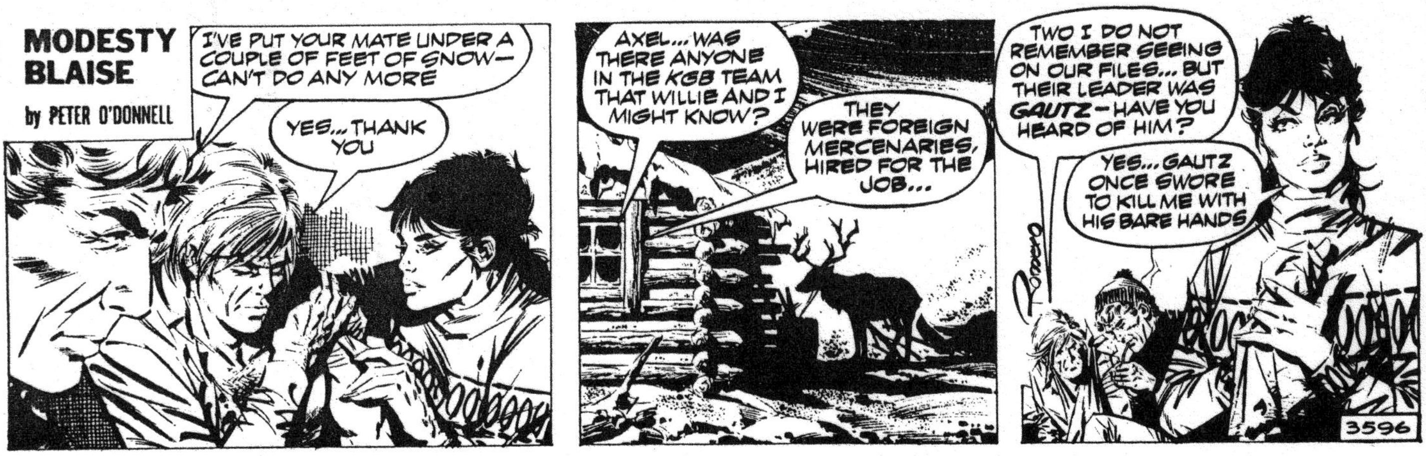
MODESTY BLAISE
by PETER O'DONNELL
I'VE PUT YOUR MATE UNDER A COUPLE OF FEET OF SNOW— CAN'T DO ANY MORE
YES... THANK YOU
AXEL... WAS THERE ANYONE IN THE KGB TEAM THAT WILLIE AND I MIGHT KNOW?
THEY WERE FOREIGN MERCENARIES, HIRED FOR THE JOB...
TWO I DO NOT REMEMBER SEEING ON OUR FILES... BUT THEIR LEADER WAS GAUTZ—HAVE YOU HEARD OF HIM?
YES... GAUTZ ONCE SWORE TO KILL ME WITH HIS BARE HANDS
3596

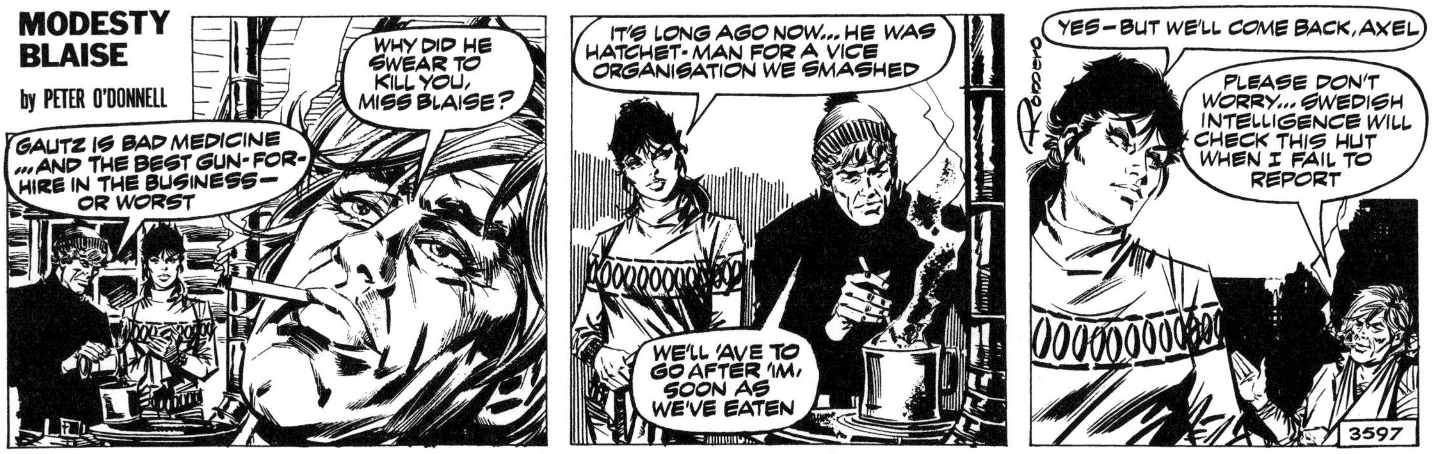
MODESTY BLAISE
by PETER O'DONNELL
WHY DID HE SWEAR TO KILL YOU, MISS BLAISE?
GAUTZ IS BAD MEDICINE ... AND THE BEST GUN-FOR-HIRE IN THE BUSINESS— OR WORST
IT'S LONG AGO NOW... HE WAS HATCHET-MAN FOR A VICE ORGANISATION WE SMASHED
WE'LL 'AVE TO GO AFTER 'IM, SOON AS WE'VE EATEN
YES—BUT WE'LL COME BACK, AXEL
PLEASE DON'T WORRY... SWEDISH INTELLIGENCE WILL CHECK THIS HUT WHEN I FAIL TO REPORT
3597

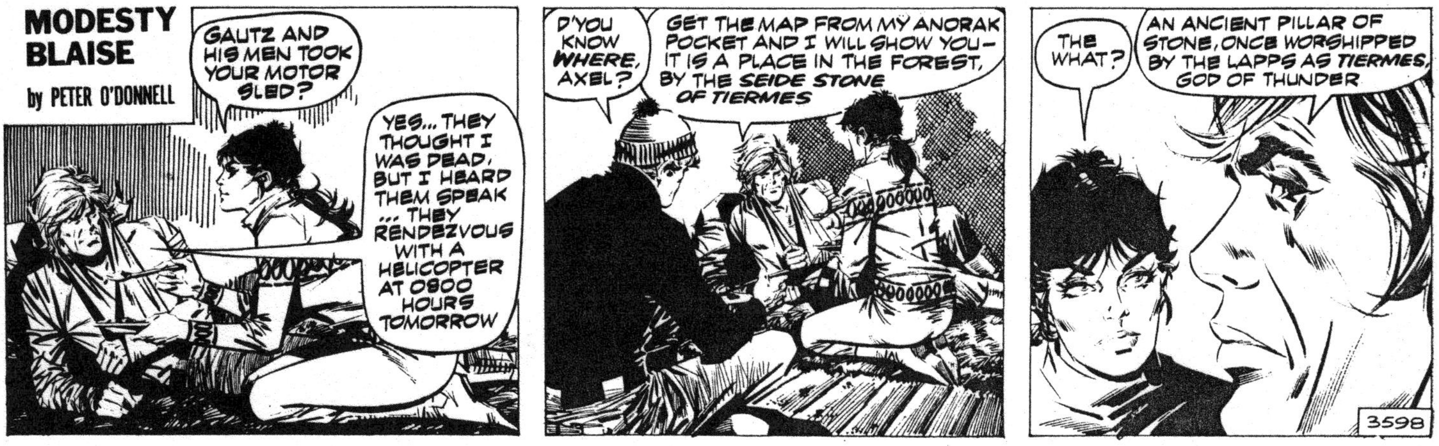
MODESTY BLAISE
by PETER O'DONNELL
GAUTZ AND HIS MEN TOOK YOUR MOTOR SLED?
YES... THEY THOUGHT I WAS DEAD, BUT I HEARD THEM SPEAK ... THEY RENDEZVOUS WITH A HELICOPTER AT 0800 HOURS TOMORROW
D'YOU KNOW WHERE, AXEL?
GET THE MAP FROM MY ANORAK POCKET AND I WILL SHOW YOU— IT IS A PLACE IN THE FOREST, BY THE SEIDE STONE OF TIERMES
THE WHAT?
AN ANCIENT PILLAR OF STONE, ONCE WORSHIPPED BY THE LAPPS AS TIERMES, GOD OF THUNDER
3598

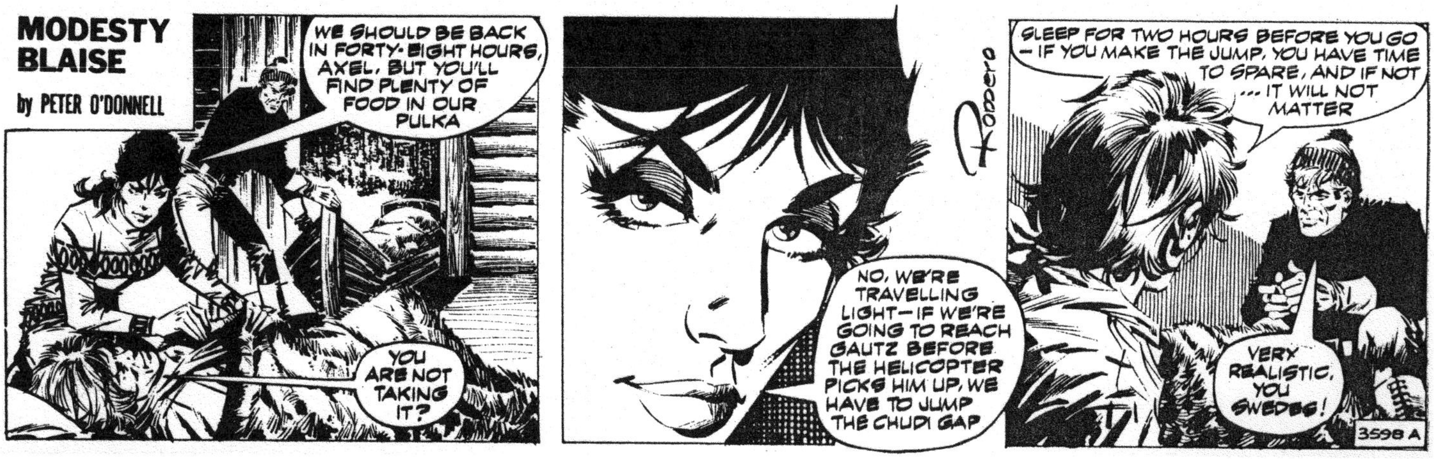
MODESTY BLAISE
by PETER O'DONNELL
WE SHOULD BE BACK IN FORTY-EIGHT HOURS, AXEL, BUT YOU'LL FIND PLENTY OF FOOD IN OUR PULKA
YOU ARE NOT TAKING IT?
NO, WE'RE TRAVELLING LIGHT—IF WE'RE GOING TO REACH GAUTZ BEFORE THE HELICOPTER PICKS HIM UP, WE HAVE TO JUMP THE CHUDI GAP
SLEEP FOR TWO HOURS BEFORE YOU GO —IF YOU MAKE THE JUMP, YOU HAVE TIME TO SPARE, AND IF NOT ... IT WILL NOT MATTER
VERY REALISTIC, YOU SWEDES!
3598 A

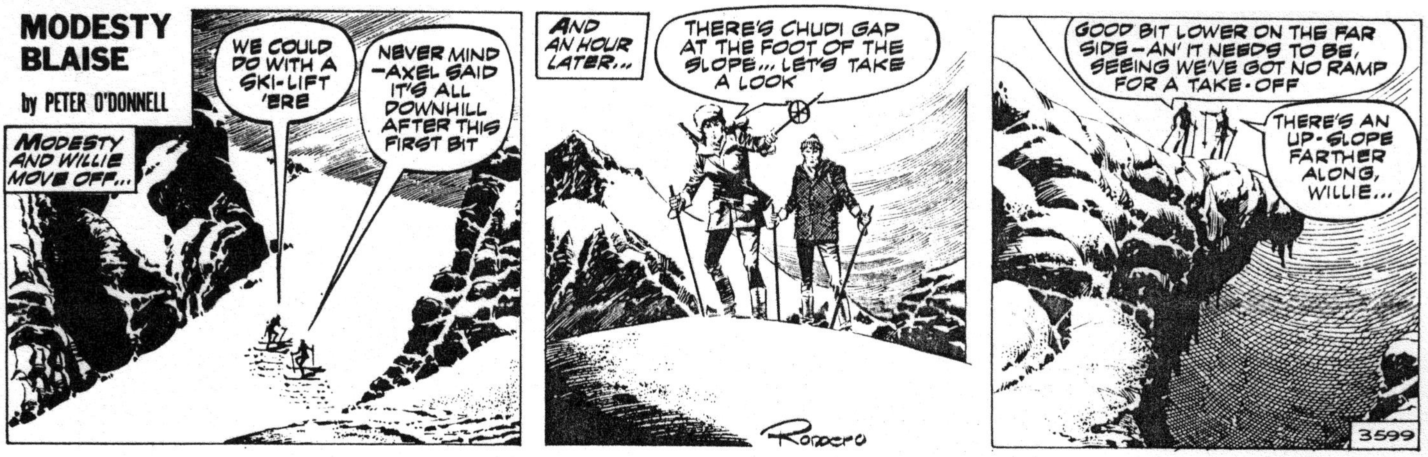
MODESTY BLAISE
by PETER O'DONNELL
MODESTY AND WILLIE MOVE OFF...
WE COULD DO WITH A SKI-LIFT 'ERE
NEVER MIND —AXEL SAID IT'S ALL DOWNHILL AFTER THIS FIRST BIT
AND AN HOUR LATER...
THERE'S CHUDI GAP AT THE FOOT OF THE SLOPE... LET'S TAKE A LOOK
GOOD BIT LOWER ON THE FAR SIDE—AN' IT NEEDS TO BE, SEEING WE'VE GOT NO RAMP FOR A TAKE-OFF
THERE'S AN UP-SLOPE FARTHER ALONG, WILLIE...
3599

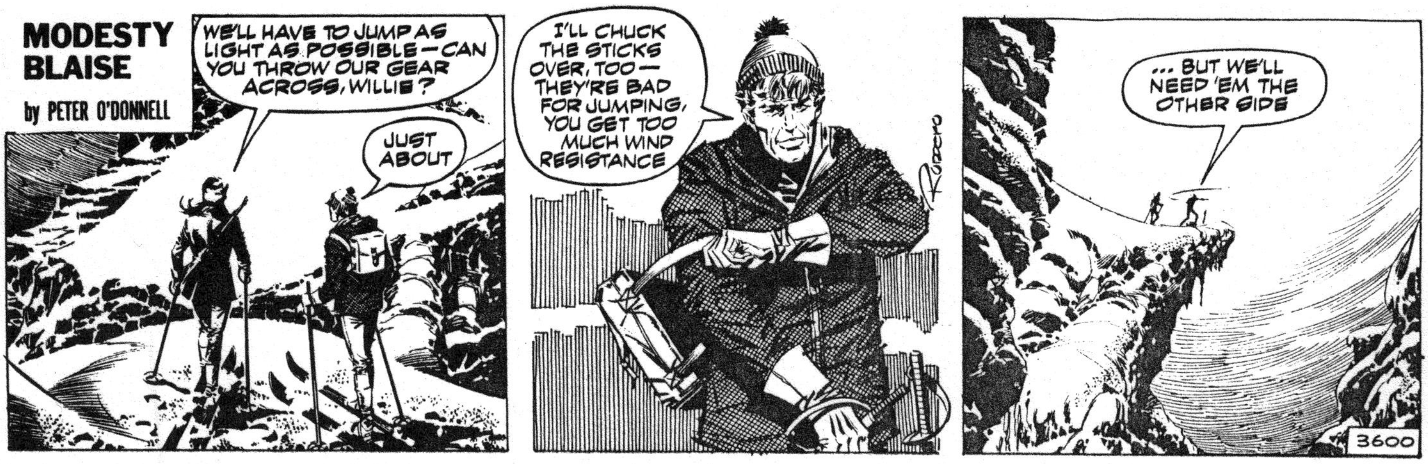
MODESTY BLAISE
by PETER O'DONNELL
WE'LL HAVE TO JUMP AS LIGHT AS POSSIBLE—CAN YOU THROW OUR GEAR ACROSS, WILLIE?
JUST ABOUT
I'LL CHUCK THE STICKS OVER, TOO— THEY'RE BAD FOR JUMPING, YOU GET TOO MUCH WIND RESISTANCE
... BUT WE'LL NEED 'EM THE OTHER SIDE
3600

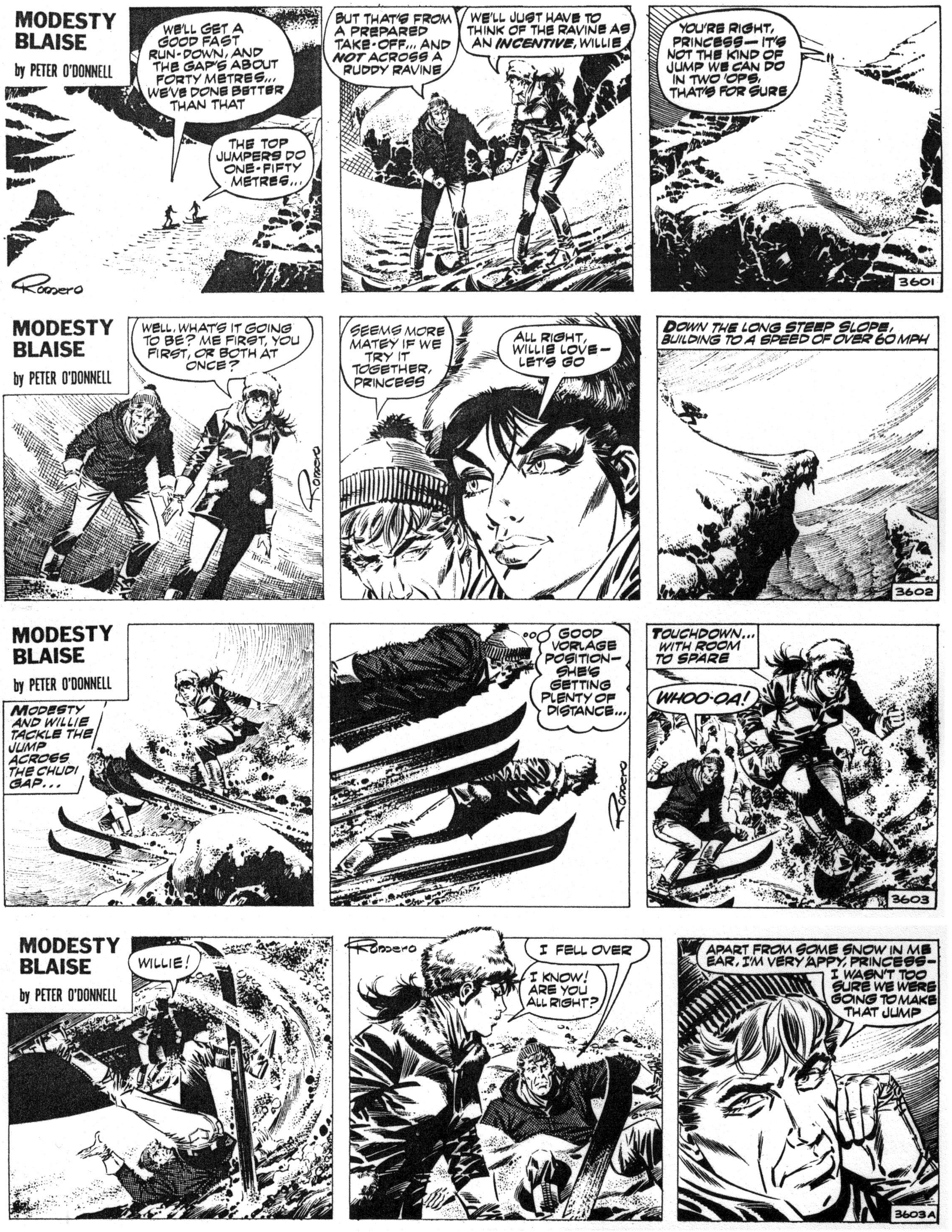
MODESTY BLAISE
by PETER O'DONNELL
WE'LL GET A GOOD FAST RUN-DOWN, AND THE GAP'S ABOUT FORTY METRES... WE'VE DONE BETTER THAN THAT
THE TOP JUMPERS DO ONE-FIFTY METRES...
Romero
BUT THAT'S FROM A PREPARED TAKE-OFF... AND NOT ACROSS A RUDDY RAVINE
WE'LL JUST HAVE TO THINK OF THE RAVINE AS AN INCENTIVE, WILLIE
YOU'RE RIGHT, PRINCESS — IT'S NOT THE KIND OF JUMP WE CAN DO IN TWO 'OPS, THAT'S FOR SURE
3601
MODESTY BLAISE
by PETER O'DONNELL
WELL, WHAT'S IT GOING TO BE? ME FIRST, YOU FIRST, OR BOTH AT ONCE?
Romero
SEEMS MORE MATEY IF WE TRY IT TOGETHER, PRINCESS
ALL RIGHT, WILLIE LOVE — LET'S GO
DOWN THE LONG STEEP SLOPE, BUILDING TO A SPEED OF OVER 60 MPH
3602
MODESTY BLAISE
by PETER O'DONNELL
MODESTY AND WILLIE TACKLE THE JUMP ACROSS THE CHUDI GAP...
GOOD VORLAGE POSITION — SHE'S GETTING PLENTY OF DISTANCE...
Romero
TOUCHDOWN... WITH ROOM TO SPARE
WHOO-OA!
3603
MODESTY BLAISE
by PETER O'DONNELL
WILLIE!
Romero
I FELL OVER
I KNOW! ARE YOU ALL RIGHT?
APART FROM SOME SNOW IN ME EAR, I'M VERY 'APPY, PRINCESS — I WASN'T TOO SURE WE WERE GOING TO MAKE THAT JUMP
3603A

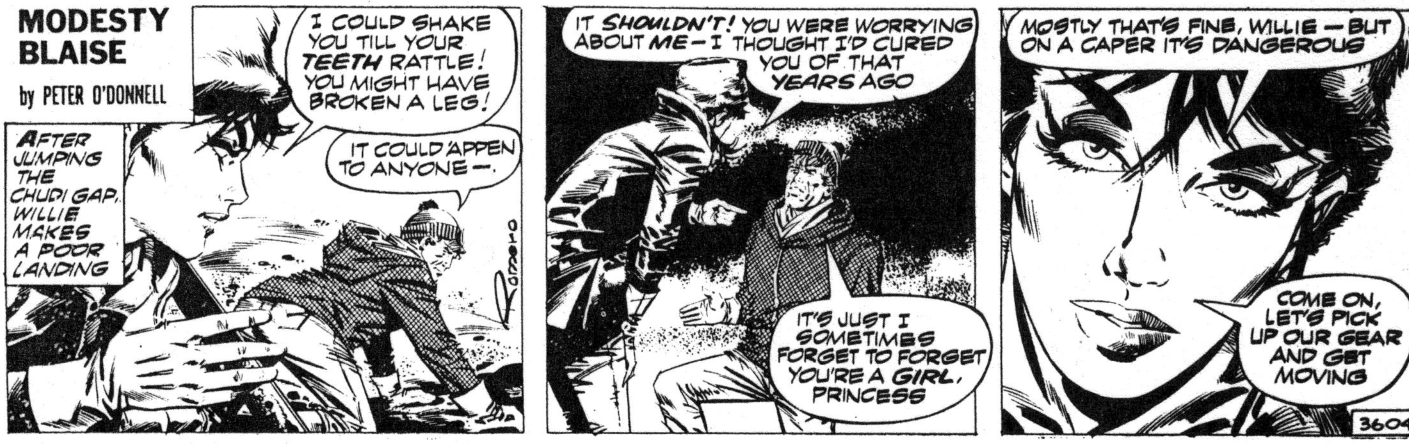
MODESTY BLAISE
by PETER O'DONNELL
AFTER JUMPING THE CHUDI GAP, WILLIE MAKES A POOR LANDING
I COULD SHAKE YOU TILL YOUR TEETH RATTLE! YOU MIGHT HAVE BROKEN A LEG!
IT COULD 'APPEN TO ANYONE—.
IT SHOULDN'T! YOU WERE WORRYING ABOUT ME—I THOUGHT I'D CURED YOU OF THAT YEARS AGO
IT'S JUST I SOMETIMES FORGET TO FORGET YOU'RE A GIRL, PRINCESS
MOSTLY THAT'S FINE, WILLIE—BUT ON A CAPER IT'S DANGEROUS
COME ON, LET'S PICK UP OUR GEAR AND GET MOVING
3604

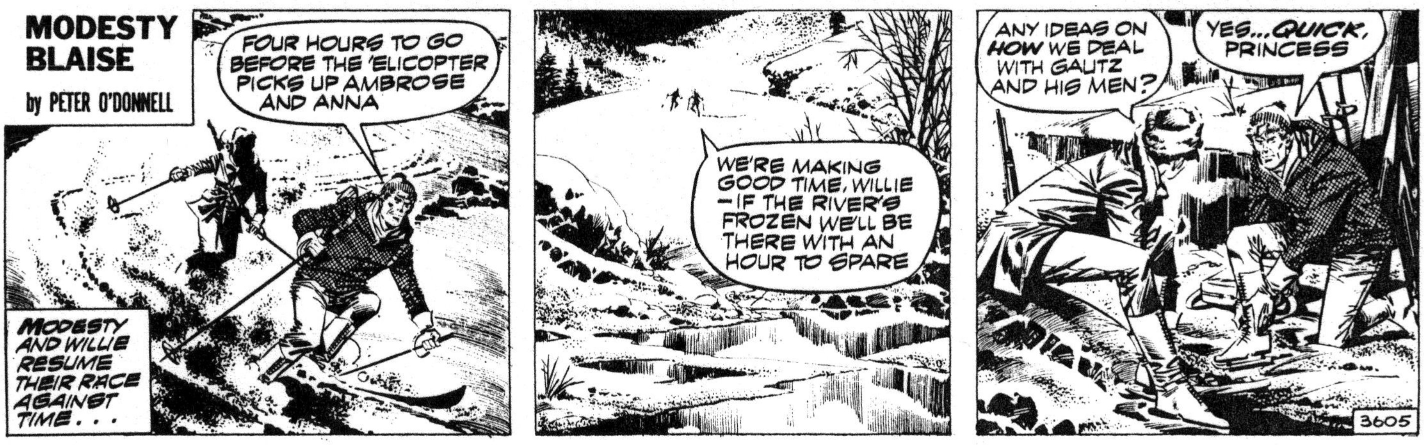
MODESTY BLAISE
by PETER O'DONNELL
FOUR HOURS TO GO BEFORE THE 'ELICOPTER PICKS UP AMBROSE AND ANNA
MODESTY AND WILLIE RESUME THEIR RACE AGAINST TIME . . .
WE'RE MAKING GOOD TIME, WILLIE —IF THE RIVER'S FROZEN WE'LL BE THERE WITH AN HOUR TO SPARE
ANY IDEAS ON HOW WE DEAL WITH GAUTZ AND HIS MEN?
YES... QUICK, PRINCESS
3605

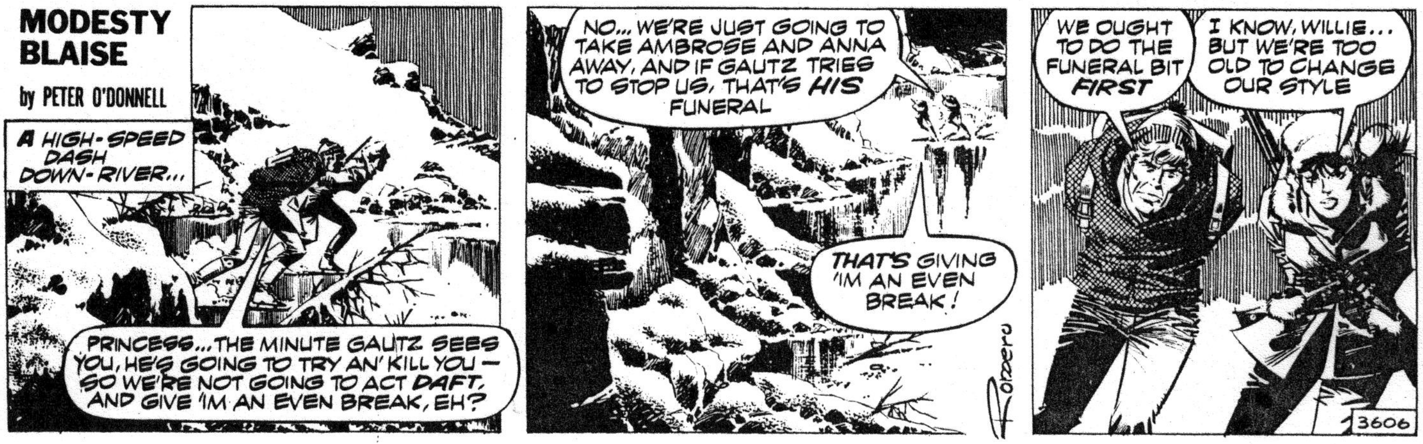
MODESTY BLAISE
by PETER O'DONNELL
A HIGH-SPEED DASH DOWN-RIVER...
PRINCESS... THE MINUTE GAUTZ SEES YOU, HE'S GOING TO TRY AN' KILL YOU—SO WE'RE NOT GOING TO ACT DAFT, AND GIVE 'IM AN EVEN BREAK, EH?
NO... WE'RE JUST GOING TO TAKE AMBROSE AND ANNA AWAY, AND IF GAUTZ TRIES TO STOP US, THAT'S HIS FUNERAL
THAT'S GIVING 'IM AN EVEN BREAK!
WE OUGHT TO DO THE FUNERAL BIT FIRST
I KNOW, WILLIE... BUT WE'RE TOO OLD TO CHANGE OUR STYLE
3606

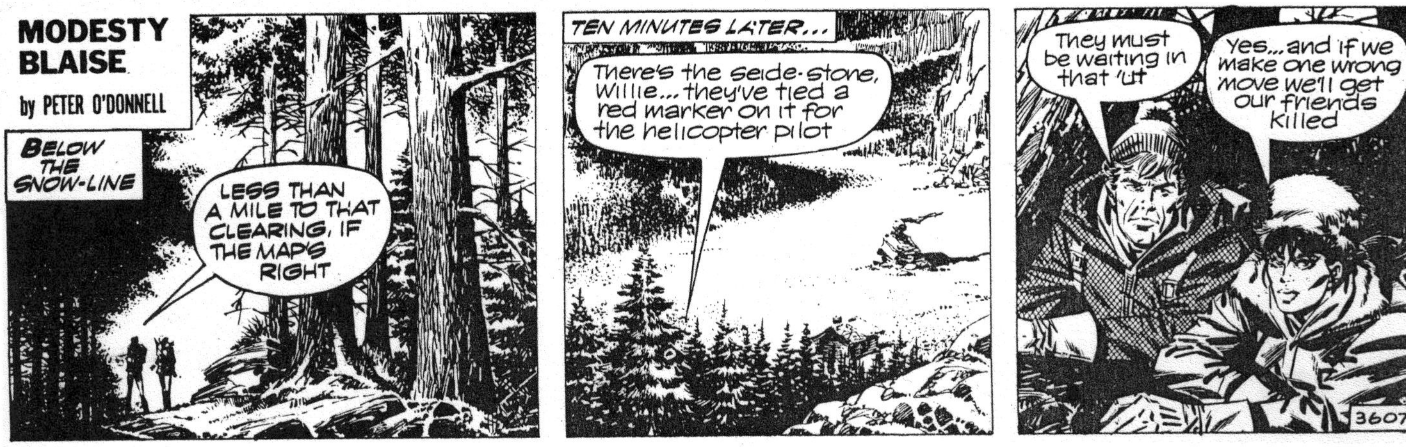
MODESTY BLAISE
by PETER O'DONNELL
BELOW THE SNOW-LINE
LESS THAN A MILE TO THAT CLEARING, IF THE MAP'S RIGHT
TEN MINUTES LATER...
There's the seide-stone, Willie... they've tied a red marker on it for the helicopter pilot
They must be waiting in that 'ut
Yes... and if we make one wrong move we'll get our friends killed
3607

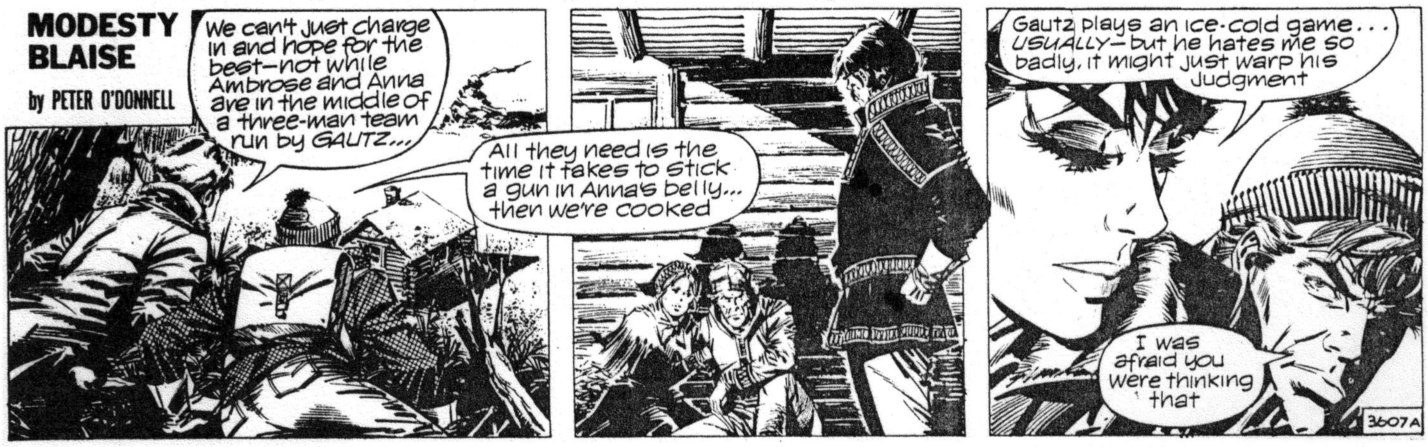
MODESTY BLAISE
by PETER O'DONNELL
We can't just charge in and hope for the best—not while Ambrose and Anna are in the middle of a three-man team run by GAUTZ...
All they need is the time it takes to stick a gun in Anna's belly... then we're cooked
Gautz plays an ice-cold game... USUALLY—but he hates me so badly, it might just warp his judgment
I was afraid you were thinking that
3607A

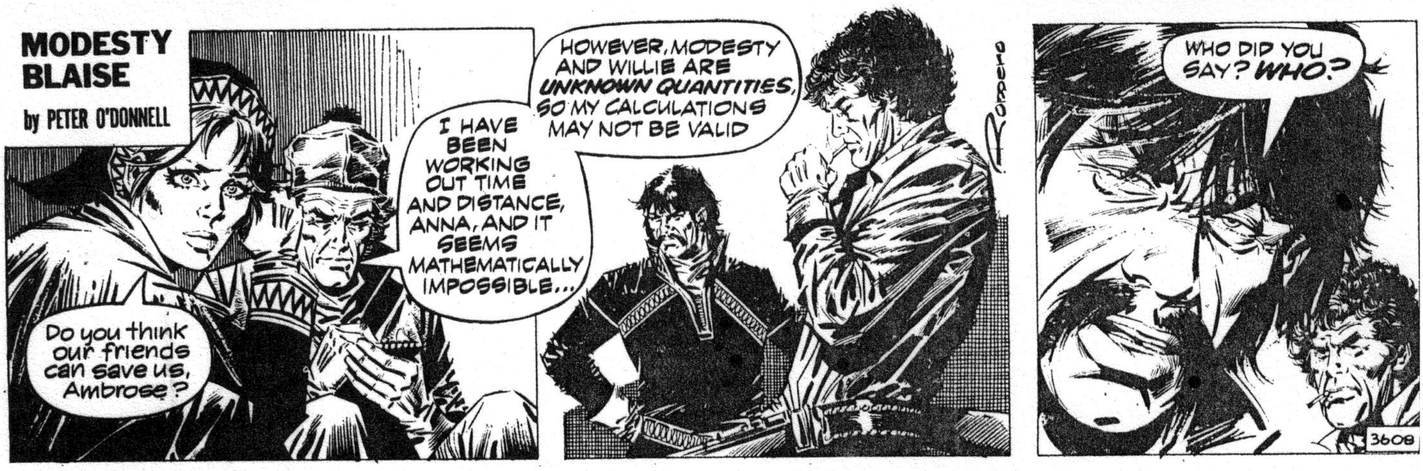
MODESTY BLAISE
by PETER O'DONNELL
Do you think our friends can save us, Ambrose?
I HAVE BEEN WORKING OUT TIME AND DISTANCE, ANNA, AND IT SEEMS MATHEMATICALLY IMPOSSIBLE...
HOWEVER, MODESTY AND WILLIE ARE UNKNOWN QUANTITIES, SO MY CALCULATIONS MAY NOT BE VALID
Romero
WHO DID YOU SAY? WHO?
3608

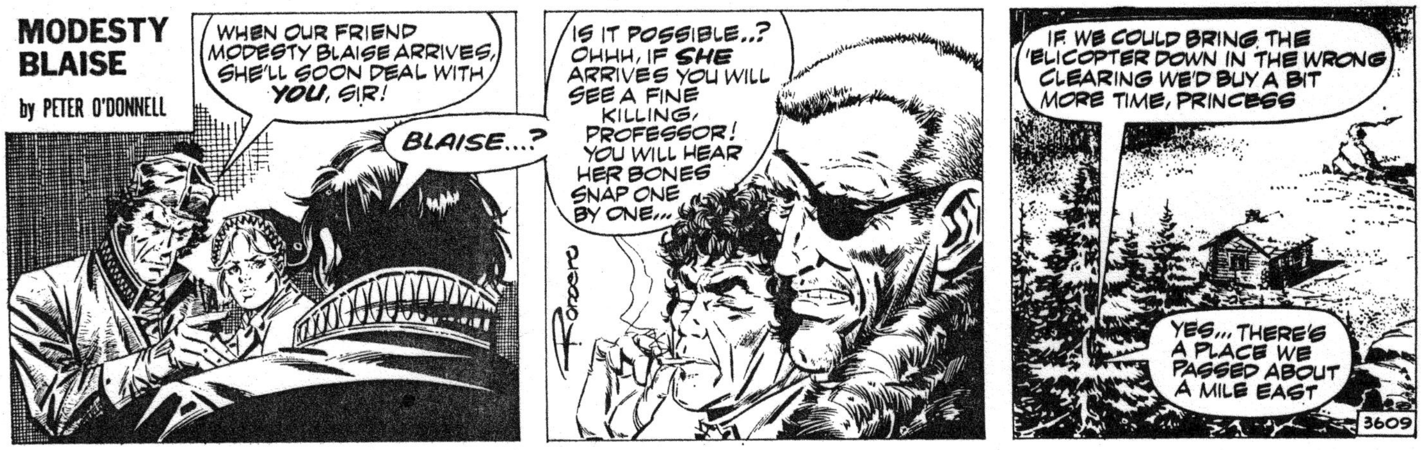
MODESTY BLAISE
by PETER O'DONNELL
WHEN OUR FRIEND MODESTY BLAISE ARRIVES, SHE'LL SOON DEAL WITH YOU, SIR!
BLAISE...?
IS IT POSSIBLE..? OHHH, IF SHE ARRIVES YOU WILL SEE A FINE KILLING, PROFESSOR! YOU WILL HEAR HER BONES SNAP ONE BY ONE...
Romero
IF WE COULD BRING THE 'ELICOPTER DOWN IN THE WRONG CLEARING WE'D BUY A BIT MORE TIME, PRINCESS
YES... THERE'S A PLACE WE PASSED ABOUT A MILE EAST
3609

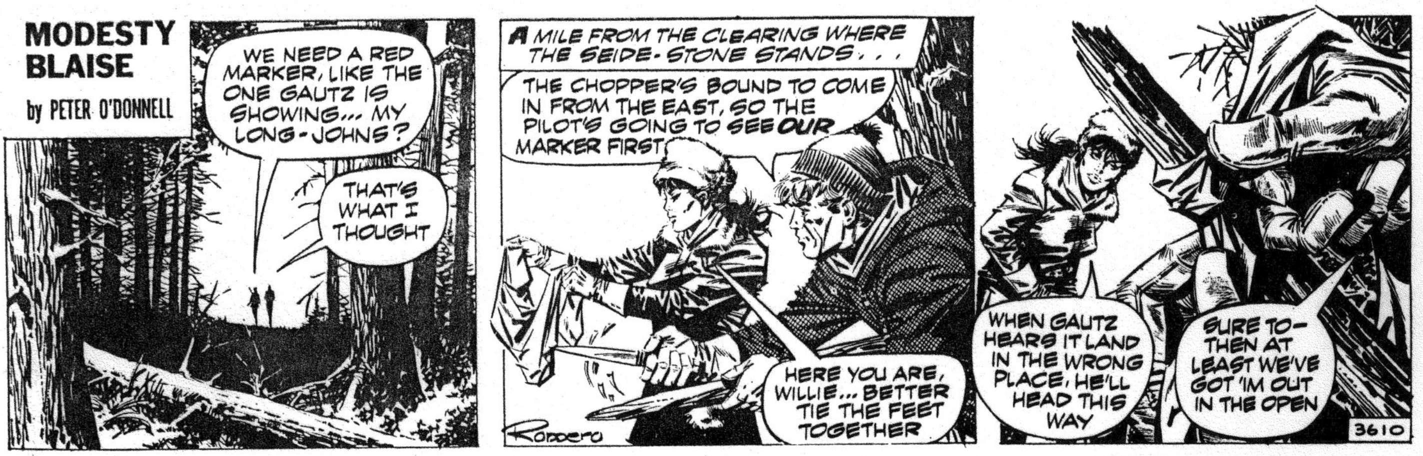
MODESTY BLAISE
by PETER O'DONNELL
WE NEED A RED MARKER, LIKE THE ONE GAUTZ IS SHOWING... MY LONG-JOHNS?
THAT'S WHAT I THOUGHT
A MILE FROM THE CLEARING WHERE THE SEIDE-STONE STANDS...
THE CHOPPER'S BOUND TO COME IN FROM THE EAST, SO THE PILOT'S GOING TO SEE OUR MARKER FIRST
HERE YOU ARE, WILLIE... BETTER TIE THE FEET TOGETHER
Romero
WHEN GAUTZ HEARS IT LAND IN THE WRONG PLACE, HE'LL HEAD THIS WAY
SURE TO—THEN AT LEAST WE'VE GOT 'IM OUT IN THE OPEN
3610

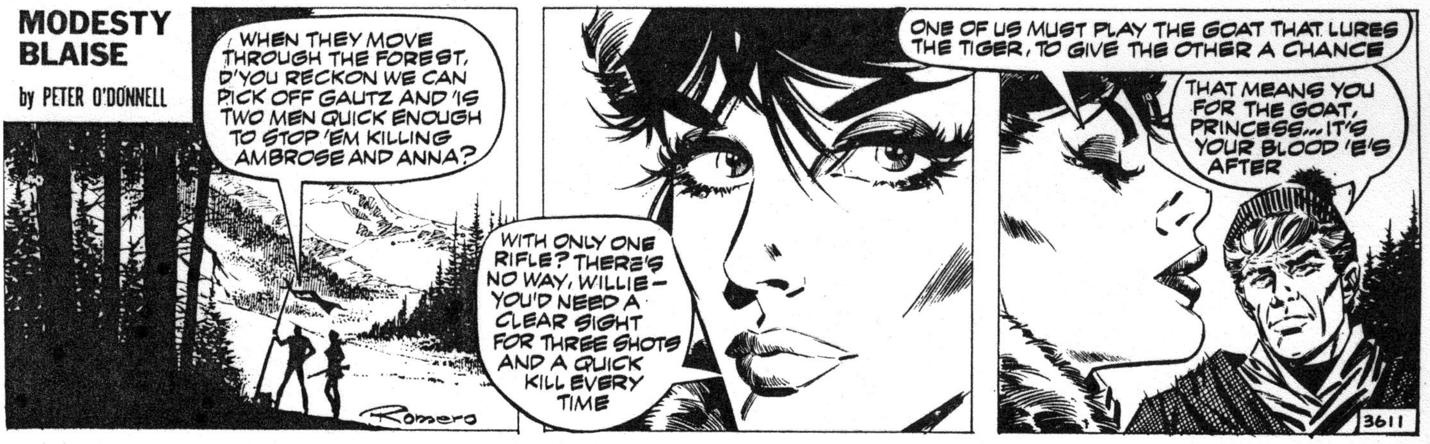
MODESTY BLAISE
by PETER O'DONNELL
WHEN THEY MOVE THROUGH THE FOREST, D'YOU RECKON WE CAN PICK OFF GAUTZ AND 'IS TWO MEN QUICK ENOUGH TO STOP 'EM KILLING AMBROSE AND ANNA?
Romero
WITH ONLY ONE RIFLE? THERE'S NO WAY, WILLIE— YOU'D NEED A CLEAR SIGHT FOR THREE SHOTS AND A QUICK KILL EVERY TIME
ONE OF US MUST PLAY THE GOAT THAT LURES THE TIGER, TO GIVE THE OTHER A CHANCE
THAT MEANS YOU FOR THE GOAT, PRINCESS... IT'S YOUR BLOOD 'E'S AFTER
3611

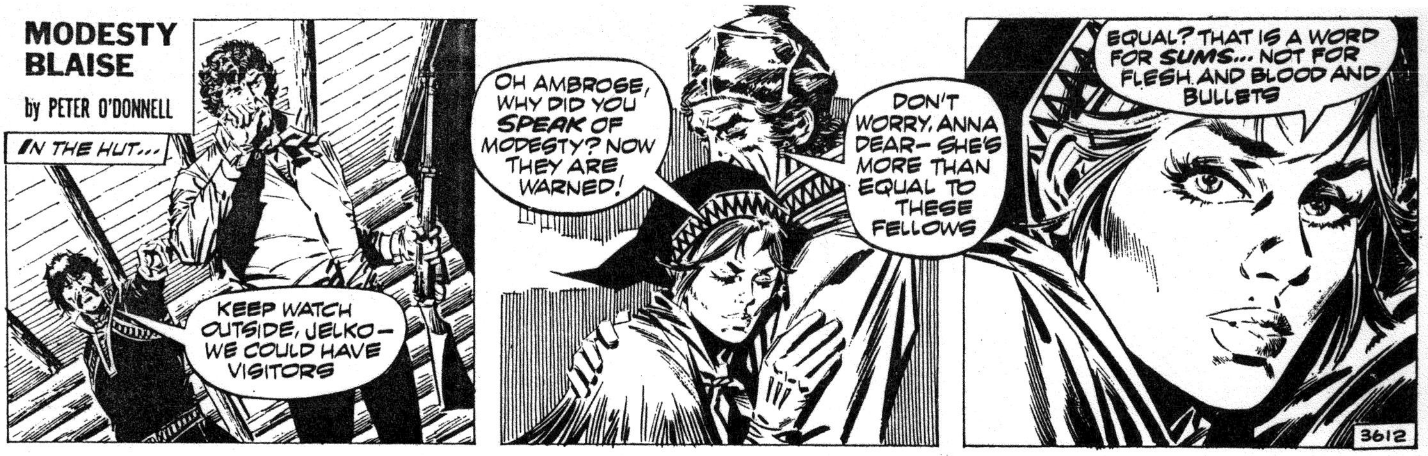
MODESTY BLAISE
by PETER O'DONNELL
IN THE HUT...
KEEP WATCH OUTSIDE, JELKO— WE COULD HAVE VISITORS
OH AMBROSE, WHY DID YOU SPEAK OF MODESTY? NOW THEY ARE WARNED!
DON'T WORRY, ANNA DEAR— SHE'S MORE THAN EQUAL TO THESE FELLOWS
EQUAL? THAT IS A WORD FOR SUMS... NOT FOR FLESH AND BLOOD AND BULLETS
3612

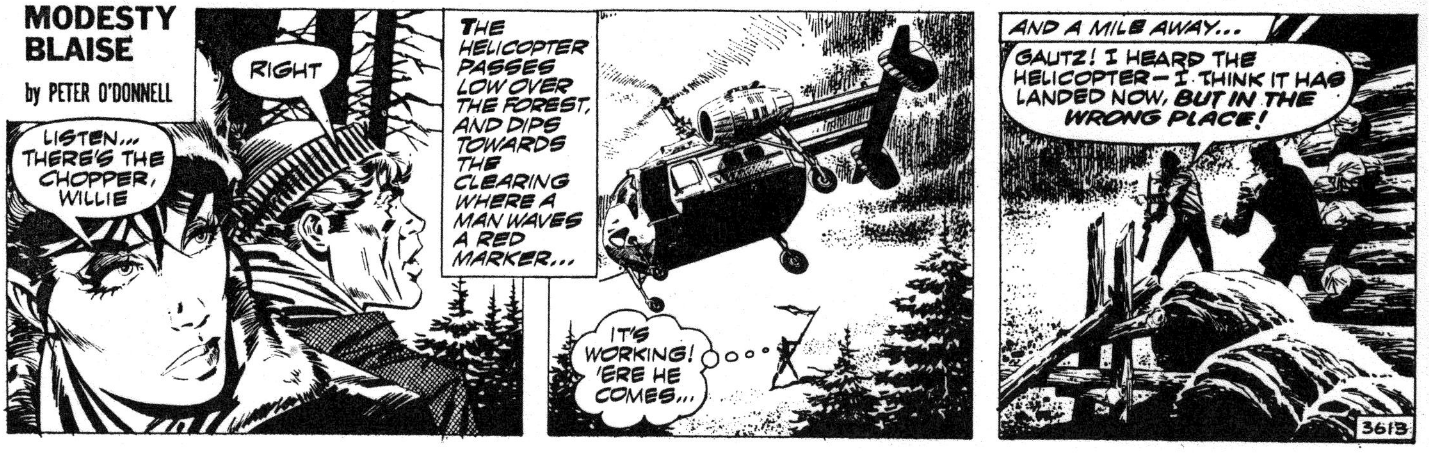
MODESTY BLAISE
by PETER O'DONNELL
LISTEN... THERE'S THE CHOPPER, WILLIE
RIGHT
THE HELICOPTER PASSES LOW OVER THE FOREST, AND DIPS TOWARDS THE CLEARING WHERE A MAN WAVES A RED MARKER...
IT'S WORKING! 'ERE HE COMES...
AND A MILE AWAY...
GAUTZ! I HEARD THE HELICOPTER— I THINK IT HAS LANDED NOW, BUT IN THE WRONG PLACE!
3613

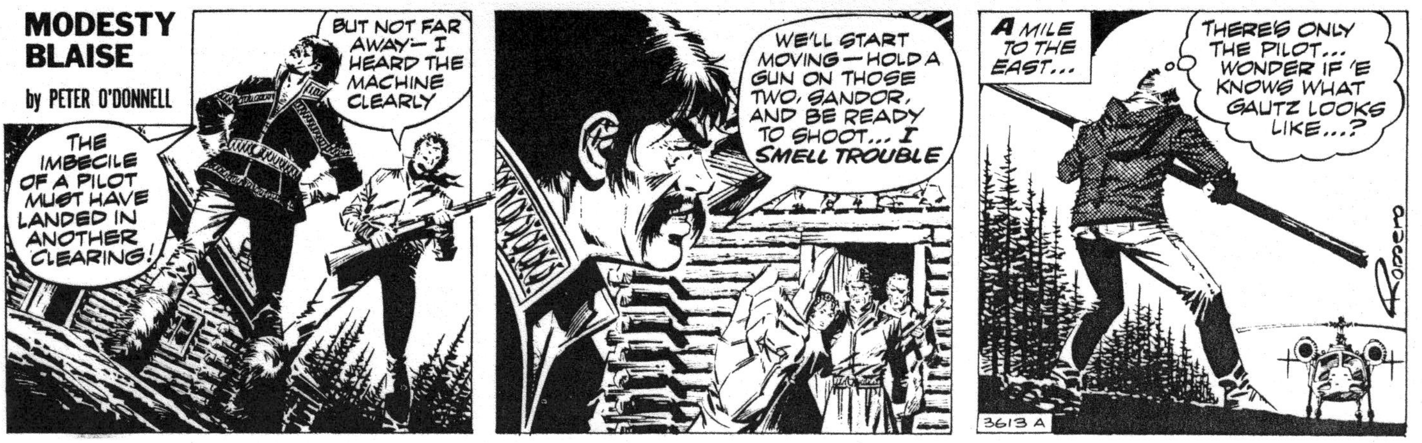
MODESTY BLAISE
by PETER O'DONNELL
THE IMBECILE OF A PILOT MUST HAVE LANDED IN ANOTHER CLEARING!
BUT NOT FAR AWAY— I HEARD THE MACHINE CLEARLY
WE'LL START MOVING— HOLD A GUN ON THOSE TWO, SANDOR, AND BE READY TO SHOOT... I SMELL TROUBLE
A MILE TO THE EAST...
THERE'S ONLY THE PILOT... WONDER IF 'E KNOWS WHAT GAUTZ LOOKS LIKE...?
3613 A

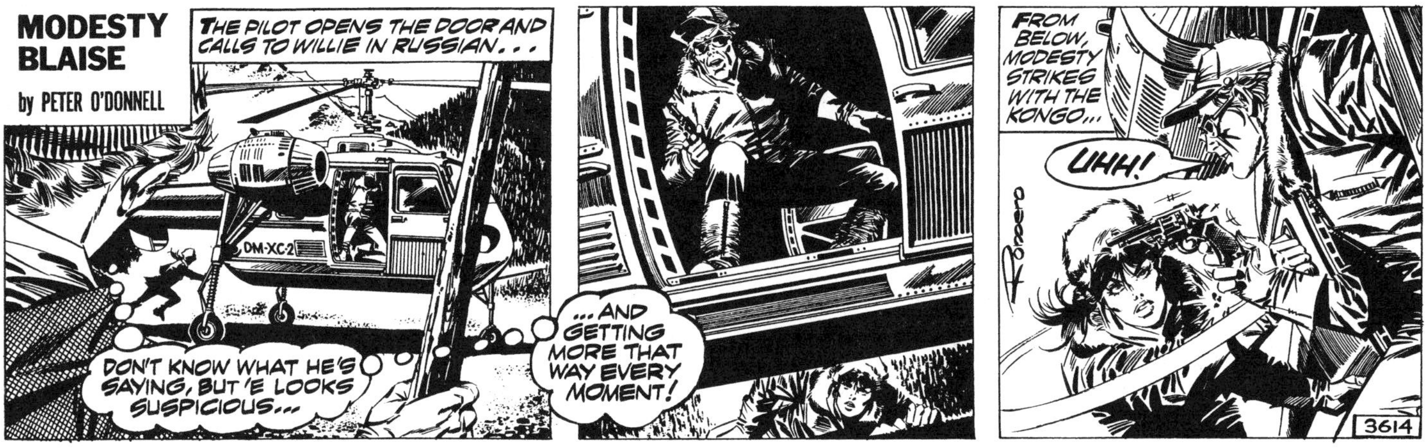
MODESTY BLAISE
by PETER O'DONNELL
THE PILOT OPENS THE DOOR AND CALLS TO WILLIE IN RUSSIAN . . .
DM-XC-2
DON'T KNOW WHAT HE'S SAYING, BUT 'E LOOKS SUSPICIOUS...
...AND GETTING MORE THAT WAY EVERY MOMENT!
FROM BELOW, MODESTY STRIKES WITH THE KONGO...
UHH!
3614

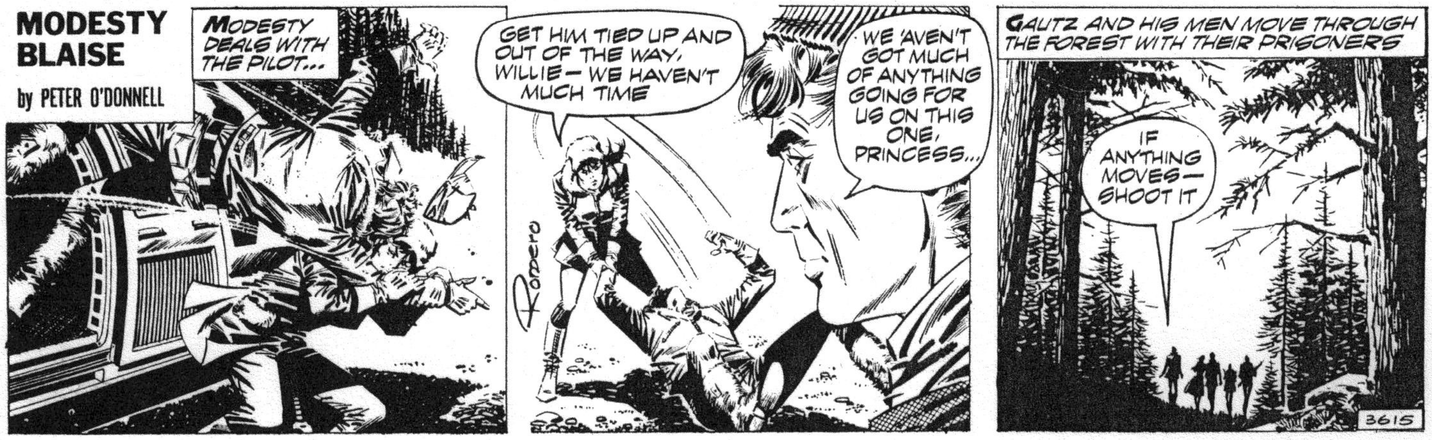
MODESTY BLAISE
by PETER O'DONNELL
MODESTY DEALS WITH THE PILOT...
GET HIM TIED UP AND OUT OF THE WAY, WILLIE — WE HAVEN'T MUCH TIME
WE 'AVEN'T GOT MUCH OF ANYTHING GOING FOR US ON THIS ONE, PRINCESS...
GAUTZ AND HIS MEN MOVE THROUGH THE FOREST WITH THEIR PRISONERS
IF ANYTHING MOVES — SHOOT IT
3615

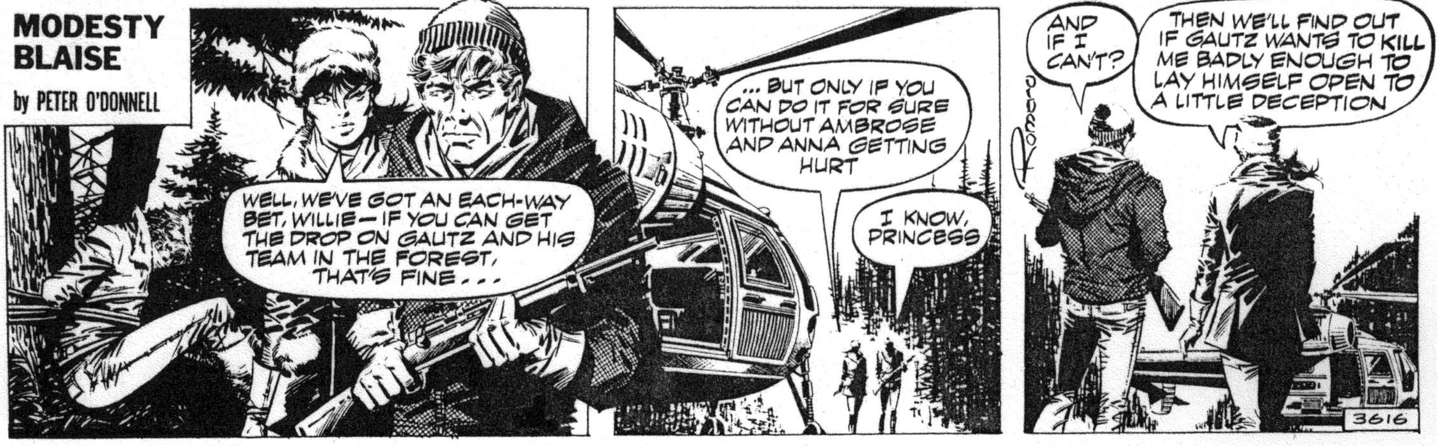
MODESTY BLAISE
by PETER O'DONNELL
WELL, WE'VE GOT AN EACH-WAY BET, WILLIE — IF YOU CAN GET THE DROP ON GAUTZ AND HIS TEAM IN THE FOREST, THAT'S FINE . . .
... BUT ONLY IF YOU CAN DO IT FOR SURE WITHOUT AMBROSE AND ANNA GETTING HURT
I KNOW, PRINCESS
AND IF I CAN'T?
THEN WE'LL FIND OUT IF GAUTZ WANTS TO KILL ME BADLY ENOUGH TO LAY HIMSELF OPEN TO A LITTLE DECEPTION
3616

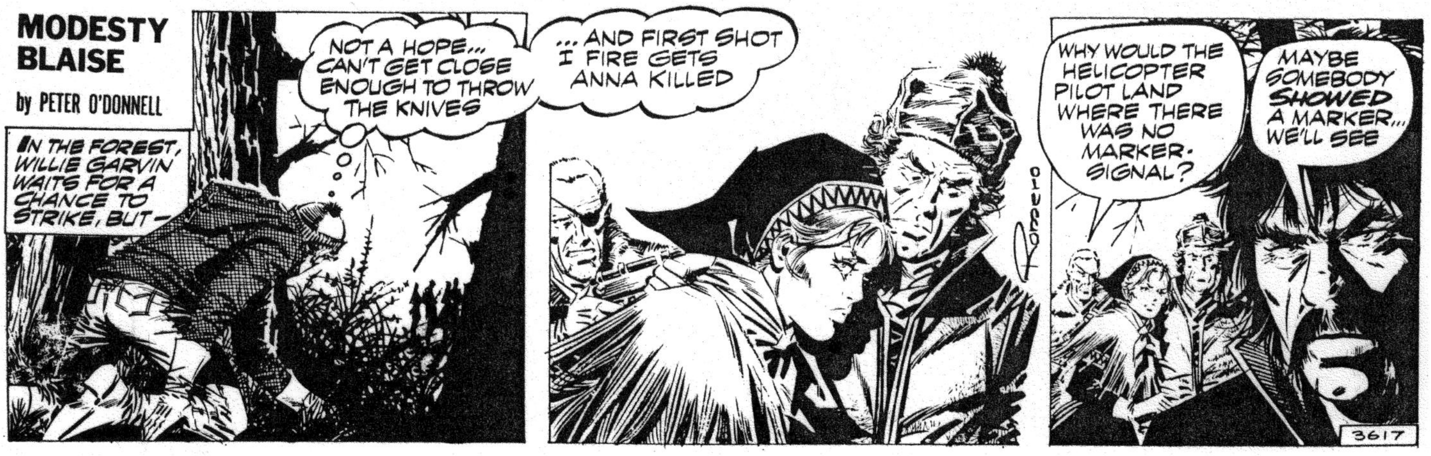
MODESTY BLAISE
by PETER O'DONNELL
IN THE FOREST, WILLIE GARVIN WAITS FOR A CHANCE TO STRIKE, BUT—
NOT A HOPE... CAN'T GET CLOSE ENOUGH TO THROW THE KNIVES
...AND FIRST SHOT I FIRE GETS ANNA KILLED
WHY WOULD THE HELICOPTER PILOT LAND WHERE THERE WAS NO MARKER-SIGNAL?
MAYBE SOMEBODY SHOWED A MARKER... WE'LL SEE
3617

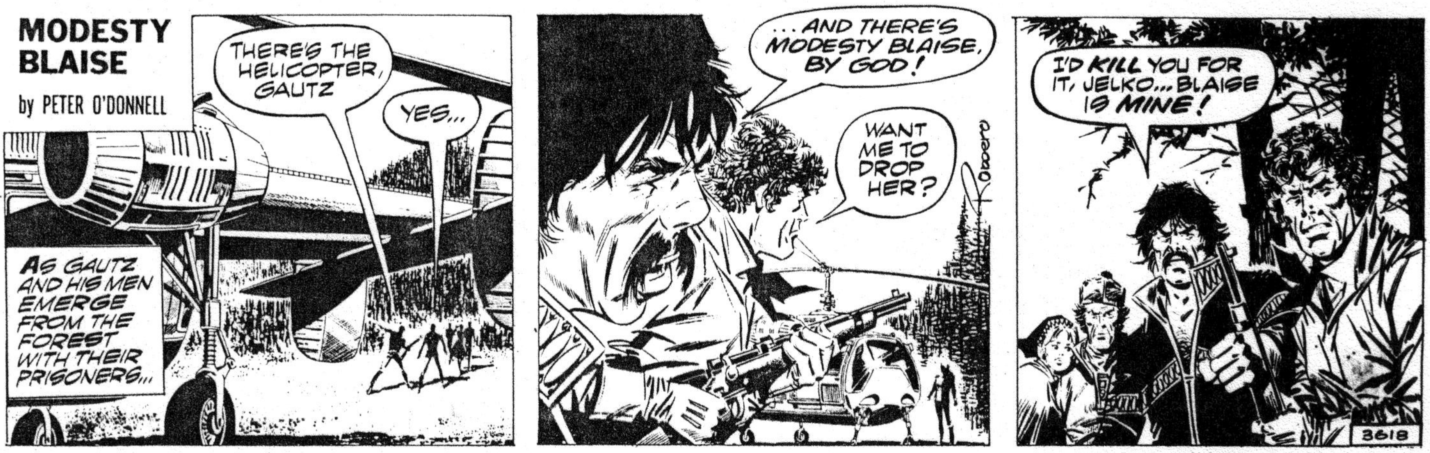
MODESTY BLAISE
by PETER O'DONNELL
AS GAUTZ AND HIS MEN EMERGE FROM THE FOREST WITH THEIR PRISONERS...
THERE'S THE HELICOPTER, GAUTZ
YES...
...AND THERE'S MODESTY BLAISE, BY GOD!
WANT ME TO DROP HER?
I'D KILL YOU FOR IT, JELKO... BLAISE IS MINE!
3618

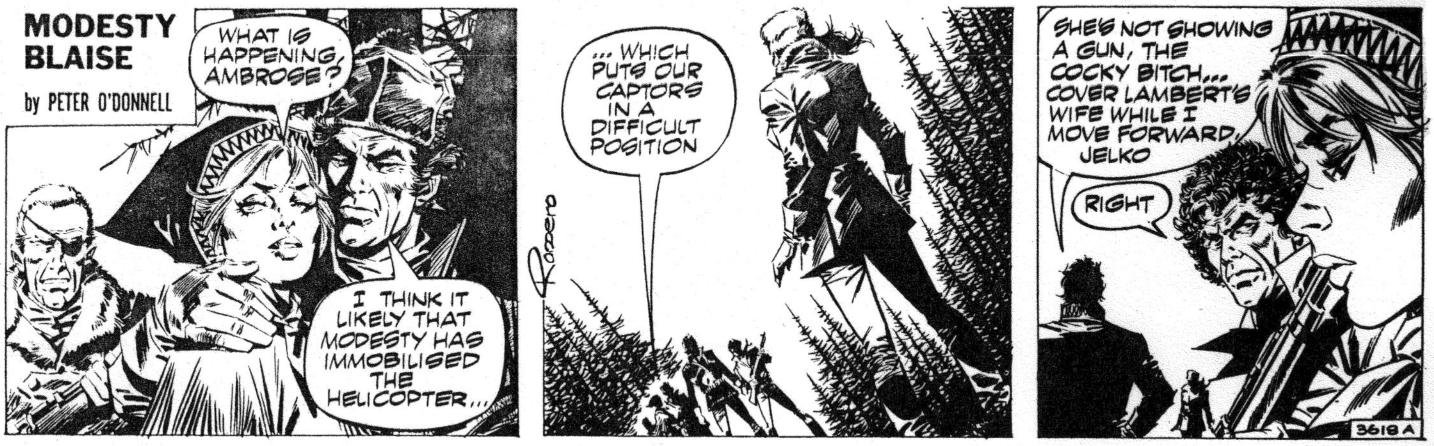
MODESTY BLAISE
by PETER O'DONNELL
WHAT IS HAPPENING, AMBROSE?
I THINK IT LIKELY THAT MODESTY HAS IMMOBILISED THE HELICOPTER...
...WHICH PUTS OUR CAPTORS IN A DIFFICULT POSITION
SHE'S NOT SHOWING A GUN, THE COCKY BITCH... COVER LAMBERT'S WIFE WHILE I MOVE FORWARD, JELKO
RIGHT
3618 A

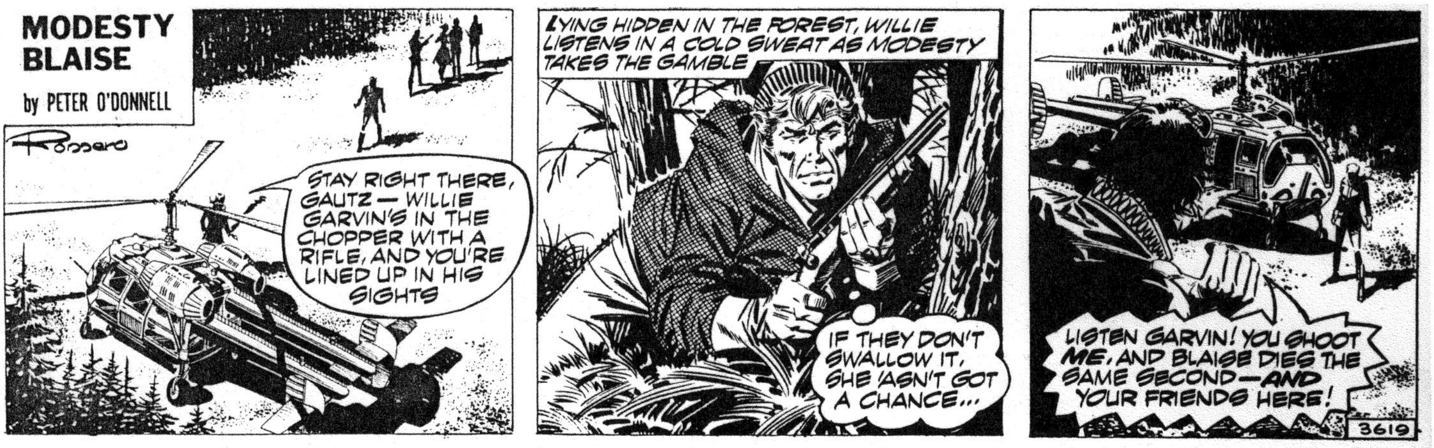
MODESTY BLAISE
by PETER O'DONNELL
STAY RIGHT THERE, GAUTZ — WILLIE GARVIN'S IN THE CHOPPER WITH A RIFLE, AND YOU'RE LINED UP IN HIS SIGHTS
LYING HIDDEN IN THE FOREST, WILLIE LISTENS IN A COLD SWEAT AS MODESTY TAKES THE GAMBLE
IF THEY DON'T SWALLOW IT, SHE 'ASN'T GOT A CHANCE...
LISTEN GARVIN! YOU SHOOT ME, AND BLAISE DIES THE SAME SECOND — AND YOUR FRIENDS HERE!
3619

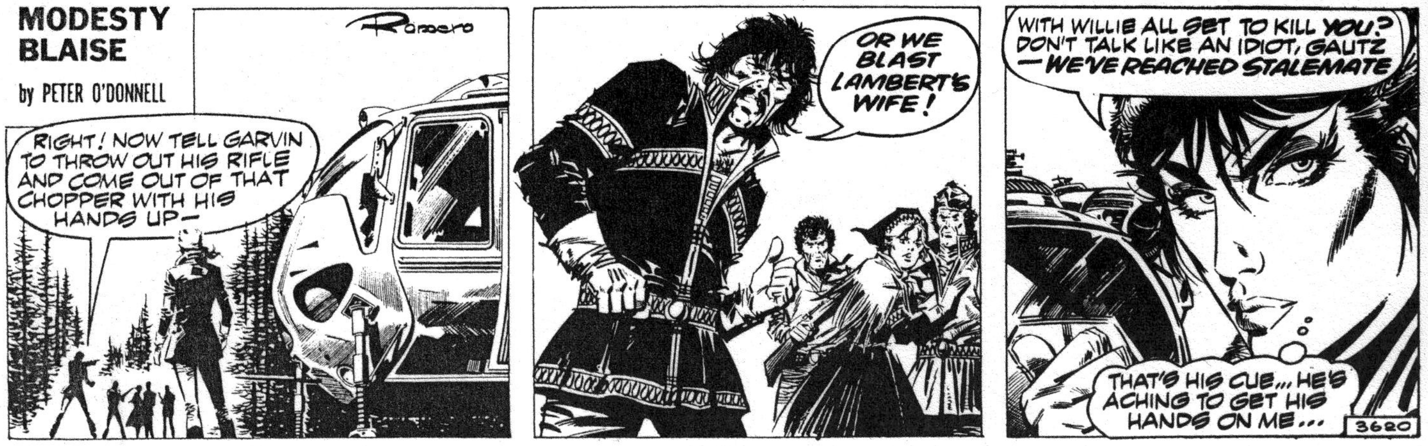
MODESTY BLAISE
by PETER O'DONNELL
RIGHT! NOW TELL GARVIN TO THROW OUT HIS RIFLE AND COME OUT OF THAT CHOPPER WITH HIS HANDS UP—
OR WE BLAST LAMBERT'S WIFE!
WITH WILLIE ALL SET TO KILL YOU? DON'T TALK LIKE AN IDIOT, GAUTZ — WE'VE REACHED STALEMATE
THAT'S HIS CUE... HE'S ACHING TO GET HIS HANDS ON ME...
3620

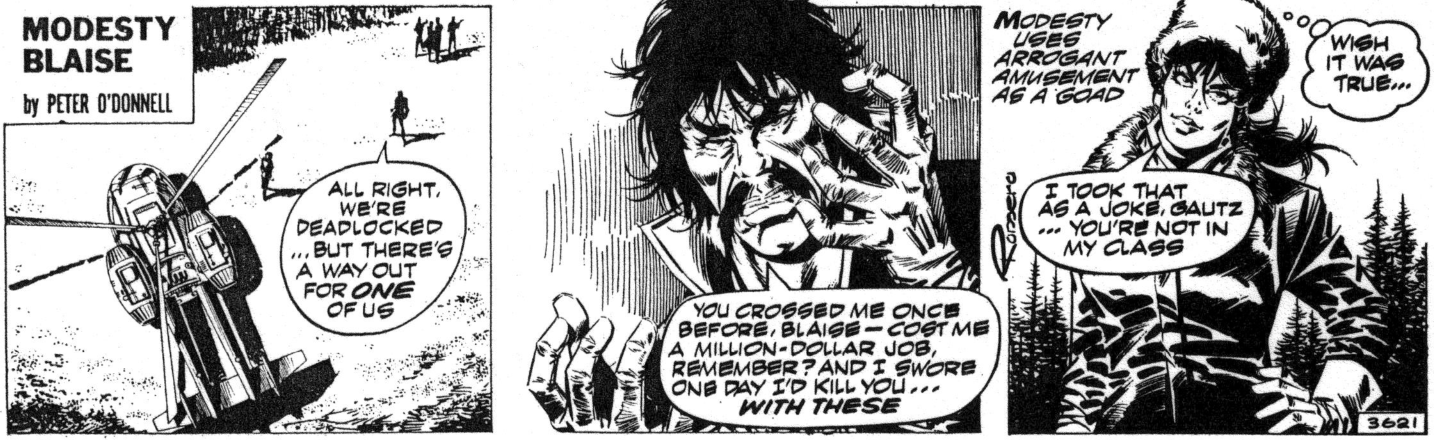
MODESTY BLAISE
by PETER O'DONNELL
ALL RIGHT, WE'RE DEADLOCKED ... BUT THERE'S A WAY OUT FOR ONE OF US
YOU CROSSED ME ONCE BEFORE, BLAISE — COST ME A MILLION-DOLLAR JOB, REMEMBER? AND I SWORE ONE DAY I'D KILL YOU ... WITH THESE
MODESTY USES ARROGANT AMUSEMENT AS A GOAD
WISH IT WAS TRUE...
I TOOK THAT AS A JOKE, GAUTZ ... YOU'RE NOT IN MY CLASS
3621

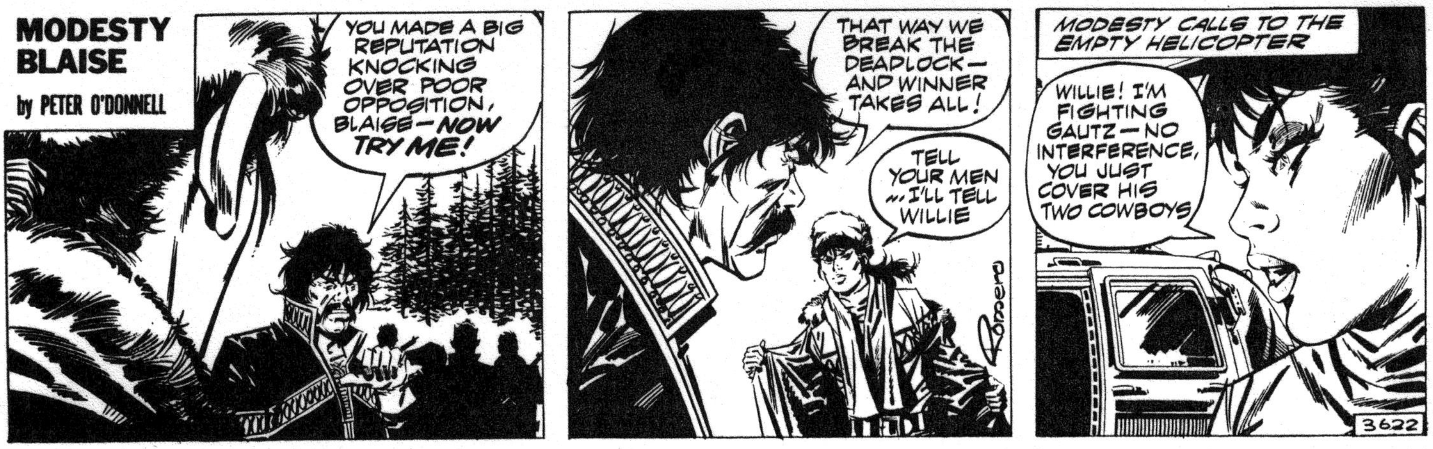
MODESTY BLAISE
by PETER O'DONNELL
YOU MADE A BIG REPUTATION KNOCKING OVER POOR OPPOSITION, BLAISE — NOW TRY ME!
THAT WAY WE BREAK THE DEADLOCK — AND WINNER TAKES ALL!
TELL YOUR MEN ... I'LL TELL WILLIE
MODESTY CALLS TO THE EMPTY HELICOPTER
WILLIE! I'M FIGHTING GAUTZ — NO INTERFERENCE, YOU JUST COVER HIS TWO COWBOYS
3622

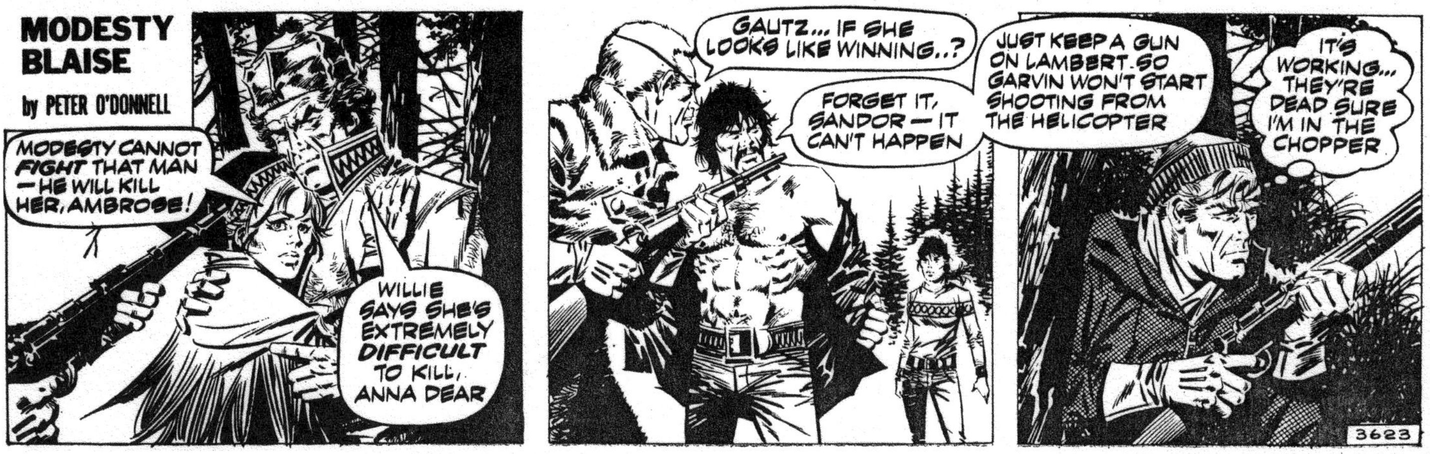
MODESTY BLAISE
by PETER O'DONNELL
MODESTY CANNOT FIGHT THAT MAN — HE WILL KILL HER, AMBROSE!
WILLIE SAYS SHE'S EXTREMELY DIFFICULT TO KILL, ANNA DEAR
GAUTZ... IF SHE LOOKS LIKE WINNING..?
FORGET IT, SANDOR — IT CAN'T HAPPEN
JUST KEEP A GUN ON LAMBERT SO GARVIN WON'T START SHOOTING FROM THE HELICOPTER
IT'S WORKING... THEY'RE DEAD SURE I'M IN THE CHOPPER
3623

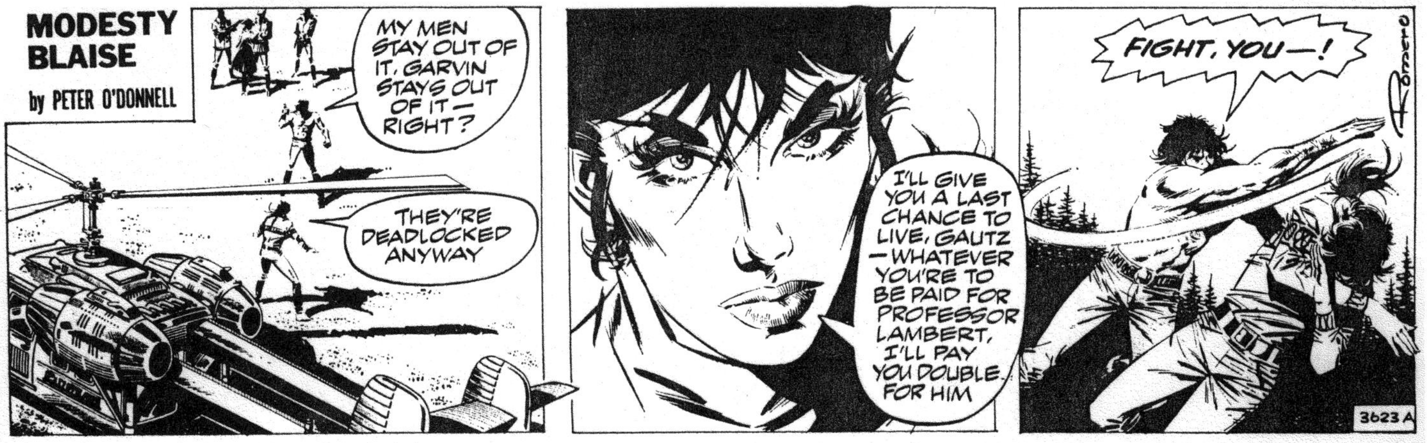
MODESTY BLAISE
by PETER O'DONNELL
MY MEN STAY OUT OF IT, GARVIN STAYS OUT OF IT — RIGHT?
THEY'RE DEADLOCKED ANYWAY
I'LL GIVE YOU A LAST CHANCE TO LIVE, GAUTZ — WHATEVER YOU'RE TO BE PAID FOR PROFESSOR LAMBERT, I'LL PAY YOU DOUBLE FOR HIM
FIGHT, YOU —!
3623 A

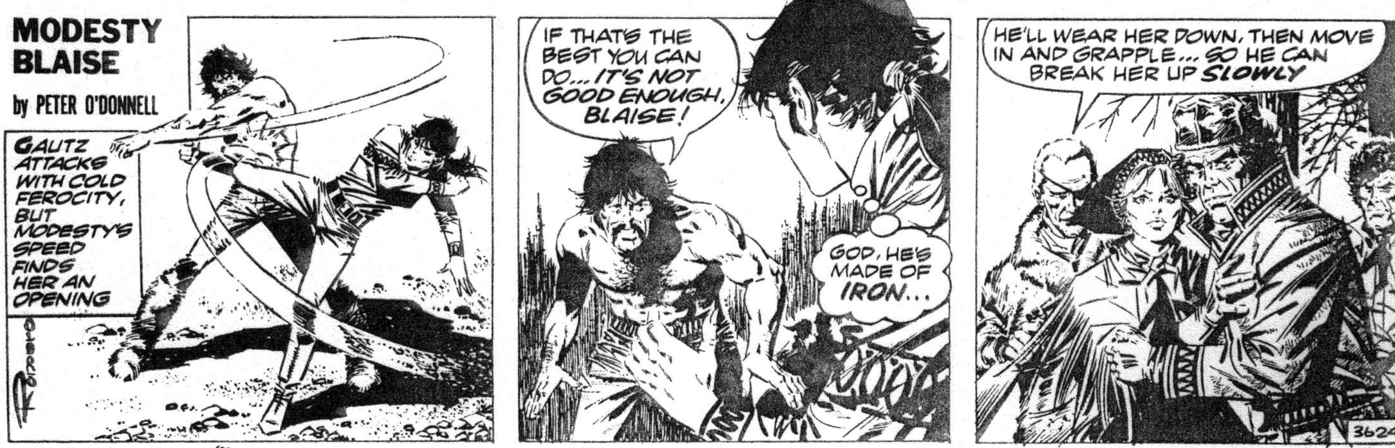
MODESTY BLAISE
by PETER O'DONNELL
GAUTZ ATTACKS WITH COLD FEROCITY, BUT MODESTY'S SPEED FINDS HER AN OPENING
IF THAT'S THE BEST YOU CAN DO... IT'S NOT GOOD ENOUGH, BLAISE!
GOD, HE'S MADE OF IRON...
HE'LL WEAR HER DOWN, THEN MOVE IN AND GRAPPLE... SO HE CAN BREAK HER UP SLOWLY
3624

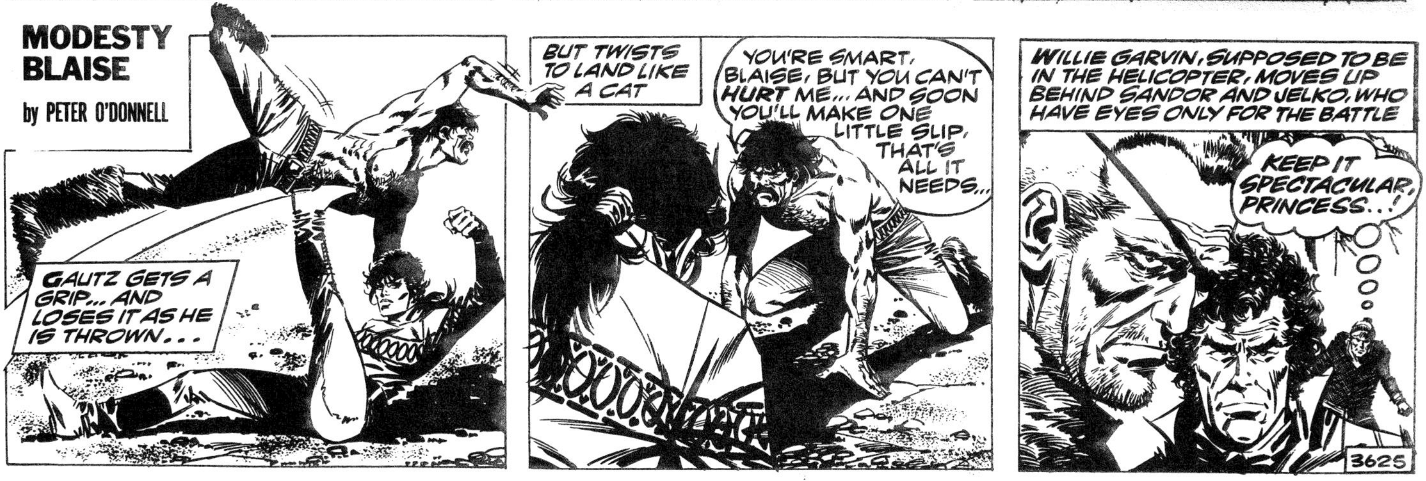
MODESTY BLAISE
by PETER O'DONNELL
GAUTZ GETS A GRIP... AND LOSES IT AS HE IS THROWN...
BUT TWISTS TO LAND LIKE A CAT
YOU'RE SMART, BLAISE, BUT YOU CAN'T HURT ME... AND SOON YOU'LL MAKE ONE LITTLE SLIP, THAT'S ALL IT NEEDS...
WILLIE GARVIN, SUPPOSED TO BE IN THE HELICOPTER, MOVES UP BEHIND SANDOR AND JELKO, WHO HAVE EYES ONLY FOR THE BATTLE
KEEP IT SPECTACULAR, PRINCESS...!
3625

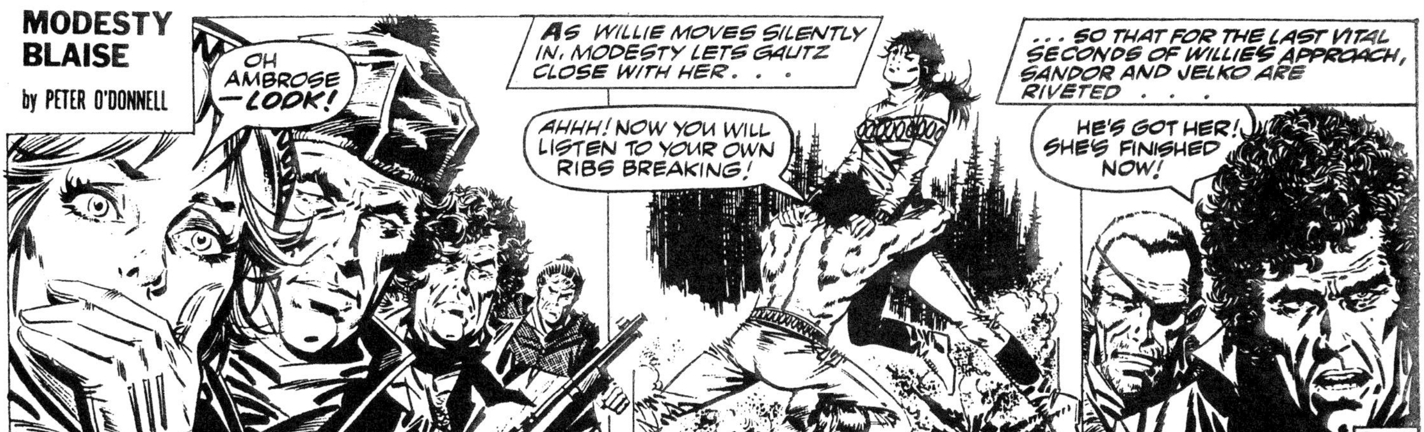
MODESTY BLAISE
by PETER O'DONNELL
OH AMBROSE —LOOK!
AS WILLIE MOVES SILENTLY IN, MODESTY LETS GAUTZ CLOSE WITH HER...
AHHH! NOW YOU WILL LISTEN TO YOUR OWN RIBS BREAKING!
... SO THAT FOR THE LAST VITAL SECONDS OF WILLIE'S APPROACH, SANDOR AND JELKO ARE RIVETED...
HE'S GOT HER! SHE'S FINISHED NOW!
3626

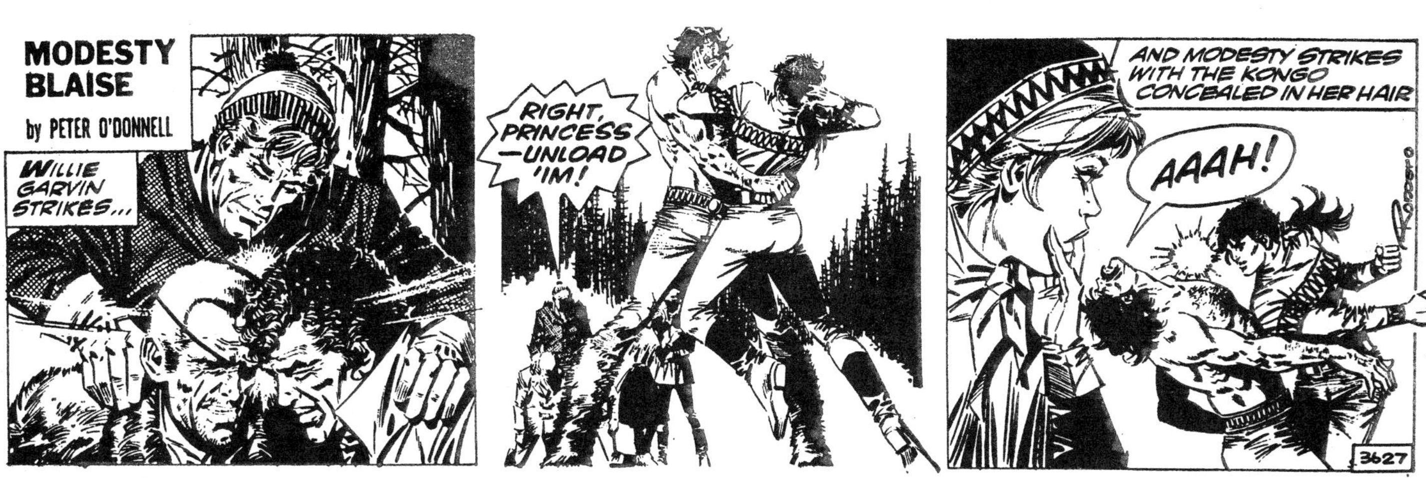
MODESTY BLAISE
by PETER O'DONNELL
WILLIE GARVIN STRIKES...
RIGHT, PRINCESS —UNLOAD 'IM!
AND MODESTY STRIKES WITH THE KONGO CONCEALED IN HER HAIR
AAAH!
3627

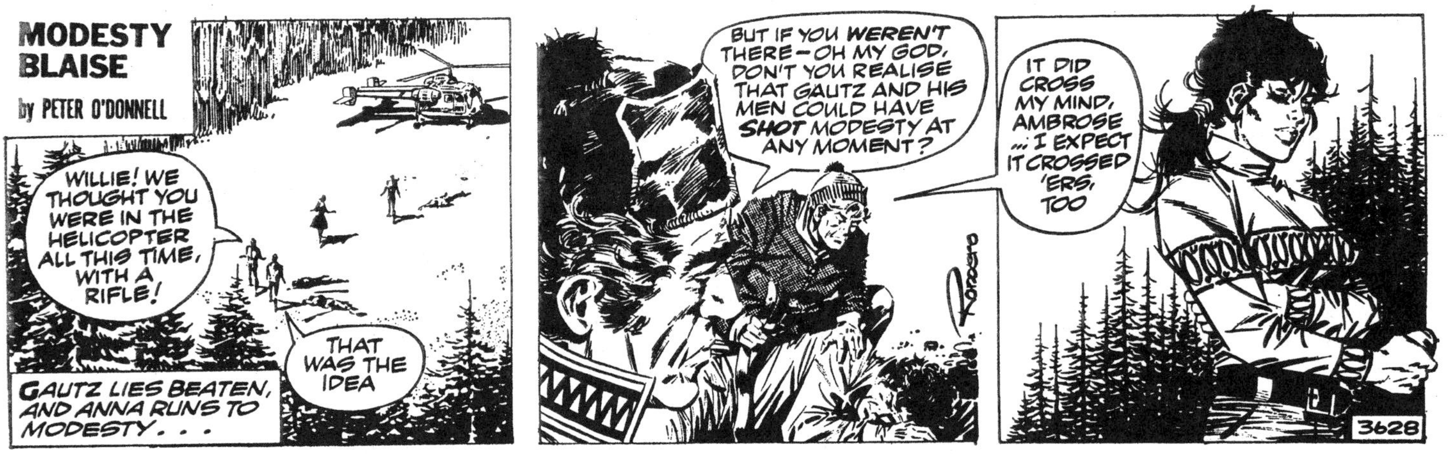
MODESTY BLAISE
by PETER O'DONNELL
GAUTZ LIES BEATEN, AND ANNA RUNS TO MODESTY . . .
WILLIE! WE THOUGHT YOU WERE IN THE HELICOPTER ALL THIS TIME, WITH A RIFLE!
THAT WAS THE IDEA
BUT IF YOU WEREN'T THERE—OH MY GOD, DON'T YOU REALISE THAT GAUTZ AND HIS MEN COULD HAVE SHOT MODESTY AT ANY MOMENT?
IT DID CROSS MY MIND, AMBROSE ... I EXPECT IT CROSSED 'ERS, TOO
3628

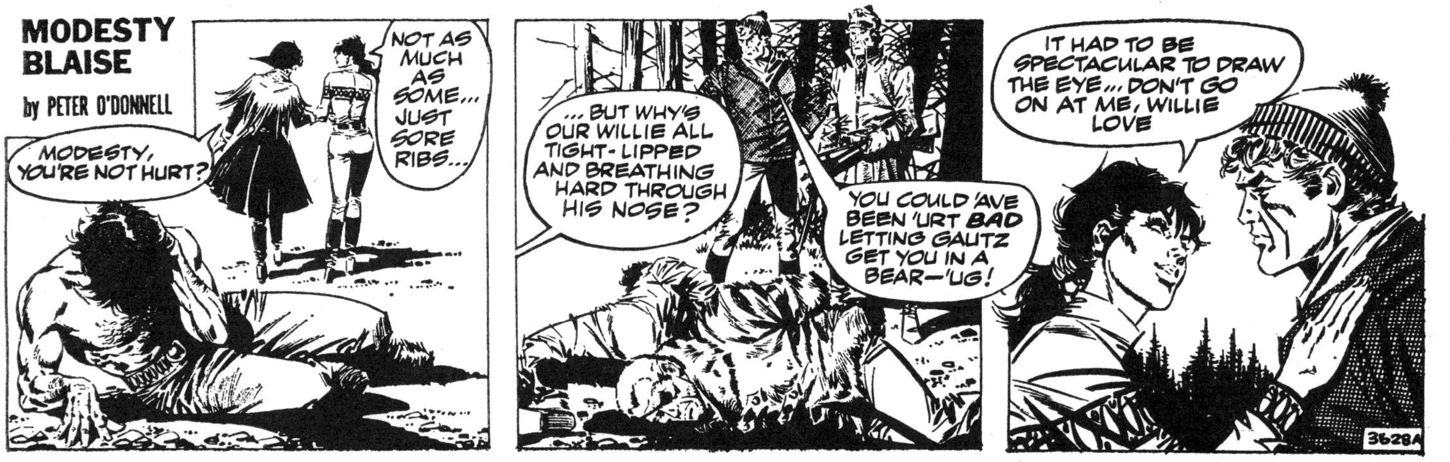
MODESTY BLAISE
by PETER O'DONNELL
MODESTY, YOU'RE NOT HURT?
NOT AS MUCH AS SOME... JUST SORE RIBS...
... BUT WHY'S OUR WILLIE ALL TIGHT-LIPPED AND BREATHING HARD THROUGH HIS NOSE?
YOU COULD 'AVE BEEN 'URT BAD LETTING GAUTZ GET YOU IN A BEAR-'UG!
IT HAD TO BE SPECTACULAR TO DRAW THE EYE... DON'T GO ON AT ME, WILLIE LOVE
3628A

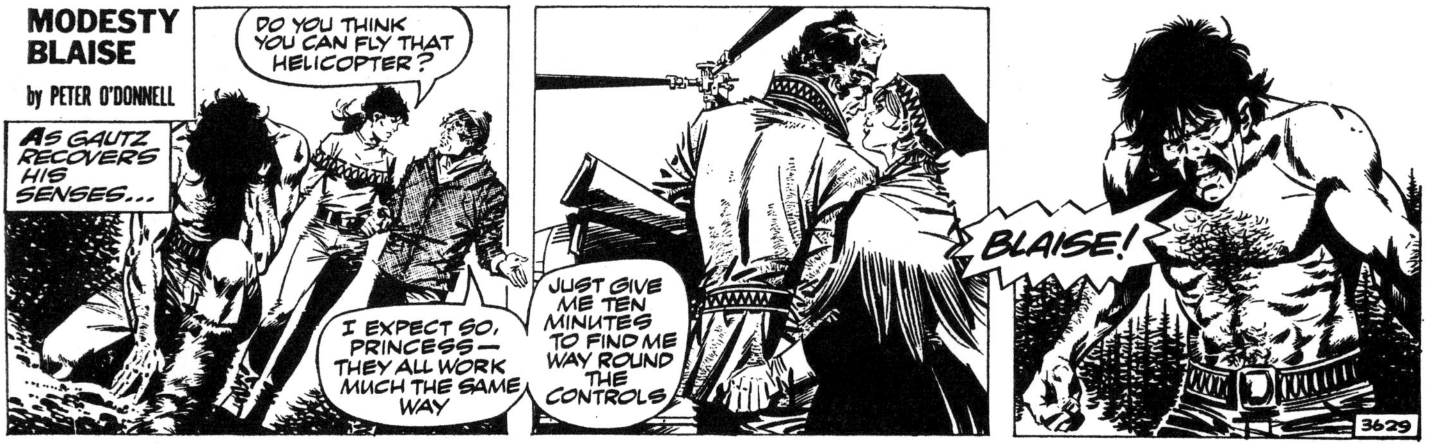
MODESTY BLAISE
by PETER O'DONNELL
AS GAUTZ RECOVERS HIS SENSES...
DO YOU THINK YOU CAN FLY THAT HELICOPTER?
I EXPECT SO, PRINCESS—THEY ALL WORK MUCH THE SAME WAY
JUST GIVE ME TEN MINUTES TO FIND ME WAY ROUND THE CONTROLS
BLAISE!
3629

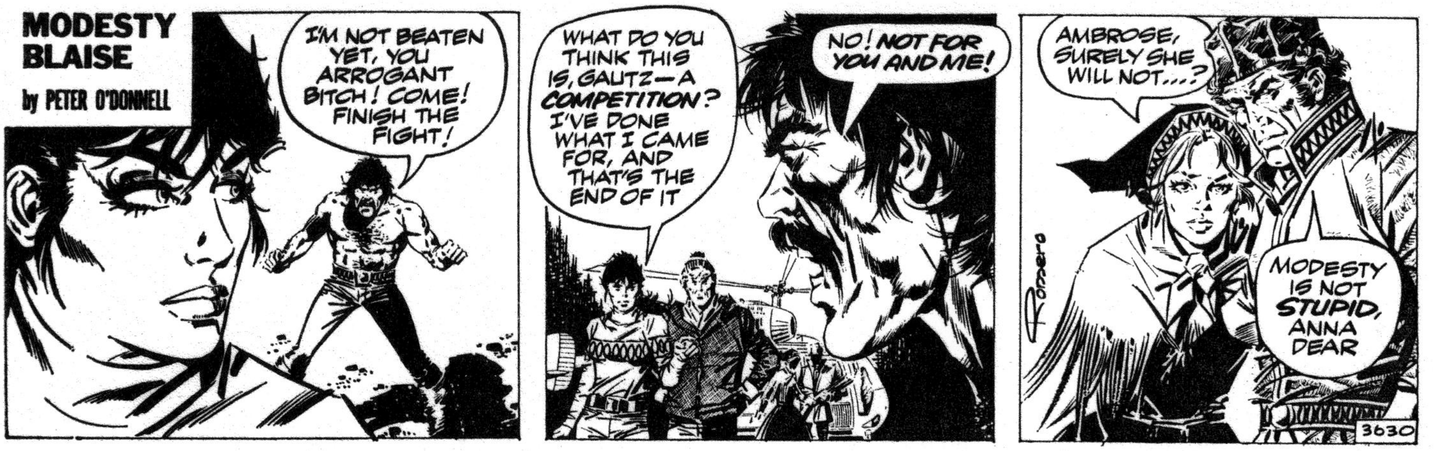
MODESTY BLAISE
by PETER O'DONNELL
I'M NOT BEATEN YET, YOU ARROGANT BITCH! COME! FINISH THE FIGHT!
WHAT DO YOU THINK THIS IS, GAUTZ—A COMPETITION? I'VE DONE WHAT I CAME FOR, AND THAT'S THE END OF IT
NO! NOT FOR YOU AND ME!
AMBROSE, SURELY SHE WILL NOT...?
MODESTY IS NOT STUPID, ANNA DEAR
3630

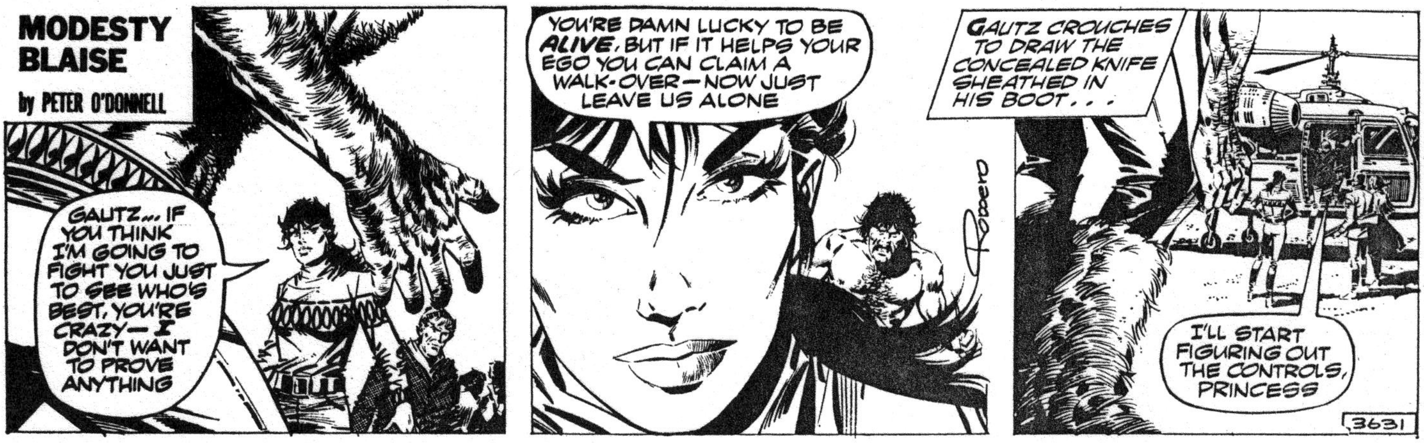
MODESTY BLAISE
by PETER O'DONNELL
GAUTZ... IF YOU THINK I'M GOING TO FIGHT YOU JUST TO SEE WHO'S BEST, YOU'RE CRAZY— I DON'T WANT TO PROVE ANYTHING
YOU'RE DAMN LUCKY TO BE ALIVE, BUT IF IT HELPS YOUR EGO YOU CAN CLAIM A WALK-OVER—NOW JUST LEAVE US ALONE
GAUTZ CROUCHES TO DRAW THE CONCEALED KNIFE SHEATHED IN HIS BOOT . . .
I'LL START FIGURING OUT THE CONTROLS, PRINCESS
3631

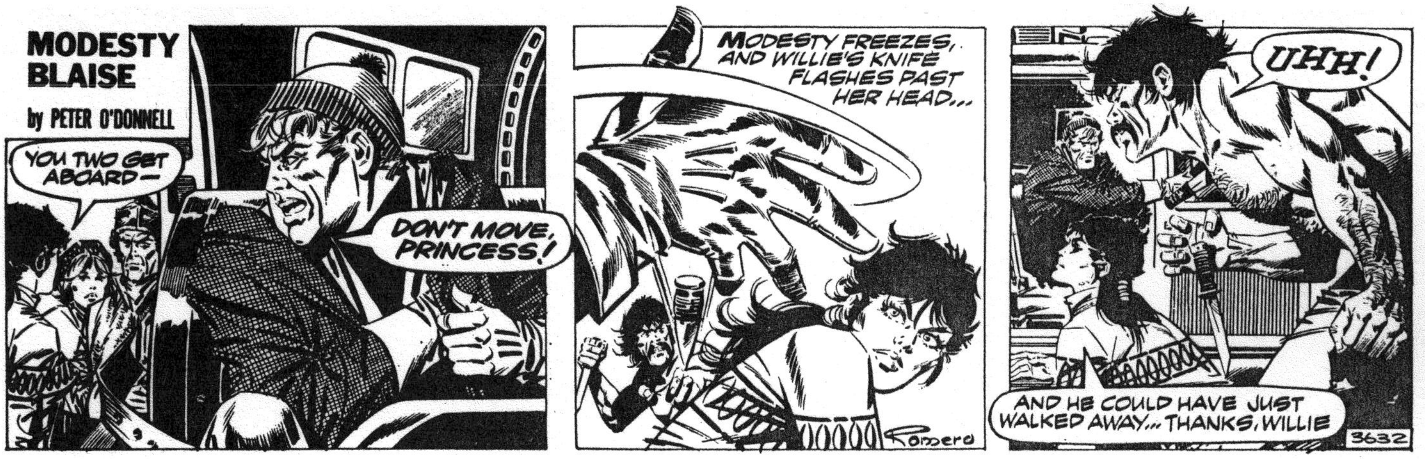
MODESTY BLAISE
by PETER O'DONNELL
YOU TWO GET ABOARD—
DON'T MOVE, PRINCESS!
MODESTY FREEZES, AND WILLIE'S KNIFE FLASHES PAST HER HEAD...
UHH!
AND HE COULD HAVE JUST WALKED AWAY... THANKS, WILLIE
3632

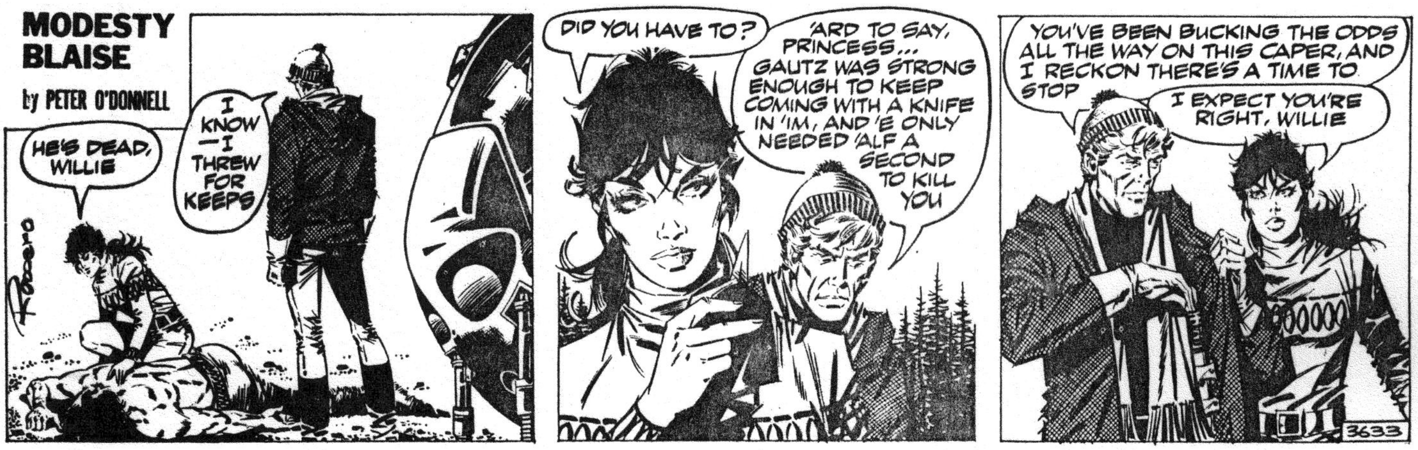
MODESTY BLAISE
by PETER O'DONNELL
HE'S DEAD, WILLIE
I KNOW —I THREW FOR KEEPS
DID YOU HAVE TO?
'ARD TO SAY, PRINCESS... GAUTZ WAS STRONG ENOUGH TO KEEP COMING WITH A KNIFE IN 'IM, AND 'E ONLY NEEDED 'ALF A SECOND TO KILL YOU
YOU'VE BEEN BUCKING THE ODDS ALL THE WAY ON THIS CAPER, AND I RECKON THERE'S A TIME TO STOP
I EXPECT YOU'RE RIGHT, WILLIE
3633

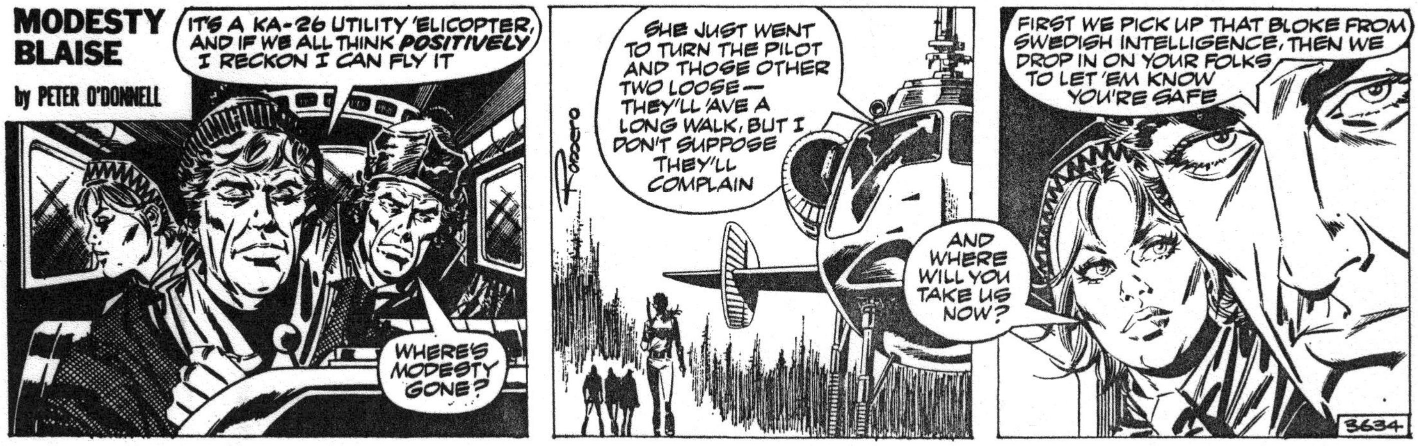
MODESTY BLAISE
by PETER O'DONNELL
IT'S A KA-26 UTILITY 'ELICOPTER, AND IF WE ALL THINK POSITIVELY I RECKON I CAN FLY IT
WHERE'S MODESTY GONE?
SHE JUST WENT TO TURN THE PILOT AND THOSE OTHER TWO LOOSE— THEY'LL 'AVE A LONG WALK, BUT I DON'T SUPPOSE THEY'LL COMPLAIN
FIRST WE PICK UP THAT BLOKE FROM SWEDISH INTELLIGENCE, THEN WE DROP IN ON YOUR FOLKS TO LET 'EM KNOW YOU'RE SAFE
AND WHERE WILL YOU TAKE US NOW?
3634

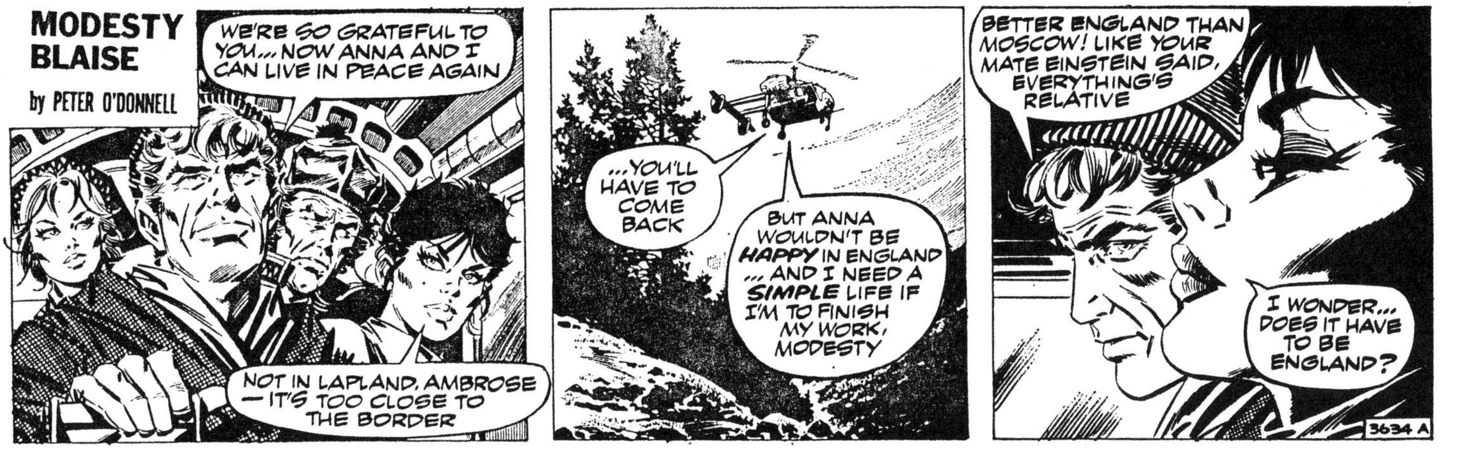
MODESTY BLAISE
by PETER O'DONNELL
WE'RE SO GRATEFUL TO YOU... NOW ANNA AND I CAN LIVE IN PEACE AGAIN
NOT IN LAPLAND, AMBROSE — IT'S TOO CLOSE TO THE BORDER
...YOU'LL HAVE TO COME BACK
BUT ANNA WOULDN'T BE HAPPY IN ENGLAND ... AND I NEED A SIMPLE LIFE IF I'M TO FINISH MY WORK, MODESTY
BETTER ENGLAND THAN MOSCOW! LIKE YOUR MATE EINSTEIN SAID, EVERYTHING'S RELATIVE
I WONDER... DOES IT HAVE TO BE ENGLAND?
3634 A

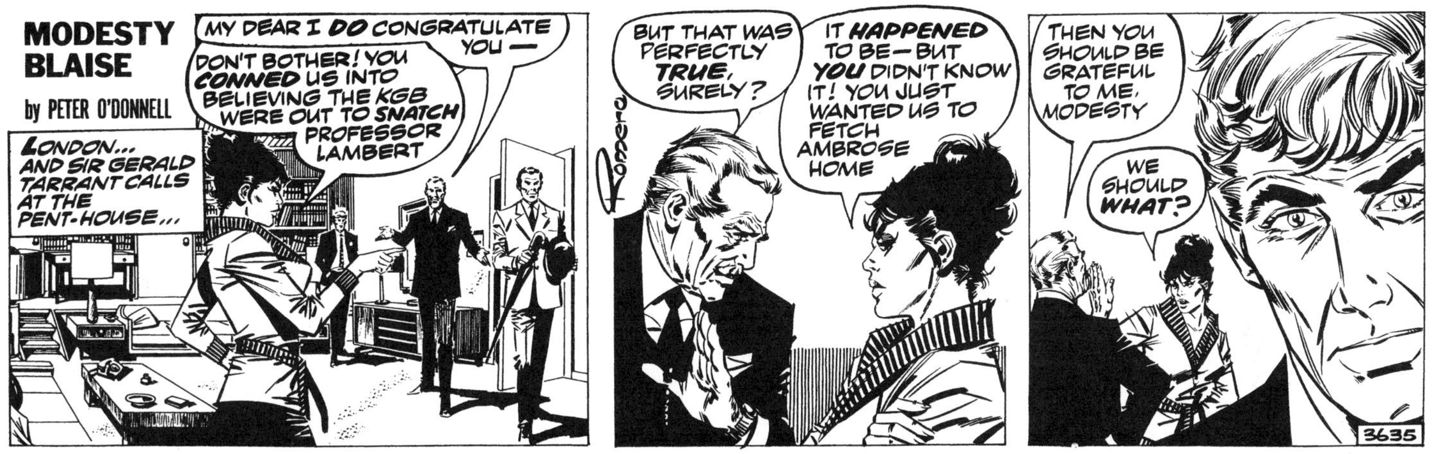
MODESTY BLAISE
by PETER O'DONNELL
MY DEAR I DO CONGRATULATE YOU —
DON'T BOTHER! YOU CONNED US INTO BELIEVING THE KGB WERE OUT TO SNATCH PROFESSOR LAMBERT
LONDON... AND SIR GERALD TARRANT CALLS AT THE PENT-HOUSE...
BUT THAT WAS PERFECTLY TRUE, SURELY?
IT HAPPENED TO BE — BUT YOU DIDN'T KNOW IT! YOU JUST WANTED US TO FETCH AMBROSE HOME
THEN YOU SHOULD BE GRATEFUL TO ME, MODESTY
WE SHOULD WHAT?
3635

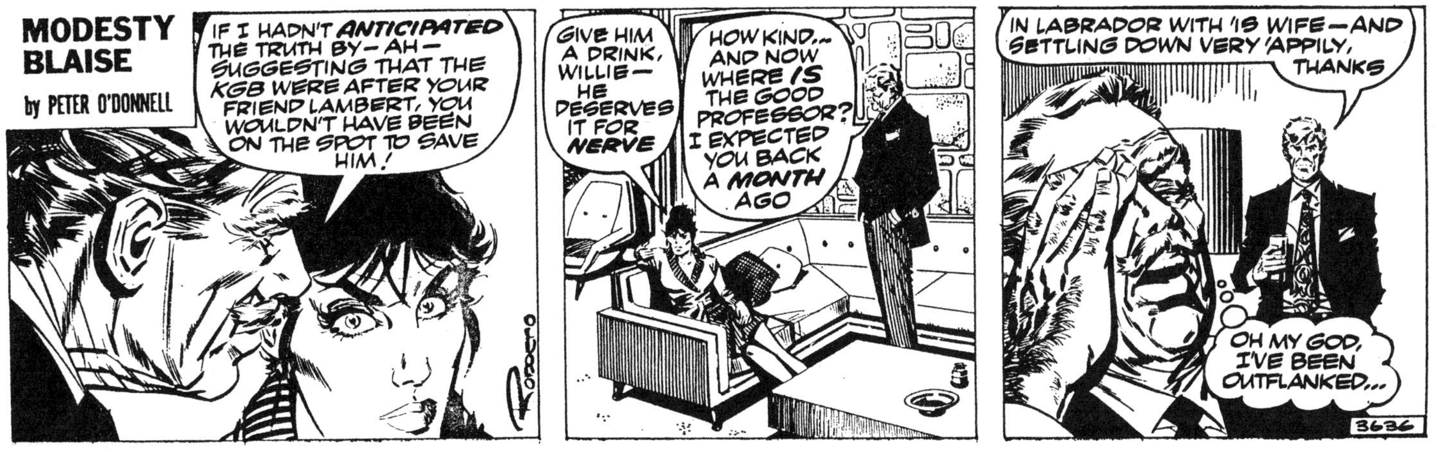
MODESTY BLAISE
by PETER O'DONNELL
IF I HADN'T ANTICIPATED THE TRUTH BY — AH — SUGGESTING THAT THE KGB WERE AFTER YOUR FRIEND LAMBERT, YOU WOULDN'T HAVE BEEN ON THE SPOT TO SAVE HIM!
GIVE HIM A DRINK, WILLIE — HE DESERVES IT FOR NERVE
HOW KIND... AND NOW WHERE IS THE GOOD PROFESSOR? I EXPECTED YOU BACK A MONTH AGO
IN LABRADOR WITH 'IS WIFE — AND SETTLING DOWN VERY 'APPILY, THANKS
OH MY GOD, I'VE BEEN OUTFLANKED...
3636

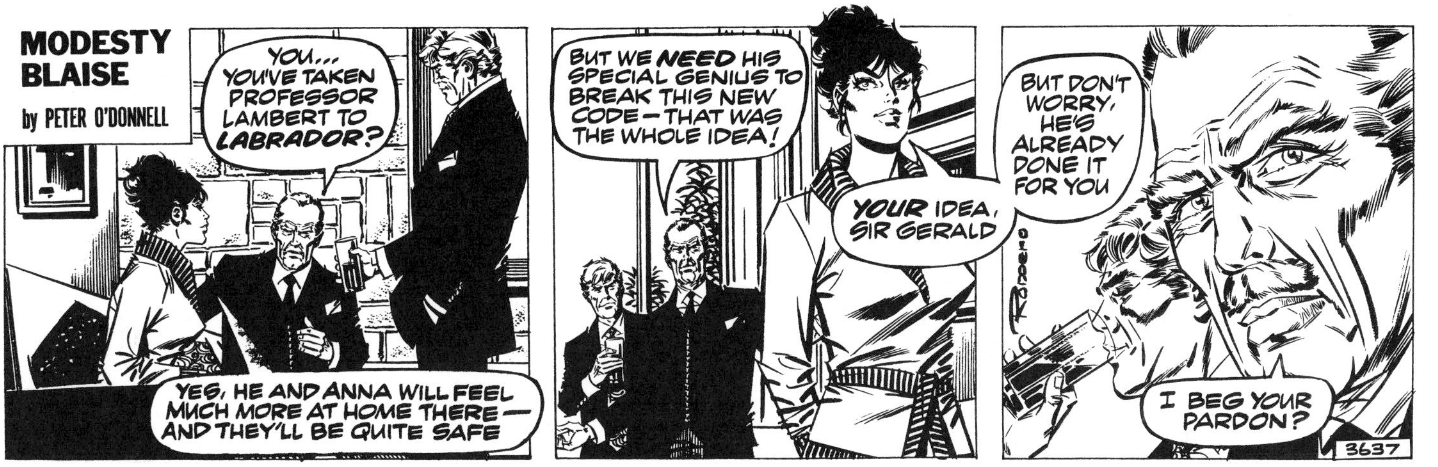
MODESTY BLAISE
by PETER O'DONNELL
YOU... YOU'VE TAKEN PROFESSOR LAMBERT TO LABRADOR?
YES, HE AND ANNA WILL FEEL MUCH MORE AT HOME THERE — AND THEY'LL BE QUITE SAFE
BUT WE NEED HIS SPECIAL GENIUS TO BREAK THIS NEW CODE — THAT WAS THE WHOLE IDEA!
YOUR IDEA, SIR GERALD
BUT DON'T WORRY, HE'S ALREADY DONE IT FOR YOU
I BEG YOUR PARDON?
3637

MODESTY BLAISE
by PETER O'DONNELL
SWEDISH INTELLIGENCE OWED US A FAVOUR, AND THEY HAD PLENTY OF SAMPLES OF THE NEW CODE... SO WE STAYED IN STOCKHOLM FOR A COUPLE OF WEEKS WHILE AMBROSE CRACKED IT
DON'T TRY FLOGGING IT TO THE CIA
BUT MY DEAR IT WILL HELP MY BUDGET — AND THEY'LL BE DELIGHTED
THEY CERTAINLY WERE, SIR G, AND THEY'RE PAYING AMBROSE
AFTER ALL, IT'S HIS WORK
3638

MODESTY BLAISE
by PETER O'DONNELL
NOW WAIT! THIS IS HIGHLY SENSITIVE MATERIAL, AND YOU HAD NO RIGHT TO SELL IT TO THE CIA!
TIME WE WERE LEAVING FOR THE THEATRE, WILLIE LOVE
YOU MEAN WE SHOULD HAVE GIVEN IT TO THEM?
NO! I MEAN THAT I HAVE THE AUTHORITY TO DEAL WITH ALLIED INTELLIGENCE SERVICES, AND YOU HAVEN'T
THEN SUE US, MY OLD DARLING, SUE US!
3638A

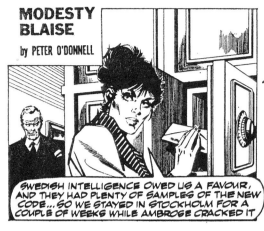

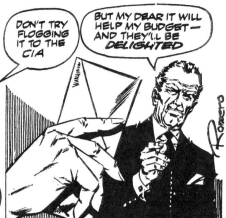

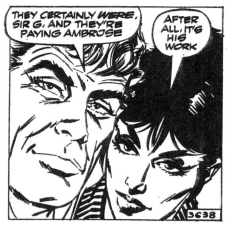

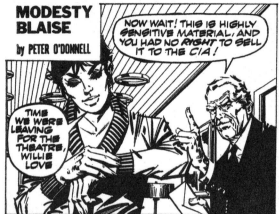

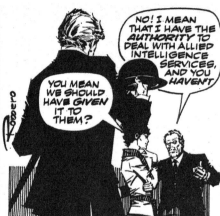

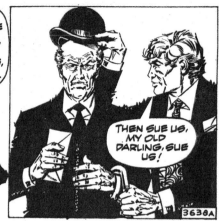

MODESTY BLAISE CHECKLIST

The following is a complete checklist of Modesty Blaise stories that have appeared in the London Evening Standard. All stories were written by Peter O'Donnell.

GLOSSARY

KEY TO ARTISTS

JH = Jim Holdaway

ER = Enrique Badia Romero

JB = John Burns

PW = Pat Wright

NC = Neville Colvin

DATES

13/5/63 = 13th May 1963

SERIAL NUMBERS

Each serial number represents a day. When the Evening Standard stopped publishing on Saturdays the suffix 'a' (e.g. 3638a) was introduced for those papers in syndication that wanted a Saturday Modesty Blaise; the Standard did not run these strips.

*This story was written and drawn in 1966 for syndication only to introduce the character to its new audience.

**This story was written for the *Glasgow Evening Citizen*, an associated newspaper of the *Evening Standard*, to cover a break in publication of Story 14 in the *Evening Standard* due to an industrial dispute in London.

Many thanks to Trevor York and Lawrence Blackmore for his help in compiling this list.

	STORY	ARTIST	DATE	SERIAL NUMBER
1.	La Machine	JH	13/5/63 – 21/9/63	1 – 114
2.	The Long Lever	JH	23/9/63 – 2/1/64	115 – 211
3.	The Gabriel Set-Up	JH	3/1/64 – 18/6/64	212 – 354
4.	Mister Sun	JH	19/6/64 – 5/12/64	355 – 500
5.	The Mind of Mrs Drake	JH	7/12/64 – 19/4/65	501 – 612
6.	Uncle Happy	JH	20/4/65 – 18/9/65	613 – 743
7.	Top Traitor	JH	20/9/65 – 19/2/66	744 – 873
8.	The Vikings	JH	21/2/66 – 9/7/66	874 – 992
8A.	In The Beginning*	JH	1966 Syndication only	(1 – 12)
9.	The Head Girls	JH	11/7/66 – 10/12/66	993 – 1124
10.	The Black Pearl	JH	12/12/66 – 22/4/67	1124 – 1235
11.	The Magnified Man	JH	24/4/67 – 2/9/67	1236 – 1349
12.	The Jericho Caper	JH	4/9/67 – 13/1/68	1350 – 1461
13.	Bad Suki	JH	15/1/68 – 25/5/68	1462 – 1574
14.	The Galley Slaves (Part 1)	JH	27/5/68 – 6/8/68	1575 – 1630
14A.	The Killing Ground**	JH	1968 (Scotland only)	(A1 – A36)
14B.	The Galley Slaves (Part 2)	JH	10/9/68 – 16/11/68	1630a – 33, 35 – 88
15.	The Red Gryphon	JH	18/11/68 – 22/3/69	1689 – 1794
16.	The Hell Makers	JH	24/3/69 – 16/8/69	1795 – 1919
17.	Take-Over	JH	18/8/69 – 10/1/70	1920 – 2043
18.	The War-Lords of Phoenix	JH/ER	12/1/70 – 30/5/70	2044 – 2162
19.	Willie the Djinn	ER	1/6/70 – 17/10/70	2163 – 2282
20.	The Green-Eyed Monster	ER	19/10/70 – 20/2/71	2283 – 2388
21.	Death of a Jester	ER	22/2/71 – 10/7/71	2389 – 2507
22.	The Stone Age Caper	ER	12/7/71 – 27/11/71	2508 – 2627
23.	The Puppet Master	ER	29/11/71 – 8/4/72	2628 – 2738
24.	With Love From Rufus	ER	10/4/72 – 12/8/72	2739 – 2846
25.	The Bluebeard Affair	ER	14/8/72 – 6/1/73	2847 – 2970
26.	The Gallows Bird	ER	8/1/73 – 12/5/73	2971 – 3077
27.	The Wicked Gnomes	ER	14/5/73 – 29/9/73	3078 – 3197
28.	The Iron God	ER	1/10/73 – 9/2/74	3198 – 3309
29.	"Take Me To Your Leader…"	ER	11/2/74 – 1/7/74	3310 – 3428
30.	Highland Witch	ER	2/7/74 – 16/11/74	3429 – 3548
31.	Cry Wolf	ER	18/11/74 – 25/3/75	3549 – 3638a
32.	The Reluctant Chaperon	ER	26/3/75 – 14/8/75	3639 – 3737a
33.	The Greenwood Maid	ER	15/8/75 – 2/1/76	3738 – 3829a
34.	Those About To Die	ER	5/1/76 – 28/5/76	3830 – 3931a
35.	The Inca Trail	ER	1/6/76 – 20/10/76	3932 – 4031a
36.	The Vanishing Dollybirds	ER	21/10/76 – 28/3/77	4032 – 4141a
37.	The Junk Men	ER	29/3/77 – 19/8/77	4142 – 4241a
38.	Death Trap	ER	22/8/77 – 20/1/78	4242 – 4341a
39.	Idaho George	ER	23/1/78 – 16/6/78	4342 – 4447a
40.	The Golden Frog	ER	19/6/78 – 31/10/78	4448 – 4542a
41.	Yellowstone Booty	JB	1/11/78 – 30/3/79	4543 – 4647a
42.	Green Cobra	JB	2/4/79 – 10/8/79	4648 – 4737a
43.	Eve and Adam	JB/PW	13/8/79 – 4/1/80	4738 – 4837a
44.	Brethren of Blaise	PW	7/1/80 – 23/5/80	4838 – 4932a
45.	Dossier on Pluto	NC	27/5/80 – 14/10/80	4933 – 5032a
46.	The Lady Killers	NC	15/10/80 – 3/3/81	5033 – 5127a
47.	Garvin's Travels	NC	4/3/81 – 27/7/81	5128 – 5229a
48.	The Scarlet Maiden	NC	28/7/81 – 16/12/81	5230 – 5329a
49.	The Moonman	NC	17/12/81 – 7/5/82	5330 – 5424a
50.	A Few Flowers For The Colonel	NC	10/5/82 – 24/9/82	5425 – 5519a
51.	The Balloonatic	NC	27/9/82 – 18/2/83	5520 – 5619a
52.	Death in Slow Motion	NC	21/2/83 – 15/7/83	5620 – 5719a
53.	The Alternative Man	NC	18/7/83 – 28/11/83	5720 – 5814a
54.	Sweet Caroline	NC	29/11/83 – 19/4/84	5815 – 5914a
55.	The Return of the Mammoth	NC	24/4/84 – 14/9/84	5915 – 6014a
56.	Plato's Republic	NC	17/9/84 – 6/2/85	6015 – 6114a
57.	The Sword of the Bruce	NC	7/2/85 – 2/7/85	6115 – 6214a
58.	The Wild Boar	NC	3/7/85 – 20/11/85	6215 – 6314a
59.	Kali's Disciples	NC	21/11/85 – 16/5/86	6315 – 6414a
60.	The Double Agent	NC	17/4/86 – 15/9/86	6415 – 6519a
61.	Butch Cassidy Rides Again	R	16/9/86 – 12/2/87	6520 – 6624a
62.	Million Dollar Game	R	13/2/87 – 8/7/87	6625 – 6724a
63.	The Vampire of Malvescu	R	9/7/87 – 3/12/87	6725 – 6829a
64.	Samantha and the Cherub	R	4/12/87 – 6/5/88	6830 – 6934a
65.	Milord	R	9/5/88 – 27/9/88	6935 – 7034a

MODESTY BLAISE CHECKLIST

STORY	ARTIST	DATE	SERIAL NUMBER
66. Live Bait	R	28/9/88 – 17/2/89	7035 – 7134a
67. The Girl from the Future	R	20/2/89 – 21/7/89	7135 – 7239a
68. The Big Mole	R	24/7/89 – 11/12/89	7240 – 7339a
69. Lady in the Dark	R	12/12/89 – 8/5/90	7340 – 7439a
70. Fiona	R	9/5/90 – 9/10/90	7440 – 7544a
71. Walkabout	R	10/10/90 – 11/3/91	7545 – 7649a
72. The Girl in the Iron Mask	R	12/3/91 – 2/8/91	7650 – 7749a
73. The Young Mistress	R	5/8/91 – 6/1/92	7750 – 7854a
74. Ivory Dancer	R	7/1/92 – 5/6/92	7855 – 7959a
75. Our Friend Maude	R	8/6/92 – 2/11/92	7960 – 8064a
76. A Present for the Princess	R	3/11/92 – 8/4/93	8065 – 8174a
77. Black Queen's Pawn	R	13/4/93 – 10/9/93	8175 – 8279a
78. The Grim Joker	R	13/9/93 – 9/2/94	8280 – 8384a
79. Guido the Jinx	R	10/2/94 – 5/7/94	8385 – 8484a
80. The Killing Distance	R	6/7/94 – 30/11/94	8485 – 8589a
81. The Aristo	R	1/12/94 – 3/5/95	8590 – 8694a
82. Ripper Jax	R	4/5/95 – 2/10/95	8695 – 8799a
83. The Maori Contract	R	3/10/95 – 1/3/96	8800 – 8904a
84. Honeygun	R	4/3/96 – 2/8/96	8905 – 9009a
85. Durango	R	5/8/96 – 3/1/97	9010 – 9114a
86. The Murder Frame	R	6/1/97 – 6/6/97	9115 – 9219a
87. Fraser's Story	R	9/6/97 – 3/11/97	9220 – 9324a
88. Tribute of the Pharaoh	R	4/11/97 – 3/5/98	9325 – 9429a
89. The Special Orders	R	6/5/98 – 4/9/98	9430 – 9534a
90. The Hanging Judge	R	7/9/98 – 10/2/99	9535 – 9644a
91. Children of Lucifer	R	11/2/99 – 13/7/99	9645 – 9749a
92. Death Symbol	R	14/7/99 – 15/12/99	9750 – 9859a
93. The Last Aristocrat	R	16/12/99 – 19/5/00	9860 – 9964a
94. The Killing Game	R	22/5/00 – 17/10/00	9965 – 10069a
95. The Zombie	R	18/10/00 – 2/4/01	10070 – 10183

The Dark Angels (This story was originally written as a graphic novel and is not a true strip story. It has only recently been published)